Beyond Slavery's Shadow

Beyond Slavery's Shadow

FREE PEOPLE OF COLOR IN THE SOUTH

Warren Eugene Milteer Jr.

THE UNIVERSITY OF NORTH CAROLINA PRESS   CHAPEL HILL

This book was published with the assistance of the Z. Smith Reynolds Fund of the University of North Carolina Press.

© 2021 Warren Eugene Milteer Jr.
All rights reserved

Designed by Richard Hendel
Set in Miller, Sentinal and Egiziano by Tseng Information Systems, Inc.

The University of North Carolina Press has been a member of the Green Press Initiative since 2003.

Cover photograph: Theodosia A. Lyons, a free person of color, was born in South Carolina but later relocated with her family to Ohio. Photograph courtesy of Warren Eugene Milteer Jr.

Library of Congress Cataloging-in-Publication Data
Names: Milteer, Warren E., Jr., author.
Title: Beyond slavery's shadow : free people of color in the South / Warren Eugene Milteer Jr.
Description: Chapel Hill : The University of North Carolina Press, [2021] | Includes bibliographical references and index.
Identifiers: LCCN 2021003644 | ISBN 9781469664385 (cloth) | ISBN 9781469664392 (paperback) | ISBN 9781469664408 (ebook)
Subjects: LCSH: Free African Americans—Southern States—History. | Free African Americans—Southern States—Social conditions.
Classification: LCC E185.18 .M55 2021 | DDC 975/.00496073—dc23
LC record available at https://lccn.loc.gov/2021003644

In memory of Doretha Skeeter Milteer

CONTENTS

Introduction *1*

1. LIBERTY IN THE COLONIAL SOUTH *13*

2. THE REVOLUTION OF FREEDOM *37*

3. THE BACKLASH *69*

4. MAKING FREEDOM WORK *104*

5. REBELLION AND RADICALISM *137*

6. RESISTING RADICALISM *179*

7. PRESERVING FREEDOM IN A DIVIDED SOUTH *220*

Conclusion *250*

Acknowledgments *259*

Notes *261*

Bibliography *305*

General Index *343*

Index of Names *351*

FIGURES

Benjamin Banneker *56*

Joseph Jenkins Roberts *86*

Jane Waring Roberts *86*

Jarena Lee *119*

Bethel Church of Baltimore *123*

Daniel Coker *125*

Leonard Grimes *147*

Daniel A. Payne *199*

John Patterson Sampson *205*

Moses Hammond *238*

Elizabeth Keckley *247*

Mary Smith Peake *247*

Hiram Revels *251*

P. B. S. Pinchback *252*

Beyond Slavery's Shadow

INTRODUCTION

Over the course of nearly eighty years, Amariah Read lived out a life that was typical of many men of his generation in the South. Born a subject of the British crown around 1762 in Nansemond County, Virginia, by age sixteen, Read had enlisted in the effort to overthrow British power in Virginia and several other colonies. After participating in various skirmishes against British forces, Read was present for the surrender of Lord Cornwallis at Yorktown. Following the war, Read returned to Nansemond County, settling down on an eighty-acre tract with his growing family by the early 1800s. Read's eighty acres eventually became the inheritance of his children, who would continue to prosper from the foundations laid by their father.[1]

Yet Amariah Read also stood apart as a man who was born free in a time when most other people of color in the future U.S. South were born enslaved. Unlike the majority of people termed "colored" in his community, Read could and did hold title to personal and real property. He could work for himself, provide for his family, and keep his wages without interference from a white master. In the courts of Virginia, he could sue and be sued. As a free person of color, however, he was also subjected to an increasing number of restrictions and forms of legal discrimination. Since the time of his birth, Virginia law prevented him from enjoying some of the civil rights possessed by his white male neighbors, including the right to vote and the ability to hold public office. When Read decided to spend the rest of his life with Betsey Skeeter, Virginia law prohibited them from marrying because he was "colored" and she was "white." By the time of his death, the state had passed laws that prohibited Read from traveling freely between Virginia and other localities, required him to obtain a license in order to own a gun, and demanded that he register with county officials in order to receive documents proving his free status. Read was wedged in the precarious position of being both free and yet a person of color.[2]

The complexity of Read's experiences reveals some of the social intricacies of life in the South from the colonial period through much of the nineteenth century. The social order of the South stood on a platform steadied by an assortment of intersecting social hierarchies that made Read and other free people of color both privileged and victimized, both celebrated and despised. During the earliest days of colonization, many of those who traveled from Europe and established themselves in North America had decided that the individuals they termed "negroes," "mulattoes," "mustees," and "Indians"—people of color—were inherently unequal to the mass of people they categorized collectively as "white." This viewpoint vindicated the denigration, enslavement, and genocide of the indigenous people of the Americas as well as provided justification for the capture and commodification of thousands of people with connections to various parts of Africa who arrived in American ports as enslaved laborers. Yet the racial hierarchy was not the only form of hierarchy helping to uphold the social order. Hierarchies based on wealth, gender, occupation, reputation, and religion coexisted with ideas promoting white supremacy and discrimination against people of color. And at no time did the hierarchical relation between legal freedom and enslavement dissipate from southern society. In so many ways, southerners expressed the constant importance of distinguishing who was free and who was enslaved, even when those people were not classified as "white."

The intersection between different forms of hierarchy ultimately led to the political and social inconsistency that characterized the South from the early days of European colonization through the Civil War years. Under the laws of Virginia, Amariah Read could sue a white man but could not testify against him in court. Although he could not marry Betsey Skeeter because Virginia law prohibited unions between persons of color and whites, law enforcement in his community allowed Read to live with Skeeter in the same house. At least some of his white neighbors recognized Betsey as his wife, even when the law would not.[3] These inconsistencies were not exceptions in the South but standard throughout the region.

Appearing in the colonial period, the theory of white superiority and proslavery ideology slowly poisoned the social and political environments in which free people of color experienced their daily lives. These ideas were part of the intellectual technology that gradually reshaped the South from Native ground to scenes of unprecedented levels of exploitation and expropriation. Over time, southern politicians found attacking free people of color and their liberties to be an expedient way to promote these ideas and uphold the projects of extraction and enslavement attached to them. During the colonial period, the politicization of free people of color in an effort to defend human bondage and land exploitation was constricted. In communities where various forms of hierarchy were well accepted and abstract discussions of freedom were infrequent, strong advocacy for proslavery and white supremacist stances were of limited necessity.[4]

Efforts to politicize free people of color became more widespread as slavery's critics became more vocal during the period of revolutions in North America. Political attacks against free people of color steadily increased with the success of antislavery efforts throughout the hemisphere. By the first decades of the nineteenth century, abolitionist forces had pushed slavery toward disintegration in the North; instances of emancipation had begun to increase in the South; and proslavery regimes had collapsed in French Saint-Domingue, in parts of Latin America, and in Great Britain's remaining North American empire. Freedom was on the rise.[5]

Politicians across the nation, but especially in the South, gradually adopted attacks on free people of color as an indirect defense of an economy propelled by slave labor and as a way to attract support from disaffected whites who saw persons of color as commercial competitors. Attacking free people of color was also a strategy for participants in the national sectional debate who argued that enslavement, not the freedom enjoyed by the majority of persons of color in the North, was the proper place for people of color. This toxic rhetoric only intensified as advocates of both slavery and white supremacy became more radical over the decades and birthed increasingly fanatical prescriptions for dealing with the South's free people of color. By the eve of the Civil War, radical politicians and their associates floated extremist bombasts about deporting or even enslaving the South's free people of color. Newspapers, petitions, legislative papers, journals, and personal letters demonstrate that the rhetoric targeting free people of color grew increasingly radical from the colonial period up to and even through the Civil War.

At the height of the radical proslavery and white supremacist alliance's ascendency, whites in the South were still sorely divided concerning the proper position of free people of color in their region, just as they remained split over many political issues. Historians of the nineteenth-century United States such as William W. Freehling and Matthew Mason have highlighted the important divides among white southerners, including on the issue of slavery. Instead of depicting white southerners as a group with a single opinion about slavery, Mason argued that scholars should focus on the "intrasectional debates in which certain groups gained the upper hand at various times."[6] Radical forces among white southerners successfully moved the discussion of the place of free people of color in extreme directions. They ushered through a variety of restrictions on the lives of free people of color, curbing their civil liberties and ability to interface on equal terms with whites in the marketplace. Extremist ideas even trickled into private settings, shaping the ways communities organized their religious institutions and social organizations.

Yet the growing influence of radical ideologies concerning free people of color did not equal complete domination. The same sets of records that highlight the growing importance of extremist ideas also reveal a concerted effort on the part of free people of color and their allies to reject denigration and discrimination. Free people of color and their allies petitioned their governments and filed suits in the courts challenging the radical agenda. Sporadic enforcement of radical restrictions further limited the impact of the extremists. Radicals were often better at pushing through legislation to serve their immediate political needs than providing the necessary infrastructure to see their ideas transformed into action. Radical legislation approved at the state level did not always reflect buy-in from local people. Furthermore, lawmakers largely failed to fund their radical mandates. Even when local officials enforced discriminatory legislation against free people of color, the reasons for that enforcement related to the political and personal interests of those local officials.

Across time, white southerners maintained a complex assortment of relations with the free people of color in their midst. From the colonial period through the Civil War, whites and free people of color lived, worked, and played together, created families, socialized, and interacted in business. At same time, they engaged in physical altercations and sued one another. Whites used slurs when speaking about free people of color and discriminated against them with and without the backing of the law. Peaceful interactions and conflict coexisted. Individual whites were commonly inconsistent in their actions dealing with free people of color. Especially during the post-Revolutionary years, when proslavery and white supremacist ideologies were most influential, white people commonly espoused causes, such as forced deportation or colonization, that threatened the liberties of free people of color while interacting courteously with free people of color in their communities and complimenting them for their contributions. These white people disconnected their actions from their rhetoric and ignored the consequences of their political choices. Surviving records from every region of the South reveal a common willingness among white people to celebrate the positive attributes of the free people of color among them, even as they allowed their elected representatives to spew inflammatory rhetoric that depicted free people of color as corrupt and threatening. Even such major events as the Nat

Turner Rebellion and the Dred Scott decision were not momentous enough to halt these fluid behavioral patterns.[7]

The people of the South, both white and of color, viewed their world through a complex web of intersecting values, which led to significant inconsistencies in their society at large, including the treatment of free people of color. Many white southerners prized their racial hierarchy that placed them above people of color in multiple facets of life. Yet they also recognized other forms of hierarchy such as gender, wealth, reputation, occupation, and family connection. These other forms of hierarchy intersected with racial categorization and influenced how white southerners evaluated the people in their neighborhoods.

White people may have discussed free people of color as one group in the halls of their legislatures, but they also interacted with them largely as individuals with unique attributes that reflected their more complicated positions in society. Societal norms about gender that extended from dress to types of education to legal rights caused free men and women of color to experience southern life differently. Whites also applied disparate forms of treatment toward free persons of color depending on their economic situation. Poor free people of color did not fare the same in the South as the region's free persons of color who held slaves or ran successful businesses. Both whites and people of color recognized and valued individuals in their communities differently based on their reputations for veracity and propriety. Whites respected the economic impact of free people of color and acknowledged the value of skilled free persons of color. Family and kin connections meant a great deal to southerners regardless of the time period. Although enslavement commonly clouded these connections and even permitted parents to sell their own children on auction blocks and to dealers of human flesh, not all white southerners accepted such extreme treatment of their kin across the artificial color line. White parents and other relatives, especially mothers, cared for and supported their children, grandchildren, and other kin of color. For some white people, certain free persons of color were their relatives and not simply part of the ambiguous mass of "colored" people. Radical speechifying was not loud enough to shatter these bonds.[8]

It should not be a surprise that such a society produced a wide span of social patterns that were often inconsistent, especially in terms of physical separation. As in the North, race-based segregation was a part of life in certain areas of the South as early as the eighteenth century. By the end of that century, physical separation had a piecemeal existence in southern life. In Spanish Louisiana and Florida, as in other parts of the Spanish Empire, free men of color and white men served in separate military units. In Charleston, South Carolina, theaters excluded free people of color from attending performances. Into the nineteenth century, segregated or white-only churches, schools, cemeteries, jails, poorhouses, and transportation systems dotted the southern landscape. The white supremacists had sown the seeds of the post–Civil War Jim Crow system into the prewar southern soil. In many ways, however, free people of color experienced a world much different from the one that would appear by the end of the nineteenth century. In the prewar South, segregated institutions coexisted with institutions in which free people of color and whites cooperated and lived together. During the American Revolution, whereas free persons of color in the Spanish colonies served in segregated units, free people of color in Virginia and North Carolina fought side by side with their white neighbors. Segregated poorhouses and jails existed in some localities but not in others. White supremacists had yet to convince white southerners more broadly that physical separation from people of color was essential to maintaining power.[9]

The South's imperfect systems of discrimination and exclusion sometimes opened up opportunities to those positioned to outmaneuver them. Free people of color exploited the vulnerabilities in the proslavery and white supremacist network to uncover paths to survive and occasionally thrive in a region increasingly influenced by radical ideas. By working with white neighbors and building their separate networks and institutions, free people of color sustained themselves in the social and political gap between white freedom and enslavement. In the colonial period, they enshrined themselves as important workers, craftspeople, farmers, and landholders. As their numbers increased through the Revolutionary period, their influence on society only grew. By the late eighteenth and early nineteenth centuries, free people of color took on roles as religious leaders, public intellectuals, business people, and advocates for political causes. In the face of discrimination and exclusion, they created their own churches and social organizations. Even during the height of proslavery and white supremacist attacks, free people of color continued to build their social networks, establish businesses, and increase their property holdings.

Personal relationships largely guided interactions between free people of color and their white neighbors. Yet important regional differences affected the lives and experiences of free persons of color, including in their relations with white neighbors. By the late eighteenth century, if not earlier, free people of color had become a population situated largely in the Upper South, which included Maryland, Delaware, Virginia, North Carolina, Tennessee, Kentucky, Missouri, and the District of Columbia.

Maryland, Virginia, North Carolina, and Delaware were always among the localities with the largest populations of free persons of color in the region. By 1860, the overwhelming majority of the South's free people of color, nearly 86 percent, lived in the Upper South. Scholars and lay historians alike have devoted significant attention to the free people of color of the Deep South, despite the fact that they made up a substantial minority of the region's population. Louisiana was the only Deep South locality with a population of free persons of color that exceeded 10,000. Surviving census data suggest that of all the Deep South states, only Louisiana, South Carolina, Georgia, and Alabama had populations of free people of color exceeding 2,500. Mississippi's population of free persons of color peaked at just over 1,000 and later collapsed. The number of free people of color in Florida, Arkansas, Texas, and Indian Territory never reached 1,000. Whereas the laws suggest that free people of color were an equal burden for the radical lawmakers in both sections of the South, population figures reveal that the free person of color was more of a political boogeyman in the Deep South than an actual presence. In many parts of the Deep South, whites would have been hard-pressed to ever meet a free person of color.[10]

The vast majority of institutions created by free people of color were concentrated in the Upper South. Especially in such metropolitan areas as Baltimore, Maryland; Wilmington, Delaware; the District of Columbia; Richmond and Petersburg, Virginia; Louisville, Kentucky; and Saint Louis, Missouri, free persons of color established numerous churches and social clubs. They could be found participating in many types of work. These patterns of behavior often extended into some of the more rural regions of the Upper South, particularly in areas that saw significant European settlement during the colonial period. Most of Maryland's rural counties; all three counties in Delaware; some areas of Virginia, including Norfolk, Frederick, Southampton, Isle of Wight, Loudoun, James City, Surry, Nansemond, and Accomack Counties; and, in North Carolina, Granville, Halifax, Hertford, Craven, Wake, Robeson, and Pasquotank Counties were centers of life for free people of color. Many of these localities had robust institutions either run by free people of color or heavily influenced by them. The population of free people of color was larger in all of these counties than in major southern communities like Savannah and Atlanta in Georgia; Pensacola, Florida; or Natchez, Mississippi. In the Deep South, only locations such as New Orleans and Saint Landry Parish in Louisiana; Charleston, South Carolina; and Mobile, Alabama, hosted significant populations of free people of color and the usual social institutions that came with such numbers.[11]

Although the South's free people of color were largely situated in the most northern parts of the region, much of the population's wealth was concentrated among those who lived in the Deep South. Free persons of color, like their white neighbors, found the greatest opportunities for wealth in areas with the greatest and fastest economic expansion, which by the nineteenth century were often in the Deep South. Free people of color in Louisiana, Mississippi, and South Carolina had the largest per capita wealth among free persons of color in the region.[12] They benefited from the economic expansion generated by the expropriation of indigenous people's lands and the transformation of those lands into fields and plantations. Many of the region's most financially successful free people of color, especially in the Deep South but also in some parts of the Upper South, built their fortunes at least in part through the exploitation of enslaved men, women, and children. Others living in cities such as New Orleans and Charleston benefited from their proximity to major slave trading markets. While proslavery ideology was a threat to free people of color, for some in the Deep South, antislavery positions were not a solution to their problems and actually posed a threat to their economic success. Many of the Upper South's free people of color lived in areas where slavery was on the decline and as a result were unable to benefit from the significant expansion of wealth directly connected to the trade in human beings and commodities derived from their labor. Free people of color in the Upper South, on average, were significantly poorer than their Deep South counterparts, making them economically vulnerable and more dependent for employment on large businesses and wealthier neighbors, most of them white. This situation, especially in such cities as Baltimore and the District of Columbia, placed free persons of color and whites in greater competition in the labor market. The existence of larger numbers of free people of color who were more dependent on others for work was a recipe for conflict.

An assortment of individuals with a variety of ancestral backgrounds fell into the "free people of color" category. Individuals labeled "negroes," "mulattoes," "mustees," "Indians," "blacks," "pardos," "morenos," "mestizos," "quadroons," and "octoroons," who possessed various ancestral connections to the Americas, Africa, Europe, and South Asia, were considered part of the populations commonly called "free people of color" in the South.[13] Historical definitions of "free people of color" reveal that southerners had an intricate understanding of the category.[14] This multifaceted understanding fits well with the ways people in other parts of the European colonial and postcolonial worlds understood racial categories. Furthermore, this book operates under the assumption that "free people of color," though commonly used as a catchall category, was never a fixed group. Those understood by their communities as falling under the category "free people of color" changed over time, as people moved from slavery to freedom, lost their freedom, and experienced processes of racial recategorization.

In addition, southerners were not always certain who qualified as a free person of color. Individuals shifted in and out of the category, just as people in more recent times have moved back and forth between racial categories.[15] Since the colonial period, the laws of many southern jurisdictions exempted people of varying degrees of whiteness from the limitations of being a person of color. In theory, members of a community could consider a person to be of "negro" or "Indian" descent but choose to categorize that person as "white" instead of a "person of color." Ariela J. Gross has demonstrated, however, that the ways southerners determined who was and was not "white" was more than a matter of simple calculation, as suggested by the language of southern laws. Instead, imprecise community discussions about physical features, character, kinship, and behavior ultimately determined the lines between "whites" and "persons of color."[16] Changes in geographic location had the ability to shift understandings of memory and kinship, further complicating the process of racializing people. A person could be considered "of color" in one community and "white" in another.[17]

The relationship between the category "Indian" and the broader category "person of color," as well as the categories "negro" and "mulatto," was equally situational. People in the pre-1865 United States commonly used the terms "persons of color" or "colored" as well as "negro," "mulatto," and "mustee" for individuals they also considered to be "Indians" or persons of "Indian descent."[18] Yet at the same time, they generally did not consider all "Indians" to be "colored," "persons of color," "negroes," or "mulattoes." Many southerners differentiated between "Indians" and "persons of color" on the basis of perceived differences in political power. They frequently classified "Indians" and persons of "Indian descent" who lacked ties to a recognized, politically sovereign nation as "colored" or even "negro" or "mulatto." This is how white southerners treated descendants of the Gingaskin, Chowan, and Mattamuskeet during much of the nineteenth century.[19] Yet most southerners did not consider people classified as "Indians" who had connections to politically stable and powerful nations, such as the Cherokee, Choctaw, Chickasaw, Seminole, and Creek nations, to be "colored" persons. The position of individuals who possessed ties to nations with severely limited political autonomy, such as the Pamunkey and Nottoway of Virginia, often switched back and forth between "Indian" and "colored," depending on geographic, social, and political contexts. Further complicating this situation was the way the more powerful indigenous nations understood the terms "colored," "negro," and "mulatto." By the nineteenth century, these nations had adopted the terms "colored" and "persons of color" as well as "negro" and "mulatto" into their lexicons. Yet their laws strongly implied that "colored" persons as well as "negroes" and "mulattoes" were people they understood to be of "negro blood," or African ancestry. Native peoples without such ancestry were not labeled "colored" as they often were among other populations in the South. Moreover, indigenous nations drew strict lines between the "colored," "negro," and "mulatto" people who they considered kin, and therefore part of the nation, and the "colored," "negro," and "mulatto" people who were social outsiders.[20] The potency of racial categories depended heavily on context.

For over a century, scholars have explored and analyzed free people of color, their place in southern society, and their relationships with their white and enslaved neighbors. The bulk of the scholarship on free people of color has focused on specific localities. During the first two decades of the twentieth century, the first major scholarly studies on free persons of color appeared. Focusing on the states with the largest populations of free people of color, Maryland and Virginia, historians provided an outline of major topics and questions that would drive much of the scholarship for the next half century. These studies focused on the origins, social lives, and economic circumstances of free people of color. Yet they also embraced bigoted undertones that sometimes poisoned their conclusions. An assortment of articles, theses, and dissertations as well as two particularly significant works by scholars of color, Luther Porter Jackson and John Hope Franklin, followed in the next quarter century. While the questions posed by their predecessors greatly influenced them, Jackson and Franklin also offered assessments of life for free people of color that recognized their ability to operate—in many ways—as the equals of their white neighbors, economically, socially, and, most importantly, intellectually.[21]

During the 1970s, Ira Berlin offered the first major attempt to synthesize the findings of the previous generations of scholarship on free people of color. The basic organization of his study was heavily influenced by his predecessors, but the conclusions he reached offered a more comparative analysis. Berlin highlighted differences between whites' ideology and the experiences of free people of color in the Upper and Lower

South. Significantly, he created the first compendium of the legislation that targeted the region's free people of color. After examining these laws and other details circumscribing life for free people of color, Berlin contended that "free negroes stood outside the direct governance of a master, but in the eyes of many whites their place in society had not been significantly altered. They were slaves without masters." At the same time, Berlin noted the important distinctions between slavery and freedom. He argued that "Southern free Negroes" were stuck between "abject slavery, which they rejected, and full freedom, which was denied them."[22]

Since Berlin's study, historians have shifted back to examining free people of color within their local confines. Additional state studies, individual biographies, family histories, and local histories focused at the county and city levels have told us much about the lives of free people of color. Historians know significantly more about elite free people of color, especially in the Deep South. Studies focused on the experiences of free people of color in former Spanish colonies that are now part of the United States and the unique struggles of free women of color have greatly enhanced the way we think about human interactions in the pre–Civil War South.[23] Yet the greatest challenges to the narratives set by Berlin and many of his predecessors have come from historians writing about free people of color at the community level. These scholars have focused less on the laws and political rhetoric used to attack free people of color and more on the ways people lived day to day. Scholarship on such topics as interracial relationships between men of color and white women in the pre–Civil War South were the prelude to the major shift ushered in by Melvin Patrick Ely's *Israel on the Appomattox*, which told a far different story than the one offered by Berlin and others. Ely found lax enforcement of discriminatory laws and fewer significant changes in the regular interactions among free people of color and whites than suggested by the extreme rhetoric that appeared in southern newspapers and political debates. A small number of scholars have followed Ely's lead. Nevertheless, the local nature of Ely's and others' studies have left some historians unconvinced of the broad applicability of their conclusions.[24] Historians continue to grapple with the proper way to characterize the collective lives of free people of color.[25]

This study seeks to take on this challenge and move us in a new direction. In this book, I do not view laws and political rhetoric as explicit evidence of the viewpoints of everyday people and instead try to place them in their proper political and social contexts. Political elites across time and place have implemented laws for a variety of reasons that extend beyond attempts to address the day-to-day concerns of the people they claim to represent. This book tries to highlight the strategic goals and importance of the increasingly radical rhetoric around the issue of slavery in the development of discriminatory legislation and behavior. It also takes seriously the many examples of social and political consternation experienced by the South's free people of color and the variety of reasons that free people of color throughout the region experienced both financial success and economic exploitation, legal flexibility and discriminatory punishment, and social integration and de facto segregation. Diverse outcomes for free people of color appeared in every section of the South. White people who were willing to defend free people of color, establish families with them, and value them as trusted neighbors lived in every state in the region. Yet in these very same localities, whites also exploited free people of color, targeted them, and treated them as less than equal. This book is designed to explain how such divergent attitudes could coexist.

Beyond Slavery's Shadow focuses primarily on the lives of free persons and not enslaved people. The experiences of free persons of color, who may have shared a common racial categorization with the enslaved, do not fit neatly with the struggles of enslaved people because, indeed, free persons had a different status. To suggest a somewhat complex yet overwhelmingly essential experience for all people of color during the pre-1865 period blinds us to the important difference between legal freedom and bondage and requires us to give superficial treatment to the multifaceted nature of human relations. Scholars who study free people of color in other parts of the world have recognized that free people of color held a flexible but largely firm status between whites and enslaved people. They have not tried to conflate the severe limitations of slavery with the contested liberty experienced by free persons of color.[26] This study highlights many of the key differences between the lives of free people of color and the enslaved population, and thus brings our understanding of life for free people of color in the South much closer to historical understandings of free people of color in other parts of the world. Thousands of people of color in the South experienced a freedom that was contested yet worth defending, a liberty worth dying for. And, as this book shows, some ultimately sacrificed their lives to preserve that freedom.

CHAPTER 1

Liberty in the Colonial South

On February 6, 1677, King Tony of Northampton County, Virginia, already knew he was unwell as he dictated his last will and testament—his time was growing short. Before he died, Tony wanted to secure everything for which he had worked so hard in order to pass on something to his family. Over the preceding century, Tony and people like him had come as servants, slaves, and settlers from Europe, Africa, and even South Asia to French, English, Dutch, Swedish, and Spanish colonies, where they tilled ground, pummeled trees, and exterminated both man and beast in order to turn indigenous lands into profits. King Tony now owned enough property to leave a legacy to his wife, Sarah, and granddaughter, Sarah Driggers. Yet as much as he shared in common with the thousands of other people living in colonial North America, King Tony was unlike much of the colonial population in a crucial way. King Tony was categorized as "Negroe," but he was also free.[1]

King Tony was one of a handful of free people of color living in the southern colonies before the outbreak of revolution in the 1770s. While many people living in these colonial settlements who were labeled "negroes," "mulattoes," "mustees," "Indians," "pardos," and "morenos" were enslaved, King Tony and others like him enjoyed various levels of freedom inaccessible to their enslaved counterparts. Free people of color came from diverse origins and experienced freedom in many forms. Their ancestral origins were African, European, Asian, and American. Many were born free, while some found liberty later in life. They spoke English, Spanish, French, German, and likely a host of African and indigenous American dialects. Their economic circumstances ranged from rich to poor. They performed a variety of different types of work and practiced a span of religions. Their diverse backgrounds produced a wide range of life outcomes.[2]

Prejudice and discrimination were inherent to the colonial systems in which free people of color lived. Within imperial settings, these practices justified the European colonial conquests and became important parts of the intellectual technology that supported the enslavement and exploitation of laborers from the Americas, Africa, and Asia. The Spanish, French, and English interspersed ideas about freedom and slavery, proper gendered behavior, relations between elites and people of lesser means, and religion with discriminatory practices tied to racial categories in order to construct the colonial social order. In theory, regardless of the colony, free persons were supposed to be above enslaved people and white people were supposed to be above persons of color. The rise of free people of color in societies in which many persons of color were enslaved and not free troubled those who sought and promoted a world with less complexity, a world in which negroes, mulattoes, mustees, Indians, pardos, and morenos were enslaved and white people, Europeans, enjoyed liberty. Prejudice against free persons of color and attacks on their freedom appeared as quickly as their population grew. No consensus developed in the colonies about the place of free people of color. Yet a small and powerful element among the white population would construct the intellectual and legal infrastructure that permitted discrimination to blossom and reproduce throughout the decades.[3]

Race-based discrimination contaminated the society but did not completely halt development for free people of color in the colonies. Laboring as servants and apprentices, free persons of color clung tightly to their sense of self-determination while struggling to fulfill their obligations to their masters. Free people of color who existed outside of the colonial servitude system had greater opportunities. They strove for and often obtained property in the form of household goods, tools, livestock, land, and, in a few cases, enslaved people. Free men of color, excluded from the direct influences of the white master class, became heads of households with their own dependents underneath them. Even as legal discrimination slowly increased against free persons of color, free status provided them with social capital and wide legal protections unavailable to the enslaved. A contested freedom was better than no liberty at all.

The Rise of Free People of Color

As early as the sixteenth century, free people of color were woven into the colonial world's social fabric. By the mid- to late seventeenth century, free people of color existed as a category of individuals legally distinct from whites and enslaved persons in the colonial order. As the children of free mothers, some of these individuals were legally free at birth. With few exceptions, elites in the Spanish, English, and French colonies considered all children born to free mothers to be free persons, regardless of their racial categorization. Of course, this rule excluded people, such as the mass of enslaved Africans, who were born free elsewhere, detained, enslaved, and then transported to the colonies. Early on, the colonizers also permitted indigenous Americans captured in war to be enslaved for life, even though they, too, were technically freeborn. When free birth led to free status, the law provided extensive privileges associated with legal personhood, though it did not offer protection from servitude, poverty, or discrimination. In colonial settings, free persons could own property and had legally recognized kin connections. Colonial lawmakers withheld these legal privileges from enslaved people, who could only gain them through manumission, a centuries-old legal procedure that permitted enslaved persons to become free. In the manumission process, masters rescinded their claims on enslaved people through pecuniary transactions and as gifts to enslaved persons.[4]

People of color were born free under a variety of circumstances, but birth to a free white mother appears to have been the most common circumstance through the colonial period. White women, many of whom were indentured servants, gave birth to a sizable number of free children of color during the colonial period. Writing in 1723, William Gooch unsympathetically declared that most "free-Negros & Mulattos" were "Bastards of some of the worst of our imported Servants and Convicts."[5] Nineteenth-century North Carolina lawmaker William Gaston, after speaking with people who lived in the colonial period, concluded that most free people of color in his region established their freedom as the maternal descendants of white women.[6] Colonial court records document the roots of a significant portion of the free population of color who were the children or descendants of white women in the southern colonies. On October 3, 1699, officials in Gloucester County, Virginia, issued an apprentice indenture for Anne, "a mulatto child," who was born to Anne Toyer, a white servant woman, and Peter, "a Negro."[7] In 1719, Mary Gibson, a "molatto child," of Queen Anne's County, Maryland, appears in the court records as the daughter of a white servant woman also named Mary Gibson.[8] Toyer and Gibson were progenitors of generations of free people of color to come.

The incorporation of Native peoples into European colonial settlements created two classifications of indigenous people: those whom colonists recognized as social insiders in their communities and those with recognized ties to sovereign or tributary Native nations. Colonists frequently treated those Native peoples whom they recognized as part of their communities as indistinct from other persons of color. They incorporated Native peoples into their settlements both as bondspeople and as free persons.[9] These Native people who became part of these colonial communities as free persons passed down their freedom in the same ways white women passed their free status to their children. The child of a free Native woman was free as well. Luke, a "free boy" of Craven County, North Carolina, owed his status to the fact that his mother, Phebe, was "an Indian woman."[10] In a similar example, James, "a boy of eight years old" in 1765, lived as a free person in Edgecombe County, North Carolina, because his mother, Jenny Zekell, was an "Indian."[11]

People of color sometimes arrived in the Americas as free persons as a result of the chase for empire that brought colonizing countries into greater contact with individuals from around the world. Trade associated with these imperial aspirations encouraged the movement of people between Europe and sites of commerce in Asia and Africa. As time passed, increasing numbers of people from trade centers and colonized areas landed in the imperial metropoles. Individuals with roots in South Asia or Africa, who came to Europe primarily as sailors and servants, became part of the social fabric of the colonizing countries. Some of these individuals eventually made their way from Europe to the Americas and thereby supplemented the growth of the colonial South's population of free persons of color.[12] Like so many white people in the colonies, many of these free persons of color came to the colonies as indentured servants. In 1671, while living in England, Thomas Hagleton, "a negroe," contracted with Margery Dutchesse to labor as a servant for four years. After making the agreement, Hagleton landed in Maryland and worked there for many years under several masters.[13] In another case, Thomas Waters, "a Mulatto Servant Man," arrived in North America from Liverpool, England. By 1745, he worked under the employ of Thomas Bantom in Virginia.[14] James Dunn's journey to North America began in the East Indies, the place of his birth. From there, a visitor to his homeland transported him to England. After spending a significant portion of his childhood in England, Dunn found himself in Savannah, Georgia, on the eve of the American Revolution. During his time in Savannah, he served multiple masters.[15]

Manumission played a role in the growth of the colonial population of free people of color, although its role became much more pronounced in the Revolutionary era. Still, the legal transformation of enslaved people into free people contributed to the gradual increase of free persons of color across the colonies. As early as the 1630s, a few Virginia masters had begun to liberate their bondspeople. In 1635, Anthony Longo, a "Negro," received his freedom from Nathaniel Littleton of Accomack County.[16] Masters manumitted enslaved people for a variety of reasons. Personal motives drove some masters to liberate those they held in bondage. By 1735, Jorge and Marie of New Orleans, Louisiana, were free after their master, Jean-Baptiste Le Moyne de Bienville, liberated them for their good and faithful service.[17] In 1741, Gideon and Elizabeth Ellis of Craven County, South Carolina, emancipated Titus, "an Indian man," whom they described as "true and trusty."[18] James Bond of Colleton County, South Carolina, purchased and liberated Peggy, a "Negro woman," and her children, Nanny, Sarah, and Ben, in 1753. Bond declared that he freed them because of the "Natural Love and affection which I have and bear unto my said wife [Peggy] and three children."[19] Persons of color also obtained their freedom through self-purchase. Sarah, a "mulatto woman," paid 101 pounds to purchase her freedom and that of her children Mary, Benjamin, and Sarah from William Snow of Craven County, South Carolina, in 1746.[20]

A small number of individuals received their freedom under atypical circumstances. Although these liberations were unusual, these paths to freedom still played an important role in the overall growth of the population of free people of color. Caesar, an enslaved man from South Carolina, won his freedom after the South Carolina General Assembly learned of his scientific discovery. Sometime before the assembly met to discuss the matter, Caesar had unearthed an antidote to reverse the effects of a poison. Witnesses relayed that Caesar had cured multiple patients. On learning of Caesar, the General Assembly decided to appropriate the funds to purchase him from his master, John Norman, and liberate him.[21] In the case of Caesar, manumission was a reward for a particular kind of behavior, one that was compatible with the larger system of enslavement. Caesar's service as a healer and his willingness to share his knowledge to the benefit of white South Carolinians demonstrated his loyalty to the very society that supported his initial enslavement. By manumitting Caesar, South Carolina lawmakers encouraged the larger enslaved population to work for the benefit of the master class. The possibility of freedom served as an incentive to motivate enslaved people to stay within the limits prescribed by their masters and lawmakers.

In reaction to constant conflict between the English and Spanish on the Georgia-Florida border, colonial officials offered freedom to enslaved people who reached their respective colony from the territories claimed by the opposing empire. People of color took advantage of this imperial conflict and fled in search of liberty within the lands of their masters' enemies. In 1738, Francisco Menendez, along with thirty other enslaved people who were escapees from Carolina, petitioned the governor of Florida, Manuel de Montiano, for their freedom. They argued that they had served faithfully on behalf of the Spanish crown, and on March 15, 1738, Montiano declared all of the runaways free. Menendez and others would go on to found the Spanish outpost Gracia Real de Santa Teresa de Mose, a settlement specifically for freedpeople.[22] Sometime before August 1748, John Dick, Kingson, Billy, and Lewis were among the enslaved people who ran from Saint Augustine, Florida, to Georgia in search of freedom. On their arrival in Savannah, each man received documents attesting to his free status from local officials. Kingson's document declared that he was "a free man he having made his Escape from St. Augustine to this Colony."[23] In these cases, manumission served an important role in undermining the efforts of opposing empires. Imperial officials worked to keep persons of color enslaved within their colonies while encouraging those enslaved by their enemies to abscond, not out of support for liberty as a general principle but because they desired to drain human resources that their enemies could otherwise use against them. Enslaved persons in the competing empires understood these conflicts well and took advantage of the situation to improve their own lives and secure a better future for their descendants.

By the mid-1700s, free people of color lived in every southern colony from British Delaware and Maryland down to Spanish Florida and west into French Louisiana. Whether born free or made free, they became important actors in colonial societies. In the 1600s, when free people of color existed only in small numbers, they attracted the attention of officials at irregular intervals. For some colonists, free people of color were simply part of the diversity of individuals in their communities, but this was not a universally shared opinion.

As the 1600s turned to the 1700s, colonial officials began to notice the presence of free people of color more regularly, and some viewed them as more than simply folks in the neighborhood. For these officials, free persons of color presented a nuisance at best and, at worst, they represented a threat to the developing economy dependent on slavery.

Legal Reaction

The debate over the legal position of free people of color in the colonial South developed during the 1600s and 1700s as lawmakers sought to balance the free status of persons of color with the demands of both slaveholders and others who desired to build stronger racial and class hierarchies. Throughout this period, lawmakers slowly chipped away at the rights and privileges of free people of color. Some laws targeted certain demographics of the population such as the poor, servants, women, or children. Other laws sought to curb the activities of all free persons of color; often these edicts were part of broader race-based initiatives targeting people of color, both free and enslaved. Through these laws, white elites attempted to balance their intersectional interests. They wanted to strengthen class and racial divisions, gender boundaries, and the legal separation between free and slave statuses.[24]

Throughout the colonies, lawmakers developed an obsession with regulating the sexuality of all people, but they especially wanted to discourage relationships between people of color and whites. These lawmakers sought to curb the blurring of lines between colonizer and colonized and between free and enslaved. Support for these hierarchical divisions was universal among the colonial powers. As early as 1662, Virginia lawmakers sought to limit mixed relations by doubling the usual fine for sex outside of marriage for "any Christian" convicted specifically of "fornication with a negro man or woman." The next generation of Virginia lawmakers expanded the scope of the attack on mixed unions through a 1691 act that declared "that for the time to come, whatsoever English or other white man or woman being free shall intermarry with a negroe, mulatto, or Indian man or woman bond or free shall within three months after such marriage be banished and removed from this dominion forever." This law also targeted mixed sexual relations outside of marriage by ordering "that if any English woman being free shall have a bastard child by any negro or mulatto, she [shall] pay the sume of fifteen pounds sterling, within one month after such bastard child shall be born, to the Church wardens of the parish where she shall be taken into the possession of the said Church wardens and disposed of for five yeares." The church wardens were supposed to sell English women who were already in servitude for five years after the completion of their original terms of service.[25]

The most consequential part of the Virginia legislation designed to control relationships between whites and people of color was a provision that punished the child for the crimes of the parent, requiring the child to "be bound out as a servant by the said Church wardens until he or she shall attaine the age of thirty yeares."[26] This law made intergenerational servitude a common experience for countless numbers of free people of color. Children of color born out of wedlock to white women automatically became part of the servant class. Virginia law limited servants' right to marry and therefore bear legitimate children. If the daughters of white women had children while under the bonds of servitude, those children also would become servants with restrictions placed on their sexual behavior.

The ideas expressed in the Virginia act soon proliferated across the southern colonies. In 1715, Maryland lawmakers required localities to sell the services of white women who bore "mulatto" children along with the labor of their children until their thirty-first birthday. "Mulatto" children born to "free negro" women were also targeted by the Maryland assembly. Maryland lawmakers required those children, like the children of white women, to serve until the age of thirty-one.[27] During the same year, North Carolina lawmakers passed "An Act Concerning Servants and Slaves," which targeted any white woman who had "a Bastard child by a Negro, Mulatto or Indyan." This law required a fine of six pounds or two years of service for white women who violated the act. The children of North Carolina white women, like those in Maryland, served until their thirty-first birthday. The North Carolina act also levied a fifty-pound fine on a white person who married "any Negro, Mulatto or Indyan Man or Woman."[28] In contrast to laws in other colonies, Delaware's restrictions sought to punish the whole family. Like the laws of the other colonies, Delaware's code called for the binding out of the child and punishment of the white mother. Unlike the others, however, Delaware lawmakers also sought to punish the men involved in relationships between whites and people of color. Delaware law directed "that the Negro or Mulatto man" who fathered a child with a white woman should receive "thirty-nine lashes on his bare back, and stand in the pillory for the space of two hours, with one ear nailed thereunto, and cropped off." Lawmakers in the colony also targeted white men who committed "fornication with a Negro or Mulatto woman." These men faced a comparatively lighter punishment of a twenty-pound fine and "twenty-one lashes, well laid on."[29] South Carolina's 1717 law mandated the punishment of a white woman or a white man who had children by a "negro." White people of either sex faced seven years of servitude if convicted. Similar to the situation in other colonies, the child of a white woman and "a negro or other slave or free negro" faced terms of servitude. However, their terms were shorter than in other colonies at the time: the courts were supposed to bind boys until age twenty-one and girls until age eighteen.[30] As one of the last colonies to be formed, Georgia did not outlaw intermarriage and sexual relations between whites and people of color until 1750.[31]

Colonial officials in Louisiana were less determined than lawmakers in other localities to restrict intermarriage between persons of color and whites. Louisiana's 1724 Code Noir banned marriage between people of color and whites. The law operated, however, in a much different manner and was arguably less strict than other colonial edicts. The Code Noir did not include provisions for placing children in servitude and did not focus specifically on controlling the sexuality of women as did the laws of other colonies. In fact, the Code Noir was primarily concerned with the behavior of white men and provided officials with the ability to levy fines on those men who engaged in sexual relations with their slaves.[32]

Free people of color and their white partners reacted in a variety of ways to these laws. Some couples simply ignored them. Under the threat of a fine, John Cotton officiated the marriage of Edward Burket, "a mullatto man," and Margaret McCartee, "a white women," on December 31, 1720. The couple had left their home in Nansemond County, Virginia, to marry in North Carolina. On finding out about the marriage nearly five years later, the general court in Edenton investigated the situation. Officials discovered corroborating information but decided to dismiss the case against Cotton for marrying the couple.[33] Tamar Smith, alias Hitchens, "a white woman" from Northampton County, Virginia, was not so lucky. After intermarrying with Edward Hitchens, "a mulatto man," local officials sought to punish her for what they perceived as an indiscretion. On October 10, 1738, the county court sent Tamar to jail with no opportunity to post bail for six months. The court also assessed a fine of ten pounds against her.[34]

The southern colonies followed precedents set elsewhere in order to shape their tax codes into tools for distinguishing people of color from whites. By the late sixteenth century, the Spanish crown required Indians as well as "negros" and "mulatos" in its American colonies to pay tribute. The law excluded Spaniards from the tax.[35] Virginia began the process of levying discriminatory taxes on people of color in 1644. Originally, Virginia law reserved taxation for men, but during that year, lawmakers declared all "negro" men and women taxable. By 1682, "Indian women servants" became taxable. In 1723, Virginia lawmakers clarified their law by declaring tithable "all free negroes, mulattoes, and Indians (except tributary Indians to this government), male and female above sixteen years of age."[36] North Carolina's General Assembly issued a similar act that same year.[37] Maryland legislators began using the tax law to target "Female Mulattoes born of White Women" and "Free Negro Women" in 1715.[38] Georgia lawmakers were among the last to impose discriminatory taxation on free people of color. In 1768, all "free Negroes, Mulattoes and Mustizoes" over sixteen years of age became subject to a fifteen-shilling head tax.[39]

For free people of color and their allies, discriminatory taxation was one of the most provocative attacks on their position in society. These taxes created significant financial consequences for free families of color. Surviving tax lists from localities in Virginia and North Carolina demonstrate that local officials executed the discriminatory policy and taxed free men of color who were heads of households along with their male and female dependents over the age of majority. Discriminatory taxation led to widespread protests, both through individual action and through collective community response. In 1758, the court in Surry County, Virginia, received the names of fourteen men described as "mulattoes" who failed to list their wives as tithable.[40] By the 1760s, both free people of color and whites in parts of North Carolina had become frustrated with the effects of discriminatory taxation. In 1762, a group of men from Northampton, Edgecombe, and Granville Counties petitioned the General Assembly on behalf of their neighbors who were "free negroes, mulattoes, mustees and such persons." They argued that the tax on "their wives and daughters" made free men of color "greatly impoverished" and "rendered unable to support themselves and Families with the common necessaries of Life."[41] A petition from Granville County with greater support landed before the General Assembly in 1771. The signatories of the petition agreed that the tithe on "all free negroes & mulato women and all wives of free negroes & mulatoes" was "highly Derogatory of the Rights of Freeborn Subjects" and called for an exemption to the levy. The signers of the petition included free men of color and their white allies.[42] In Virginia, these acts of protest swayed lawmakers, and in 1769, the legislature repealed the tax on free women.[43]

Colonial lawmakers moved beyond using taxation as a way to favor white men over free men of color. By restricting the right of suffrage to white men, these officials further privileged white men through the law. Although the process of preventing free men of color from voting across the South was not complete until 1835, the colonial legal precedents foreshadowed the battle lines that would be drawn decades later between opponents and supporters of disfranchisement. In 1723, Virginia's General Assembly prevented any "free negro or Indian" from having "any vote at any election."[44] As in many future debates over the right to vote, each side issued statements explaining their rationale. In a letter to the Lords Commissioners of Trade and Plantations, Richard West wrote, "To vote at Elections of officers ... is incident to every Freeman who is possessed of a Certain proportion of Property." He continued, "Several Negroes have merited their Freedom and obtained it and by their industry have acquired the proportion of property so that ...

Rights of liberty are actually vested in them." West therefore concluded "that it cannot be just be a generall Law without any allegation of Crime or other demerit whatsoever to strip all free persons of a black Complexion (Some of whom may perhaps be of Considerable substance) from those Rights which are so justly valuable to every Freeman."[45] Several years later, William Gooch described the rationale for disfranchisement. He linked the denigration of the status of free men of color to their alleged inherent connection to slaves, a charge that would remain part of attacks against free people of color for many years to come. He argued that the assembly sought "to fix a perpetual Brand upon Free-Negros & Mulattos by excluding them from that great Priviledge of a Freeman, well knowing they always did, and ever will, adhere to and favour the Slaves." Gooch also admitted that bigotry and a desire to affirm the racial hierarchy drove proponents of the disfranchisement campaign, stating, "And 'tis likewise said to have been done with design, which I must think a good one, to make the free-Negros sensible that a distinction ought to be made between their offspring and the Descendants of an Englishman, with whom they never were to be Accounted Equal." He continued, "It seems no ways Impolitick ... to preserve a decent Distinction between them and their Betters, to leave this mark on them."[46] A similar rationale may have driven the disfranchisement movement in other colonies such as North Carolina and South Carolina. South Carolina lawmakers disfranchised free men of color in 1721. North Carolina legislators moved to prevent free men of color from voting, but the crown overturned the colonial lawmakers' decision.[47]

An assortment of other laws rounded out colonial lawmakers attempts to create legal distinctions between people of color and whites. As early as 1639, Virginia lawmakers passed an act providing all people with arms except "Negroes." In 1670, Virginia law prohibited "Negroes and Indians" from purchasing "Christians." Assemblymen updated the law to specify "white servants" instead of "Christians" in 1705.[48] A 1715 Maryland act distinguished among runaways based on racial categorization. It declared that people taken up as runaways could not be held longer than six months in jail except "mulattoes and negroes."[49] Maryland lawmakers evidently assumed that "mulattoes and negroes" were likely to be slaves. Delaware legislators permitted local officials to hire out "a free Negro, or Mulatto" who could not pay a fine after being convicted of a crime.[50] Several colonies prohibited people of color from testifying against whites in court. In 1717, Maryland assemblymen banned "Indians, Negroes, and Mulattoes" from appearing in cases concerning whites.[51] North Carolina lawmakers were late to adopt this type of discriminatory legislation and did not prohibit "all Negroes and Mulattoes, bond or free, to the Third Generation, and Indian Servants and Slaves" from standing as witnesses against whites until 1754.[52]

Lawmakers in some colonies not only sought to discriminate against free people of color but also desired to limit their numbers more generally. They placed several checks on the manumission process and issued tight immigration restrictions in an attempt to limit the increase of free people of color. Virginia led the tide of discrimination in 1691 by enacting a law stating, "No Negroes, or mulattoes be set free by any person whatsoever, unless such person pay for the transportation of such Negro out of the country within six months after such setting free."[53] In 1715, North Carolina legislators required recently emancipated persons to leave the colony within six months of manumission. After realizing that freed persons were bypassing the law by moving out of North Carolina only temporarily, lawmakers, in 1723, required manumitted persons who returned to the colony to spend seven years in servitude.[54] South Carolina legislators passed a manumission law in 1722 and demanded that each recently manumitted person leave the colony within twelve months or "lose the benefit of such manumission, and continue to be a slave" unless granted a waiver by the General Assembly. In 1735, South Carolina lawmakers revised their law and gave recently freed people six months to leave the state. South Carolina's legislators were likely dealing with the same problems faced by their North Carolina counterparts when they required the reenslavement of freed persons who returned to South Carolina within seven years of their initial freedom.[55] The 1724 Code Noir required Louisiana masters who wished to manumit their enslaved persons to receive approval from the Superior Council before any bondspeople could become free.[56]

Freedom in Its Many Forms

Although discrimination based on racial categorization was an important feature of the law, people in southern communities used other forms of hierarchy in conjunction with racial classification to organize their society. Other modes of distinction such as wealth, gender, occupation, and reputation intersected with racial categorization to create a wide range of experiences for free people of color in the colonial South. The lives of free persons of color who were servants contrasted greatly with those free people of color who were property owners. Free women and girls of color, both poor and well-to-do, experienced their liberty differently than free men and boys of color. No single racialized experience can encapsulate the range of capabilities, sufferings, triumphs, and challenges of free people of color in the colonial South.

The frequent appearance of servants of color, in comparison to free people of color in other stations, in the records of the colonies suggests that servant status was likely the most common position for free people of color in the colonial period. Most free families of color, including those who eventually became financially successful in later generations, likely had ties to servitude if not slavery. Colonial laws constrained the lives of free people of color in servitude and blighted their prospects for economic improvement. Their masters owned their work and the tools they used, and, in some instances, they had the power to transfer their bodies like property. Indenture agreements commonly prevented servants from marrying, and the law bastardized their children, even when servants were in committed relationships.

Large numbers of free people of color entered the colonial systems of servitude as the result of lawmakers' control over servant women's reproductive lives. Laws declaring the children of servant women illegitimate, and therefore targets of local apprenticeship systems, placed countless numbers of free people of color into what often became generational cycles of servitude. Even those children who were products of rape could be pushed into decades of servitude simply because they were born out of wedlock. Colonial lawmakers were more concerned with protecting the interests of masters, who were responsible for supporting pregnant servants, than the women themselves, who may have been victims of assault.[57]

The significant number of children of color born to white mothers were among those most greatly affected by the lack of privileges granted to them by colonial lawmakers. The laws punishing white mothers and their children of color indeed influenced the life trajectories of innumerable free people of color. Local courts bound out many free children of color with white mothers soon after their births. In 1709, Queen Anne's County, Maryland, officials bound Catherine Hawkins's two-year-old "mallatto" daughter as a servant to Catherine's master, John Hawkins, until the little girl reached "the age of one and thirty years." Officials also punished Catherine by requiring her to serve John Hawkins for an additional seven years.[58] In another case, the court for North Carolina's Currituck Precinct placed Sarah Williamson with William and Joanah Parker to serve for five years as part of her punishment for "having a mulatto child" on October 17, 1715. In addition to punishing Williamson directly, the court also targeted her "mulatto child" and forced the child into servitude for "the full term & space of thirty one years."[59] At its June 1755 session, the court of Baltimore County, Maryland, bound Martha Miers until age thirty-one because of her mother's conviction for "Mallatto Bastardy." Martha's mother, Ann Miers, also faced seven years of servitude as a result of her conviction.[60] White political elites specifically targeted white women who participated in sexual acts across racial boundaries as a way to enhance their patriarchal authority. Punishing white women who challenged elite ideas about proper racial boundaries enhanced the power of white men over white women. It also enhanced the power of white men over men of color who were the partners of white women and supported the idea that white men, alone, had the right to access the bodies of white women.[61] The desire to control white women and their bodies had dire consequences for generations of free people of color.

The laws requiring "mulatto" children born to white women to act as servants well into their prime reproductive years made servitude an inherited status for many free children of color. Servitude became passed down from mothers to their children as many free women of color could not protect themselves from pregnancy and childbirth until after their thirty-first birthday. Mary Graves, "a free mullatto," of Kent County, Maryland, was already entangled in servitude when she gave birth to children out of wedlock. Mary's master, Arthur Miller, brought her before the county court in November 1733 to face charges for bastardy. Like so many before her, Mary received additional years of service for giving birth while unmarried. Moreover, her children faced long futures in servitude as the court during its March session bound the "mullatto children," one of whom was two years old and the other six weeks old, to Mary's master until they turned thirty-one.[62] John Power successfully pushed the Lewis family into multigenerational servitude when he reported Mary Lewis, his "mallatto" servant woman, to Bertie County, North Carolina, officials for delivering a "Bastard Female Child called Dinah." In response to the complaint, the court bound Dinah to Power as "an apprentice" in May 1735.[63]

While out-of-wedlock birth was one path to servitude, debt or lack of pecuniary resources also forced some free persons of color into the colonial servitude system. Like many white servants, some free people of color came under the control of masters through indenture agreements that placed them in servitude for a specified number of years, typically in exchange for paid passage from Europe to North America or a reward at the end of service. On April 8, 1690, "Alexander an Indian," who "was imported into this Country," agreed to serve Mary Scot of Perquimans Precinct, North Carolina. In exchange for Alexander's services, Scot agreed to provide him with "lodging, diet, & cloathes."[64] In 1764, Jean Benoit, a "negre libre," or free negro, contracted with Pierre Huberdeau to work on a boat set to travel from New Orleans to Illinois. Benoit agreed to serve for six years in exchange for monetary compensation and food.[65] A law permitting the hiring out of debtors in colonial Delaware pushed some free persons of color into the servitude system. During its May 1771 session, the New Castle County court ordered the sheriff to hire out Jo and Ann Sip, "Negroes," for up to seven years to pay their jail fees. Jo and Ann Sip had spent nearly six months in jail "as Vagrants" before the court forced them into servitude.[66]

Apprentice agreements made between potential masters and parents or local courts frequently placed children in servitude. Officials did not necessarily create these agreements specifically to punish parents of illegitimate children. Children born out of wedlock, orphans, and some children with both parents served as apprentices. Gendered expectations often drove the types of work assigned to apprentices. At the June 1761 court session in Somerset County, Maryland, "Mulatto Leah" became the apprentice of Mary Hobbs. In exchange for Leah's service, which was set to end on her sixteenth birthday, Hobbs agreed to teach Leah the "trade of a weaver" and to "sew and spin." Hobbs also guaranteed to provide the girl with "meat, drink, washing, lodging, and cloathing sufficient for such an apprentice." Leah was supposed to "keep her commandments Lawfully and honestly everywhere" and "demean herself towards her said mistress."[67] In 1764, James Hutt, a two-year-old "mullatto boy" from Kent County, Delaware, became the apprentice of James Voshell. With the alleged consent of Hutt's mother and father, Voshell promised to provide the boy with "sufficient meat, drink, washing, lodging and wearing apparrel" and to teach him farming. He also promised Hutt "two suits of good working cloaths" on the completion of his apprenticeship.[68]

Local officials sometimes abused their power to apprentice children of color and seized children from their parents without consent. These actions challenged the role of apprenticeship as simply a method of youth education and poverty prevention. In 1733, the Committee of Propositions and Grievances of the North Carolina General Assembly received reports of serious abuses taking place in the Bertie Precinct and Bath County. According to the reports, justices of the peace in the counties had apprehended "free Negros & Mollattos" and bound them "until they come to thirty-one years of age contrary to the consent of the parties bound out." These activities concerned some North Carolinians who feared that free people of color would "desert the settlement of those parts fearing to be used in like manner so unlawfully." The committee responded to the reports by requesting the assembly to declare "the illegality of such practice" and order the return of the children to their parents or guardians.[69]

White people used the guise of education and instruction as a justification for placing indigenous children in servitude. During the first century of colonization in Virginia, lawmakers permitted individuals to take "Indian children" in order to provide them with "education or instruction in the Christian religion or for learning English." These children could not be "assigned or transferred" and had to be freed by the age of twenty-five.[70] Accomack County, Virginia, officials permitted local whites to take on Native children as servants during the seventeenth century. In 1669, Edmund Scarburgh made claim to Oliver, Arthur, and Darby, each described as "an Indian servant." In November of that year, the Accomack County court assessed the age of each child and ordered Scarburgh to provide them with "corne & clothes" until their twenty-fourth birthday.[71]

Once free persons of color became entangled in the servitude system, masters obtained considerable power over their lives. Masters commonly treated free people of color as movable property as long as they were under indenture contracts. They bargained, traded, and sold the contracts of their servants at leisure. In August 1687, the Lancaster County, Virginia, master of William Grandy, a "Molatta man," and Andrew Wilson, "a Christian man," transferred them to settle his debts.[72] Captain James Mitchell sold the time of an unnamed "East India Indian" to Michael Miller of Kent County, Maryland, for a five-year term in 1698.[73] In 1736, the Charleston, South Carolina, master of Johny Holmes, "a free negro" carpenter and wheelwright, sold Holmes's services to Kennedy O'Brien in Savannah, Georgia.[74] Servants of color also appeared in the estate accounts of their masters. Robin, a "malato man," Jimmy, a "malato boy," and Nancy, a "malato woman," appeared in the 1713 inventory of property belonging to Richard Marsham of Prince George's County, Maryland. While the appraiser listed these three individuals among the "Negroes" in Marsham's estate, he distinguished them by including information about their terms of service. The other people listed as "Negroes," however, were bound for life.[75] In 1746, the administrator of John Hubard's Amelia County, Virginia, estate included Anne, a "molatto servant girl," in an inventory of Hubard's property. Anne's name showed up on the list along with livestock, tools, and furniture.[76] Servitude represented a major challenge to free people of color hoping to assert control over their lives. Colonial laws or, in some cases, the lack of regulation permitted masters to exert very similar, though not exactly the same, forms of power that they exercised in their relations with enslaved people.[77]

Although colonial lawmakers gave masters significant power over the lives of servants, local courts provided free persons of color with opportunities to lodge complaints against their overlords. As free people and not slaves, these individuals had the right to seek recourse for excessive behavior, such as physical abuse and the violation of contractual agreements.[78] A "Mollattoe girl" servant suffered greatly under the hand of her master, Thomas Courtney of Saint Mary's County, before the Maryland Assembly learned of her case. According to the assembly's records, Courtney had "cut off both the Ears" of the girl. In response to Courtney's crime, the assembly's Council Board ordered the girl "manumitted and sett free from her said Master" on June 4, 1692.[79] In November 1745, Will and Hannah, "an Indian man and woman," petitioned the Kent County, Maryland, court for their freedom, declaring that John Spencer illegally held them as slaves. After hearing the complaint, the court ordered Will and Hannah to "go free" and awarded them five hundred pounds of tobacco in damages.[80] Sarah, "an Indian," charged Patrick White with "assault and battery and false imprisonment" in a complaint to the Norfolk County, Virginia, court in 1750. At an October 19, 1750, session, the court found in favor of Sarah and assessed a fifty-shilling fine against White.[81] In 1769, Alexander Anderson, "a free mulatto," reported to the Court of General Sessions in New Castle County, Delaware, that his master had agreed "to learn him to read, write, and cypher" when the court originally bound him as an apprentice. He explained, however, that his master had "never sent him to school during his apprenticeship" and detained him in service beyond the period of the apprenticeship. The court ordered Anderson to return to his master and declared that his master must send him to school.[82] Although servants of color sometimes were unable to realize the objectives of their complaints, their ability to seek legal recourse separated them from the enslaved people who may have shared similar problems but held a different legal status.

Parents and grandparents who were free played a central role in lodging complaints against masters who they believed crossed the line of acceptable behavior in dealings with their bound children. Their free status allowed them to advocate on behalf of their children and grandchildren, and although they lacked custody, their ability to approach the court on behalf of these youth provided the children with a layer of protection despite their dependent status. Their advocacy provided a voice to the children who were otherwise not in a position to defend their basic rights as free persons. Mary Gibbs, who was also known as "Mulatto Moll," won her freedom from illegal detainment after proving that she was the daughter of Fleetwood Gibbs, a "Scottish woman." In 1758, after her own victory, she petitioned officials in Kent County, Delaware, on behalf of her children, Grace, Mary, Joseph, and Flora Gibbs, whom Waitman Sipple and Andrew Caldwell held as slaves.[83] During the same year, Thomas Carter, a "mullatoe," lodged a complaint against James Wright for illegally detaining five of his grandchildren in Cumberland County, North Carolina. Carter asked the local court to remove the children from Wright's possession. Following the complaint, officials removed at least two of Carter's grandchildren and assigned them to new masters.[84]

When servants of color recognized that they could no longer find recourse through the courts or other legal means, they often took their fates into their own hands by running away from their masters. Facing the possibility of brutal physical punishment and extended terms of service if caught, these free people of color challenged the power of their masters and the laws that gave those masters wide authority over the everyday lives of those in servitude. Roger, "an Indian," made his escape and evaded his master's grasp for six months before his capture. Following his arrest, his master, Richard Bradford, brought Roger's behavior before the December 1689 session of the court in Charles City County, Virginia, which sentenced Roger to one month of additional service.[85] In 1740, Rose Hugin, "a Mulatto Girl" about twenty-six years old, ran from her master, Valentine Robinson, of Brandywine Hundred in New Castle County, Delaware. Robinson reported that Hugin left his employ with "an ash-coloured homespun Gown of worsted Drugget, a striped linsey-wo[o]lsey Petticoat, good Stockings and wooden heel'd Shoes, a Platt Bonnet lined with light read Silk, good linen Shifts, Aprons and Handkerchiefs."[86] Thomas Gilbert, "a Mustee" apprentice with "a broad Face ... full Set of Teeth," and "thick bushy Head of hair," ran from his master, John Brown, in 1745. Brown offered a pistol to anyone who returned Gilbert to Williamsburg, Virginia.[87]

While stuck in servitude, free people of color developed alliances with those who shared similar experiences as bound laborers. These alliances sometimes transformed into long-term relationships, allowing free persons of color to enjoy a sense of stability within a larger social situation that was compromised by the undue influence of the master class. They established relationships with other servants, frequently bridging the artificial racial divide. Isaac Cromwell, "a Mulatto Servant Man," and Anne Green, "an English Woman," developed a long-lasting romantic bond and built a family while they were servants of Thomas Cresap of Frederick County, Maryland. By the early 1750s, the couple had a daughter named Susanna. Working together to create a different life, the couple ran away from Cresap on at least two occasions.[88] Free people of color in servitude also struck up relationships with enslaved people in their neighborhoods. Rachel Overton, "a mallatto" servant of Aaron Jackson of Pasquotank County, North Carolina, had an enslaved "negro Husband." Together the couple had at least three children, Daniel, Samuel, and Parthenia Overton, by 1755.[89]

Occupying a position just steps away from servitude's lack of self-determination was a class of poor free people of color. These free persons of color struggled to make ends meet and lived on the verge of falling back into lives of servitude. Jane Webb's poverty put her in the tough position of sacrificing her children's freedom in order to keep her family together. Sometime before 1711, Webb, "a free malatto," negotiated with Thomas Savage, the enslaver of her partner, Left, to bind her children to him in exchange for permission to marry Left and the eventual emancipation of her husband. Years after making the agreement, Savage's failure to uphold all aspects of the contract forced Webb to sue him in a Northampton County, Virginia, court.[90] Toney, a "Negro," was on the verge of financial collapse in 1748, when Bennett Morgan, a Pasquotank County, North Carolina, constable, confiscated all of his property. Before the confiscation, Toney had borrowed a canoe from James Cleeves but failed to return the canoe after losing it. When Toney was unable to produce the canoe on demand, Morgan collected "all the things" Toney "had in the world," including a small stock of animals, a tub, hooks, and a rundlet. In Toney's case, luck was on his side. Before Morgan could sell his possessions, Toney recovered the canoe in "good order." After petitioning for the return of his property, Toney received a favorable judgment from the court, which ordered Cleeves to compensate him for his losses.[91] Toney shared a common lot with inestimable numbers of free people of color across the colonial world. Many free persons of color struggled to improve themselves within a system that depended on lifting some people through the exploitation of others.

Free people of color who were small property holders lived an often-fruitful existence under the slaveholding class in their communities. These free people of color frequently owned small farms and an assortment of valuable personal property. They accumulated enough wealth to keep their immediate families outside of the colonial servitude system and in some cases maintained a small cadre of apprentices. Some smallholders, such as Emanuel Cambow of James City County, Virginia, a "Negro," acquired their property through the colonial land grant systems. Virginia officials issued a grant of fifty acres to Cambow in 1667.[92] Edward Nicken of Lancaster County, Virginia, purchased multiple plots of land during his lifetime. By the time of his death around 1735, Nicken possessed an assortment of livestock, furniture, and tools and could afford to leave each of his children a small inheritance.[93] Neither wealthy nor eager enough to purchase slaves for profit, John Owen of South Carolina accumulated sufficient money to purchase at least three of his sons out of enslavement. When he dictated his will in 1748, Owen could afford to leave an estate composed of both real and personal property to his sons, John and Thomas.[94] Till Williams, "a free mollatto," owned enough assets to employ William Travis, "a free Negro" apprentice, in 1764.[95] To take on an apprentice, Williams would have needed enough money to post a bond with the Norfolk County, Virginia, court as well as extra resources to feed and clothe Travis.

Free women of color often experienced life as part of more economically privileged families in much different ways than their male counterparts. In the British colonies, coverture commonly disfranchised women and prevented them from making contracts and controlling financial assets directly. Married women in particular had at best a second-class legal personhood, subsumed by their husbands' identities. Uncovering the original surnames of married women during the colonial period is often an impossible task because they took on their husbands' surnames on marriage. When their husbands died, free women of color often maintained some part of their husbands' property, but only as long as they stayed single. Edward Nicken's will dictated that his wife, Mary Nicken, receive his whole estate. Yet if she decided to remarry, the Nicken children were to seize control of the property. John Owen gave his wife, Mary Owen, property that would revert to his sons on Mary's death or remarriage.[96]

The slaveholding elite among free people of color remained relatively small in colonial times. Yet the existence of slaveholders among free persons of color highlights important contrasts between the majority of free people of color and a tiny group of privileged persons. Slaveholding among free people of color emerged as early as the 1600s with individuals such as Anthony Johnson of Northampton County, Virginia. Johnson experienced a peculiar relationship with a man named John Casar, who challenged Johnson's right to hold him as a slave. Even with these challenges from Casar, Johnson successfully maintained control over Casar's life and likely profited from his labor.[97] Although slaveholding appeared among free people of color by the 1600s, the mid-eighteenth century was likely the high point during the colonial period for slave ownership among them. By this time, free men of color like William Chavis, William Johnson, and James Lowry were among the slaveholders in their communities. Chavis accumulated over a thousand acres of land, operated a tavern, and held nearly a dozen people in bondage. In his section of Granville County, North Carolina, Chavis was among the most successful individuals. In 1758, Chavis, as the owner of six enslaved persons, was the largest slaveholder in his tax district. Only one person had surpassed Chavis three years later. Unlike many people, both white and of color, Chavis was literate and owned an inkstand and books. At the time of his death, Chavis possessed land, livestock, and eleven enslaved people.[98] The historical record provides comparatively less insight into the life of William Johnson, "a free Negro man" of Saint Bartholomew's Parish in Colleton County, South Carolina. At his death in the early 1770s, however, Johnson's estate included livestock and a number of enslaved people, including four men, three women, and seven children.[99] James Lowry of Bladen County, North Carolina, whom officials counted as a "mulatto" in tax lists, held a smaller yet significant estate that also included enslaved people. In 1771, Lowry was taxed on one enslaved man named Jack. By the time of the Revolution, Lowry had added a man named Hansom to his holdings.[100] The existence of slaveholders of color in the colonial South revealed that at least under certain circumstances, free status and the rights of one group of people to own another prevailed over a strict racial hierarchy. Such situations appeared throughout the European colonial world.[101]

Regardless of their economic status, free people of color found ways to navigate the barriers of racial categorization, wealth inequality, and gender norms to contribute to their communities and work together with their neighbors. Social necessity and reliance on understandings of family connection and reputation provided free people of color with the opportunity to cooperate with some white southerners. While farming and common labor were the primary focus of colonial southerners including free persons of color, some of these individuals contributed to the economic and practical needs of their communities as business owners and tradespeople. Their contributions helped to keep their neighbors fed, housed, and healthy. During the 1690s, Chrispin de Tapia, a free pardo, operated a grocery store in Saint Augustine, Florida. Jean Baptiste Marly, a "negre libre," or free negro, worked as a cook in Pointe Coupee, Louisiana, during the 1740s.[102] Doctor Caesar, a "Negro" man mentioned earlier in this chapter, described himself as a "Practitioner of Phisick," or a doctor. During the 1750s, the South Carolina General Assembly provided Caesar with one hundred pounds annually for "discovering an Antidote against poison."[103] In 1760, William Hill, a "mulatto bricklayer," received a construction contract from George Butler of Charles County, Maryland.[104] Aaron Bird, a "mulatto," was working as a carpenter in Northampton County, North Carolina as of 1771.[105]

A few free people of color became closely immersed in the business of their white neighbors and became subject to their wills. When Adam Seagrove, a white man, of Currituck Precinct, North Carolina, dictated his will in 1723, he included instructions for John Smith, a "free negro." Seagrove described Smith as his "freind" and declared that Smith would serve as his executor on his death. He also left to Smith his plantation, household goods, and an assortment of livestock.[106] Before Anthony Neale of Charles County, Maryland, died in 1722 or 1723, he dictated a lengthy will that included James Gates, "a Mollatto Man." Neale granted Gates "one thousand pounds of Tobacco." Neale left other men equal or lesser amounts of tobacco. The beginning of Neale's will suggests that these payments were part of his attempt to pay off several debts that would exist against his estate on his death.[107] The appearance of John Smith and James Gates in these wills highlights the deep ties some free persons of color shared with their white neighbors. Both men enjoyed the respect of their white counterparts and benefited from their interactions with them. Their relationships with these white neighbors further reflect the importance of the diverse social positions held by free people of color. The social positions of John Smith and James Gates allowed them to become the beneficiaries of white neighbors. In stark contrast, white people sometimes treated free people of color who were poor servants as only a step above chattel by listing them as property in their inventories.

Living in a world in which slaves and mercenaries commonly served in armies across the globe, officials in southern colonies permitted the enlistment of free people of color in militias. The enlistment of free men of color in the colonial forces demonstrates that free people of color played an important role in the defense of their respective empires and reveals that these empires were at least at some level dependent on the same people who were sometimes the targets of discriminatory policies. The French and Spanish developed segregated militias composed of free men of color and sometimes enslaved men as well. As early as 1580, people of color had served in Spanish units stationed in Florida. In 1683, Governor Juan Márquez Cabrera organized a militia unit consisting of free "pardos" and "morenos" in Saint Augustine. Three years later, this militia defended Saint Augustine from pirate attacks.[108] Free people of color mustered alongside their white neighbors in the British colonies that permitted them to serve. The 1754 muster rolls for militia companies from Granville County, North Carolina, include the names of individuals denoted as "mulatto" and "negro."[109] In these instances, whites and free people of color were interdependent; circumstance and common objectives required them to consider their mutual interests.

Common religion was a catalyst for community in the colonial South and created connections between free persons of color and their white neighbors. Religion gave people of color and white people a shared set of beliefs, a collective understanding of the origins of power, and a basic framework of human evolution. Religious organizations also provided southerners with social validation. By marrying, burying, and blessing the births of people across various social boundaries, religious organizations afforded even persons with the lowest social standing the opportunity to assert the legitimacy of their unions, their families, and their lives. Free people of color, especially in the French and Spanish colonies, sought out the Catholic Church to do all of these things. At Saint Augustine, the Catholic diocese united numerous free persons of color with their chosen partners. The church married Pablo, a free "negro" from the "Congo," to Agustina Nutinez, a "mulata esclava," or mulatto slave, in 1701. In 1713, Nicolas Romezo, a free "pardo," united with Agustina, a "negra esclava," or negro slave.[110] The Catholic church in Saint Augustine also baptized several free people of color, including Antonio, a free "moreno," in 1738, and Juana, the daughter of Juan and Maria, "negros libres," or free negroes, in 1739.[111] In the British colonies, the Anglican church drew together people of various backgrounds, giving free people of color opportunities to become part of religious communities. The register of baptisms for the Saint Peter's Parish in New Kent County, Virginia, contains the names of several free people of color, including Mary and George, the children of Ann Holt, a "free mulatto woman," whom the rectors baptized during the 1730s.[112] White church officials worked diligently to bring people of all backgrounds into the church. John MacDowell reported in a letter to Daniel Burton, dated June 15, 1762, that he had successfully recruited to the church people of numerous backgrounds in North Carolina, including "a free negro man, who after proper instructions" had "become a constant communicant."[113] Religion served as one of the many ways people in the colonies organized their societies and defined the lines between insiders and outsiders. By joining these religious institutions with their white neighbors, free people of color strengthened social connections with their neighbors and established alternative ways to understand societal hierarchies and structures. Free people of color were not simply nonwhite persons but also fellow Christians, fellow Catholics, or fellow Anglicans.

By the middle of the eighteenth century, free persons of color had established themselves in many facets of colonial life. They held a diversity of positions in the economy, social life, political debates, and religious communities. Their lives were intertwined with those of their neighbors, white as well as enslaved. In many ways, their existence in the southern colonies was similar to the experiences of free people of color in other colonial settings. The colonial South's free persons of color consistently defied attempts to create an inflexible society stratified solely on the basis of racial categorization.

From the earliest generations, including individuals like King Tony to those living at the dawn of the American Revolution, free people of color made important strides to shape the societies of which they were part. Free persons of color outside the bonds of servitude experienced life based on a variety of factors, including wealth, gender, work, and reputation. The colonial period offered a few free people of color great prosperity while many others occupied the economic margins of society and barely scraped by. A significant number of free people of color were positioned in the social space between the slaveholding elites and the destitute. Many free persons of color worked hard to create lives for themselves and their families and in doing so promoted the development of their communities.

The presence of free people of color in the colonies did not go unnoticed. White lawmakers concerned with creating and sustaining both racialized and wealth-based hierarchies sought to define proper social boundaries, which included restrictions on marriage, sexual behavior, and political privileges. These restrictions, however, did not prevent all free people of color from progressing economically and socially. Legislation could be important in dictating white people's attitudes about free people of color. Many whites clearly accepted ideas about white superiority. Yet the law could not completely dictate the ways that white people reacted to the free persons of color in their midst. Free people of color and whites broke the law together, and occasionally they came together to challenge the law in formal ways. Even though the law largely invalidated their unions, free people of color and whites still sought to build families on their own terms. These patterns of behavior would continue as life in the British, Spanish, and French colonies gradually shifted toward political and social revolution.

CHAPTER 2

The Revolution of Freedom

As early as the 1760s, revolutionary ideas were trickling into the neighborhoods of Baltimore. These revolutionary ideas, like so many other concepts floating through society at the time, focused on the issue of freedom. Yet they were not about freedom for the colonists or freedom from a supposedly tyrannical monarch in distant England. These ideas were about freedom for the truly oppressed: freedom for the enslaved and freedom for thousands of men, women, and children held in oppressive bondage in every corner of the colonial world. For over a century, slaveholders across the colonies had offered their bondspeople liberty in exchange for monetary considerations and occasionally because of familial affection. In this period, however, a new set of ideas would pave the road to freedom for thousands of enslaved persons. On April 9, 1768, Baltimore resident James Rigbie manumitted his bondspeople after "having undergone much uneasiness and Trouble of Mind on account of the Bondage & Captivity of those poor distressed people" and "Under a Sense of Duty Conscienciously Scruple to keep them & In Justice to them." In the same year, William Cox, also of Baltimore, freed several women and children because holding them in slavery was "inconsistent with the rules of Christianity."[1] The statements by Rigbie and Cox represent the new grounds on which people in the colonial South fought the first full-fledged war against slavery.

Since slavery's establishment in the Americas, people of color had battled against bondage: on the decks of slave ships, on the plantations of their masters, and in local courtrooms. By the middle of the eighteenth century, some white people, too, were viewing slavery as an enemy to battle, a despotic demon to destroy. The combined efforts of people of color, enslaved and free, and white allies would permanently alter the lines of slavery and freedom in North America. These changes would reshape the world of free people of color and transform their composition and position in society. By the beginning of the 1800s, slavery was dead or near collapse in several northern states. Slavery's gradual deterioration in the North ultimately led to its strong association with the South. The population of free people of color began to explode in the late 1700s in the South as well as in the North. Even as the South became more firmly associated with slavery, the numbers of free persons of color increased.[2]

White people's goodwill played only a part in the revolution of freedom that swept across North America during the late eighteenth century. People of color paved their own paths to liberty by increasingly negotiating with their enslavers for self-purchase. Some people of color, who thought their enslavers held them in bondage against the dictates of nature but more importantly against the laws of their country, hauled their oppressors to courts across the land. In front of judges and juries, they told stories of their families' once cheerfully held freedom and how their oppressors stole their liberties and unjustly detained their bodies. They demanded freedom, and in many cases, they obtained the freedom they sought.[3]

The rise of antislavery ideologies coalesced with changes in the French and Spanish Empires to make the South home for thousands of free people of color. The Spanish takeover of Louisiana after the Seven Years' War created new opportunities for freedom among the enslaved people of the region. Spanish officials offered a more flexible manumission policy than their French predecessors. French colonial failures in the Caribbean at the end of the eighteenth century further increased the population of free people of color. Led by Toussaint Louverture, former bondspeople pushed out the slaveholding class, who had exploited their labor to make Saint-Domingue one of the most profitable colonies in the world. Among the exiled slaveholders and refugees of the war were free persons of color. These free people of color, who were among the living vestiges of French colonialism, found their way to port cities across North America, including in the South. They arrived in cities like New Orleans, Savannah, Charleston, Norfolk, and Baltimore. In these localities, they set down roots and became an important and influential subsection of the free population of color.[4]

The battle for independence from Great Britain was born alongside the war against slavery and would subsume the energies of free people of color across the colonies. The participation of free persons of color served to support their demands for continued freedom and their claims to social privileges and political rights through the decades of the nineteenth century. Free people of color simultaneously contributed to American independence and brought about opportunities for greater freedom across the country. The ideas of liberty regularly recited during the war against Great Britain became the demands of the postwar generations. If the United States truly stood for liberty, free people of color called for all Americans to prove it through their treatment of those already free and to demonstrate it by providing freedom to the enslaved.

Organizing the War against Slavery

In the British colonies, the formal war against slavery began in the Quaker churches scattered across the land as early as the 1750s. The Pennsylvania Yearly Meeting published the antislavery tract *An Epistle of Caution and Advice, Concerning the Buying and Keeping of Slaves* in 1754. The tract pointed out the inconsistencies between Christianity and enslavement by declaring, "If we continually bear in Mind the royal Law, of doing to others, as we would be done by, we shall never think of bereaving our Fellow Creatures of that valuable Blessing Liberty; nor endure to grow rich by their Bondage."[5] By the end of the decade, Pennsylvania Quakers punished their members for importing, purchasing, or selling their fellow human beings. Following years of consideration and debate, the Pennsylvania Friends finally prohibited their members from owning slaves in 1776. Quaker meetings across North America, including those in the South, followed the lead of their Pennsylvania brethren. Thomas Nicholson of Perquimans County, North Carolina, was speaking out against slavery by 1767. During that year, he professed to an audience of Friends that "the Slave Trade is a very wicked and abominable Practice, contrary to the natural Rights and Privileges of all mankind."[6]

The most adamant antislavery Quakers not only spoke against slavery but worked to spread the idea of liberty beyond their home communities. David Ferris of Wilmington, Delaware, spent the last years of his life arguing diligently for emancipation. During the 1760s and 1770s, he wrote to slaveholding Friends and asked them to reconsider holding other human beings in bondage. He also made visits to the homes of slaveholders. Citing the Bible, he contended that neither God nor Jesus condoned slavery but spoke against it. He warned fellow Quakers that holding others in bondage was a threat to their own salvation, as the Bible suggested that those who failed to follow the teachings of Jesus would not see him in the afterlife. Ferris worked to protect the interests of those bondspeople whom he helped to free by asking emancipators to make out their manumissions in writing. This action was meant to protect the emancipated people from reenslavement. After freeing his bondspeople and adopting the causes of human equality and abolition, Warner Mifflin of Kent County, Delaware, dedicated much of his life to convincing others of the righteousness of liberating the enslaved. Beginning in the 1770s, Mifflin initiated a years-long tour of Friends meetings, traveling from New England to the Carolinas and advocating for the antislavery cause. To those he was able to convince, he offered instruction in how to manumit bondspeople. Going beyond the standard doctrine of his sect, Mifflin also encouraged would-be emancipators to provide their soon-to-be liberated bondspersons with some form of compensation for their time in bondage, such as land or money. He preached against emancipating people without providing them with basic necessities like housing and food. Back home in Delaware, he worked with other Quakers to build community with recently emancipated people. He assessed the freedpeople's needs and sought to address their grievances.[7]

By the 1770s, the antislavery gospel had spread beyond the Quakers to the Nicholites and Methodists. Religious abolitionists joined with other activists to build antislavery societies tasked with executing the assault on slavery and protecting the interests of free persons of color. In 1775, activists came together to form the Society for the Relief of Negroes, which eventually became the Pennsylvania Society for Promoting the Abolition of Slavery and the Relief of Free Negroes, Unlawfully Held in Bondage. This organization spawned numerous affiliated antislavery organizations, including some in the South. Of the southern organizations, the societies in Delaware and Maryland were the strongest and most active. Maryland was the home to a state organization, the Maryland Society for Promoting the Abolition of Slavery, as well as to local associations such as the Baltimore Society for the Abolition of Slavery and the Chestertown Society for Promoting the Abolition of Slavery. Delaware's antislavery organizations included the Dover-based Delaware Society for Promoting the Abolition of Slavery and the Delaware Society for the Gradual Abolition of Slavery, which met in Wilmington. Antislavery societies also existed in Virginia and North Carolina.[8]

As the desire to end slavery gained traction, southern activists sought to improve existing manumission laws. The laws of multiple localities required "meritorious service" from candidates for emancipation and demanded that they leave their jurisdictions on liberation. In order to secure the liberty of their bondspeople, southern Quakers sought to repeal the limitations on manumission. In 1780, Virginia Quakers asked the House of Delegates to permit them to free their bondspeople.[9] By the outbreak of the American Revolution, antislavery activists made serious inroads toward changing the political environment and laid a path to freedom for thousands of liberty-seeking enslaved persons. They persuaded many localities to reform their manumission laws. Virginia lawmakers in 1691 had required freedpeople to leave the state on emancipation, but by 1782 a new generation of legislators permitted manumissions by will or deed without insisting on the removal of the recently emancipated persons. In 1796, Maryland lawmakers removed restrictions on manumission by will and permitted anyone to emancipate enslaved persons by will as long as those persons' manumissions would not counter the interests of creditors.[10]

Antislavery advocates found less success in the North Carolina General Assembly. After 1777, North Carolina lawmakers continued to require "meritorious service" for emancipated persons. State law provided county courts with the power to decide which appeals for manumission were meritorious. People emancipated without court approval faced arrest and possible sale.[11] North Carolina law made manumission largely a local issue, although the General Assembly heard petitions for freedom as well. While North Carolina lawmakers did not grant potential emancipators the liberties enjoyed by that group in other states, the new regulations in North Carolina were an improvement over the old system. North Carolina's new legislation no longer required expulsion from the state for emancipated persons. If a master could convince the court of his or her enslaved person's meritorious service, the emancipated person could legally remain at home, a privilege denied to previous generations of freed persons in North Carolina.

The combination of social and political changes led slaveholders across the South to reconsider the enslavement of their bondspeople. Manumissions driven by antislavery thinking were common in the Upper South. Slaveholders cited ideas such as natural rights and moral qualms as driving their decisions to manumit their bondspeople. Thomas Blades of Caroline County, Maryland, emancipated a man named Harry in 1781 because of the "good will and affection" he held for Harry and to "satisfy" his "conscience." The idea of keeping "any slave or slaves from their freedom" troubled Blades.[12] Immediately following the passage of manumission reform in Virginia, several Southampton County slaveholders moved to liberate a cadre of women, men, and children. In late 1782, members of the Denson, Jones, Stanton, Pretlow, Butler, Eley, Ricks, and Smith families emancipated ninety-five people because they believed that "freedom is the natural right of all mankind." The adults received their freedom immediately while most of the liberated children remained under the guardianship of their former enslavers until reaching maturity.

Nineteen of the emancipated people had enjoyed nominal independence under Thomas Pretlow's guardianship for several years. The change in the manumission laws and Pretlow's formal deed of emancipation now made them legally free.[13]

Emancipators drew explicit connections between their antislavery sentiments and their religious ideologies to justify the manumission of their bondspeople. For these individuals, antislavery acts were the fulfillment of religious sentiment. Daniel Mifflin, a Quaker from Accomack County, Virginia, and the father of antislavery warrior Warner Mifflin, freed one hundred people in 1775, "being convinced of the Enequity and injustice of detaining my fellow creatures in bondage it being contrary to the standing and perpetual command enjoyned by our blessed Lord to his followers to do unto others as we would they should do by us." Mifflin feared that "continuing in violation thereof will incur his displeasure and debar me of the Enjoyment of the peace promised to his faithfull followers."[14] Allen Young of Mecklenburg County, Virginia, was among the fieriest religious emancipators of his time. On June 14, 1790, he issued a deed of emancipation for Ann, Rachel, Richard, Ephraim, and Pompey with the "sincere desire to do Justly, love mercy, and walk humbly before God." Concerned with the futures of the five emancipated people, Young explained that "feeling myself deeply concerned about their present and eternal welfare, I do most earnestly and humbly beseech Thee O thou compassionate father of all mercies to guide them by thy glorious spirit that they may travel through this impetuous world so in thy fear & love that they may stop the mouths of bloody oppressors." To support further the religious justification for his actions, Young also cited passages from the Bible, including Romans 8:16 and Luke 16:20.[15]

Antislavery ideas did not find the same success in the English-speaking Deep South. Economic trends increasingly tied the future of this area to slavery. The political environment in the Deep South, however, still permitted masters to exercise basic discretion over the futures of their bondspeople, and there were some who acted to emancipate their bondspeople citing antislavery justifications. On August 18, 1796, James Leggitt of Green County, Georgia, manumitted Bob, Peggy, Sam, Cleoeke, Luke, and Isabele on the grounds that "all men by nature are equally free and have a right to liberty."[16] The 1799 will of Thomas Wadsworth of Charleston, South Carolina, included a section manumitting his bondspeople. Wadsworth explained that he was "induced from Motives of Humanity to set free and emancipate all the Negro Slaves that have been intrusted to my care or that I may die possessed of." He delegated the task of caring for the soon-to-be-emancipated people to "the Society of Quakers or Friends." Wadsworth bequeathed land to the Quakers, who would then divide it among the emancipated persons.[17]

Antislavery advocates organized relief efforts to purchase and liberate enslaved people. They united to raise funds to purchase and emancipate enslaved individuals. As a collective, they made a greater impact than if they tried to work individually. Following the death of Thomas Cooch of New Castle County, Delaware, Solomon and Elizabeth Maxwell, Robert and Mary Middleton, and Dorcas Armitage joined together to purchase a woman from Cooch's estate with "the sole purpose and humane desire of setting the said Jemima free from her slavery." On procuring Jemima from the estate, the group executed a deed of manumission on December 15, 1788.[18] In 1798, Tommey Thomas, Charles Campbell, Hannah T. Lorimer, Thomas Fauntleroy, and Isabella Fauntleroy of Middlesex County, Virginia, "actuated by humanity," came together to liberate Sam, "a negro slave belonging to James H. T. Lorimer, an infant under the age of twenty one years." The group agreed to pay Lorimer's guardian, James Ross, fifty pounds for Sam's freedom. On April 22, 1799, Ross accepted the payment and issued a deed for Sam's emancipation.[19]

Reciprocity continued to play an important role in the growing number of emancipations in the South. Throughout history, manumission had served as an incentive for enslaved people to follow their masters' directives and perform to their highest abilities with the hope of someday becoming free.[20] Slaveholders were ultimately left to consider the value of their bondspeople's services, and they defined the behavior that merited liberty. While dictating that his executors divide most of his bondspeople among his heirs, George Weedon of Fredericksburg, Virginia, requested that his coachman Bob, whom he described as "my faithful servant," remain with his wife and receive his freedom after her death.[21] The executors followed the instructions laid out in Weedon's 1793 will and emancipated Bob on November 25, 1797.[22] Due to North Carolina's requirement that masters liberate only people who performed "meritorious service," county courts often defined the term broadly and allowed slaveholders to liberate their bondspeople for a wide variety of equally ambiguous reasons. In his 1790 will, Francis Clayton of New Hanover County, North Carolina, freed Brunetta in consideration of her "fidelity."[23] Ichabud received his liberty from Samuel Jackson of Pasquotank County, North Carolina, in 1799 for simply being "a faithful servant."[24] Each master created a slightly different set of criteria to define meritorious service. In states where the law required meritorious service, masters not only set their own standards but then had to convince legal arbiters that their process of evaluation was sound.

Some slaveholders who were willing to emancipate their bondspeople were reluctant to liberate them immediately. Slaveholders often provided a path to freedom that required a set term of additional service before the enslaved would be unconditionally free. Such arrangements benefited masters who sought to extract additional labor from bondspeople while attempting to incentivize good behavior. Some enslavers opted to provide a semblance of freedom to their bondspeople in order to fulfill their personal beliefs about human liberty or demonstrate their willingness to follow neighbors who emancipated their bondspeople, all the while retaining soon-to-be emancipated people as assets who could be hired out or sold if needed. When Cassandra Sheredine of Harford County, Maryland, issued a deed of manumission for her bondspeople in 1775, she required them to serve for several additional years before obtaining their freedom. Sheredine forced the adults to serve her until January 1, 1779, except for Samuel, whom she demanded serve additional time to make up for a period when he ran away. The enslaved people who were minors were to stay with Sheredine until reaching majority.[25] Absalom Ridgely's 1789 deed of manumission required Joshua, Phillis, and Thomas to serve him for several years before receiving their freedom. Although Ridgely claimed to be "conscienciously concerned," he demanded that Joshua and Phillis remain his slaves until the beginning of 1794. Ridgely's deed required Thomas to remain with him in Anne Arundel County, Maryland, until January 1, 1801.[26]

When masters failed to provide a more immediate path to liberation, enslaved people took advantage of the new political and social environment to arrange for self-purchase even though such arrangements were risky. Under the laws of the U.S. South, enslaved people could not enter into agreements that were enforceable, nor could they expect their financial interests to be protected. A master could easily renege on a promise of liberty and fail to deliver freedom documents after an enslaved person presented the money to the master for self-purchase. Nevertheless, some enslaved people were able to conduct exchanges with their enslavers in good faith. The possibility of self-purchase, like other forms of manumission, incentivized productive behavior on the part of enslaved persons by providing them with monetary goals to work toward. Self-purchase also benefited masters who could take the hard-won earnings of their bondspeople and use the funds for their own purposes.[27] In 1789, Abraham Skipwith of Richmond, Virginia, purchased himself from James Warington and Thomas Keene for forty pounds.[28] At the age of thirty-five, Stephen obtained his liberty from John Freeman of Dover, Delaware, after paying thirty pounds.[29] Henrietta James of Baltimore emancipated

Jack after he paid her eighty dollars for his freedom in 1794.[30] Even in the Deep South, where the antislavery cause failed to gain significant traction, a few fortunate enslaved people convinced their masters to liberate them. In 1777, Scipio purchased his liberty from Hugh and Mary Brown of Charleston, South Carolina, for nine hundred pounds.[31] These transactions were made at a time when many people received fewer than ten to fifteen dollars or pounds per month in wages.[32]

Family and friends also played an important role in guiding many enslaved people to liberty. The free status of family and friends provided an extra layer of protection for the enslaved during negotiations to obtain their liberty. Unlike enslaved people who sought to purchase their liberty directly from masters, friends and family who were free had basic property rights and the ability to enter legally binding contracts with the masters of the enslaved. William Blamyer of Charleston, South Carolina, manumitted Nancy, a "mulatto girl," in 1780 after Nancy's mother, Kate, a "free negro woman," paid him five hundred pounds.[33] On September 7, 1796, Thomas Sylvester, "a free man of colour," purchased his wife, Joan, and their three children—Abba, Nancy, and Jerry—from Jeremiah Symons of Pasquotank County, North Carolina, for one hundred pounds. The following year, Sylvester petitioned the county court to liberate his wife along with their now four children. At the June 1797 session, the court granted Sylvester's request.[34] Caesar King, "a black man" living in Cecil County, Maryland, procured his son David from James McCoy for forty-five pounds in 1798. Following the purchase, King manumitted David.[35]

By the late 1700s, some of the South's most affluent and influential slaveholders had decided to adopt the war against slavery as their own. Their actions demonstrate that antislavery ideology influenced even those who had the most to lose if slavery collapsed in the U.S. South. Unwilling to sacrifice the benefits provided to them in life by their bondspeople, however, some of these slaveholders waited until their death before offering liberty to the enslaved. Before his passing in 1785, Joseph Mayo of Henrico County, Virginia, requested that his executors emancipate his bondspeople. His estate included 176 individuals spread over the counties of Mecklenburg, Henrico, Goochland, Chesterfield, and Cumberland. On Mayo's death, his executors petitioned the state legislature to ask for a law permitting such a large manumission. The legislature granted the request.[36] When George Washington dictated his last will and testament in 1790, he declared, "Upon the decease of my wife, it is my will and desire that all the slaves which I hold in my own right shall receive their freedom." Washington also instructed that those suffering from "old age or bodily infirmities" and those in their "infancy" be "fed and clothed by my heirs."[37] Unlike some of his wealthy counterparts, Robert Carter of Nomini Hall in Westmoreland County, Virginia, did not wait until his death to free his bondspeople. Throughout the 1790s, he issued deeds of manumission freeing dozens of people at a time. In three deeds dated January 2, 1792, Carter emancipated a total of twenty-nine people. On the first day of 1793, Carter freed an additional fifty-seven women and men.[38] The example of these well-to-do slaveholders, however, did not sway all of their peers toward the cause of emancipation. Their large-scale manumissions still created important precedent and led to the development of significant populations of free people of color that would grow and thrive into the nineteenth century.

Revolutionary Freedom

Efforts to provide people of color with liberty extended beyond collective and individual acts of manumission. In localities across the South, people of color and their white allies fought against the illegal bondage of free persons. Since the earliest days of the colonies, unscrupulous masters and kidnappers had attempted to hold free people of color as slaves. For generations, free persons of color had battled in the courts against those who held them in bondage. As the effort to expand liberty to thousands of enslaved people accelerated, however, some antislavery advocates also decided to dedicate attention to the plight of individuals who claimed to be free but faced continued oppression under the authority of masters.

Across the United States, people of color with assistance from white associates sought liberation from what they considered illegal bondage.[39] The coexistence of slavery and long-term servitude allowed crooked masters to blur the line between enslavement and freedom. Local governments in the colonial period had also failed to create a legal procedure for free people of color to document their freedom. Instead, local knowledge and public memory were important tools in the process of establishing the free status of one's ancestors. The lack of accurate information concerning dates of birth for free persons of color also led to disputes about the appropriate terms of services. Furthermore, local record keepers did not always record ages on indenture documents. Those who claimed to be illegally held declared descent from an assortment of free female ancestors—"white," "Indian," and "East Indian women"—and demanded freedom on those grounds.

Robert Thomas of Anne Arundel County, Maryland, was one such individual, and in 1794, Thomas sued Henry Pile for his freedom. Thomas declared that he was a lineal descendant of a white woman named Elizabeth Thomas, who, he asserted, was his great-great-grandmother. The district court heard testimony from dozens of witnesses, both white and of color, in Thomas's case. Several witnesses claimed that they had known Thomas's family only as slaves. Others claimed that they had heard that the mother of Thomas's great-grandmother, whom many witnesses knew before her death, was a white woman. After taking the evidence into consideration, the court liberated Robert Thomas.[40] Around the same time Robert Thomas received his liberty, officials in Kent County, Delaware, learned about the case of a woman named Phillis. They received a petition from her claiming that she was "born free" but was being held as a slave by Evan Lewis, "her pretended master." Sarah Ward of Somerset County, Maryland, provided the court with important details about Phillis's heritage. Her April 4, 1796, deposition explained that Phillis's grandmother Sarah and mother, Binah, were servants to the Ward family until Binah removed to Delaware. Ward described Phillis's grandmother as "an East Indian" who "was of a complexion rather darker than any of the natives of this country, and still different from the common mulatto color." According to Ward, Sarah, Phillis's grandmother, also had "straight black hair very much unlike the hair of the negroes imported from Africa." With Sarah Ward's support, Phillis established the free status of her ancestors and gained her liberty.[41]

Numerous people of color filed charges against their masters for holding them beyond their terms of service or keeping them as slaves. Some of these individuals were freeborn while others had been emancipated. In 1782, James Manly, "an Indian," petitioned the justices of Craven County, North Carolina, for his liberty. He declared that "he was free born at Edenton and that he never has been guilty of any action by which his freedom can be forfeited." Manly further explained that John Garland came to his "dwelling house" and "forcibly drove him away and sold him as a slave to Colonel Levi Dawson." He asked the county court to "pass an order for liberating or setting him free." After reviewing the request, the court demanded that Dawson release Manly.[42] In a different situation, the chancery court in Accomack County, Virginia, in 1790 heard the case of London, a "negro" man, held as a slave by John Kellam. London claimed that, with the help of friends, he acquired his liberty from his former master, John Savage, who was Kellam's father-in-law. Following his emancipation, London "by his honest industry" bought property and reimbursed his friends who helped purchase his freedom. London also cared for the daughters of Savage, who left the country, leaving his children behind in Virginia. After London had acted as a free man for many years, Kellam, the husband of one of Savage's daughters, decided to claim London as his property. In response to his aggression, London filed a suit against Kellam. Several witnesses, including some who knew of or participated in the purchase from Savage, testified on London's behalf. On hearing the totality of evidence, a jury declared London free.[43]

Only a few years before the outbreak of the American Revolution, southern lawmakers had begun to take seriously abuses against people of color in the servitude system. Officials in several localities recognized that some masters and kidnappers were exploiting the servant status of free people of color to hold them beyond their original terms of service or to present them as slaves instead of free persons. In 1760, Delaware lawmakers observed that "the children of white women and Negro or Mulatto fathers, and the descendants of such children and Negroes, entitled to their freedom, are frequently held and detained as servants, or as slaves, by persons pretending to be their masters and mistresses." They also understood that some of the people "frequently are sold as slaves by such pretended masters or mistresses to persons who reside in other governments, with a fraudulent design to prevent them procuring proof of their being entitled to their freedom." The legislators described Delaware's laws concerning the problem as "defective" and decided to pass new protections for people of color. They created a legal process for people of color who wanted to make claims against those who allegedly held them illegally. Those convicted of selling free persons out of Delaware faced fines of one hundred pounds plus the cost to restore the trafficked persons back to Delaware. If they failed to pay the fines, offenders could be imprisoned until the fines were paid.[44] A 1765 Virginia act explained that "ill-disposed persons" in the colony had been "guilty of selling certain mulattoes and others as slaves, who are by law subject to serve only to thirty-one years of age." Virginia lawmakers reacted to the problem by passing legislation fining offenders "fifty pounds" to be paid to the purchasers of the illegally trafficked free persons. An individual found guilty of a second offense of illegally selling free persons was supposed to "forfeit the residue of the time due from such servant, who shall thereupon be bound to serve until twenty-one years of age, in the same manner as is directed for orphan children." If the offender could not meet this condition, lawmakers required that "he must serve the buyer the time that would have been due from the servant." Unlike Delaware legislators, Virginia lawmakers did not give people of color who claimed to be free a clear legal process to make their claims until 1795.[45] Legislators in other jurisdictions took action during the American Revolution. North Carolina lawmakers addressed the issue of selling free people of color as slaves relatively late, not passing legislation tackling the issue until 1779. The state's lawmakers, however, made up for the delay with one of the strictest kidnapping laws. Persons found guilty of illegally transporting "any free negro or free negroes, or persons of mixed blood, out of this state to another, with an intention to sell or dispose of such free negro or free negroes, or persons of mixed blood," faced a felony conviction and "death without benefit of clergy."[46]

Spanish Freedom

The expansion of freedom in the South extended well beyond the English-speaking regions. Political change in Louisiana ushered in new opportunities for freedom for hundreds of enslaved people. Following the Seven Years' War, the French transferred Louisiana to the Spanish. By 1769, the Spanish had begun to reorganize the legal and political system in Louisiana by implementing the Spanish legal codes. The Spanish brought new ideas about manumission and the rights of enslaved people to pursue their liberty. Spanish law gave enslaved persons the ability to negotiate with their masters to purchase their freedom. These negotiations could involve a simple agreement between a slaveholder and enslaved person or could also include the court. Spanish law provided slaveholders with greater flexibility to liberate their bondspeople. Unlike French colonial law, the Spanish legal code allowed slaveholders to emancipate the enslaved without the consent of government officials. Enslaved people also had the right to seek their freedom without their masters' agreement. A bondsperson or agent could request a *carta de libertad*, or letter of freedom, from the governor's tribunal. The carta de libertad provided an enslaved person with an assessed self-purchase price. Spanish law required slaveholders to accept the valuations and liberate enslaved people who could pay the assessed costs.[47]

Enslaved people and slaveholders took advantage of the new legal system under the Spanish regime and transformed the social landscape of Louisiana, particularly in New Orleans. Hundreds of bondspeople obtained their liberty through self-purchase. In 1775, Maria purchased her freedom and that of her daughter Carlota from Father Barnabe, who had acquired Maria and Carlota from their former master with the expressed purpose of providing Maria with the opportunity to liberate herself and her child. In 1788, Juan Santiago Mangloan bought his freedom from his master, Marcos Olivares, for 1,050 pesos. While self-purchase was an important mechanism in the pursuit of freedom, some enslaved people secured their liberty without engaging in direct financial transactions. As a reward for faithful service, Angelica obtained her freedom from the heirs of Mariana Hervieux in 1770.[48] In New Orleans alone, over nineteen hundred bondspeople obtained their liberty during the Spanish colonial period.[49] The liberalization of Spanish manumission policies transformed societies across the Atlantic. Populations of free people of color were rapidly increasing in other parts of the Atlantic, including Havana, Santiago de Cuba, and Bayamo, at the same time freedom was expanding in Louisiana.[50]

The annexation of Louisiana to Spain created a new path to freedom for enslaved people who could demonstrate indigenous heritage. Spanish officials, unlike their French counterparts, sought to curb the enslavement of indigenous persons and provided enslaved Native people with avenues to obtain their liberty. In 1769, Governor Alejandro O'Reilly issued an ordinance prohibiting Indian slavery.[51] As Spanish law replaced the French legal code, some enslaved persons grabbed the opportunity to sue for their freedom based on their "Indian" ancestry. In 1790, Pedro Morsu, an "Indio Mestizo," or Indian Mestizo, demanded his liberty in the colonial court. Although held as the slave of Don Francisco Cruzat, Morsu claimed to be free. Morsu supported his assertion by explaining that he was the son of Catalina, a woman of the Chi Nation. As the son of an indigenous woman, he was supposed to be free under Spanish law. On presenting his case to the court and proving his familial connection to Maria Paget, another child of Catalina who was already free, Morsu gained his liberty.[52] In another case occurring in 1791, Mariana, an "India," or Indian woman, sued Francisca Pomet, a "mulata libre," or free mulatto, for illegally keeping her as a slave. Mariana sought to establish that she was an Indian and therefore unable to be enslaved by Pomet under Spanish law. After hearing the case against Pomet, the court liberated Mariana.[53]

The expansion of freedom continued in parts of the South long dominated by the Spanish, although not at as fast a pace as in Louisiana. The Spanish briefly lost control of Florida after the Seven Years' War, but after the Spanish reclaimed the territory from Great Britain following the American Revolution, the opportunities for bondspeople to become free persons increased. Following the death of Jacob Femmie of Galvez Town, West Florida, Magdelena, a "mulatto" woman, obtained her freedom. Before he died in 1782, Femmie willed Magdelena her liberty along with all of his clothing and half of his movable goods. In 1787, Maria Ana Decoux appeared before Don Francisco Rivas at Fort Bute in order to liberate Jacobo, an enslaved "Indian" man. At age twenty, Jacobo was finally able to enjoy his freedom.[54]

Immigrants

A wave of immigration accompanied the expansion of manumissions in the late eighteenth century. While several parts of the world were experiencing political and social volatility, free people of color from those places landed in southern ports as refugees and workers. The instability brought about by revolution and rebellion in France and its dependencies pushed many of these free persons of color to seek new homes in the fledgling United States.[55] In 1793, Catherine, a free "mollatto woman," arrived in Wilmington, Delaware, from Hispaniola.[56] During the same year, Felicite Barran, a "mulatresse libre," or free mulatress, left Saint Mark in Saint-Domingue on board the schooner *Eliza Cape Wheeler* and relocated to Baltimore. Barran was accompanied by her bondspeople Azou Najo, Virginia Arada, and Sophia Poryo.[57] Born in Saint-Pierre, Martinique, Nicholas Cammel, "a free Black Man" and sailor, departed in 1793 for Alexandria, at that time part of the District of Columbia. After his arrival in Alexandria, Cammel set down roots in the community by finding a wife and working on vessels stationed in the community.[58] Azou, an eleven-year-old "mullatto Boy," arrived in Baltimore as the servant of David Williamson sometime shortly before September 1790. Williamson professed to have purchased Azou as a slave in the Isle of France, a French colony off the eastern coast of Africa, but he made no claim on him as a slave. Following their arrival in Maryland, Williamson had Azou formally bound to him as a servant until Azou's twenty-second birthday. Williamson promised to provide Azou freedom dues at the end of his term of service.[59]

The benefits of the revolutionary environment extended to immigrants of color who arrived on the shores of the United States as slaves but gained their liberty on landing in the country. Sanette or Sophie, a "mulatress" and "creole" originally from "the Northern parts of Saint Domingue," along with her daughter Marie Francoise, received their freedom during their residence in Baltimore. Their master manumitted them in 1795 as repayment for Sophie's "services and attentions."[60] While living in Savannah, Georgia, Marie Jeanne Destres, formerly of Plaisance in Saint-Domingue, emancipated Cité, a "negresse creole" who was originally from the town of Grosmorne and the daughter of Jeanne, a "negresse" from Congo. Destres also liberated Cité's two-month-old child. The 1797 emancipation decree explained that Cité received her liberty as a reward for performing great and important services.[61]

Societies in Flux

The revolutionary changes taking place across the South forced free people of color, both the recently emancipated and those born free, to navigate unsettled social landscapes. The social flux created opportunities for some while others experienced continued suffering. The American Revolution created unity among some free people of color and their neighbors while at the very moment severely dividing others. The transformations driven by increased opportunities for freedom and immigration influenced political debates about the social hierarchy and power. Social and political activism created opportunities for freedom even as some people sought to define the South as a white man's country. As emancipations increased in certain localities, slavery continued its westward expansion. Expanded opportunities for freedom for some and the prospect of generations of enslavement for others set the stage for political conflict.

The American war for independence initiated important changes for all southerners, including free people of color. Numerous free persons of color participated in the war, serving as soldiers, sailors, and support personnel for the allied U.S. and Spanish forces.[62] Free people of color from Delaware, Maryland, Virginia, North Carolina, South Carolina, and Louisiana fought against the British and their allies. State militias functioning as part of the broader U.S. force enlisted free men of color to fight side by side with their white neighbors. Philip Savoy of Anne Arundel County, Maryland, remembered enlisting in the state militia at a tavern in his home county in 1778. During his first tour of duty, Savoy participated in battles at Monmouth, White Plains, and Elizabethtown, where he was captured by British forces. Following a period of imprisonment in New York, Savoy returned to Maryland, where officials drafted him for a second tour of duty. He recalled that during this final enlistment that he was "at the taking of Cornwallis" in Yorktown, Virginia.[63] Isam Carter, a man "descended from an Indian woman and a negro man," served with a South Carolina artillery regiment. He recalled participating in battles at Stono Ferry, Savannah, and Charleston.[64] Joseph Ranger of Northumberland County, Virginia, joined the navy of his state early in the war and served on several ships throughout the conflict. He survived an explosion on board the brig *Jefferson* before his capture by British forces following a skirmish on the James River. Ranger and several of his compatriots remained in confinement until the British surrender at Yorktown.[65]

Some free men of color, instead of engaging directly in battle, held noncombat roles as part of the U.S. forces. Solomon Bibby of Franklin County, North Carolina, who served at Eutaw Springs, Camden, and

Guilford Courthouse, cared for horses and guarded baggage wagons. Barnet Stewart joined the U.S. forces while living in Brunswick County, Virginia. On joining the army, Stewart marched with his fellow servicemen to Norfolk, where he worked as a cook. After being stationed in Norfolk, Stewart returned to Brunswick County, only to be drafted several times. During each term of service, he continued in his capacity as a cook. Drury Walden recalled being drafted in Bute County, North Carolina, as a musician for his company and marching to Georgia, where his company engaged in battle. A second deployment followed a short return home. During his second enlistment, Walden constructed gun carriages for cannons, created canteens for soldiers, and helped to build barracks to house the troops. In 1781, he enlisted for a third time as a substitute and acted as a guard for a jail that held British prisoners of war.[66]

The ideals of freedom and revolution failed to motivate every free person of color engaged in the U.S. war for independence. For some, military service was a burden worth trying to escape. Charles Smith, a "Mulatto" from Henrico County, Virginia, ran away from his unit during a July 1777 march through his home state.[67] In 1778, Charles Peters, an "East-India Indian," deserted from the Fifth North Carolina Battalion along with William Watson, a man of "dark" complexion with "black hair." The men, who both had ties to New Bern, absconded while their battalion was on the march toward Halifax, North Carolina.[68] In 1779, Charles Valentine, a "free negro" from Surry County, Virginia, abandoned the U.S. forces and became one among an assortment of men wanted by Major Edward Waller for desertion. Phillip Miller, "a German," Thomas Johnson, "an Irishman," Andrew Wilson, "a Scotchman," William Thompson, "an Englishman," and Thomas James, "a Portuguese," had committed the same offense as Valentine. Waller offered "free pardon" to Valentine and his fellow runaways if they returned on their own accord. If they failed to return, Waller threatened that "they shall be punished as deserters by the rigour of the martial law." He placed a bounty of thirty pounds on each man.[69]

The Spanish enlisted free men of color in segregated units during the war with Great Britain. Over one hundred free pardos and morenos, including at least eighty from New Orleans, fought for Spain against the British in contests on the Mississippi River and at Mobile and Pensacola. Free men of color acted as soldiers and officers in these operations. Francisco Fortiere, a gunsmith, and Carlos, a carpenter, both free men of color, accompanied the Spanish forces during the war. For their service, Simon Calpha, Juan Bautista Hugon, Francisco Dorville, Felipe Rueben, Manuel Noel Carriere, Nicolas Bacus, and Luis la Nuit received recommendations for commendations from Louisiana governor Bernardo de Gálvez. The Spanish crown granted ten medals of honor to members of the free pardo and moreno militia. Following the American Revolution, free men of color continued to protect Louisiana and serve the Spanish crown as members of the militias.[70]

While cooperating with the forces of the United States or Spain was strategically beneficial for some of the South's free people of color, others placed their lives in the hands of the British forces during the war. Some entered the British lines as single persons while others sought refuge for themselves and their families. Virginia native Robert James left his home and joined the British fleet on the Chesapeake Bay in 1777. He remained with the British through the war. Lewis Carter, a "mustee" man, ran from his Virginia master, Archibald Gilbert, and sought refuge with the British troops. By 1783, Carter had been with the British army for four years, traveling with them from Virginia to New York. Andrew Hilton, a "mulatto" man and son of an "Indian" mother, and Charles Allen, who was described as a mixture between an "Indian & Spaniard," escaped their Maryland masters and joined the British. Both served as pioneers in the army. George Lacey, Fanny Lacey, and their daughter Kate, who were originally from Virginia, took refuge with the British forces during the conflict. George had spent most of his life serving the Churchill family in Virginia. As the daughter of a white woman, Fanny had worked under George McCall of Tappahannock, Virginia, until sometime around 1781, when her indenture expired. Their positions in the class hierarchy of the South left them with little hope for social mobility under the new U.S. regime. Following the British defeat, these free people of color joined the British evacuation to Nova Scotia.[71]

Although some free people of color left the South following the conclusion of the American Revolution, the overall population of free people of color increased in the region. During the final years of the eighteenth century, the population exploded, especially in the Upper South. In 1790, just over 30,000 free people of color lived in the southern United States. Census takers counted 12,766 in Virginia, 8,043 in Maryland, 4,975 in North Carolina, and 3,899 in Delaware. The Deep South states of South Carolina and Georgia along with the western territories had much smaller populations. By 1800, the free population of color had increased to 61,241 people. Virginia and Maryland were virtually tied for the largest populations of free people of color at 20,124 and 19,587 persons, respectively. Delaware temporarily replaced North Carolina as the state with the third largest population of free people of color with 8,268 people compared to North Carolina's 7,043. Between 1790 and 1800, Delaware became the only southern state with a population of free people of color larger than its enslaved population. The presence of free people of color in the Deep South remained limited, with just 3,185 people in South Carolina and 1,019 in Georgia in 1800. Still, these figures represent a near doubling of the population in South Carolina and a tripling of Georgia's free population of color. Nearly half of each states' free people of color lived in Charleston and Savannah, the states' most important cities.[72]

The ingenuity of free people of color helped to drive innovation in the Revolutionary South. While some struggled to obtain a basic education, others became leaders in the South's intellectual life. Thomas Stewart gained prominence in Dinwiddie County, Virginia, as the result of his medical expertise. In 1778, his acumen in medical matters came to the attention of many Virginians after he saved the life of Tom, an enslaved boy who had been kicked in the head by a horse. Nathaniel Hobbs, the boy's master, explained that Tom had "lost a quantity of blood" and "many ounces of matter, supposed to be part of his brains." "By the assistance of Dr. Thomas Stewart, of Dinwiddie, and his specific balsam," Hobbs declared, Tom was "perfectly well."[73] A decade after saving Tom's life, Stewart continued to receive wide acclaim. In 1788, Henry Willis, who was familiar with the doctor's career, described Stewart as a "free black man of a very respectable character." He explained that Stewart had "acquired an estate worth some thousands of pounds and his medical skill is taken notice of even by the Faculty [of a college]."[74] Indeed, Stewart had obtained an estate of unusual significance for a free man of color in late eighteenth-century Virginia. His holdings included a plantation and numerous enslaved people. In 1790, he paid taxes on 845 acres, a tremendous sum of land.[75] James Derham had risen to become a highly respected physician in New Orleans by the 1780s. Before gaining his freedom, Derham trained under several doctors, including surgeon George West. After obtaining the confidence of Robert Dove, a doctor and his last master, Derham procured his liberty and continued to work "under the patronage" of Dove. Benjamin Rush, a distinguished physician and signer of the Declaration of Independence, noted Derham's expertise in the common diseases of his region and the methods to deal with those ailments. In addition to his medical expertise, Derham spoke three languages. He was fluent in English and French and had "some knowledge of the Spanish language."[76]

Benjamin Banneker, an astronomer and mathematician, was likely the most famous free person of color in the United States during his lifetime. In 1791, Banneker released his first almanac, *Benjamin Banneker's Pennsylvania, Delaware, Maryland and Virginia Almanack and*

Benjamin Banneker was a famed astronomer and mathematician and an outspoken advocate for the rights of people of color. In 1791, he published the first edition of his almanac, which provided readers with weather predictions, movements of the sun and moon, and other important dates. (Courtesy of the Maryland Historical Society)

Ephemeris for the Year of Our Lord, 1792. Published in Baltimore, the almanac on its title page promised readers information about the movements of the sun and moon, weather predictions, and information about eclipses, festivals, and other important dates.[77] Advertisements for Banneker's almanac appeared in newspapers in some of the country's most important cities, including Baltimore, Philadelphia, and Alexandria, Virginia.[78] Banneker's work even reached the attention of Thomas Jefferson, who received a copy of the almanac directly from the author. Jefferson responded, "Nobody wishes more than I do, to see such proofs as you exhibit, that nature has given to our black brethren, talents equal to those of the other colours of men."[79] In other correspondence, Jefferson described Banneker as "a very respectable mathematician" and "a very worthy & respectable member of society."[80]

Other free people of color discovered success in more modest ways—by becoming property holders and business owners. Benjamin and Dinah York moved from slavery to become respected members of their Cecil County, Maryland, neighborhood. By the 1780s, the couple had purchased one hundred acres of land and established a farm. Benjamin also obtained a wagon, four horses, and a stock of cattle.[81] The former bondsmen, Abraham Jackson, a "liberated black Man of St. Paul's Parish Colleton County" in South Carolina, had accumulated a large assortment of property in the years after gaining his liberty. Jackson's 1785 will reveals the extent of his success. In his last testament, he left three head of cattle to his wife, Daphne, an enslaved woman named Sue to his daughter Hannah, a horse to his nephew Abraham, and an enslaved boy named Caesar to Paul Hamilton Jr. According to the same document, Jackson also owned a woman named Sarah, who he declared would be free on his death.[82] A man named Ames of Worcester County, Maryland, accumulated a smaller but still significant estate. Before his death in 1798, Ames left his household furniture, livestock, and money to Leonard Jones, his wife's father. He hoped that after his death, Jones could sell some of the property in order to procure the freedom of his wife, Dianah, who was still enslaved.[83]

Although many free people of color achieved success during the Revolutionary years, some continued to struggle under the pressures of poverty. Ideological freedom did not guarantee opportunity to all. In the English-speaking South, local officials and potential masters continued to use the apprenticeship system to interfere in the lives of free people of color. In some parts of the region, the percentage of free children of color entangled in the apprenticeship system increased while the percentage of white children apprenticed decreased.[84] In April 1789, the court in

Baltimore County, Maryland, bound out Jesse Creek, "a free Black Boy aged Eight Years in December Next," to Edmund Ford in order to learn the trade of a farmer. The county clerk described Creek as the son of a "slave" father and a "mother so poor that he [Creek] is likely to become an expense to the county."[85] Although Creek had two living parents, his father's status as a slave without parental rights, his mother's poverty, and the fact that his parents could not be recognized as a married couple brought him to the attention of local officials, who commonly targeted poor children they considered born out of wedlock. Soon after obtaining her liberty, Catharine, a recently emancipated woman, surrendered her children Thomas, John, and Violet to the Baltimore County court to be bound as apprentices. Absalom Butler promised to teach Catharine's sons to farm and to instruct Violet in sewing; he also promised to provide the children with "sufficient meat[,] drink[,] and apparel[,] lodging[,] washing[,] and all other things necessary." Instead of working together to establish an at least partially independent life, Catharine and her children shifted from one form of dependent status to another.[86]

While the apprenticeship system continued to intrude in the lives of poor free people of color, changes made during the social and political revolution provided many apprentices bound during the last third of the eighteenth century with greater protections than those indentured through most of the British colonial period. North Carolina and Virginia legislators reformed their laws and declared that apprenticeships could not last beyond the apprentices' twenty-first birthday. Legislation passed in 1760 nullified North Carolina's colonial law permitting the binding of children of color born to white mothers until the age of thirty-one. The new law dictated that an "Orphan shall by direction of the Court be Bound apprentice, every male to some Tradesman, Merchant, Mariner, or other person approved by the Court, until he shall attain to the Age of Twenty-one Years." Girls were supposed to serve until the age of eighteen except "all free base born children, and every such Female Child being a Mulatto or Mustee, until she shall attain the Age of Twenty-one Years."[87] A 1785 Virginia act declared that "Infants under fourteen years shall serve until twenty-one or for such shorter term as is fixed."[88] The North Carolina law was more discriminatory than the Virginia act, yet both laws afforded apprentices greater protections. Children were no longer trapped under the authority of their masters into their prime adult years. These changes were especially important for young women who were often ensnared by regulations that prevented them from marrying but punished them for bearing children out of wedlock during their prime reproductive years.

The new political and social environment of the Revolutionary years was especially fruitful for free people of color living under the more liberal laws of the Spanish government. Many free people of color acquired land and houses. Before the end of her life, Naneta Colet, a "negra libre," or free negro woman, had acquired a home and lot on Chartres Street in New Orleans.[89] Free people of color in Spanish Louisiana also invested in slaves. George Bolard, a "mulatre libre," or free mulatto, of Saint Landry Parish, purchased a woman named Zaire from Jean Baptiste Lacour in 1790.[90] By the time of his death around 1797, Joseph Casanova, a "mulato libre," or free mulatto man, of New Orleans, owned a large estate, including a home and nine enslaved people.[91]

In Mobile, which was at the time part of Spanish West Florida, free people of color received grants for town lots, purchased them, and sold them. On October 7, 1792, Julia Vilars, a free "mulatto" woman, received a grant for a lot bounded by Saint Charles Street and Saint Jago Street. Nearly six years later, Vilars acquired a grant for another lot on Saint Francis Street beside a lot owned by Martha Triton, a free woman of color. On March 16, 1794, Augustin Colin, a free man of color, submitted a petition to the governor for a vacant lot on Conception Street. Later that year, the government granted Colin's request. Angelica, a free woman of color, received a grant for a lot on Conception Street in 1798. The next year, Angelica added to her estate by purchasing a lot and small cabin from the estate of Mary Josephine, a free woman of color. A debt forced Mary Josephine's executors to sell the land, which ultimately benefited Angelica. The same year, Euphrosine Andry, a free "mulatto" woman, procured a lot between Saint Jago Street and Royal Street. Phillip, a free "negro" and former slave who had purchased his freedom, sought out and received a land grant for a town lot that he hoped would allow him to build a house, settle down, and marry. On November 5, 1799, Charles, Madelon, and their children, free people of color, agreed to care for Julia de la Brosse, a sickly woman. In exchange, they were promised a twenty-by-forty-arpent section of de la Brosse's plantation. Charles had already constructed a house on the land before receiving the deed of gift.[92] These grantees became the forebears of generations of free people of color and creoles of color in Mobile.[93]

Legal Debates

The social flux brought about by the American Revolution helped to produce an inconsistent legal environment for free people of color. Free people of color were gaining opportunities in some places even as some whites contested their hard-won freedoms in others. As in earlier generations, white southerners continued to struggle with defining the proper position of free people of color within their communities. At several important moments, white southerners offered equal access regardless of racial categorization. Yet in a slowly increasing number of cases, their adherence to the theory of white superiority and desire to provide preferential treatment to white people left free people of color disfranchised and excluded. During the American Revolution, conventions in the various southern states ratified constitutions outlining the rights of their citizens. All southern states discriminated against women by privileging men, but only some used racial categories as a way to draw distinctions among their citizenry. The original constitutions of North Carolina, South Carolina, Maryland, and Virginia did not mention racial categories or privilege specifically white men with any rights.[94] The Delaware constitution only mentioned racial categories in the state's prohibition on the importation of slaves "from any part of the world."[95] Restrictions, however, appeared in the constitution of Georgia. Georgia's 1777 constitution combined racial, gender, age, and wealth restrictions to define the electorate. Only "male white inhabitants, of the age of twenty-one years, and possessed in his own right of ten pounds value, and liable to pay tax in this State, or being of any mechanic trade, and shall have been resident six months" in Georgia had the right to vote.[96] South Carolina's second constitution, which representatives ratified only two years after the issuance of the state's first constitution in 1776, also restricted voting rights to white men who were twenty-one years of age and older. The state's third constitution, adopted in 1790, included similar language.[97]

While some features of the post-Revolutionary United States indicate that democracy was on the rise, the increasingly discriminatory language in the South's, and eventually the nation's, voting laws suggest that something more complex was taking place.[98] The expansion of white men's democracy frequently came with disfranchisement for free men of color. The antidemocratic sentiments of South Carolina and Georgia that appeared during the American Revolution eventually became the dominant ideology among southern lawmakers to the north. With the expansion of manumission came constraints on the right to vote in parts of the Upper South. Maryland lawmakers targeted recently freed persons. In 1783, they prohibited people manumitted after that year from "the privilege of voting at elections, or of being elected or appointed to any office."[99] Two years later, Virginia lawmakers went a step further and excluded all "free Negroes or Mulattoes" from the franchise.[100] Delaware lawmakers used the language of white preference instead of direct exclusion to disfranchise free persons of color. The authors of the state's 1792 constitution restricted voting to "every white free man of the age of twenty-one years." When Kentucky broke away from Virginia in 1792, the original constitution did not prohibit free people of color from voting. The state's 1799 constitution, however, explicitly disfranchised "negroes, mulattoes, and Indians."[101]

Racial discrimination was absent from most eighteenth-century southern states' original constitutions but remained a facet of those states' legal codes. Most of the discriminatory laws passed during the colonial period continued to be in force after U.S. independence. During the early national period, lawmakers in some states further doused their laws with the taint of prejudice. In 1782, Virginia legislators targeted recently emancipated people who failed to pay taxes and permitted local officials to hire them out. Ten years later, Virginia assemblymen prohibited "free negroes" from owning more than one gun. In an obvious attempt to limit the number of free people of color in the state, Virginia lawmakers passed a series of acts restricting their movement. Virginia law now prohibited "free negroes and mulattoes" from migrating into the state. Lawmakers also levied a tax of one hundred pounds on vessels that brought free negroes into Virginia. To keep track of the free people of color already resident in the state, lawmakers now required "free negroes and mulattoes" to register with their local county.[102] Georgia legislators passed multiple laws in the 1780s and 1790s levying discriminatory taxes on "free negroes and mulattoes."[103] Furthermore, when new states formed from territories, they adopted parts of their parent state's legal frameworks. Therefore, when Kentucky was created from the western section of Virginia and gained statehood in 1792, its lawmakers adopted Virginia's restrictions on court testimony and gun ownership.[104]

City leaders occasionally took the lead in curtailing the liberties of free people of color, particularly in the Deep South. In 1783, the city council of Charleston, South Carolina, targeted "free Negroes, Mulattoes and Mustizoes" with an ordinance requiring them to register with the city clerk. The same ordinance also demanded that "every free negro, mulatto, or mestizo, above the age of sixteen years ... obtain a badge from the Corporation of this City, for which badge every such person shall pay into the City Treasury the sum of Five Shillings, and shall wear it suspended by a string or ribband, and exposed to view on his breast." The ordinance threatened fines for any person who sought to counterfeit the badges or wore them without paying the registration fee. Moreover, the ordinance attacked the right of "any free negro, mulatto, or mustizoe" to host more than seven male slaves in their homes at one time.[105] In 1790, officials in Savannah, Georgia, followed those in Charleston with an ordinance requiring "every free negro, mulatto, or mestizoe, of the age of sixteen years and upwards, living or residing within this city," to register with the city clerk.[106] By 1797, the commissioners of Fayetteville, North Carolina, had also instituted a badge and registration requirement for "all free negroes, mulattoes, and other persons of mixed blood."[107]

Charleston officials were likely among the pioneers of creating racialized public spaces in the U.S. South.[108] They attempted to shape the behaviors of Charlestonians through an exclusionary policy that created white-only spaces. On November 24, 1795, a comedy titled "The Jew" was scheduled to play at the City Theatre on Church Street. The production's backers welcomed white people to attend the performance of the comedy but explained that "agreeably to the regulation of the city council, no people of color to be admitted to any part of the house."[109] A 1796 advertisement for the production of "The Tragedy of Alexander the Great: Or, the Rival Queens" playing at the Charleston Theatre informed readers that the Charleston City Council required that "no People of Color can be admitted in any Part of the Theatre."[110] Regardless of their level of success, free people of color could not enter the city's theaters. The appearance of white-only spaces, such as theaters, reflected an important moment in the construction of white supremacy. By excluding people of color, Charleston officials had initiated the slow process of configuring their city's geography to reflect their desired social hierarchy.

In response to the expansion of freedom for persons of color in the South and the United States as a whole, proslavery radicals began to develop ways to advocate for slavery by attacking free people of color. They viewed expanded freedom as a threat to slavery and, in response, propagated the idea that persons of color were corrupt and unworthy of freedom. Through a combination of petitions and political speeches, slavery's most loyal advocates spread the seeds of hate that would begin to germinate in pockets of the South. Only two years after Virginia lawmakers passed a 1782 act liberalizing the manumission process, proslavery advocates in Henrico and Hanover Counties decided to go on the offensive. Two groups of petitioners complained to the General Assembly "that many Evils have arisen from a partial Emancipation of Slaves under the Act entitled an act authorizing the manumission of slaves." They labeled "free negroes" as "agents, factors, and carriers to the Neighbouring Town for Slaves of property by them stolen from their masters and others." They requested that the legislature repeal the manumission law.[111] In 1788, a Chatham County, Georgia, grand jury targeted the "free negroes" in their jurisdiction. The body declared, "We present, as a grievance, a number of free negroes, or those who pass as such, being permitted to wander about the country and this town, without any inquiry being made into their right or title to such claim of freedom." Members of the grand jury requested "that the Magistrates of this county, and Wardens of the town of Savannah, examine the credentials of all such persons."[112] On June 10, 1795, a grand jury in Richmond, Virginia, described "free negroes" as purveyors of "disorderly houses," places which "we conceive are highly dangerous to the peace and happiness of the community, inasmuch as they encourage idleness, dissipation, and immorality."[113] In 1790, Congressman William Loughton Smith of South Carolina took the fight against manumission and free people of color to the national stage. There, he labeled "negroes" an "inferior race" and argued that "free negroes never improve in talents, never grow rich.... They will after manumission continue [as] a distinct people, and have separate interests."[114]

At least some of the legal restrictions passed during the 1790s, in particular, originated as part of the reaction to the ongoing Haitian Revolution. In 1791, rebellion broke out in Saint-Domingue and continued through the dawn of the new century. Thousands of refugees escaped the island and resettled in various parts of the Americas, including such cities in the U.S. South as Charleston, Norfolk, and Baltimore. These bands of refugees included free people of color and enslaved people. Some whites feared or stoked fears that free persons of color and slaves might bring a bloody antislavery revolution to the shores of the United States.[115] By 1793, South Carolina politicians at the state and local levels began to speak out publicly against this new influx of people. During that year, Governor William Moultrie stated, "Whereas it has been represented to me that a number of free negroes and people of colour, natives of, and heretofore residents in the Island of Saint Domingo, have arrived in this state ... there are many characters amongst them which are dangerous to the welfare and peace of the state." In response to the alleged presence of "dangerous" individuals among these refugees, he demanded, "All free negroes and people of colour who have arrived from Saint Domingo, or who have arrived within 12 months from any other place to depart from this state within ten days from the date hereof." Moultrie threatened arrest and confinement for "every person or persons of any of the above descriptions who may be found in this state after the expiration of the time herein limited."[116] At the same time Governor Moultrie issued his proclamation, officials in Charleston and Georgetown began to target immigrants of color. Charleston officials passed resolutions to create a committee tasked with taking "immediate measures to send out of the state all free people of color and free negroes, who have come from St. Domingo, or who have come from any other place within twelve months."[117] Georgetown officials adopted an identical resolution.[118] Leaders in the Beaufort District backed the Charleston resolutions and pledged to assist Charlestonians, especially regarding the parts of those resolutions related "to the free negroes and people of colour brought into this state from St. Domingo and other parts of the world."[119]

The actions taken by Governor Moultrie and the town councils of Charleston and Georgetown were only the beginning of the backlash toward people of color fleeing the revolution in Saint-Domingue. Some politicians sought to make the site of the Americas' first revolution an unwelcoming and even hostile environment for refugees of color escaping the hemisphere's second major revolution. Across the U.S. South, lawmakers enacted restrictions on persons of color coming from the Caribbean. At the end of 1795, North Carolina legislators passed an act addressing the immigration of people of color from Saint-Domingue and the surrounding area. This act made it unlawful "for any person coming into this state, with an intent to settle or otherwise, from any of the West-India or Bahama Islands, or the settlements on the southern coast of America, to land any negro or negroes, or people of colour, over the age of fifteen years, under the penalty of one hundred pounds for each and every such slave or persons of colour." The law also directed "that if any free person of colour shall come into the state, by land or water, or any slave shall hereafter be emancipated, he, she or they shall be compelled to give bond and security to the Sheriff." The prescribed bond was enormous at two hundred pounds. Those who failed to post bond were supposed to face confinement, trial, and, if convicted, sale "at public auction."[120] In 1796, Georgia lawmakers enacted legislation authorizing "officers of the militia" to "apprehend any negro, mustee or mulatto freeman or freemen, slave or slaves, who shall hereafter arrive in any port of this state, from any of the West-India or Bahama Islands, and to keep such mustees, negroes or mulattoes in close and safe custody." Individuals arrested by the militia officers were supposed to remain in custody until officials in Savannah or a body of three justices of the peace in any county could meet and authorize their deportation "at the expence of the importer or owner."[121]

Following the passage of laws at the state level, officials continued to instigate unrest by politicizing the plight of refugees of color. Georgia governor James Jackson issued a proclamation on June 11, 1798, that explained, "I have received information from the Mayor of the City of Savannah that certain Negroes or people of color are shipped off from

Port au Prince, in the West Indies, for the ports of South Carolina and Georgia, and many of them are on board vessels bound directly to Savannah." Drawing on feelings of distrust of these potential arrivals, the governor continued, "Policy dictates that persons of color, used to the horrid scenes of massacre which of late years have been so barbarously practiced in the West Indies, without respect to age or sex, should be prevented from coming within the limits of this state, to diffuse their seditious and cruel tenets." He requested "all Officers, Civil and Military, to be vigilant in apprehending and exporting all and every other Negro, Mustee, Mulatto freeman or freemen, slave or slaves, who has or may have come within the limits of this state" in defiance of the act of 1796. The governor also used his proclamation as an opportunity to increase suspicion of people of color without ties to the West Indies and other restricted areas. The governor called on local officers "to keep a watchful eye over all and every suspicious slave or slaves, free Negroes or Mulattoes, although not within the description of the said law."[122]

The connections of people, language, and heritage that continued to bind Louisiana and Saint-Domingue in the years following the Spanish annexation of Louisiana gave colonial officials legitimate reasons to fear the contagion of rebellion disseminating from the Americas' latest center of revolution. In response, colonial officials sought to quiet and, if necessary, shackle those free people of color who publicly sympathized with the cause of the insurrectionists. Pedro Bailly, a member of the pardo militia, found himself arrested for publicly supporting the rebellion and calling for equality between militiamen of color and white troops. After an initial trial in 1791, Bailly avoided imprisonment. By early 1794, however, Governor Baron de Carondelet ordered Bailly imprisoned in Havana, Cuba. One of Bailly's fellow officers had testified that he had continued to preach about equality, the newfound possibilities of citizenship, and an egalitarian future developing in revolutionary Saint-Domingue. In 1795, Carondelet ordered the deportation of Antonio Coffi and Louis Benoit, free men of color accused of supporting a plot of rebellion among the slaves of Pointe Coupee. After officials discovered the plot, they learned that the insurrection in Saint-Domingue may have inspired it. Benoit's origins in Saint-Domingue only motivated Carondelet further to take action.[123]

Although the restrictions concerning free people of color were slight compared to what was to come in the nineteenth century, free persons of color did not turn a blind eye to their own oppression. The South's free people of color organized to defend their rights and pressed against discrimination. In 1791, bricklayer Thomas Cole, along with butchers

P. B. Mathews and Mathew Webb, petitioned the South Carolina Senate "on behalf of themselves & other Free Men of Colour." These men declared that under the Constitution of the United States, they were "part of the Citizens of this State." They also recognized that the laws of the state, including the so-called "Negroe Act," prevented them from accessing certain "Rights and Privileges of Citizens," such as the right to give testimony in certain cases and the right to trial by jury. They were also "subject to Prosecution by Testimony of Slaves without Oath." Although free men of color were not treated equally under the law, the petitioners declared, "they have at all times since the Independence of the United States contributed and do now contribute to the support of the Government by cheerfully paying their Taxes proportionable to their property with others who have been during such period and now are in full enjoyment of The Rights and Immunities of Citizens Inhabitants of a Free Independent State." They further exclaimed, "As Free Citizens of this State they hope to be treated as such." The petitioners asked lawmakers to pass legislation "relieving" them from the "grievance they now Labour under." Lawmakers, however, decided to reject their appeal.[124]

The idea that free people of color were citizens drove another group of free men of color to make a passionate appeal to South Carolina lawmakers in 1794. The petitioners expressed their displeasure with the continued enforcement of "a poll tax on all free Negroes, Mustees, and Mulattoes." The group professed "having the honor of being your citizens" and expressed a willingness "to advance for the support of the government anything that might not be prejudicial to us, it being well known that we have not been backward on our part in performing any other public duties." Their current legal situation left them "grieved." They had "frequently discovered the many distresses occasioned by your act imposing the poll tax." According to the petitioners, the tax placed a particularly difficult burden on "widows with large families & women scarcely able to support themselves." They requested that lawmakers repeal the poll tax.[125] Compared to many other forms of bigotry found in the southern law books, discriminatory taxation had a greater impact on the lives of free people of color across the spectrum of wealth, gender, reputation, and occupation. Free persons of color could avoid some of the negative effects of discriminatory legislation by staying out of legal trouble or hiring effective counsel. Neither good behavior nor a strong legal challenge, however, could protect free persons of color from a discriminatory tax in the eighteenth-century South. Protesting discrimination at the highest levels of government was the only possibility for removing the financial burden caused by prejudicial tax policy.

Benjamin Banneker took advantage of the fanfare brought about by the release of his almanac to lobby on behalf of his "brethren." On August 19, 1791, Banneker wrote directly to Thomas Jefferson, who was at the time secretary of state. He declared, "I am fully convinced of the greatness of that freedom which I take with you on the present occasion; a liberty which seemed to me scarcely allowable, when I reflected on that distinguished and dignified station in which you stand, and the almost general prejudice and prepossession which are so prevalent in the world against those of my complexion." Banneker complained "that we have long been looked upon with an eye of contempt, considered rather as brutish than human, and scarcely capable of mental endowments." Drawing attention to the conflict between the reality of so many Americans and the words of the Declaration of Independence and ideology of the American Revolution, he explained "that if your love for yourselves, and for those inestimable laws which preserve to you the rights of human nature, was founded in sincerity, you could not but be solicitous that every individual, of whatever rank or distinction, might with you equally enjoy the blessings there of." Furthering the argument, Banneker pointed directly to Jefferson's own failings and noted "that although you were so full convinced of the benevolence of the Father of mankind, and of his equal and impartial distribution of these rights and privileges which he had conferred upon them, that you should at the same time counteract his mercies, in detaining by fraud and violence so numerous a part of my brethren under groaning captivity and cruel oppression; that you should at the same time be found guilty of that most criminal act, which you professedly detested in others, with respect to yourselves."[126] Banneker's personal successes did not blind him to the human struggles of the Revolutionary period. His analysis of Jefferson's alleged adoption of natural rights doctrine and the continued enslavement and oppression of people of color under the banner of freedom highlighted an inconsistency that people fighting for equal rights and the end of discrimination would repeatedly observe and protest.

The revolution for freedom transformed the social landscape of the South. The number of free people of color exploded across the South from Delaware to New Orleans. Revolutionary ideas about Christianity, natural rights, and equality converted slaveholders into emancipators. Changes in manumission laws permitted ever-increasing numbers of people to purchase themselves and their families out of bondage. The courtrooms of the South became sanctuaries of freedom for people of color illegally held in servitude. Growing numbers of free people of color became property holders and respected members of society. The small number of individuals freed during the middle of the eighteenth century in places like Baltimore had become thousands scattered across the region by the end of the century.

The moving tide of freedom, however, did not eradicate the ideas of old. Wealth disparities continued to divide free people of color. Gender inequalities persisted and in certain situations became worse as southern statesmen embedded gender qualifications for political rights in their constitutions. The concept of racial hierarchy and the inequalities attached to it continued to persist, especially in the Deep South, and became more widespread. Although a few white people decided that people of color were their equals, another group of white people began to advance the opposite view. They constructed a prototype of a free person of color who was inferior by descent and threatening in action. In the nineteenth-century South, proslavery advocates built on this prototype and used its construction to fight back against the tide of revolutionary freedom.

CHAPTER 3

The Backlash

On August 30, 1791, Thomas Jefferson had described Benjamin Banneker, a free man of color, as "a very respectable mathematician" and praised the publication of his soon-to-be-famous almanac.[1] Eighteen years later, however, Jefferson expressed a different view of Banneker. In an October 8, 1809, letter to Joel Barlow, Jefferson asserted that Banneker "had a mind of very common stature" and circulated the rumor that Banneker received "aid" in producing his almanac.[2] In less than two decades, Jefferson had moved from praising Banneker's work as evidence of equality among people of different colors to raising suspicion about Banneker's almanac and denying Banneker's intellectual authority. Jefferson, like so many white people of his generation, struggled to determine the proper place for free people of color in society. The rising importance of slavery to the southern economy in the early nineteenth century only made the debacle worse.[3]

The parallel growth of slavery and freedom during the early nineteenth century exacerbated disputes over the position of free people of color that had existed since the earliest days of European colonization. Slavery's near extinction in the northern United States stimulated questions about the proper place of free people of color in the minds of white southerners, who also witnessed an explosion of manumissions in their own region. White southerners were experiencing a moment of uncertainty. While increasing numbers of northerners found slavery distasteful and called for its demise, white southerners with political power and those with a vested interest in the development of the southern regional economy grew more attached to the expansion of slavery. Some southern politicians prescribed attacking free people of color as a solution to the conundrum. By targeting free people of color, they could place a legislative check on a population whose growth was tied to the collapse of slavery in the northern states. Attacking free people of color ultimately became a way to protect slavery from the forces of freedom and promote its expansion.

Radical proslavery politicians and their backers successfully imposed a variety of restrictions on the lives of free people of color during the early 1800s. These forces were particularly successful in the Deep South and other parts of the country with the most to gain from slavery's extension. Proslavery ideas influenced politics in every part of the region from the Upper South states to the territories acquired from the French and Spanish to the South's indigenous nations. Advocates of the proslavery agenda created a patchwork of bigoted policies across the region. Radicals also developed a number of extreme ideas including expulsion, which failed to gain traction but nevertheless helped cement their position as the ultimate defenders of slavery. The enemies of free people of color were willing to challenge the concept of freedom in order to promote slavery's growth and protect the intellectual and legal underpinnings of human bondage. They created an environment in which attacks on the rights and liberties of free persons of color were increasingly more acceptable. These assaults could be verbal, written, or occasionally physical. The heartless aggressions expressed toward free people of color provided the perfect breeding ground for illicit attacks on free persons of color. Instances of kidnapping free people of color increased alongside the expansion of the slave-based economy. Kidnappers emerged as a growing threat to free people of color as slave valuations increased throughout the nineteenth century. Using trickery, drugs, and violence, kidnappers transformed free men, women, and children into illicit commodities.[4]

Proslavery politics collided with increasing demands to enshrine preferential treatment for whites in the law. Politicians across the country sought to build coalitions and create political advantage by promoting white supremacy. In all sections of the country, including the South, they called for white-only restrictions on the franchise and preferential treatment for white businessmen and laborers. White preference was an important facet of Jeffersonian Republican party politics as Republicans rapidly pushed the Federalists to the fringes of power and, in effect, nearly transformed the United States into a one-party state.

The paradox of American freedom rings true, at least in this sense: the expansion of slavery came with a growth in opportunities and freedom for many Americans. Yet at the same time, the growth of freedom for white men came with a constriction of the political rights of free persons of color. Together, the expansion of liberty for white men and the growth of slavery across the southern landscape contributed to a corresponding reduction of legal protections for free people of color in the early nineteenth century.⁵

Closing Freedom

The first decades of the nineteenth century constituted a period of unprecedented attacks on the rights of free people of color. As the most ardent proslavery politicians and ideologues began to expand their influence in state legislatures, newspapers, and local meetinghouses, the position of free people of color increasingly became consumed in discussions about the best ways to defend slavery. Since the American Revolution, enslaved persons had become free people in record numbers in the South. In the northern states, lawmakers had laid the groundwork for slavery's demise through immediate emancipation programs and gradual abolition laws. Slaveholders saw federal lawmakers restrict the expansion of bondage in the Northwest Territory. History's grandest slave rebellion transformed the slaving colony of Saint-Domingue into Haiti, a nation built and run by former bondspeople. Even in the British Empire, formal slavery was on the decline.⁶

Ardent proslavery men refused to see the U.S. South gradually emancipate its enslaved population or, worse, become the next Haiti. They argued that government at every level needed to check the growth and influence of free people of color. During the first three decades of the nineteenth century, they began to craft and implement plans to do just that. Placing a check on free people of color was a gradual process that took many decades to implement. Radical proslavery voices had to convince moderates, whom they considered potential allies, that the free people of color who lived among them, mostly as peaceful neighbors, presented a burden and a threat. The radicals' ability to persuade was mixed, but they were most successful in places with relatively small populations of free people of color such as Georgia and South Carolina. With the exception of Louisiana, the Deep South was, in legal terms, the most unfriendly area of the country for free people of color by the 1830s. In places like North Carolina and Tennessee, radicals had limited success, but their most extreme agenda items failed to gain traction.

Although proslavery radicals had many successes in the first decades of the nineteenth century, free people of color and their allies were able to check the radicals in some instances. They successfully highlighted the extreme nature of the radical agenda and prevented the passage or implementation of certain extremist proposals. Citing the Constitution, ideas about fairness and liberty, and the contributions of free people of color to their communities, the alliance challenged the radicals' justifications for denying free persons of color the rights and privileges enjoyed by other free people.[7]

The faulty manner by which radicals sought to implement discriminatory laws also dealt a blow to their agenda. Lawmakers often passed regulations attacking free people of color without providing the necessary resources to realize their stated objectives. They talked about expulsion and colonization but were disinclined to fund those projects adequately. They sought to police their states' boundaries without creating checkpoints on the state lines. They depended on often unwilling partners at the county and municipal levels to enforce their policies. Seemingly aware of the overly harsh or impractical nature of their legislation, they commonly created loopholes that negated the supposed aims of their laws. The passage of discriminatory legislation in order to score points for short-term political gains appears to have been more important than seeing the regulations enforced.

Since the colonial period, proslavery advocates and white supremacists had attempted to limit the number of free people of color in their midst. Expulsion riders attached to manumission laws were the most direct attempts to curtail the free population of color. The revolutionary tide of freedom washed away many of these restrictions on manumission, providing free people of color, regardless of their origins, with the liberty to travel to and from the various states and territories. Just as lawmakers loosened restrictions, however, organized opposition to the expansion of freedom emerged. Radical proslavery and white supremacist elements complained of lazy free people of color, who allegedly crowded their communities. The outbreak of the Haitian Revolution and subsequent migration that brought free people of color from the Caribbean to the shores of mainland North America further invigorated calls to corral and control the free population of color.[8]

As an essential part of their strategy to check the growing free population of color, proslavery advocates and white supremacists sought to restrict or eliminate avenues to liberty for enslaved people. Opposition to the liberalization of manumission laws emerged as soon as the laws appeared in southern legal texts. Defenders of slavery in Virginia organized as early as the 1780s to launch attacks against the state's liberal manumission policy. Organized opposition in places like Mecklenburg, Hanover, and Henrico Counties petitioned the General Assembly to reverse the tide of manumission and bring a halt to the increasing numbers of free people of color in the state. In 1805, lawmakers received a petition directly from Petersburg's city leaders, including Mayor William Prentis, who complained that the presence of a significant number of free people of color caused white residents to be "forever on watch" and would "prove at some future period dangerous to our peace and safety." Prentis and his allies attempted to draw a connection between Petersburg's growing free population of color and the outcome of the Haitian Revolution. Underemphasizing the contrasting positions of people of color in Petersburg and those in Haiti during the nation's war for independence, they contended that "free people of color" were responsible for laying "a mine spring in St. Domingo that totally annihilated the whites."[9] Following two decades of lobbying, Virginia lawmakers approved their state's first major restriction on manumission since the Revolutionary period liberalization. On January 25, 1806, legislators passed an act requiring "any slave hereafter emancipated" to leave Virginia within twelve months of the original manumission. The new law stipulated that any emancipated person who failed to leave the state "shall forfeit" the right to freedom and "may be apprehended and sold by the overseers of the poor of any county or corporation in which he or she shall be found, for the benefit of the poor of such county or corporation."[10]

Though such language appears quite harsh, a more contextual examination of the 1806 law reveals that the wording represented compromise rather than a clear victory for those who advocated for the end of manumission. Before the passage of this act, some lawmakers had proposed eliminating manumission altogether, but their efforts failed.[11] The 1806 law did not outlaw manumissions but simply attempted to impose roadblocks on the manumission process. Potential emancipators still had the right to liberate the enslaved, but the 1806 law gave communities tools to expel unwanted freed persons from their localities. The law attempted to protect the interests of both masters who wanted to retain the power to do what they pleased with their human property, including manumit them, and slaveholders who viewed emancipated persons as disruptive and desired to remove perceived threats from their communities.

The 1806 law had an immediate effect on the pace of manumissions but failed to stop the growth of Virginia's free population of color. Scholars have observed a noticeable decline in the number of emancipations following passage of the 1806 act. In some communities, the practice of manumitting slaves nearly vanished.[12] At the same time, the overall number of free people of color in the state continued to surge. Between 1800 and 1810, Virginia's free population of color increased from 20,124 to 30,570. By 1820 the population had increased further to 36,889. Enumerators counted 47,348 free people of color by 1830. Even in the face of the 1806 law, whites and free people of color alike proceeded to manumit enslaved persons, often without making provisions for the newly emancipated people to leave the state. In her 1810 will, Nancy Lee of Richmond, "a free woman of colour," liberated several children and grandchildren whom she held as slaves. Lee left her estate to her daughters and granddaughters but made no specific plans for their removal from Virginia.[13] Many people emancipated after 1806 continued to live in Virginia beyond the twelve months allotted by the law, creating a new class of illegal residents. Some of these free people of color sought legal remedies to this dilemma by seeking out permission from the General Assembly to remain in the state. With the support of their neighbors, John Dungee and Lucy Ann Littlepage Dungee of King William County petitioned the General Assembly for permission to allow Lucy Ann to remain in Virginia. John Dungee was freeborn and a descendant of "the aborigines, of this Dominion," but Lucy Ann was the "illegitimate daughter of the late Edmund Littlepage Esq., a highly respectable and wealthy citizen, who by his Testament & last will ... bequeathed to his innocent offspring the boon of freedom & a pecuniary legacy of $1,000 consisting of stock of the Bank of Virginia." As a person emancipated after 1806, Lucy Ann was not supposed to stay in the state without lawmakers' consent. After reviewing the Dungees' appeal, lawmakers approved the request and granted Lucy Ann permission to remain in Virginia.[14] Another group of emancipated people simply ignored the 1806 law. Local officials across the state turned a blind eye to emancipated persons living illegally in their communities. George Selby remained in Accomack County, Virginia, nearly two years after the execution of his former master's 1821 will before local officials took notice of him. Adah Bagwell continued to reside in the same county well after her emancipation in 1817. Her case did not appear in the local court until almost seven years after her manumission.[15]

Virginia's restrictions on manumission certainly created problems for those seeking to become free.[16] Politicians in the Deep South, however, proved more extreme in their opposition to manumission. They created almost impenetrable barriers to manumission for freedom seekers and would-be emancipators. Georgia politicians led the movement against manumission when they passed restrictions in 1801, stating that "it shall not be lawful for any person or persons to manumit or set free any negro slave or slaves, any mulatto, mestizo, or any person or persons of colour, who may be deemed slaves at the time of the passing of this act, in any other manner or form, than by an application to the Legislature for that purpose." Some emancipators worked with lawmakers to free their bondspeople in spite of the difficulties imposed by the legislature. In 1803, the executors of Sally Harper of Elbert County received legislative approval to emancipate eleven people formerly held by Harper.[17]

Officials in Richmond County at least partially ignored the will of lawmakers and recorded deeds of manumission without legislators' approval. In 1815, the county clerk recorded a deed from 1804 for the freedom of a woman named Betty. Betty purchased her liberty from John Willson for $350.[18] By recording the deed, Richmond County officials formally recognized Betty's freedom even though Betty was not properly emancipated under Georgia law. While some Georgians were successful in using the law to their advantage or ignoring the law entirely, Georgia lawmakers' restrictions on manumission were generally effective. The number of free people of color in Georgia grew at a trickle's pace, and between 1810 and 1820 the population in fact declined.[19]

Following the lead of Georgia assemblymen, other Deep South legislators adopted laws designed to discourage emancipations. In the Deep South, new restrictions made manumission a privilege that only the most well-connected and, in some cases, only the wealthiest potential emancipators could confer on their bondspeople. Manumissions could never take place at the pace they proceeded at in the northern states or even the Upper South. Beginning in 1805, lawmakers in Mississippi Territory required a "meritorious act" from the enslaved person seeking manumission in addition to approval from the General Assembly.[20] Legislators in Alabama and Mississippi, which the federal government carved from Mississippi Territory, adopted the same restrictions on manumission when their states entered the union. Emancipators in Alabama and Mississippi were at the mercy of lawmakers to give final approval to liberate their bondspeople. Like Georgia, neither Alabama nor Mississippi had a significant population of free people of color. By 1830, Alabama's free population of color had reached only 1,572 while Mississippi's lingered at 519, the second lowest population in the South. In 1820, lawmakers in South Carolina restricted the power of manumission to the General Assembly. Their action curbed the growth of free people of color in South Carolina, but the restrictions were not as effective as they had been elsewhere in the Deep South. By 1820, South Carolina already had 6,826 free people of color in its borders, making it the state with the second largest population of free persons of color in the Deep South. Limiting manumissions alone could not eliminate the effects of natural population increase, especially in Charleston, where a plurality of the state's free people of color resided.[21] In 1829, officials in Florida Territory sought to dissuade potential emancipators by requiring them to pay two hundred dollars for each manumitted person. Furthermore, Florida law required each emancipator to post a bond for the slave value of the manumitted person, a cost approved by a county justice, ensuring the removal of the liberated person "within thirty days after the manumission."²² During the Spanish colonial period, Florida had been a refuge for people of color seeking freedom. Under U.S. rule, lawmakers discouraged those desiring to expand access to liberty. Florida's population of free people of color remained negligible throughout the pre–Civil War nineteenth century, never reaching 1,000 souls. During the decade following the passage of manumission restrictions, Florida's free population of color actually decreased.²³

Like so many trends concerning free people of color, serious restrictions on manumission did not catch on in every southern state. Strong opposition to the presence of free people of color could be found throughout the region, but radical proslavery politicians failed to muster enough support to make drastic changes to the manumission laws. Delaware by far represented the worst defeat for radical proslavery politicians on the issue of manumission. A combination of strong antislavery forces and the most liberal manumission laws in the region turned Delaware into the only southern state in which free people of color outnumbered enslaved persons. Radical proslavery forces also failed to turn back the trend of manumission in Maryland and the District of Columbia. Following the passage of Virginia's manumission restrictions, Maryland overtook Virginia as the southern state with the largest population of free people of color. The District of Columbia trailed only Delaware as the southern jurisdiction with the highest percentage of people of color living outside of bondage. Missouri lawmakers failed to impose serious restrictions on manumission. Yet the state's population of free people of color remained negligible throughout the early 1800s. The manumission laws in Kentucky mirrored those in Virginia before 1806. North Carolina and Tennessee lawmakers continued to require emancipators to receive approval from county officials in order to formalize manumissions.²⁴

The proslavery and white supremacist battle to control the growing free population of color not only focused on curbing manumissions but also targeted immigration. By the late 1790s, lawmakers in some cities and states began to propose and pass legislation limiting the movement of free people of color. The migration of free people of color from Saint-Domingue to the U.S. mainland provided agitators and politicians with a concrete target for their proslavery and white supremacist agendas. The actions taken by a few localities in the late 1700s became the blueprints for a better organized effort to limit the movement of free people of color in the nineteenth century. Restrictions that focused on free people of color from beyond the United States transformed into broader attacks on all free persons of color coming from the outside. Radicals were willing to allow the free people of color who were their neighbors to remain but focused on those whom they could depict as potentially dangerous strangers. State after state, and sometimes local governments, gradually shut down the legal migration of free people of color into their jurisdictions.

Until the beginning of the nineteenth century, Virginia remained the only southern state to prohibit free people of color from entering its borders. In 1800, the tide turned for advocates of immigration restrictions, and the rest of the South began to follow suit. That year, after much fanfare over the immigration of free people of color from Saint-Domingue, South Carolina lawmakers prohibited "any free negro, mulatto or mestizo" from entering the state.[25] In 1806, William Hebb, a Federalist delegate from Saint Mary's County, introduced an immigration restriction bill before the Maryland General Assembly. After considering the bill, a majority of lawmakers agreed to ban free people of color from coming into their state's boundaries to settle. The next year, Delaware and Louisiana legislators added similar provisions to their law books. Kentucky followed the other three states by shutting down the legal immigration of free persons of color in 1808.[26] As immigration restrictions became part of a growing trend in the early nineteenth-century South, a parallel anti-immigration movement took place in other parts of the country. In 1807, the Ohio General Assembly stiffened its immigration regulations and required a hefty two-hundred-dollar bond for "negroes" and "mulattoes" entering the state.[27] Virginia's 1806 law requiring emancipated people to leave the state on receiving their liberty likely provided proslavery and white supremacist forces in other states the political clout needed to push through immigration bans. They could depict their stance against immigration as a proactive step to control an inevitable flood of free people of color ready to pour out from the borders of Virginia. If Virginia lawmakers were trying to flush out their emancipated populations, legislators in neighboring states could guarantee that their communities would not become repositories for the rush of free people of color leaving Virginia.

The text of the immigration legislation for Orleans Territory, the predecessor of the state of Louisiana, clearly connected immigration restrictions to the exodus of people leaving the Caribbean for mainland North America and more specifically, New Orleans. Orleans Territory's 1807 law served as a replacement for an 1806 law targeting "free people of color coming from Hispaniola." The 1807 law demanded that "no free negro or mulatto shall emigrate to, or settle in this territory ... under the penalty of twenty dollars for every week any such person shall remain in the territory." Those who refused to pay the fine faced jail time, public sale "for a term sufficient to pay the fines," or forced labor "at public works."[28] Political and social transformations that took place outside of Orleans Territory largely made its restrictions ineffective. Nearly two years after lawmakers in Orleans Territory prohibited the immigration of free people of color, shiploads of refugees from Saint-Domingue via Cuba, including many free persons of color, challenged authorities' ability and willingness to enforce their immigration laws. Between 1809 and 1810, nearly three thousand free people of color arrived in New Orleans. In 1810, free people of color made up over a quarter of the city's population, and New Orleans became the U.S. city with the second largest free population of color in the South. After the 1807 ban largely failed to achieve its objectives, more than two decades would pass before some white Louisianans seriously attempted to limit the growing free population of color through immigration policy.[29]

For years, Georgia lawmakers at the state and local levels had passed piecemeal regulations that made their state an unfriendly destination for free persons of color. Yet small numbers of free people of color continued to trickle into the state. Finally, in 1818, Georgia lawmakers passed a comprehensive immigration ban as part of a larger package of restrictions on free people of color. The new act declared, "It shall not be lawful for any free person of color, (Indians in amity with the state, and regularly articled seamen or apprentices arriving in any ship or vessel excepted,) to come into this state." Offenders faced jail time, a fine of up to one hundred dollars, and possible enslavement for failure to pay a conviction fine.[30] Lawmakers in Mississippi and the Cherokee Nation, which neighbored Georgia, followed by approving comparable legislation in 1824. North Carolina legislators passed a similar act during the 1826–27 General Assembly session. Their counterparts in Florida Territory shut down legal immigration in 1829.[31]

In 1820, South Carolina lawmakers decided to strengthen their immigration restrictions on free people of color. That year, they passed a comprehensive immigration ban along with the previously discussed manumission restrictions. They contended that "the great and rapid increase of free negroes and mulattoes in this state, by migration and emancipation, renders it expedient and necessary for the Legislature to restrain the emancipation of slaves and to prevent free persons of colour from entering into this State." Their law prohibited "any free negro or mulatto" from moving into South Carolina. An individual who failed to abide by the law faced "a fine of twenty dollars." If the person could not pay the fine or remained in South Carolina after paying the penalty, the law required the sale of the individual "for a term not exceeding five years." The act also penalized "every master of a vessel or other persons" convicted of bringing "any free negro or mulatto" into the state by water with a five-hundred-dollar fine. Lawmakers, however, provided exclusions for "any free negro or mulatto" who worked on vessels or who entered the state as servants of white persons. The act also shielded from prosecution natives of the state who left and returned within two years.[32]

By 1823, a more extreme political agenda took hold in the South Carolina General Assembly. Following the exposure of the alleged 1822 plot by Denmark Vesey and others to overthrow slaveholders and free the enslaved people, proslavery lawmakers sought to tighten their grasp on the enslaved population and their potential allies, free people of color.[33] That year, South Carolina lawmakers replaced the 1820 act with a more aggressive set of regulations. The new act made it unlawful "for any free negro or person of colour, to migrate into this state, or be brought or introduced into its limits, under any pretext whatever, by land or by water." A "free negro or person of colour" who failed to abide by the law faced "corporal punishment" instead of a fine. The 1823 law no longer exempted free persons of color who worked on board watercrafts except for those in the service of the United States. Lawmakers required local sheriffs to jail any "free negro or person of colour" working on board a visiting vessel. They demanded that a jailed ship worker remain imprisoned until the vessel was prepared to leave the state and the captain paid the ship worker's jail fees. Captains who failed to pay the jail fees faced a thousand-dollar fine and imprisonment. Legislators also eliminated the protections for free persons of color who were South Carolina residents. If a free person of color left South Carolina for any period of time, that person could never return legally.[34]

At the time of its passage, the 1823 South Carolina immigration law was one of the toughest laws on the books. The imprisonment of free people of color who worked on vessels received a great deal of negative attention. Yet the cleverest free persons of color found their way around the prohibition. In the 1823 law, legislators left a loophole that some sailors quickly exploited. The act included a clause excluding "free American Indians, free Moors, or Lascars, or other coloured subjects of countries beyond the Cape of Good Hope" who worked on ships. By 1825, legislators began to recognize that some persons of color who lawmakers perceived were not part of the excluded categories were claiming protection from the law by declaring themselves to be "Indians," "Moors," and "Lascars." Lawmakers reported that "many coloured persons from the northern states and elsewhere, have arrived in the ports and harbours of this state, under the pretence of their being descended from free Moors, Indians and Lascars, on both father's and mother's sides." These persons of color brought "with them certificates and papers purporting that they are of such descent, when on such inspection, they appear to be mulattoes or mustizoes, by means of which false papers, many persons of color are introduced into this state, contrary to the intention of the act." Legislators designed an 1825 law to address the loophole, and this new legislation no longer exempted "Indians," "Moors," and "Lascars" from the migration ban unless they served on vessels from foreign countries of which they were natives.[35] This change helped South Carolina maintain its relationship with foreign nations while targeting free people of color from the United States, especially the North.

The limitations of the South Carolina immigration law did not dissuade others from following the lead of the state's radicals. Georgia lawmakers gradually adopted stricter rules about free people of color working on ships that attempted to dock in the state. An 1826 law prohibited "colored seamen" from anywhere except South Carolina from leaving their vessels to come on land between 6:00 P.M. and 5:00 A.M. The act also required captains of vessels to register all their employees with the appropriate port city or town and post bonds on each of the "colored seamen" who were part of their crews. The following year, lawmakers added a hundred-dollar penalty for captains who did not comply. By 1829, Georgia legislators had decided to replace the strong but flexible policy on "colored seamen" with a law that placed restrictions on free people of color working on visiting vessels and strongly resembled South Carolina's act. Instead of jailing free people of color, as the law required in South Carolina, Georgia's 1829 act mandated a forty-day quarantine for "vessels with free persons of color." The law even applied to vessels from Georgia moving within the state. Like South Carolina's law, the Georgia regulations provided exemptions for "free American Indians, free Moors, Lascars, or other colored subjects of the countries beyond the Cape of Good Hope."[36]

While radicals could claim victory with the passage of every measure prohibiting free people of color from entering their states, lawmakers, merchants, and other interests were less than enthusiastic about the South becoming an increasingly costly and hostile environment for business. Legislation that demanded the imprisonment of free people of color at the cost of shippers and the quarantine of vessels presented a threat to free enterprise. By 1824, the British crown had begun to petition the federal government in response to these restrictions. American business interests, including shippers, asked Congress for relief from a situation that permitted free persons of color employed on their vessels to be "taken from the vessels, thrown into prison, and there detained at their own expense, greatly to the prejudice and detriment of their interest." As local officials in the South continued to detain free people of color at ports of entry, lawmakers at the federal level struggled to deal with the response from home and abroad. The conflict brought about by the restrictions did not dissuade lawmakers in other southern seaboard states from following the lead of South Carolina. Lawmakers in North Carolina, Florida Territory, Alabama, Louisiana, and Mississippi all adopted similar measures. Nearly twenty years after the passage of the South Carolina restrictions, the federal government continued to deal with the backlash, but it was ultimately to no avail. Southern representatives defended the radicalism at home.[37]

The legislative successes on the immigration issue were only one part of the solution to a larger challenge for supporters of immigration bans. As with so many of the laws targeting free people of color, the passage of a law did not guarantee full enforcement. Except for slave patrols, state governments had provided localities with few mechanisms to enforce the immigration bans. Illegal immigration continued to be a problem, especially in places where interstate commerce was common, such as port cities and border regions. Many years after the passage of Kentucky's immigration ban, free people of color from other jurisdictions continued to cross into the state. Jefferson County became a prime destination for border crossers, given its location on the Ohio River across from Indiana and the fact that it was home to Louisville, the state's largest city and commercial hub. In the late 1820s, Jefferson County officials sought to curb illegal immigration through sporadic roundups, arrests, and prosecutions, but out-of-state free people of color continued to cross the state line. Free people of color sometimes illegally resided in states with the full knowledge of officials. In 1822, officials in Mecklenburg County, Virginia, which shared a border with North Carolina, granted permission to Nancy Garnes, a free woman of color, to reside in the county even though she was from North Carolina. County leaders also had to deal with free people of color like William Kersey, who owned property in Virginia and North Carolina. Kersey moved back and forth across the border with ease. In the South, sporadic enforcement of immigration restrictions was possible, but strict application of immigration restrictions was an impossible task. Historians have noted that officials in northern localities dealt with similar issues.[38]

Bounding Freedom

Proslavery and white supremacist lawmakers did not limit their mission to removing free people of color from their communities or preventing them from entering their borders. They also sought to control the movements and activities of free persons of color within their jurisdictions. Throughout the South, policymakers passed registration laws as a preferred method of control.

As noted in the previous chapter, registration laws began to appear in a few southern localities at the end of the eighteenth century. Virginia was the first state to authorize a statewide registration system in 1793. During the early nineteenth century, several other states adopted registration requirements for free people of color, including Maryland, Tennessee, Georgia, and Mississippi. While southern lawmakers adopted registration laws in order to address local concerns, the idea of forcing free persons of color to register with governments had been in practice in other parts of the Americas for several decades. As early as 1761, officials in Jamaica had demanded the registration of free people of color.[39]

Registration laws were tough on paper but difficult to implement in practice. In Virginia, forced registration of free people of color was a massive failure in the early days. The town of Petersburg had a relatively significant registration rate. In 1800, the census enumerator counted 428 free people of color living in Petersburg, and by the end of that year, 210 individuals, or about 49 percent of the free population of color, had registered with the town clerk. The vast majority of those registrations, however, occurred during two particular years, 1794 and 1800. In 1794, the first year Petersburg residents complied with the registration law, 97 free people of color registered with the town. From 1795 to 1800, a total of only 53 people attempted to register. The pace of registration in 1800 remained relatively slow, with only two registrations from January until August, when the number of registrations exploded. An additional 58 people registered in Petersburg between August and September 1800, the period immediately before and immediately after the discovery of Gabriel's planned slave uprising. Issues of more local importance may have caused this uptick in registrations. Yet the increasing registration numbers also offer the possibility that at least a few free people of color knew of Gabriel's plot and secured documentation in preparation for the looming conflict.[40]

The registration trend in Petersburg, even during the plotting and ultimate collapse of the rebellion, did not extend to the state as a whole. In Charlotte County, located in central Virginia, only 4 free people of color had registered with county officials by 1800, even though the census taker had counted 123 free persons of color in the county that year. If Gabriel's plot affected registrations in Petersburg, it did not have the same impact on registration in Charlotte County. From 1800 to 1804, not a single free person of color registered with the county. Charlotte County was not the only locality that failed to enforce Virginia's registration law. Officials in Goochland County, the home of 413 free people of color in 1800, did not begin to keep a register of "free negroes" until 1804. In Mecklenburg County, a locality with 553 free people of color in 1800, free persons of color did not begin registering with the clerk until 1809. Even as the number of registrations increased into the nineteenth century, compliance continued to be a problem across the state. The state mandate for registration effectively became a government identification service for free people of color. Free persons of color could register and receive freedom documents that provided them with proof of their free status for the purpose of traveling or moving through a place where they were not known.[41]

Registration in other parts of the early nineteenth-century South was piecemeal. Free people of color in Maryland treated the registration process in a fashion similar to those in Virginia. In 1806, the first year Maryland clerks implemented the registration law, only ten free persons of color registered in Baltimore County, nine registered in Dorchester County, six registered in Washington County, and just two registered in Frederick County. Annual registrations generally increased after this point. Yet overall, free people of color registered at an unhurried pace.[42] Unlike the initial registration systems in Virginia and Maryland, which recorded detailed information about each registered person, including how he or she obtained his or her free status, Georgia's registration system, in some localities, operated more like a census, with details about the registrant's age, occupation, and place of birth. Local courts in Georgia appear to have updated the registrations sporadically. Before lawmakers at the state level required registration, officials in Savannah mandated yearly registration for "all free negroes, mulattoes or mestizos ... age of sixteen years and upwards" as early as 1800.[43] Attempts to register free people of color in Tennessee were largely ineffective. In 1806, Tennessee lawmakers passed an act requiring county clerks to register "every free negro or mulatto" residing in the state in a book, but no such volumes survive if they ever existed.[44]

Controlling the movements of free people of color was insufficient for some white southerners who called instead for the removal of free people of color from the country. Their cries coincided with clamors for the removal of Native nations. In both cases, politicians portrayed these peoples as dangers to civilization and, particularly in the South, threats to slavery. Many southern proponents of westward expansion also endorsed the removal of free people of color. By the early 1800s, Virginia politicians were considering removing persons whom they deemed troublesome, including enslaved convicts and free people of color, beyond the boundaries of their state and the nation. In 1802, members of the General Assembly along with Governor James Monroe and President Thomas Jefferson, discussed proposals to relocate free persons of color and others to Africa or South America. The proponents of colonization eventually organized under the American Colonization Society, which led the charge to convince lawmakers to remove and colonize free people of color abroad. Founded in 1817, the society counted among its early members some of the nation's most elite white men, including Bushrod Washington, Henry Clay, Andrew Jackson, and Francis Scott Key. Jackson was not only a colonizationist but would also become the face of the movement to purge the eastern United States of its Native inhabitants. The society encouraged the establishment of a colony outside of the United States to receive the country's free population of color. With the support of President James Monroe, a Virginian, the organization gained enough support at the federal level to establish the colony of Liberia on the west coast of Africa.[45]

Although the colonization movement had significant support from the South's political elites, funding and implementing the removal of free people of color were difficult tasks. By the mid-1820s, the organization had only successfully colonized "several hundred" free persons of color in Liberia. Under the leadership of Bushrod Washington, the society lobbied state assemblies across the nation to support colonization with mixed results. In an 1826 petition to state lawmakers across the country, the society contended that the removal of nearly a quarter million free persons of color to Africa "would be a blessing to themselves and a relief to us." The organization's advocates begged the states for funds and promised that their support would eventually make removal more cost effective. As the number of emigrants increased, they argued, the expense to ship them would decrease.[46]

The American Colonization Society persuaded numerous individual donors to support colonization, but securing the backing of state governments was much more difficult. State legislators were willing to advocate for colonization with their words but not necessarily with their dollars. On February 3, 1825, the Delaware General Assembly endorsed an effort to lobby the governors of the different states to back colonization. In 1826, Maryland's house of representatives called for the state's U.S. senators to support federal funding for colonization. The next year, Kentucky lawmakers passed a resolution requesting that the state's congressional delegation champion colonization at the federal level.[47] Eventually, Maryland lawmakers capitulated to the demands of the colonizationists and appropriated a meager thousand dollars to the colonization society during the 1826–27 assembly session. Yet one thousand dollars was far from enough money to remove Maryland's thousands of free people of color.[48] The backers of colonization influenced the debate over the proper place of free people of color in the South but failed to alter southern lawmakers' general habit of espousing radical ideas without providing the resources necessary to transform those ideas into widespread realities.

The colonization movement captured the attention of the South's free people of color, and while some looked favorably upon the project, the majority rejected it. The reaction in the North was similar.[49] Most free people of color found the prospect of leaving behind all that was familiar—family, friends, and community—largely unappealing. When white North Carolina colonizationists surveyed free people of color to find individuals willing to leave the country in 1826, David Moore told them he did not "want to go anywhere." Moore had an enslaved wife and child whom he was unwilling to abandon. Jenny, a free woman, told them that she was not interested in crossing the water and had heard bad things about Liberia. She also had family that she did not want to leave behind.[50] In contrast, some free people of color viewed relocating to Africa as a chance to expand their economic and political opportunities. Joseph Jenkins Roberts and William Colson left Petersburg, Virginia, and relocated to Liberia, where they established an import and export business. Christian missionaries sought to take advantage of the colonization movement in order to increase their orbit of influence. The Richmond African Baptist Missionary Society, organized in 1814, sent free men of color, including Lott Carey and Colin Teague, to proselytize to the people of West Africa. By 1822, the organization had raised nearly a thousand dollars to support the Christian missionaries.[51]

For those free people of color seeking better futures, other sections of the United States, not Africa, were generally their preferred destinations. They left the states of the Eastern Seaboard for every part of the expanding nation, especially areas in the old Northwest Territory: Ohio, Indiana, Illinois, and Michigan. Many established themselves near settlements of white Quakers, who left the South to live in a land free from human bondage. In the Midwest, in particular, free people of color had access to fertile land and did not have to contend with the everyday influences of slaveholders.[52] James Roberts relocated from Northampton County, North Carolina, to Indiana to provide his family with better

*Joseph Jenkins Roberts and Jane Waring Roberts were among the early colonists who relocated from Virginia to Liberia. For several years, Joseph Jenkins Roberts operated a successful business in Liberia before becoming the first president of a newly independent Liberia. Jane Waring Roberts served as the new nation's first lady.
(Courtesy of the Library of Congress)*

opportunities. He wrote to his kinsman Willis Roberts that he did not want his future children to live in a place where they could not "speak fore thear rits."[53] For James Roberts the Midwest represented the future and the South was the site of a dreary past.

Even as many white Virginians favored colonization, others sought to take more radical steps to remove the state's free people of color. In 1823, Virginia lawmakers adopted some of the most extreme measures attacking the residency rights of free people of color. They passed an act permitting the sale and banishment of "any free Negro" originally sentenced to "more than two years" of imprisonment as punishment for a crime.[54] This act, like other radical laws passed by Virginia statesmen, operated with vicious but ultimately narrow effect. Ellick Sparrow became the first free person of color sentenced to be transported out of the state in 1823, and by 1827, the courts had sentenced at least forty-four free persons of color to sale and banishment. County courts convicted these free people of color for an assortment of alleged crimes ranging from larceny to rape of a child to second degree murder. The governor granted clemency to five of these individuals, and two others died in the penitentiary before the execution of their sentences, leaving thirty-seven subjects of this harsh legislation.[55] Sale and transport may have been effective deterrents for would-be criminals, but they were less useful as methods to remove free persons of color from the state.

Legislators in Georgia and South Carolina took extreme steps to limit the rights of free persons of color to act in their own interests in legal matters, including civil suits. In 1810, Georgia lawmakers required a "free negro or person of color" to seek out a court-approved white guardian to pursue or defend that person in "all suits." Lawmakers amended this law in 1829 to permit the selection of a "next friend" in lieu of a guardian. The "next friend" did not require court approval.[56] Although the 1829 act relieved obstacles imposed by the 1810 act, both laws shifted the status of free persons of color, regardless of sex or age, closer to that of dependents such as children, who also needed guardians to pursue their legal interests. In 1822, South Carolina lawmakers designed a more extensive guardianship requirement for free people of color in their state. The 1822 law required "every free male negro, mulatto or mestizo in this state, above the age of fifteen years," to have a guardian. It also demanded that every guardian appear before the local clerk of the court to declare the "negro, mulatto or mestizo, for whom he is guardian, is of good character and correct habits." Those individuals who failed to secure a guardian risked the same punishments as free persons of color who resided illegally in the state.[57]

Although the South Carolina guardianship law placed the state's free people of color in a similar legal situation to their neighbors in Georgia, the context for the South Carolina law was quite different. South Carolina lawmakers passed the guardianship act in the same year as the failed Denmark Vesey conspiracy, in which Vesey, a free person of color, allegedly planned to lead a rebellion against the slaveholders of Charleston. South Carolina lawmakers were clearly more interested in controlling free people of color and trying to identify any threatening characters among them than amending civil suit procedures. South Carolina's 1822 guardianship law was the legal manifestation of a much greater effort by proslavery forces to consolidate control. In addition to passing the guardianship law, proslavery actors forced the shutdown of the African Methodist Episcopal Church in Charleston. The impact of the 1822 guardianship law was similar to that of other restrictions placed on free persons of color during the period. Many free people of color obeyed the law and obtained court-approved guardians. Officials in Charleston County kept a register of the free people of color in the community.[58]

Nevertheless, some free persons of color slipped through the gaps of the system, as they had in so many other instances, and lived for years without ever obtaining guardians. Furthermore, free people of color transformed a law meant to lessen their power into a tool for their own means. Just as free people of color in states that required registration turned the registration laws into acts providing them with government identification, so South Carolina's free people of color used the guardianship laws for their own benefit. Guardians became important allies in efforts to overcome the manumission restrictions passed by the legislature earlier in the century. Free people of color placed enslaved family members and property in trust with their guardians in order to provide their relatives who could not be emancipated with a form of unsanctioned personal liberty. Throughout the antebellum period, persons of color who were considered slaves under the law were able to operate in a similar fashion to free persons by virtue of their relatives' guardians. On their deaths, free persons of color bestowed upon their enslaved relatives land, money, and provisions to be held by their guardians. The guardians remained the legal owners of the enslaved people and the property, but in day-to-day life the enslaved persons were the actual beneficiaries of the property given by their deceased free family members.[59]

Proslavery radicals and white supremacists continued their efforts to control free people of color by pressing for restrictions on their ownership of guns and other weapons, but the idea was slow to catch on. The earliest of these regulations were relatively mild compared to the stricter laws that appeared on the books by the middle of the nineteenth century. Again, Virginia lawmakers took the lead in limiting the rights of free people of color. A 1792 Virginia regulation permitted "every free negro or mulatto, being a housekeeper ... to keep one gun, powder and shot." "All Negroes and mulattoes" had the right to "keep and use guns, powder, shot, and weapons" when living on the "frontiers" if granted a license from a justice of the peace. Kentucky lawmakers passed a similar law following the state's separation from Virginia. By 1806, legislators began to require that free people of color obtain licenses in order to own guns and other weapons. That year, Virginia lawmakers required every "free negro or mulatto" to acquire a license in order "to keep or carry any firelock of any kind, any military weapon, or any powder or lead."[60] During the same year, Orleans Territory lawmakers implemented an act requiring free people of color to procure certificates as proof of their freedom in order to carry guns. Mississippi lawmakers followed their counterparts in Virginia and Louisiana with a gun registration law in 1822, but they were the only southern state lawmakers to pass a licensing requirement between 1807 and 1830. Florida Territory's governor and legislative council passed a similar restriction in 1828. Between 1800 and 1830, lawmakers across the South were slow to adopt gun registration laws and likely even slower to enforce such laws. Early restrictions on weapons, like so many other acts targeting free people of color, came without a clear path to implementation.[61]

Georgia lawmakers took restrictions on property to the extreme by passing an act in 1818 prohibiting "free persons of color" from purchasing or acquiring "any real estate" or "any slave or slaves." This law was the most radical piece of legislation passed against the property interests of free people of color in the early nineteenth century. Within a year, support for certain aspects of the property law had collapsed in the Georgia legislature. On December 22, 1819, lawmakers restored the right of free people of color to hold real estate owned before the passage of the 1818 act. They also permitted free persons of color to obtain real estate throughout Georgia, except in the towns of Savannah, Augusta, and Darien. The 1819 repeal did not restore their right to hold slave property.[62] Even with the passage of the 1819 repeal legislation, free persons of color continued to face significant obstacles to their ability to own real estate. Chatham County, which encompassed Savannah, and Richmond County, which included Augusta, contained the largest populations of free people of color in Georgia during the nineteenth century. As a result, large swaths of the population still could not purchase or obtain real estate in their own names. Some free people of color attempted to get around the real estate ownership prohibition by placing land for their use in the hands of white guardians. The white guardians became the legal title holders of the land, but free persons of color used the property under guardianship. These arrangements allowed free people of color to continue to have access to real estate. At the same time, these arrangements left free people of color at the mercy of the guardians. Unscrupulous guardians could easily break their agreements and seize the real estate paid for or obtained through the efforts of those free persons of color under their care.[63]

Further chipping away at the rights of free persons of color, radical lawmakers in southern states ushered through legislation severely limiting the protections granted to free persons of color involved in civil and criminal litigation. Their acts generally sought to shift the legal status of free people of color closer to that of enslaved people than that of whites. In 1815, free persons of color in Georgia lost their right to a jury trial. Legislators required free persons of color who faced criminal charges to sit before a tribunal composed of three justices of the peace. Georgia lawmakers had first established the tribunal system for slaves in 1811. Two years after eliminating their right to a jury trial, lawmakers prohibited free people of color from seeking clemency after a capital conviction by barring the governor from commuting the death sentences of free persons of color and slaves.[64] In Maryland, North Carolina, and Florida Territory, lawmakers permitted enslaved persons to testify in court against free people of color, a practice that free persons of color and some whites viewed as a threat to the integrity of the legal system. The 1801 law passed in Maryland allowed slaves to testify "in all cases in which a free negro or mulatto, or other person of colour, free or freed, [is] charged with stealing goods or with the receipt of stolen goods."[65] In the 1820s, North Carolina and Florida Territory lawmakers passed more comprehensive acts that permitted enslaved persons to offer evidence in any case in which the defendant was "bond or free" and "a negro" or "mulatto." The North Carolina law also applied to any "Indian" or "person of mixed blood, descended from negro or Indian ancestors, to the fourth generation inclusive."[66]

Although the North Carolina law permitting enslaved persons to testify against free people of color remained in operation through the Civil War, the act did not go into effect without opposition. In 1822, a group of fifty-two free men of color from Hertford County petitioned the General Assembly and asked for a repeal of the law. They declared that the law consigned "their lives & liberties" to "the mercy of slaves." The group asked their legislators "whether their situation even before the Revolution was not preferable to one in which their dearest rights are held by so slight a tenure as the favour of slaves and the will & caprice of their vindictive masters." For them, the testimony of slaves was a threat because enslaved people were "bound to a blind obedience and know no Law, but the will of their masters."[67] A group of white neighbors, which included many slaveholders, joined the free men of color in their opposition because they recognized that the law could "in many cases be productive of the most serious mischief."[68] Both the free men of color and their white allies understood that the testimony of bondspeople against free persons jeopardized the integrity of the judicial system. Under the threat of the whip, slaveholders had a unique power over enslaved persons, and that power in the wrong hands could both ruin the lives of respectable free persons and make a mockery of the judiciary. Neither the free men of color nor their white neighbors declared themselves to be defenders of human equality. The slaveholders among the petitioners were likely not interested in supporting such a cause. Instead, they simply wanted to protect the important legal boundary between slavery and freedom. They were petitioning on behalf of legal certainty and political stability over the change sought by radical proslavery and white supremacist firebrands.

Reaching back into the discriminatory tool kit of the colonial period, proslavery and white supremacist lawmakers weaponized tax laws against free people of color as an alleged method to discourage their presence or support their removal. Under the leadership of Mayor W. B. Bulloch, Savannah officials passed an ordinance levying discriminatory taxes against free people of color in 1811. They demanded "each and every free negro, or person of color," who engaged in "any trade or handicraft, or the business of a huckster, carter or drayman," to pay a ten-dollar tax in addition to any property taxes owed. Their ordinance also charged a five-dollar head tax on "each and every other free negro or person of color, males from the age of sixteen to forty-five years, and females from the age of fourteen to forty-five years." Individuals who failed to pay their taxes could have their property seized by the city. The mayor and aldermen required those unable to pay the tax and without sufficient property to cover the tax burden to work on the city streets.[69] In 1817, New Orleans mayor Augustin de Macarty instituted new regulations on balls and public performances, including a five-dollar tax on "every ball of free persons of colour."[70] Virginia lawmakers succeeded in making tax discrimination a state mandate. During the 1814 assembly session, they passed an act placing a one-and-a-half-dollar poll tax on every "free negro."[71]

Proslavery and white supremacist forces combined race-based initiatives with wealth discrimination to target the most vulnerable free persons of color, the poor. By appealing to elite concerns about controlling the poor, lawmakers gained support for greater restrictions on impoverished free people of color. In 1807, Tennessee lawmakers permitted local officials to arrest any "free negro" found loitering. Virginia legislators attacked destitute free people of color with an 1820 act requiring overseers of the poor to examine the condition of all "free negroes and mulattoes" and deem as vagrants those who were unable to "procure sufficient means for substinance."[72] In 1825, Maryland's General Assembly required constables to report to the justices of the peace "any free negro or mulatto living idle, without any visible means of maintenance, or going at large through their counties or cities without any visible means of support." The justices had broad authority to haul any alleged offenders before them and judge their cases. If the justices thought a "free negro or mulatto" was guilty, they could assess a fine "not exceeding thirty dollars." Those individuals who could not pay the fine were supposed to "depart the state within fifteen days." If they failed to leave, the law permitted the justices to hire out the offenders.[73]

Moving beyond the gendered apprentice laws of the colonial period that targeted the children of impoverished, unwed women, nineteenth-century lawmakers targeted poor free families of color regardless of the parents' marital status. In 1808, Georgia lawmakers permitted justices of the peace in collaboration with "any three freeholders" to bind out "any male free negroes or persons of color, over the age of eight years, until he arrives to the age of twenty one years."[74] During the same year, Maryland legislators approved an act authorizing the state's orphan courts to force "the child or children of lazy, indolent and worthless free negroes" into apprenticeships. By 1818, lawmakers had decided to give the Maryland orphan courts greater discretion over the lives of free children. That year, they passed an act permitting the courts to bind out "any child or children of free negroes or mulattoes not at service or learning a trade, or employed in the service of their parents."[75] An 1811 Delaware law enabled constables to pick up any "free negro or mulatto" with a child or children and bring that person before a court to determine if the individual could provide for the child or children. If a court determined that a parent was unable to provide support, the child or children could be bound out by county justices or trustees. To incentivize the rounding up of poor children of color, the masters of apprenticed children were supposed to pay the constables three dollars for every child bound out.[76] During the 1826–27 session, North Carolina legislators followed other lawmakers with a slightly weaker act that permitted justices "to bind out the children of free negroes and mulattoes, where the parent ... does or shall not habitually employ his or her time in some honest industrious occupation."[77] Mississippi lawmakers passed a similar law targeting "free negro and mulatto children" with parents who were "incapable of supporting and bringing them up in honest ways."[78]

Radical legislators' obsession with denigrating the position of free persons of color led to a restructuring of the apprenticeship system in parts of the South. After years of requiring basic literacy and computation training as part of apprenticeship agreements, lawmakers gradually moved away from demanding the teaching of such skills to free people of color. In 1805, Virginia lawmakers freed masters from the legal obligation to provide apprentices who were "free negroes or mulattoes" with "reading, writing or arithmetic" skills.[79] Maryland legislators in 1818 permitted masters to pay "a sum not exceeding thirty dollars" to "free negroes or mulattoes" on the completion of their apprenticeships in lieu of providing them with literacy skills. Six years later, Maryland lawmakers dropped education requirements entirely.[80] In 1807, lawmakers in Mississippi Territory had implemented education requirements as part of the apprenticeship system. After the territorial period, however, Mississippi state lawmakers shielded masters from such obligations.[81]

In a scattering of localities, proslavery and white supremacist factions were unsatisfied with merely limiting the movements, rights, and privileges of free people of color. They sought to create far less ambiguous power divisions between free persons of color and whites and stripped the legal option of self-defense from free people of color in cases involving whites. During the 1806 assembly session, Orleans Territory legislators demanded that free persons of color speak respectfully to whites and prohibited them from insulting or striking whites. Ten years later, Louisiana state lawmakers reinforced the 1806 law with an act prescribing imprisonment or fines for free people of color convicted of insulting or assaulting white persons.[82] Mississippi lawmakers adopted the spirit of Louisiana's legislators by banning free persons of color from assaulting or using "insolent or abusive language, without provocation," against whites in 1820. Florida Territory's legislative council and governor adopted similar legislation in 1828.[83] In 1823, Virginia assemblymen permitted the banishment of "a slave or free Negro" who "willfully" assaulted and beat a white person with "an intention to kill." If the person returned to Virginia after banishment, the law stipulated "death without benefit of clergy."[84]

At the beginning of the nineteenth century, the majority of southern states prohibited free persons of color from voting, and advocates of white supremacy sought to extend the reach of suffrage restrictions. As Jeffersonian Republicans gained power in the early 1800s, they argued for an expansion of the franchise for white men while depicting the votes of free men of color as illegitimate. Enfranchised free men of color represented the traditional system of voting in which men received the right to vote based on their wealth and not their racial classification. The Jeffersonian Republicans, in contrast, promised to lift up all white men, including those excluded by the old system. They were willing to sacrifice the rights of free men of color in order to gain the support of larger numbers of poor white men who had been at least partially disfranchised. In 1803, after the Jeffersonian Republicans took over the Maryland General Assembly, legislators pushed through reforms that restricted voting rights to free white males. An anonymous article published in a Hagerstown newspaper explained, "This law gives to all free white male citizens of full age, the right of voting in all instances, when by the law or constitution, the people have the right of election." The anonymous author further declared that "the former law gave this right to every free man, whether of colour or not who would swear he was worth thirty pounds. The superiority of the last, over the first provision, is, that it excludes free negroes and mulattoes."[85] Attacking the rights of free men of color was a tool for partisan advantage. Frederick's *Republican Advocate* described the old voting system as a vestige of Federalist rule. A writer for the partisan newspaper stated that "a poor, industrious man, under the federal state administration, was prevented from voting, because he was not worth thirty pounds. Under the present law, which was enacted by Republicans, if a citizen is not worth one farthing, he is entitled to a vote—Which of these is most accordant with the principles of freedom?" At least some Jeffersonian Republicans did not see free men of color as "industrious" or "citizens." Furthermore, they forced the Federalists into a defensive position by depicting them as supporters of suffrage for free men of color and opponents of suffrage for some white men, even though property qualifications actually disfranchised men across racial lines.

The Jeffersonian Republicans in the national government also worked to shape suffrage in the federal territories in a way that favored white men. Between 1804 and 1805, the U.S. Congress, under the leadership of Speaker of the House Nathaniel Macon of North Carolina and Senate presidents Joseph Anderson of Tennessee and John Brown of Kentucky, passed legislation with the approval of President Thomas Jefferson to grant the franchise exclusively to the "free white male citizens" of Alexandria and Georgetown in the District of Columbia.[86] In 1808, Congress, with Jefferson's support, also limited voting to "every free white male person" of age who could meet residency and property qualifications in Mississippi Territory.[87]

Under the Jefferson Republicans, new southern states entered the union with constitutions that contained provisions limiting the franchise to white men. Kentucky, which became a state in 1792, was the last southern state to join the union without restricting the vote to white men. Beginning with Louisiana in 1812, every southern state that entered the union before the Civil War limited the franchise to white men. Moreover, these restrictions were not exclusive to the South. In 1820, Maine became the last state to enter the union without white-only restrictions on voting until after the Civil War.[88]

Using a combination of white supremacist ideology and proslavery scare tactics, southern lawmakers created local monopolies for whites in certain sectors. The early 1800s initiated a developing movement to centralize control of liquor production and distribution to white people. In 1816, lawmakers in Mississippi Territory prohibited "free negroes" from keeping taverns and retailing spirits. Alabama legislators eventually banned free persons of color outright from selling liquor in 1822. Mississippi followed suit in 1830. In 1826, Virginia lawmakers allowed white boat pilots to monopolize control of traffic on the Rappahannock River. Free people of color could no longer serve as pilots on that waterway. The laws passed during the early decades of the nineteenth century represented just the beginning of the implementation of a growing white supremacist agenda.[89]

While several facets of de jure discrimination were the work of lawmakers at the state and federal levels, the physical separation of whites and people of color was largely a matter taken up at the local level. Through acts of exclusion and the development of separate facilities, local officials in a handful of communities implemented policies that separated persons of color from whites in public spaces. Officials in Charleston, South Carolina, continued to lead the region in creating discriminatory social arrangements. In 1807, they required the segregation of burials in the new burial ground in Cannonborough, designating one section for "negroes and persons of colour" and another for "white persons." To further the separation of the dead, they called for the construction of a fence to split the two sections.[90] Local jurisdictions with smaller populations joined Charleston in adopting discriminatory measures designed to achieve social separation. Trustees of the poor in Talbot County, Maryland, excluded people of color from the county poorhouse during the 1810s. In 1811, Abraham Adams, "a coloured man," sought to send his wife, Fanny Adams, to the poorhouse because she was "entirely deranged." On receiving Abraham Adams's request, the trustees determined that they could not "accommodate coloured people." In lieu of access to the poorhouse, the trustees gave Abraham Adams sixteen dollars toward his wife's care.[91] By 1825, separate accommodations for prisoners appeared in Craven County, North Carolina. That year, when the new county jail opened, the structure included a single room expressly for "negroes & coloured culprits."[92]

Politicians frequently drove discriminatory policy, but ordinary white southerners, particularly small business owners, were an important part of the coalition that supported white supremacy and race-based physical separation. Political beliefs extended beyond the realm of southern legal institutions. Business owners in urban and rural areas of the South implemented exclusion and separation in their establishments and at their events. In an 1806 advertisement, the operator of the Richmond Bath, located in Virginia's capital city, announced that the establishment was in "readiness to receive customers." The posting touted the establishment's supply of "Hot and Cold Waters" and separate bathing rooms. Yet these amenities were available only to whites. The advertisement also informed newspaper readers that "no people of color" were "admitted."[93] When Mr. Guille exhibited his hot air balloon at the Charleston Museum in Charleston, South Carolina, he designated specific days, Tuesday and Saturday, for "people of color" to see the balloon.[94] At least a few tavern keepers in western Virginia implemented various forms of separation and discrimination in their businesses during the late 1820s. When Ellis Mitchell, a free man of color from Guilford County, North Carolina, traveled through the region on a return trip from Indiana with two white companions, he encountered several forms of discrimination imposed by owners of establishments. The proprietor of one tavern placed Mitchell in the "negro quarters," where the enslaved people slept, while Mitchell's white companions were permitted to sleep in the tavern. Although Mitchell received inferior accommodations, the tavern keeper charged Mitchell and his white companions the same amounts for their lodging. At an inn in Patrick County, Virginia, the owner of the establishment prohibited Mitchell from eating at the same table with his party. When one of his companions protested the arrangement, the landlady exclaimed, "Niggers can't eat with white folks at my table." After further protests, the proprietress set a separate table for Mitchell with the exact meal enjoyed at the table for whites.[95] She preferred the burden of setting a second table to compromising her views on white supremacy. The proprietress created the myth that Mitchell and his companions were unequal within the confines of her inn, despite the fact that they operated as equals outside the establishment.

By the end of the first three decades of the nineteenth century, physical separation had not become commonplace. Yet its mere existence demonstrated the extent to which advocates of white supremacy were willing to go to make their ideas a physical reality. White people were not superior to persons of color in actuality, but by reshaping the social landscape through exclusion and separate, unequal facilities, the advocates of white supremacy created spaces inaccessible to persons of color and therefore privileged white people through segregation.

Kidnapped

Proslavery radicals and white supremacists used the new political environment to stir up support for their attacks on free people of color. Yet the developing national slave market that they sought to defend posed one of the greatest if not the utmost direct threat to free persons of color across the country. The traffic in kidnapped free persons of color, an illicit segment of the domestic slave trade, threatened countless lives. Those who participated in this trade unlawfully enslaved unknown numbers of people who were legally free. The illegal enslavement of free people of color had been a problem in the South since the colonial period. However, what started as the informal holding of free persons of color beyond their terms of service in the 1700s had transformed into a full-scale system of unlawful human trafficking by the 1800s. As the prices for slaves increased with the nation's continued westward expansion, the motivation for would-be kidnappers only grew. Protecting themselves and their families from kidnappers became one of the most important challenges for free people of color during the nineteenth century.[96]

Notices of likely kidnappings appeared in southern newspapers in the early 1800s. The details of John Carter's kidnapping appeared in the Baltimore *Federal Gazette* on June 14, 1803. The paper notified readers that "John Carter, a free dark mulatto boy about 19 or 20 years of age, a resident of St. Mary's County in the state of Maryland, was kidnapped on the 26th day of March last." The prime suspects in the crime were slave traders who came from South Carolina or Georgia to purchase people for shipment south. The notice encouraged readers to look out for Carter and intercede on his behalf. In an attempt to rally the emotions of readers, the announcement explained, "As liberty is one of our greatest blessings, and the crime of kidnapping one of the most atrocious acts that human nature can be guilty of, it is to be anticipated that every virtuous citizen will interest himself in detecting the villain or villains."[97] An 1812 advertisement announced that Grailen Moore, "a dark mulatto" who was "about nine years of age," fell victim to kidnappers near Core Creek in Craven County, North Carolina. The notice reported that "two men, unknown," visited the house of Celia Moore, "a free woman of color," and one of the men asked to hire her son Grailen to help "bring away some goods." The men presented themselves as acquaintances of her neighbor, and she consented. Grailen went off with the man who pretended to hire him and never returned. The other man later snuck away from Celia Moore's house. Witnesses claimed to have seen the men one day later in Wayne County, to the west of Craven County, and the newspaper reported they were last seen in Johnston County, directly west of Wayne County.[98]

Free people of color fell victim to kidnappers with varying levels of sophistication who worked for different purposes. Some kidnappers sought to make a quick profit by kidnapping a person or two and hurriedly selling that person or persons within miles of the original crime. In 1833, William Stringer, a white laborer from Nansemond County, Virginia, abducted Nancy Scott, a "free negro woman," and her son James Scott from neighboring Isle of Wight County. Stringer then transported them back to his home county for sale. He sold James Scott before officials arrested him and returned him to Isle of Wight County for prosecution.[99] Other abductors sought to benefit from the higher demand for enslaved people in the Deep South by kidnapping free people of color in the Upper South and then transporting them hundreds of miles away. Morgan Smith, a "free man of color" originally from Buckingham County, Virginia, landed in Williamson County, Tennessee, after Samuel Morris illegally sold him to a man headed south. Smith passed through the hands of several masters in Tennessee before regaining his liberty.[100]

Kidnappers ensnared free people of color of all ages and backgrounds in their illicit trade. Children were particularly vulnerable to the illicit trade because they were easy to hide away and some were too small to know anything about their status as free people. "Shelby or Shelvy, Julia, Timy, and Eliza," the children of Patience, a free woman of color, ranging in age from fifteen to two years, became victims of the traffic in 1832. Philip Shirkey of Boonville, Missouri, suspected that a man named Costello and his associates had transported the children from Saline County, Missouri, to Arkansas Territory "to sell or enslave them."[101] Kidnappers also targeted young adults, who were generally the most valuable on the slave market. An unknown person abducted Solomon Sharp, also known as Solomon Atkins, "a free negro man," from his home in Indian River Hundred, Sussex County, Delaware, in 1827. Sharp was about twenty-two at the time of his disappearance.[102]

Antislavery organizations in the Upper South as well as in the northern states took a lead in the movement to recover the victims of the illicit slave trade. The Abolition Society of Delaware raised funds to support the court cases of free persons of color illegally held in bondage. In 1803, the society organized and executed the rescue of "a free black woman" trafficked out of Wilmington and into another state. Nearly two years later, the society filed suit against William Goldsborough and his accomplices "for violently assaulting and attempting to carry off two black men" from New Castle County. Although technically located outside of the South, the Pennsylvania Abolition Society and its agents made fighting the illicit slave trade in the region a main objective.[103] Nevertheless, their efforts countered only a small number of the schemes devised by kidnappers.

By the early nineteenth century, antislavery forces realized that concentrating on individual abduction cases would not halt kidnapping or the illicit trade in free people of color. Instead of focusing solely on advocating for individual free people of color in the local courts, they moved to persuade lawmakers to take serious action to curb these crimes. In 1811, Elisha Tyson wrote to Alexander McKim, a member of Maryland's delegation to the House of Representatives, to educate him about the illicit trade in free persons. In his letter, Tyson provided several "proofs of the existence of an unlawful trade in people of colour." He explained that kidnappers were entrapping free people of color in such Upper South states as Maryland and Delaware as well as in northern states like New York and transporting them south through criminal networks using forged bills of sale. Kidnapping victims eventually found themselves as far south as Mississippi Territory and Louisiana, where the criminal networks cashed in on their heists.[104] During the same year, the Baltimore Meeting of the Society of Friends lobbied both houses of Congress for greater restrictions on the internal slave trade that would protect free persons of color from illegal transport across state lines. The Friends called for a system to certify the enslaved status of people transported through the different states. They also suggested that Congress provide custom houses with greater authority over the trade to ensure that traffickers were not illegally transporting people entitled to their freedom.[105]

Attempts to protect free people of color from kidnapping at the federal level largely failed. Yet those seeking to shield free persons from illegal trafficking had some success at the state level. Within a few decades of the nineteenth century's opening, kidnapping had become so problematic that lawmakers, even in some of the South's most proslavery regions, passed new legislation against the practice. The strength of this legislation, however, varied widely. North Carolina lawmakers had passed antikidnapping legislation in 1779 but issued new legislation in 1801. People convicted of kidnapping or selling "any free negro or free negroes, or persons of mixed blood, knowing the same to be free or stolen," faced fines ranging from fifty to five hundred pounds and prison sentences ranging from three to eighteen months.[106] Maryland lawmakers concluded that their earlier laws concerning kidnapping were "insufficient" and passed new legislation in 1817. They authorized new restrictions on who could buy slaves and required detailed documentation for every interstate transaction. People convicted of breaking the law faced up to two years' imprisonment, which was less time than required by both an 1809 law and legislation passed in 1819, which required five to twelve years' imprisonment for someone convicted of kidnapping a white child.[107] South Carolina lawmakers proved particularly stubborn about giving free people of color recourse in kidnapping cases. They provided no criminal penalty for kidnapping but passed legislation in 1820 permitting an agent of a kidnapped "free negro" or "free person of colour" to sue an accused kidnapper for civil damages of one thousand dollars.[108] Missouri policymakers offered incentives for the return of kidnapping victims in their 1825 legislation. Those convicted of kidnapping people to sell them as slaves faced ten years' imprisonment and up to thirty-nine lashes. If the victims of kidnapping were "restored to freedom," however, convicted kidnappers could face much lighter punishments. Missouri law permitted courts to liberate this particular class of kidnappers on paying a fine of no more than one thousand dollars and legal costs.[109] Arkansas lawmakers passed comprehensive kidnapping legislation in 1838, which protected all people from kidnapping regardless of color and guaranteed a prison sentence of three to twelve years for a person convicted of kidnapping. Arkansas's laws also clearly specified that kidnapping included hiring, persuading, enticing, decoying, or seducing by "false promises, misrepresentations and the like, any negro, mulatto, or colored person, not being a slave," to leave the state or be removed from the state.[110]

Legislation failed to dissuade many would-be kidnappers, and in some parts of the country, these criminals became more vicious and better organized. Joseph Johnson's kidnapping syndicate, headquartered in Delaware and the Eastern Shore of Maryland, epitomized the level of ruthless forethought some abductors put into their criminal efforts. Johnson and his associates were already involved in the slave trade and kidnapping by the late 1810s, and Johnson may have continued in the illicit business well into the 1830s. On several occasions, officials in Sussex County, Delaware, hauled Johnson and his associates into court on kidnapping charges or to face suits from victims. Johnson sometimes received punishment for his crimes but managed to avoid any serious consequences, and, as a result, he continued with his insidious plots. Early in his career, both Johnson and his father-in-law, Jesse Cannon, received public whippings and spent time in the pillory for kidnapping convictions. Johnson's associate James Jones was also fined around the same time for illegally selling a manumitted person out of state. In 1821, a party that included sheriff's deputies rescued thirteen people held by Johnson in Jesse Cannon's house in Sussex County, just yards from the Maryland border. The rescue party found the victims chained inside the house. Johnson's associates had captured some of the victims from as far away as Wilmington, Delaware, and Baltimore. The actions of the rescue party did not stop Johnson. Throughout the early 1820s, Thomas Spenser, a "free negro," pursued Johnson on charges of assault and battery and false imprisonment and sued him for damages.[111] Over the years, people trafficked south by Johnson and his associates turned up claiming to have been kidnapped and illegally sold into slavery. During the latter part of 1825, the Johnson gang abducted several free people of color, including Mary Fisher from Elkton, Maryland, and five boys, Joseph Johnson, Enos Tilghman, Alexander Manlove, Samuel Scomp, and Cornelius Sinclair, from Philadelphia. Ebenezer F. Johnson, brother of the ringleader, proceeded south with his victims. He sold Cornelius Sinclair in Tuscaloosa, Alabama, and continued to Mississippi, where local officials apprehended him. They found Tilghman, Manlove, Scomp, and Fisher along with the body of the boy Joseph Johnson in Ebenezer F. Johnson's possession. The boy's corpse showed signs of a "cruel and severe beating."[112]

By 1829, the tide had turned against Johnson and his gang. That year, authorities charged Johnson, his mother-in-law, Martha "Patty" Cannon, and Cyrus James with murder after discovering bodies on the Cannon farm. Officials threw Patty Cannon in jail, where she died awaiting trial. The Sussex County court convicted Johnson, but officials tried him in absentia since he had left the state. After the trial, Johnson does not seem to have returned to Delaware or Maryland. Yet as late as 1837, newspaper reports suggested that Johnson was still free and alive. Although he had long since left the region, Michael Millman, the man who lived at his house on the Eastern Shore, continued to ply the nefarious trade. In 1836, people in the community discovered several kidnapped people concealed and chained under Millman's guard.[113] Johnson's role in Millman's criminal activities is unclear.

Many of the individuals who participated in the illicit trade of free persons of color were white. Yet a few free people of color found the rewards of trafficking too tempting to cede the trade exclusively to white criminals.[114] An 1801 newspaper notice from Baltimore reported that officials had apprehended a "free mulatto fellow" who had abducted "two negro children" for the purpose of selling them to "Georgia men."[115] "Georgia men" were slave traders who purchased people in the North and Upper South at a low price with the goal of transporting them and selling their enslaved prisoners for a profit in the Deep South. In 1832, the Sussex County, Delaware, Court of General Sessions sentenced Isaac Tyre, a "free mulatto," to a public whipping and three years' imprisonment "for aiding and assisting" in the kidnapping and illegal transport of a "negro boy" from Delaware to Maryland.[116] During the same year, the court in Mecklenburg County, Virginia, sentenced Granderson Cousins, a free man of color, to five years in the penitentiary for kidnapping William Cole, a free boy of color, with the intent of selling him as a slave. Witnesses in the case explained that Cousins abducted Cole from his father, Bartlett Cole, in Mecklenburg County and then transported him across the state border, where the boy was later recovered by his father. Soon after William Cole's recovery, officials located and arrested Cousins.[117] The examples of the unnamed "free mulatto fellow," Isaac Tyre, and Granderson Cousins highlight the extent of the corruption directly tied to the nineteenth-century domestic traffic in human beings. These free persons of color chose the possibility of profits over any sense of race-based comradery. Their actions demonstrate the limitations placed on people of color who attempted to challenge social inequality through the concept of racial unity. The illicit kidnapping and commodification of free people of color was a threat to all free persons of color. Nevertheless, some free people of color chose to chase the short-term benefits of kidnapping rather than recognize their role in perpetuating a form of human trafficking that endangered their liberty.

By the beginning of the 1830s, slavery and white supremacy had influenced a gradual reshaping of southern society and altered the possibilities for free people of color in the region. Proslavery ideologues and white supremacists had successfully restructured the legal code of the South from one that permitted the growth of the free population of color into a collection of laws that tried to regulate, sometimes unsuccessfully, the movements and activities of free people of color. Lawmakers used strict manumission laws, registration requirements, restrictions on gun ownership, and anti-immigration legislation to make their localities appear less attractive to free people of color seeking a haven and home. Attacks against the rights of free persons of color became fodder for constituencies seeking the reification of white authority and increased protection of slave property. For the Jeffersonian Republicans, these attacks were part of the plan to consolidate power. Even if their laws failed to produce tangible results, lawmakers could argue that they had taken serious steps to defend slavery and protect the South from becoming like the increasingly slaveless northern states or, worse, like Haiti, a nation run by former bondspeople.

The actions of proslavery and white supremacist lawmakers in the early 1800s slowed the progress of freedom but failed to contain it fully. They were unable to provide definitive evidence that free people of color were the threat they portrayed them to be. Many white southerners still needed to be convinced that the free people of color who were their neighbors, associates, local business people, and sometimes relatives were the equivalents of Toussaint Louverture, Jean-Jacques Dessalines, or their comrades in the Caribbean. Furthermore, white people in some communities found themselves increasingly dependent on free people of color in order to complete daily tasks. Throughout the early 1800s, the numbers of free people of color in such cities as Baltimore; Wilmington, Delaware; Richmond and Petersburg, Virginia; and New Orleans were booming, not declining. Kidnapping was a threat to free people of color, but many of their white neighbors did not condone such acts and offered at least piecemeal protections to victims of this illicit traffic.

The discriminatory laws of the early 1800s reflected some lawmakers' growing focus on racial categories as a means to delineate status in the South and also highlighted the continued importance legislators placed on wealth disparities. Many of the early nineteenth-century laws focused on certain segments of the free population of color: poor, transient people and the recently emancipated. Lawmakers targeted the most disadvantaged free persons of color. By highlighting certain segments of the free population, proslavery and white supremacist lawmakers could bring into their coalition legislators who were primarily interested in controlling the poor and curbing the number of transients. The discriminatory laws of the early 1800s often appeared haphazard because they were the products of a sometimes-disjointed process. The people who proposed discriminatory legislation rallied support for their acts but could not secure the funding to make their laws effective. They could push through restrictions on the movements of free people of color but often had to include provisions that left loopholes for free persons of color and their allies to exploit.

CHAPTER 4

Making Freedom Work

Early national newspaper editors generally reserved the obituary sections of their publications for the famous or the infamous. Yet on January 22, 1822, the *American Watchman* of Wilmington, Delaware, published a memorial for Andrew Noel, a local barber who had arrived in the city from Saint-Domingue during the Haitian Revolution. The newspaper reported that "on Sunday morning last, Andrew Noel, Barber, a man of colour, in the 48th year of his age," died in the city. The obituary further explained that Noel's "uniform obliging disposition and suavity of manners during a long residence in this town secured him the respect and esteem of all his acquaintances." It reported that his funeral procession to "the Roman Catholic burying ground" included "a train of respectable white inhabitants as well as coloured people." This formerly enslaved man had risen from bondage to respectability.[1] As white radicals argued that free people of color were a burden to society and a threat to their preferred social hierarchy, other whites viewed their world through a different lens. While not necessarily egalitarians, these white people still had the ability to see the free people of color among them as more than members of a pariah class.

The radical agenda of the early nineteenth century succeeded on many fronts, but challenges to attacks against free people of color kept the extremists at bay. For more than a century, free people of color and whites had lived as neighbors, worked together, prayed together, and fought together. The radical agenda could not erase these bonds overnight or even over a few years. Moreover, many southern whites could not afford to expel free people of color from their midst. In the early nineteenth century, free people of color played a key role in keeping the southern economy in motion. Working as laborers, farmers, artisans, and business owners, free persons of color provided their neighbors with important services.

The ways free people of color helped shape the institutions within their communities varied as greatly as their economic situations. The social networks of some free people of color were extensive and included other free people of color, white neighbors, and enslaved persons. Especially in the early nineteenth century, neighborhoods and many public institutions remained unsegregated. Kinship could blur the importance of other differences. Free people of color commonly attended church services with whites and enslaved people, sometimes as equals and sometimes under less-than-optimal circumstances. In some localities, free children of color went to school with white children and more commonly received their educational instruction from white teachers. The work lives of free people of color, enslaved persons, and whites regularly intersected. In other instances, free people of color focused specifically on building connections with other persons of color. Together, they established churches, schools, and social organizations that focused on their own needs and interests. Devoting their energies to building relationships with other people of color provided them with opportunities to discuss issues pertinent to persons of their station and to establish themselves as leaders.[2]

The population explosion that had begun during the late eighteenth century continued into the early nineteenth century, making free people of color ever more important to the social and economic fabric of southern communities. Census takers counted 61,241 free people of color in the southern United States in 1800. The inclusion of free people of color living in parts of the 1803 Louisiana Purchase, along with continued growth in other southern locales, drove the population to 108,265 in 1810. The population growth slowed slightly in 1820. The numeration of free people of color in the South that year was 134,223. By 1830, however, the number of free people of color had nearly tripled since the beginning of the century. Enumerators tallied 182,070 free persons of color, most of whom lived in the Upper South states of Maryland, Virginia, Delaware, and North Carolina. Throughout the pre-Civil War period, Louisiana was the only Deep South state with more than 10,000 free persons of color.[3]

The forces that drove population growth in the eighteenth century continued to increase the number of free people of color in the early 1800s. Manumissions that occurred through self-purchase, the assistance of friends and family, and the willingness of reforming slaveholders sustained the population explosion. Natural growth through the birth of children to free mothers played an essential role as well. Immigration supplemented the growth driven by other factors. The results and aftermath of the Haitian Revolution had a significant impact on the population numbers in the first decade of the nineteenth century as refugees evacuated from Haiti and their temporary homes in Cuba to mainland North America, especially Louisiana.[4] Free people of color found a place within a rapidly changing South.

Family

The social connections that free people of color developed during the 1700s continued to blossom into the early 1800s. Family formed the core of their social connections. As one of the most important social institutions among southerners in the early nineteenth century, family connected southerners in complicated and complex ways. Free persons of color built familial bonds among themselves, with the enslaved population, and with their white neighbors.

Ties among free families of color served as the roots of strong social networks. In places like Virginia and North Carolina, where significant populations of free people of color existed before the establishment of the United States, free people of color were already bound together in tight familial webs by the early nineteenth century. The laws of most southern states promoted intermarriage between free persons of color over other marriage combinations by prohibiting or strongly discouraging unions between free persons of color and whites or between free people of color and enslaved persons. Without legal sanction for other forms of marriage, free people of color found the greatest security in unions with persons of their same freedom status and racial designation. Legitimate unions between free people of color protected their collective interests, including their socioeconomic status and property rights.

Early nineteenth-century family networks frequently originated from social connections formed during the colonial period. Before the outbreak of the American Revolution, the Lowry, Oxendine, Locklear, Cumbo, Braveboy, Hammonds, and Chavis families were among the free persons of color settled in the part of Bladen County that became Robeson County, North Carolina, in 1787. By the early 1800s, several of these families were heavily intertwined. Farther north in parts of Granville County, North Carolina, heavy intermarriage created a similar web of kinship among the Anderson, Bass, Pettiford, and Chavis families.[5] In some parts of Louisiana, selective marriage patterns led to the formation of tight family networks. In Saint Landry Parish and the surrounding area, the Donato, Lemelle, and Meuillon families became heavily intertwined as the century progressed.[6]

Common language and culture connected some of Louisiana's free people of color, allowing them to continue speaking French without learning English well after their homeland became part of the United States. Adelaide Isidore, a free woman of color, was born at least a decade after France ceded Louisiana to the United States, and yet one witness who encountered Isidore in her adult life recounted that she "understands English so little that she can make herself understood in that language only through interpretation." Adelaide Isidore and other Francophone free people of color tended to marry and socialize among themselves. Baptiste Isidore, Adelaide's husband, also came from a family with ties to the old French Empire.[7]

The mass expansion of freedom that started during the late 1700s and continued into the 1800s increased the number of free persons of color with enslaved spouses and relatives. Through ownership of their enslaved kin or careful negotiation with the enslavers of their loved ones, free people of color navigated through slavery's murky legal terrain to build and preserve relationships with their enslaved relatives. Free people of color and bondspeople were entwined through a wide variety of familial connections. Amorous feelings drew free persons of color and enslaved people into long-term relationships. These bonds sometimes led to the birth of children, complicating the family's status. Free women of color bore free children regardless of whether the children's fathers were enslaved. A free man of color with children born to an enslaved mother, however, was the father of enslaved people. Sets of siblings could share common parentage but not necessarily the same legal position because individual manumissions created different freedom statuses among family members. Children with the same free father but mothers of different statuses could end up in a similar situation.

Familial bonds between free people and enslaved persons made for less-than-ideal circumstances. Southern legal codes denied sanction to unions between free persons and enslaved people. Free people of color who had enslaved relatives, including children and grandchildren, had no legal familial connection to their relations in much of the South. Ownership of their enslaved kin was the only way to formalize the attachments between free people and their enslaved descendants, whether children or grandchildren. Failure to gain legal title to relatives placed free people of color in situations familiar to generations of bondspeople. At a moment's notice, with the death of a master, the collection of a debt, or the simple desire of an enslaver to transform human chattel into cash, free persons of color could find their family members on the auction blocks or tied to coffles headed south.[8]

As in earlier periods, free people of color sometimes overcame the challenges of their relatives' enslaved status and secured the freedom of their loved ones. Throughout the 1800s, free people of color continued to be among the most frequent emancipators in the South. In 1816, Caty Posey and Milly Shorter, free women of color from the District of Columbia, executed a plan to liberate their sister Jenny Carroll, who was enslaved by Richard Queen. Capitalizing on their ability to own personal property, the sisters hired a slave trader to purchase Carroll from Queen who in turn transferred her to Posey and Shorter. Following the purchase, Posey and Shorter liberated their sister.[9] On September 7, 1814, Hannah Kain, a "free black woman" from Baltimore County, Maryland, freed her grandson Harry Pinnion, a "yellow or mulatto boy," from the bonds of slavery. After purchasing her grandson from Archibald Beaty of Harford County, Kain took advantage of the opportunity to formalize Pinnion's liberty. In consideration of her "Love & Natural Affection" for her grandson, Kain issued a deed of manumission to Pinnion, discharging him from "all manner of servitude or service."[10]

Liberating family members in order to preserve family bonds was a costly venture for free persons of color. They were often left with little money after spending hundreds and sometimes thousands of dollars to purchase and free their relatives. Caesar Hope, a free man of color, affectionately known as "Barber Caesar," was a highly respected businessman in Richmond, Virginia. John Wickham described him as "one of the most industrious, orderly and respectable men of colour I ever knew." Hope's attention to his business allowed him to accumulate enough money to purchase several family members, but the price of doing so left him with little property.[11]

The expense of purchasing enslaved persons along with masters' unwillingness to part with their bondspeople prevented some free persons of color from gaining legal title to their enslaved kin. These free people of color had to learn to navigate familial relationships in which masters had the right to interfere with their most intimate affairs. Before his death in 1828, Frank Tasco, a free man of color from Harford County, Maryland, had accrued enough savings to buy his wife, Nancy, and sons, Santy and William Henry. By borrowing against his assets, he was able to procure Anna, the wife of his son Santy. Yet he failed to purchase and liberate his daughter Susan Hobles, who remained enslaved after his death.[12] Levin Tilmon, his mother, and three sisters, all of Caroline County, Maryland, received their freedom when Tilmon was a small child. Although Tilmon was free, his father and four older siblings remained enslaved. Their bondage disrupted the cohesion of Tilmon's family and forced him to struggle with the power others held over his family's future. He recalled that "my two sisters, in connection with all other female slaves in the South, were deprived of the protection of their virtue, which is disregarded and trampled in the dust, by the amorous aspirant, who delights in seducing the character of the helpless female." Tilmon's eldest sister "became a mother by the son of her own master." This situation "created a very unpleasant state of feeling in her master's family." As a result, the master sold her away. Soon after this sale, Tilmon's family suffered another blow when the master of his sister, Violette, sold her. Nearly thirty years after these events took place, Tilmon reported that he had not heard from his sisters since their sales.[13]

Unable to bring their relatives out of bondage, free people of color worked diligently to keep their families together despite the situation. In 1829, Britton Jones moved from Bertie County, North Carolina, to Alabama in order to follow his enslaved wife and children, who had been relocated to Alabama by their master. Instead of accepting the loss of his family, Jones chose to leave Bertie County, the place of his birth and residence for nearly thirty years, and relocate to the Deep South. By moving to Alabama, Jones faced the possibility of losing his residency in North Carolina and being subjected to the penalty of North Carolina's 1826 immigration restrictions, which prohibited free people of color from immigrating into the state and blocked reentry for free persons of color who had lived outside of the state for more than a year. Still, Jones risked all of this to keep his family together.[14]

Free people of color who could not find ways to purchase their relatives had to develop ingenious methods to care for their enslaved loved ones. By 1808, Bella Clark of New Hanover County, North Carolina, had obtained her freedom, but her husband, John Lillington, alias McAuslan, remained in bondage as the slave of John McAuslan. The different legal statuses of Clark and Lillington challenged their ability to act as free people would in a similar relationship. While Clark, as a free woman of color, could legally hold real and personal property, her husband could not obtain legal title to land or any other type of property. She was unable to consign her property, including her lot, house, furniture, and an enslaved girl named Sylvia, to her husband. Clark therefore entrusted her possessions to her executor to be used by her enslaved husband as a way to maneuver around the law.[15] Before his death in the 1820s, Jacob Armstrong of Worcester County, Maryland, placed some of his property in trust with his "friend" George Hayward in order to provide for his enslaved children's future. Armstrong's wife, Comfort, along with his children Harry, Elizabeth, Ebben, and Hannah were free. Yet his sons Jacob and Elijah, along with his daughter Comfort, remained enslaved by Dr. William F. Selby. Armstrong's will instructed Hayward to rent or sell several tracts of land as needed to support his children who were still in bondage.[16] Although free people of color could not always secure the liberty of their family members, they still attempted to use the privileges of their free status to improve the predicaments of their relatives in bondage. Free persons of color used their relationships with friends and allies to protect the interests of enslaved family members. Extending the benefits of freedom to their enslaved loved ones required trusted assistance and cooperation.

The legal situation in South Carolina created unique challenges for free people of color who owned enslaved relatives and sought to care for them after their deaths. Starting in 1820, South Carolina severely restricted manumissions, which left the enslaved relatives of free people of color in legal limbo. Even if a free person of color gained ownership over an enslaved relative, that person could not free this family member or pass on legal title to property to the enslaved relative. Sylvia Emanuel, "a free black woman," encountered these problems when trying to decide the fate of her adopted daughter Nancy Emanuel. Although Sylvia Emanuel owned Nancy, she could not free Nancy under the laws of the state, nor could she give Nancy title to any of her property. Like free people of color in other states who had enslaved relatives owned by others, Sylvia Emanuel had to devise a scheme in order to maneuver around the law and provide for Nancy's future well-being. Sylvia left much of her property in the hands of her guardian John J. Lafae for Nancy's benefit. Sylvia Emanuel's 1823 will also made Lafae Nancy's legal owner.[17] The situation of Sylvia Emanuel reveals the perseverance of free people of color to care for their enslaved relatives regardless of the legal limitations.

Familial connections to enslaved people sometimes created serious trouble for free persons of color by raising the suspicion of their loved ones' enslavers. Newspapers across the South printed runaway slave advertisements that implicated the free relatives of enslaved people in escape plots. After Solomon Rodgers ran away from his Anne Arundel County, Maryland, master in 1810, a local newspaper circulated an advertisement requesting his return. The advertisement suggested that Rodgers's free family members might have been involved in his plans to escape. Horatio Ridout, Rodgers's master, explained in the advertisement that his bondsman had brothers, "James and John Richardson," who were "freemen" living in Baltimore. Ridout suspected that Rodgers might have sought shelter in their community.[18] In 1827, John Guimarin of Augusta, Georgia, accused Jemima Armwood, "a free mulatto woman," of running off with her enslaved husband, Dick Youngblood, as well as the couple's three children, who were bound to Guimarin as servants. Guimarin described Armwood and her family as "thieves and runaway Mulattoes" and offered the hefty sum of two hundred dollars for their return.[19]

The familial ties that bound together free people of color and whites in the 1700s continued into the nineteenth century and were supplemented by the blossoming of new relationships established in the 1800s. Although the laws of the South gave their relationships no sanction, free people of color and their white partners challenged the very existence of an indelible color line in the South. Their relationships exposed the contrast between the laws on the books and the actual human interactions that took place in everyday life.

Free men of color established long-term relationships with white women in many parts of the South. The image of men of color as a direct threat to white womanhood had not fully developed in the early 1800s, allowing these relationships to exist without the level of scrutiny that similar relationships received from white conservatives following the Civil War.[20] Silas Shoecraft, a free man of color and veteran of the War of 1812, maintained a long-term relationship with Mary Teaster, a white woman. Shoecraft and Teaster lived together for multiple decades in North Carolina and raised their family. All the couple's children took the Shoecraft name, and Silas also shared his surname with Mary's son Abram, who was born out of wedlock before the couple began their relationship.[21] Jordan Edge, a free man of color, and Lurana "Raney" Hewitt, a white woman, lived together for nearly twenty years in Pasquotank County, North Carolina. Although county officials prosecuted them for living in an "unlawful manner," the couple persevered. Their relationship lacked legal sanction, but Jordan Edge publicly recognized Raney Hewitt as his "wife" and left his property to her and their daughter Rebecca on his death.[22]

Relationships between men of color and white women left generations of free people of color with close connections to white ancestors. By the beginning of the nineteenth century, Jane Tate, "a native of Scotland," had produced a large family of children and grandchildren whom her neighbors in Stafford County, Virginia, recognized as free persons of color. In 1808, Tate testified on behalf of her granddaughter Rachel Bales, who sought to obtain papers proving her free status. She explained to local officials that her granddaughter, although a woman of color, was free because Tate herself was "born as free as other British subjects."[23] Nancy Clarke, a "molatto woman" who spoke both "the German and English languages" and lived in Washington County, Maryland, during the 1810s, claimed her freedom as the daughter of Molly Clarke, "a white woman."[24]

Across the South, free women of color built long-lasting relationships with white men. These relationships, like those between free men of color and white women, were unrecognized by the laws of most southern locales. Nevertheless, they were a significant part of family life for free persons of color in the early nineteenth century. Historians have correctly noted that many of the relationships between women of color and white men were exploitative, especially in the context of slave-master relationships. There were some free women of color, however, whose white partners acted as trustworthy providers and supportive fathers to their children.[25]

Tales of plaçage, mulatto balls, and concubinage have long clouded the genuine connections between free women of color and white men, especially in the context of the Deep South. More recent scholarship, however, has pushed back against these simplified narratives and revealed more complex relationships between free women of color and white men.[26] In several parts of the old Spanish Empire, free women of color and white men established relationships based on affection and respect.[27] Isabelle, "a coloured woman," lived with Hilaire Dubroca, a white man, in Mobile County, Alabama, for "many years" before the couple's relationship ended with Hilaire's death. During their time together, Isabelle and Hilaire produced at least five children: Bazille, Louise, Arsene, Cephire, and Arthur. Before his death in the 1820s, Dubroca granted all of his property, including a cattle ranch, to Isabelle and their children. In the context of early nineteenth-century Mobile County, the connection between Isabelle and Hilaire was typical for individuals in such a family relationship. Other couplings between free women of color and white men operated in a similar fashion. Louison, "a free negro woman," lived with John Chastang for over twenty years. Although Louison and John could not recognize each other as wife and husband under the law, Chastang still declared that Louison was his "beloved worthy friend and companion." Like Isabelle and her family, Louison and her children inherited the property of her white partner. Nanette Pouche, a "free woman of colour," found an equally faithful partner in Geanty Mejat, a white businessman. Mejat publicly proclaimed his connection to the couple's two sons not only by providing for them but also by giving them family names. The couple named their elder son Geanty after his father. Their younger son carried the name of Mejat's brother, Leon. Mejat's affection for Pouche extended well beyond his concern for her and their two sons. He also provided for Pouche's two children who were born before the blossoming of their relationship as well as for her brother Nicole, leaving them with real estate on his death.[28]

Free women of color and white men may have found the greatest acceptance of their relationships in Louisiana, especially in New Orleans. Mathilde Gaillare, a free woman of color, cohabited for many years with Narcissus Broutin, a white man, in Gaillare's New Orleans home. The couple had three children: Appoline, Rosalie, and Augustin. Before his death around 1819, Broutin willed half of his assets to his children, leaving the other half to his legal heirs. Broutin's will also denoted Gaillare's legal title to the home they shared as well as the furnishings within the home. Broutin sought to protect his partner's interest by clearly distinguishing the property legally held by Gaillare from his own. Such a move preserved Gaillare's rights and defended her from challenges that Broutin's heirs might bring against her for the property. By the 1820s, Anne Marie Blandin, a free woman of color originally from Jeremie in Saint-Domingue, had settled in New Orleans and was living in a long-term relationship with Manuel Santos, an immigrant from Portugal. During their cohabitation, Blandin gave birth to at least three children: Manuel Francisco, Joseph Antonio, and Marie Jeanne. At age forty, Santos became sick and died, leaving Blandin to care for herself and their three children. Showing himself to be a considerate partner and father, Santos granted Blandin four hundred dollars and left the rest of his estate to their children. Further demonstrating his respect for and trust in Blandin, Santos named her as the coexecutor of his will.[29]

Relationships between free women of color and white men were not limited to parts of the old Spanish Empire. Although much of the historical scholarship as well as the mythology of these relationships have focused on traditionally French- and Spanish-speaking regions of the Deep South, free women of color established affectionate and stable relationships with white partners across the region.[30] Silvia Harwood, a "free woman of colour," lived with John McEnery, a white man, in Richmond, Virginia, during the 1810s. The couple had three children, Thomas, Peggy, and Nancy. Like his counterparts in other parts of the South, McEnery left his property to Silvia and their children.[31] In Wilkes County, North Carolina, Elizabeth Culms, a free "woman of colour," and John P. Waters, a white man, lived together for many years and raised six children. Although the couple's living arrangement lacked legal sanction, their neighbors overlooked the situation until fourteen years after the beginning of their relationship, when a neighbor driven by "envy and malice" reported the couple to the authorities. Even after the local court convicted the couple for their living situation, Waters declared that the "love" he had for his "little children and their kind mother" still motivated him to keep his family "together" and "do a fatherly & husbands part by them."[32]

On rare but important occasions, free women of color developed relationships with some of the most important and elite white men in their communities. Although public officials commonly shunned relationships between free people of color and whites, some officials lived private lives that contrasted with the alleged white elite consensus. Mary Buchanan, "a free mulatto woman," partnered with George Morgan, a British diplomat based in Norfolk, Virginia. The couple had at least two children before Morgan's death in 1812.[33] Hannah Mitchell, a free woman of color, established a relationship with John Jeffers, the mayor of Petersburg, Virginia. The couple's daughter, Sylvia, carried the surname of her father, and the Jeffers family, along with many residents of Petersburg, recognized Sylvia's connection to John.[34]

The failure of southern lawmakers to provide sanction for relationships between free persons of color and whites created an array of challenges for those engaged in these partnerships and their children. Free people of color sometimes encountered complicated legal obstacles after the death of their white partners or parents. The legal relatives of white partners and fathers occasionally worked to prevent their relatives of color from collecting assets granted to them by will or other means. After the death of his brother Pierre Bouthemy in 1812, Cyprian Bouthemy of France filed suit against his brother's executor, Francis Dreux, and two free women of color, Sanette and Barnette. He claimed that the will promising property and assets to Sanette, Pierre Bouthemy's partner, and Barnette, the partner of Charles Ellinghaus, was null and void. Cyprian maintained that he and his brother Florentine were the only lawful heirs of Pierre Bouthemy. Yet after pushing the case through several levels of Louisiana's judicial system, Cyprian failed to sway the courts, and Sanette and her children retained rights to the property entrusted to them in Pierre Bouthemy's will.[35]

White fathers also faced difficulty trying to maintain normal relations between themselves and their children. Fathers in mixed relationships occasionally encountered problems gaining custody over their children. Conflict disrupted once stable relationships, and free women of color asserted their rights to custody over the objections of their children's fathers. After the collapse of her relationship of eleven years with Antoine Acosta, a white man, Caliche Robin, a free woman of color, took their daughter and left their shared home in New Orleans. On learning that

Robin had abandoned him, Acosta sued her for custody of their daughter. In 1828, a judge for the New Orleans court ruled against Acosta, who then appealed to the Louisiana Supreme Court and lost again.[36] In most cases it was the law, and not mothers, that stood as the main impediment to fathers' abilities to establish control over their children. Since the law granted them no legal right to their children, fathers sometimes had to find creative ways to make claim to their daughters and sons. The apprenticeship laws became important tools for fathers seeking legal custody over their children. During the November 1821 session of court in Gates County, North Carolina, John Brady, a white man, had his son Joseph Rooks, a "boy of colour," bound to him.[37] By having their children apprenticed to them by the courts, fathers gained legal custody. They could therefore protect their families from malicious neighbors who might seek to break up the family in order to gain control of the children's labor.

Recognized kinship connections between free people of color and white persons sometimes extended beyond the relationships between parents and children or intimate partners. The 1821 will of Ignatius Wheeler, a white resident of Georgetown in the District of Columbia, reveals the extraordinary bonds between Ignatius and his siblings, Charles Wheeler, "a free man of colour," and Elizabeth Peck, "a free woman of colour." After donating one hundred dollars to two schools, Ignatius Wheeler devised his remaining real estate, stock in the Union Bank of Georgetown, and other property to his "beloved" siblings and their children.[38] While Ignatius Wheeler's will does not reveal his deeper philosophy about the general interactions among free people of color and whites in the South, his decision to acknowledge his siblings publicly and gift them the bulk of his estate demonstrates the value he placed on kinship connections. For Ignatius Wheeler, differences in racial classification did not trump family bonds.

Building Community

During the early nineteenth century, free people of color worked with their neighbors, both white and of color, to shape the daily patterns of southern life. Free people of color and their neighbors expressed a sense of community through social institutions as well as the physical and economic structures that fulfilled their basic needs. These institutions and structures transformed families and broader kinship networks into webs of interlinked people. Class differences, gender, and the legal divides that emerged around the concept of race created significant rifts among free people of color and their white neighbors, and these ideas influenced the social and political configurations of communities. Although various forms of inequality were rampant through the South, free people of color found ways to convey their societal importance and contribute to the development of their neighborhoods, towns, cities, and states.

As discussions of the slavery problem drew them into increasingly unfavorable political debates, free people of color still found ways to cultivate relationships with their white neighbors. Statements given by white compatriots on behalf of free persons of color reveal decades and sometimes generations of familiarity between free persons of color and their white neighbors. On March 6, 1814, John D. Barnes, "a white man," provided testimony before a Baltimore County, Maryland, justice of the peace concerning the freedom of several members of the Clark family. Barnes explained that Rachel Hill, Nancy Clark, Mary Clark, Hannah Edwards, and George Clark were all children of Martha Clark, whom he knew to have been "born free in Accomack County Commonwealth of Virginia" and "was descended from a white woman." Beyond knowing Martha Clark and her children, Barnes was familiar with Martha Clark's mother, who he knew "always past for a free woman."[39] David Hamilton demonstrated a similar level of familiarity when he testified on behalf of the Cook family before a District of Columbia justice of the peace on August 18, 1821. Hamilton explained that he had known Hannah Cook, "a coloured woman," and her daughter Ann Cook before they relocated to the District of Columbia. In Virginia, he recalled, the Cooks had lived about three miles from Ellicott's Mills, where Hannah Cook maintained "a house for the accommodation of waggoners." Hamilton further testified that the Cooks were "always considered as free people" and that Hannah Cook's "mother was of Indian descent."[40]

Neighborhood estate sales brought together people of color and whites in search of good deals on the property of departed neighbors. Estate executors permitted buyers of all backgrounds, white and of color, to peruse and purchase the assets of the deceased. On December 14, 1805, Nathaniel Newsom, a free man of color, sold the effects of his late father, Moses Newsom, of Northampton County, North Carolina, to a diverse group of family, friends, and neighbors. Members of the Newsom family purchased a wide assortment of items, including furniture, livestock, crops, and tools. Howell Wade, a free man of color, obtained a cow and calf, a horse, a gun, pewter kitchenware, and miscellaneous other goods. Thomas Faison, a neighboring white slaveholder, bought two bushels of wheat and iron wedges. Another white neighbor, James Garris, acquired two bushels and three pecks of peas and an ax.[41]

Free persons of color who were veterans of the American Revolution commonly called on their white neighbors to support their applications for pensions. White neighbors provided important details that affected the outcome of their war claims. Adam Adams, a "free black citizen" of Charles County, Maryland, received a pension with the assistance of Edmund Key, a white neighbor. On March 28, 1818, Key testified that he was "personally acquainted with Adam Adams" and knew "Adams while belonging to the Army during the Revolutionary War, and saw him often and for a long time serving in the first Regiment of the Maryland line in the continental service."⁴² Anthony Garnes, a "free man of couler" living in Wilson County, Tennessee, secured his petition with the assistance of Howell Tatum, a white man who lived in neighboring Davidson County. Tatum met Garnes while both men served in North Carolina's Continental regiment. In his 1818 statement, Tatum remembered that Garnes "was taken prisoner at Charlestown" during the war.⁴³

As in previous generations, free people of color contributed to the defense of their communities by serving in local militias, participating in military campaigns during times of war, and shipping out with the navy. Free people of color were essential to the defense of Spanish Florida until Spain ceded the territory to the United States in 1821. During an attempt by forces from the United States to invade and seize Florida in 1812, Juan Bautista Witten, a free man of color, led troops against U.S. marines who laid siege on Saint Augustine. The men under Witten's command pushed back the U.S. forces and helped to save Saint Augustine. In North Carolina, free men of color served in local militias side by side with their white neighbors into the early years of the War of 1812. Free men of color mustered in the militias of several North Carolina counties, including Halifax, Northampton, Hertford, Robeson, and Granville. Moses Pettiford, a free man of color, served as the fourth sergeant in a Granville County regiment, making him seventh in command in a company of seventy-eight men, both of color and white.⁴⁴ John Thompson of the District of Columbia was an ordinary seaman on board the frigate *Congress* during the war.⁴⁵

Following the transfer of Louisiana from France to the United States, free men of color from the area entered the service of their new country. During the War of 1812, free men of color aided in the defense of New Orleans.⁴⁶ Pierre Laborissiere stated that he "served as a private" and "participated in several engagements at and near New Orleans" after enlisting in September 1814.⁴⁷ Raynal Auguste, a resident of New Orleans, recalled serving among the "colored troops" during 1814 and 1815. During the early part of 1815, he participated in a police patrol in Saint John the Baptist Parish, Louisiana, tasked with "checking an outbursting negroe slaves insurrection."[48] Celestin Baham, who lived in New Orleans during the war, remembered serving in a company "made up principally of French (or of those who spoke the French language)." Although Andrew Jackson offered bounties to "free colored" volunteers, Baham explained that he was "pressed into the service" under Jackson. He served with many others of his background in the Battle of New Orleans.[49]

Religious institutions tied individual free persons of color and their families to wider networks of people who subscribed to similar beliefs and ideologies. Free people of color participated in almost every Christian denomination that could be found in the South. The Protestant denominations predominated through most of the region. During the early nineteenth century, free persons of color joined the Baptist, Methodist, Episcopal, Moravian, and Presbyterian churches. Under these denominations, free people of color were both adherents and leaders. Some mixed congregations had only a few free people of color among their membership. Before 1830, Sally Toulson and a woman denoted by the church clerk as "Leah" were the only free persons of color among the membership of Coan Baptist Church of Northumberland County, Virginia. In contrast, free people of color were a significant portion of the membership at First Baptist Church in Washington, District of Columbia. Throughout the early 1800s, they were a noteworthy part of the young congregation's development. Free persons of color joined the congregation by transferring their memberships from other congregations and through baptism.[50]

Although they were more likely to act as congregants in the churches of the South, a small group of free persons of color served among the Christian clergy during the early nineteenth century. These clergy members brought people of color and whites together under a common worldview. John Chavis and Jarena Lee were among the Protestant preachers of color traveling throughout the region ministering to and converting audiences of whites and persons of color. John Chavis, a licensed Presbyterian minister, trekked through Virginia, North Carolina, and Maryland, sharing the gospel and bringing new adherents to the church. During the 1790s and early 1800s, Chavis moved from hamlet to hamlet as a representative of his denomination. Whites and people of color alike supported Chavis's ministry. Jarena Lee was originally from New Jersey and made Philadelphia her permanent residence but spent a significant amount of time ministering to people of color and whites in the upper reaches of the South, including Delaware and Maryland, during the 1820s. Although Lee was a lay minister of the African Methodist Episcopal church, people across the region received her message, including fol-

During the 1820s, Jarena Lee preached before audiences of people of color and whites across the mid-Atlantic states, including Delaware and Maryland. Although Lee was a lay minister of the African Methodist Episcopal church, she also visited houses of worship belonging to Quakers, Presbyterians, Baptists, and Methodists.
(Courtesy of the Library of Congress)

lowers of such other denominations as the Society of Friends, Methodists, Baptists, and Presbyterians. She visited small houses and preached in crowded churches. She also participated in the circuit of camp meetings across the region.[51]

Henry Evans and Joseph Willis established churches for their denominations in regions of the South previously untapped by parishioners of their faith. William Capers, a white minister, described Henry Evans as "the most remarkable man in Fayetteville" and branded him "the father of the Methodist Church, white and black, in Fayetteville" after encountering Evans during his 1810 appointment in North Carolina. Evans was originally from Virginia but relocated to Fayetteville, where he started to preach among the people of color in the community. During his initial ventures, Fayetteville's town council attempted to stop Evans from preaching. Pushed out of town, Evans resurrected his ministry in the sandhills on the outskirts of town and held meetings in the woods, moving from place to place in order to avoid interference. The results of Evans's ministry included wider observance of the sabbath and temperance among his followers. Such successes eventually convinced town officials to allow Evans to return. On his return to Fayetteville, Evans expanded his ministry to include whites as well as new adherents of color. The construction of a permanent place of worship followed the growth of Evans's ministry.[52] In the early 1800s, Joseph Willis traveled to Louisiana to spread the message of the Baptist church and continued his work throughout the first half of the century. Willis helped establish some of the first Baptist churches west of the Mississippi River. His congregations included people of color as well as white people. The regard for Willis among Baptists in Louisiana was so great that delegates to the first meeting of the Louisiana Baptist Association elected him moderator in 1818. He continued in this position for several years.[53]

The Catholic Church had served as a social bridge between free people of color and whites in parts of the South since the colonial period and continued to do so into the nineteenth century.[54] Free people of color were a key constituency for the church, especially in communities with historic ties to Catholicism. An assortment of free persons of color in Baltimore became part of the Catholic religious community during the early decades of the 1800s. The Reverend Fesser baptized Marie Jeanne, alias Rosalie, "a free Black woman about 40 years old native of Congo," on February 16, 1812. On June 20, 1812, the Reverend Babaad baptized William, the five-year-old "lawful son of William & Christina Howard free col[ore]d." Two days later, Mary Ann Julia, a free woman and "native of the East Indies," joined the church at age twenty-two.[55] Free people of color also entered the Catholic Church in locales such as Savannah, Georgia, the District of Columbia, and Mobile, Alabama.[56] The church found its greatest audience, however, among free people of color in New Orleans, a city with deep historic ties to the Catholic-dominated French and Spanish Empires. Following the annexation of Louisiana to the United States, free people of color continued to look to the Catholic Church for their spiritual needs. Every year, New Orleans's Saint Louis Cathedral received free people of color as members through baptism. On August 15, 1809, Friar Antonio de Sedella baptized Luisa, a free "negra," and Yrene, a free "negra," daughters of Maria del Carmen, a free "negra," and Antonio Bouligni, a free "negro." During the next month, the friar baptized Luisa Dupart, a free "mulata" and daughter of Carlos Dupart and Victoria Millon, free "mulatoes." Some Catholic free persons of color also permitted church officials to baptize their slaves. On July 8, 1809, Friar Antonio de Sedella received Maria Estephania Delphina, the slave of Sophia Mansantos, a free "mulata."[57]

Although free people of color and whites commonly attended the same churches, the treatment that free persons of color received within these mixed congregations varied widely. Some southern churches provided free people of color with opportunities equal to those afforded to white congregants. At the turn of the century, officials of the Protestant Episcopal church of the Parish of Saint Philip in Charleston, South Carolina, permitted Sophia Smith, "a free woman of colour," to purchase a pew.[58] Elsewhere, however, white leaders transported the spirit of inequality into the region's churches. During the early national period, discrimination was a contagion gradually seeping into religious life in the South as well as other parts of the country.[59] Although the free man of color Henry Evans served people of all backgrounds at his Methodist church in Fayetteville, his white congregants enforced a policy of physical separation between themselves and people of color.[60] Some Protestant churches in Maryland etched gender and racial exclusion into the official documents of their congregations. The 1829 church charter for Ebenezer Methodist Episcopal Church in Talbot County, Maryland, limited voting rights to "free white male persons above the age of twenty one years."[61] The trustees of the Methodist church in Clear Spring, Maryland, had issued similar restrictions on voting as part of their founding document seven years earlier.[62] Sometimes exclusionary practices shifted from denying people of color a role in church decision-making to excluding them as members. In 1823, a group of free people of color and enslaved persons in Richmond, Virginia, complained that they were "excluded from the churches, meeting houses, and other places of public devotion, which are used by white persons, in consequence of no appropriate places being assigned for them, except in a few houses."[63] Even in integrated churches, the white leadership sometimes imposed segregated burial practices. By 1822, none of the free people of color affiliated with Saint Stephen's Chapel in Charleston, South Carolina, were buried in the church cemetery. Instead, the families of free people of color interred their loved ones in one of the city's cemeteries for people of color, such as MacPhelah Cemetery, the Brown Fellowship Graveyard, and the local potter's field.[64] The white supremacist ideology spreading through society had gradually manifested itself in the churches of the South.

White people's unwillingness to work as coequals within religious institutions as well as the desire of people of color for self-determination sometimes drove the creation of churches that catered specifically to the needs of free persons of color and the enslaved. The movement began in the northern states and gradually spread throughout the South, especially in the cities but also in some rural locales.[65] By developing their own religious organizations, free people of color revealed that they could build institutions without dependence on whites. Early churches for people of color in Baltimore included the African Church on Sharp Street and Bethel Church. By the 1820s, Wilmington, Delaware, had African Zion, African Baptist, African Episcopal, and African Methodist churches. In 1818, Joseph Shiphard, Sterling Mann, World Sykes, Henry Boyd, Colston M. Waring, Richard Jarrett, Jacob Howell, and Luke Taborne, "free people of colour," purchased the site for Gillfield Baptist Church in Petersburg, Virginia.[66] During the same year, Abraham and Susanna Brown transferred a tract of land containing a "meeting house" called "Elam" to Cornelius Brown, John Brown, James Brown, Henry C. Harris, and Dixon Brown Jr., free men of color, for the site of a Baptist church in rural Charles City County, Virginia.[67] These churches provided free people of color, as well as enslaved persons in some instances, with religious instruction, leadership opportunities, socialization, and discipline. Free people of color found leadership opportunities unavailable in many of the South's mixed congregations. At Gillfield Baptist Church and Elam Baptist Church, free people of color could serve as church trustees and deacons. Church secretaries were also free persons of color.[68]

When working with whites as equals was not possible or desirable, free people of color sought greater autonomy through the creation of civic and social organizations. Through these institutions, they attempted to develop and promote their ideas about the proper direction of their society. The exclusive Brown Fellowship Society of Charleston, South Carolina, had admitted over one hundred free men of color by 1830. Founded

Bethel Church was among the earliest churches founded by free people of color in Baltimore. This image depicts the Reverend Darius Stokes's presentation of a gold snuff box to the Reverend R. T. Breckenridge inside Bethel Church.
(Courtesy of the Library of Congress)

by James Mitchell, George Bampfield, William Cattle, George Bedon, and Samuel Saltus in 1790, the organization provided a social outlet for some of Charleston's most prominent free persons of color. The society also maintained a burial ground for the exclusive use of members and their families. The organization's leadership kept a strict line of decorum, even excluding from membership Samuel Saltus, one of the founders.[69] After a thorough investigation, the society removed George Logan from membership in 1817 following allegations that he had assisted in the kidnapping and illegal sale of another free man of color.[70] Around 1803, elite Charlestonians Joseph Humphries, William Cooper, Carlos Huger, James Mitchell, William Clark, Thomas S. Bonneau, and Richard Holloway established the Minors' Moralist Society. The organization's members charged themselves with providing for the city's poor and orphaned children of color.[71] In 1820, free men of color in Wilmington, Delaware, established the African Benevolent Association of Wilmington. By 1825, the association's thirty members united for the promotion of "the diffusion of knowledge, the suppression of vice and for the inculcation of every virtue that renders man great, good, or happy." These free men of color offered assistance to the greater public as well as the families of their membership. After participating in the organization for at least a year, members were entitled to support during periods of sickness and to death benefits for their widows and children. By providing for their members and their families, Wilmington's free men of color protected their interests and those of the public at large.[72] In the neighboring town of New Castle, Joseph Manly, Robert Jackson, Levi Finney, Peter Jackson, James Finny, and Caleb Darby organized themselves as the Sons of Benevolence in the Town of New Castle. Similar to their counterparts in Wilmington, they tasked themselves with "suppressing vice and immorality, burying the dead, and taking care of the indigent and sick among their coloured brethren."[73]

By the early nineteenth century, free people of color and their white allies created means for the formal education of free children of color in many parts of the South, especially in the region's cities. Free people of color often took the lead in the development of institutions for their children. By 1809, Daniel Coker and George Collins, free men of color, were operating an evening school for persons of color out of the African Church on Sharp Street in Baltimore.[74] During the following year, Hannibal Bishop opened a school for children of color on North Street, where he offered classes on "reading, writing, and arithmetic."[75] Thomas S. Bonneau, a free man of color, operated a school for children of color in Charleston, South Carolina. At Bonneau's school, pupils received les-

Rev. Daniel Coker.

During the early 1800s, Daniel Coker operated a school for children of color out of the African Church on Sharp Street in Baltimore. In addition to his educational activities, Coker was a minister and an author. (Courtesy of the Library of Congress) sons in spelling, reading, writing, speech, history, and basic mathematics. The Presbyterian minister John Chavis taught both children of color and white children in Raleigh, North Carolina. Chavis initially instructed pupils of color and white students in the same classroom before deciding to offer evening courses exclusively for children of color.[76] The District of Columbia hosted several schools for children of color in the early 1800s. George Bell, Nicholas Franklin, and Moses Liverpool, free men of color, helped establish the capital's first school for children of color in 1807. The organizers employed a white teacher, Mr. Lowe, to instruct children in the community. In 1818, operating as the Resolute Beneficial Society, William Costin, George Hicks, James Harris, George Bell, Archibald Johnson, Frederick Lewis, Isaac Johnson, and Scipio Beens created a school for the "ladies or gentlemen" among the capital's free persons of color who sought to have their children "instructed in reading, writing, arithmetic, English grammar or other branches of education apposite to their capacities" by an "active and experienced teacher." John Adams, a free man of color, was one of the school's instructors.[77]

White allies supported the efforts of free people of color to educate their youth. They taught children and raised money to support schools. In Alexandria, in the District of Columbia, Mrs. Cameron and Mrs. Tutten, both Virginians, established schools for children of color sometime before the War of 1812. Following the war, the Reverend James H. Hanson, the white minister at the Methodist Episcopal church for people of color, taught at a school founded by free people of color in the same city. Mary Billing, originally from England, operated a school in Georgetown and one at a home owned by Daniel Jones, a free man of color, in Washington during the 1810s and 1820s. At the beginning of the nineteenth century, the Abolition Society of Delaware sponsored a school for people of color in Wilmington. By 1812, whites in Delaware had organized the Wilmington Association for Promoting the Education of the People of Colour. The association collected and oversaw donations to support the schooling of free persons of color. By the 1820s, the association had incorporated as the African School Society of Wilmington.[78] In the same city, a "spirited and philanthropic gentleman" sponsored the Colored Infant School. An 1829 exhibition of the school received wide public praise. One observer remarked, "The examination of the Infant School of colored children . . . was one of the most interesting spectacles we ever witnessed. . . . There were about sixty scholars of both sexes, present, and so crowded was the large room on the first floor, with spectators, that many were unable to gain admittance. The answers of the children to questions in Geography, History, &c. and their recitations and singing, excited the admiration and delight of those who heard them."[79] Another onlooker reported, "These little coloured children, who, but a few months ago, were collected from our streets and are of the poorest of our coloured population, passed a better examination, than the scholars in any common school in the State would pass.... The extent of the useful knowledge, which these children have acquired, is matter of astonishment to one, who reflects upon what is acquired in common schools, and the length of time consumed."[80]

While free people of color obtained formal education in private schools, others received the most rudimentary skills through the tutorship of friends and acquaintances. G. W. Offley grew up in early nineteenth-century Queen Anne's County, Maryland, with parents who were free but illiterate and unable to provide him with the most basic education. He depended on a wide range of people to obtain a basic education. As a young adult, Offley received his first reading lessons from an "old colored man" employed by his father. Working at nights and on Sunday mornings, the man instructed Offley, teaching him the alphabet. After losing the assistance of this man, Offley struck up a relationship with the eighteen-year-old son of a local white slaveholder, who helped him continue his lessons. Offley instructed the young man in "the art of wrestling, boxing and fighting," and the young man taught Offley how to read. On relocating to Delaware, Offley established a relationship with a "white boy" who taught him basic math, writing, and ciphering three nights a week in exchange for food.[81]

Economic Dependence

Many southern locales depended on free people of color to keep their economies in motion. During the early nineteenth century, free people of color became increasingly integral in localities across the region and demonstrated their importance in a variety of ways. As their numbers increased from a few to several thousand people, free people of color gained more opportunities to participate in and sometimes shape their home communities. Depending on their wealth, gender, age, and occupation, they influenced the patterns of community life to different degrees. Thousands of free people of color worked the most difficult jobs as servants and common laborers. They cleaned the chamber pots, cooked their employers' bread, shoveled the city streets, and hoed their masters' dirt. Free persons of color who had skills but occupied the lower rungs of the social ladder switched back and forth between menial labor and their trades. The labor of people of this rank, often performed for the benefit of others, was at the heart of early nineteenth-century economic development. A more fortunate group of tradespeople were the proprietors of their own businesses, and many of them thrived. Some of the most successful tradespeople, along with those who inherited a greater economic station, enjoyed the benefits of wealth as members of the planter class.[82]

The labor of enslaved people was an important part of the mechanism that kept southern agriculture in motion. Yet free people of color played key roles in all sectors of agricultural work. Free persons of color commonly worked as farm laborers for their families or people in the community. Robert A. Jones, a white man, hired Buck and Dolphin Francis, Thoroughgood Dempsey, Arthur Manly, and Billy Taylor, all "Mulatto Labourers," to toil for wages on his Halifax County, North Carolina, farm in 1821. Jacob Howard, a "Negro," worked on an operation on the Eastern Shore of Maryland "mowing grass & clover." Free people of color also took on more specialized agricultural tasks. In 1826, John Butler, a free man of color from Charles County, Maryland, signed an agreement with the Reverend Francis Neale to operate a windmill on Saint Thomas's Manor. Butler's contract required him to keep the windmill in good order, including making repairs when needed, and to collect the toll from people in the community who used the mill to process their grain. In exchange, Butler received a portion of the toll corn and use of the land around the windmill.[83] Free people of color stuck in menial agricultural positions rarely moved up the economic ladder. This was not necessarily the case for free people of color who owned and operated their farms, which varied in size from small garden plots to large plantations. During the early 1810s, Benjamin Wiggins managed a farm on his plot outside of Saint Augustine, Florida. He raised cattle and kept horses and oxen. In addition, Wiggins cultivated such crops as corn, peas, pumpkins, and potatoes. By 1828, Andrew Durnford, a free man of color living in Plaquemines Parish, Louisiana, had established a sugar plantation along the Mississippi River. Like many southern planters, Durnford employed a force of enslaved men, women, and children to perform the substantial tasks required to keep his plantation in motion.[84]

Business managers looking for short-term workers or people to toil in industrial settings depended on free people of color who were willing to act as laborers or hirelings. In many parts of the region, the position of laborer was the most common occupation among free persons of color. Free people of color working as laborers could be found throughout the South's more urban areas. According to an 1803 list, common labor was the second most frequent type of work among free persons of color in Petersburg, Virginia. Nearly 49 percent of free people of color in Wilmington, Delaware, who were heads of households in 1814 were laborers.

Common labor was also a widespread occupation among free people of color in some rural localities. In the Upper District of Lunenburg County, Virginia, most free people of color were hirelings in 1803. Free people of color working as common laborers performed many essential tasks. An 1826 announcement in a New Orleans newspaper sought "Negro Men Laborers" to work for monthly wages with the Orleans Navigation Company.[85] In urban areas, common laborers kept factories in motion. In 1803, at least eighteen free people of color in Petersburg, Virginia, worked in tobacco operations as stemmers. The same city also employed at least three free persons of color as oakum pickers, a form of tedious labor requiring workers to pick apart rope fibers or fibrous plants to be used in a fiber-tar preparation that filled the gaps in boats.[86]

Free persons of color who could perform domestic chores were in high demand across the early nineteenth-century South as white people in the region sought individuals who could take on some of the most important but difficult household tasks. House servants, both enslaved and free, kept the homes of those who could afford their labor in good order. As in the colonial period, many free people of color landed in servitude as a result of the apprenticeship system. At the age of twelve years, Nancy Adams, "a black girl" with no living parents, became the apprentice of Thomas Hyde of Georgetown in the District of Columbia. Until her sixteenth birthday, Adams was supposed to work under Hyde, or more likely one of the women in his household, to learn "the business of House-wifery."[87] White people also recruited servants, especially those with more specialized domestic skills. In 1824, "a gentleman going to the North" from New Orleans wanted a "free coloured man servant" to accompany him on his trip.[88] Around 1820 or 1821, Henry Smith, a free person of color, traveled with John Scott from Missouri to the District of Columbia. Scott believed Smith to be "faithful, honest, temperate, and correct" and trusted the young man with the most important tasks, including carrying "large sums of money" on his behalf.[89]

People of various backgrounds relied on the expertise of free people of color to deliver their babies, feed their children, and care for their sick, feeble, and less fortunate relatives and neighbors. Southern newspapers circulated announcements regarding the services of free women of color as wet nurses. Someone placed an advertisement in a Savannah, Georgia, newspaper seeking "a Wet Nurse, white or black," on September 29, 1804.[90] In an 1828 advertisement, an unnamed "free mulatto" woman "aged 19 years" offered her services as a wet nurse. Her notice informed readers of the *New Orleans Argus* that she had "fine breasts of milk" and was "healthy, cleanly, and well recommended."[91] Free women of color's role in delivering newborns complemented their employment as wet nurses. While the public demanded the services of young women to feed babies, women in their reproductive years desired older, experienced women to attend them in labor and guide them through safe deliveries. Lucy Wiggins was supposedly eighty-two years old in 1803 when she was helping expectant mothers in Petersburg, Virginia. Wiggins's contemporary Betty Mead was approximately ten years younger and worked as a midwife in Petersburg throughout the early 1820s.[92] Free women of color also worked as nurses and assisted a wide variety of people in their communities. Lydia Williams nursed sickly people in the District of Columbia during the early 1820s.[93] A handful of free men of color worked as doctors in the early nineteenth-century South, supplying their communities with essential health care services. Cato Sabo served the people of Wayne County, North Carolina, in the first decade of the 1800s. Monroe Anthony was active in the Fredericksburg, Virginia, community during the 1810s. Lewis G. Wells was busy assisting the people of Baltimore as a physician in the 1820s. Wells also held the roles of lecturer and minister in the African Methodist Episcopal church. Wells's position as a doctor led to an appointment with the city's health services. Along with several others, Wells was in charge of policing the sanitation practices of Baltimore's inhabitants.[94]

Southerners always found themselves in need of free people of color, especially women, who could wash, mend, and create clothing and textiles. During the first decade of the nineteenth century, washerwoman was the most frequent form of labor among free women of color in Petersburg, Virginia. It was also the most common form of labor among all free persons of color.[95] Washerwomen completed the hard labor of drawing water, scrubbing clothes, and preparing garments for another round of use. Newspaper advertisements searching for women to work as seamstresses were commonplace in the South. Susan Brister and Rebecca Pamilla were among the seamstresses serving the people of Baltimore in 1829.[96] Tailoring was a service typically provided to the public by men. Free men of color like Louis Cornie offered their communities the latest fashion. In 1821, Cornie's tailor shop in New Orleans retailed "a complete assortment of cloths and cassimeres" as well as "vestings of black silk."[97] The Maryland Penitentiary in Baltimore employed prisoners, including free people of color, to work in textile manufacturing. Following a conviction for larceny in 1812 at age eleven, Rachel Cupid of Baltimore worked for four years in the penitentiary as a spinner. While serving a four-year sentence for stealing between 1816 and 1820, John Anderson of Baltimore labored as a dyer. In 1816, sixteen-year-old Lucretia Davis of

Hagerstown began working off an eighteen-month sentence for stealing by laboring as a weaver.[98]

Across the early nineteenth-century South, free people of color were important participants in the food services industry. They participated in every facet of food production from cooking and serving to marketing and proprietorship. A June 1814 wanted advertisement in a Baltimore newspaper called for "a coloured woman, who is a good Cook, and can come well recommended." The notice promised "good wages."[99] Food also provided free people of color with independence. Free men of color established businesses retailing liquors, confections, preserves, and seafood. By 1819, Joseph Chain had established a business selling "porter, ale, and cider." Chain promised a "superior quality" of liquor to his Easton, Maryland, customers.[100] During the early 1820s, Chain expanded his business to include foodstuffs, including crackers, cheeses, and preserved meats such as sausages and cured beef tongues.[101] Free men of color across the region operated oyster houses, offering their customers a variety of seafood options. Joseph Trusty and Morgan and Company sold oysters in Wilmington, Delaware, in the 1810s. By the 1820s, Charles Middleton had launched a seafood business that served people in Georgia and South Carolina. Middleton established an oyster hall in Savannah, but he also had customers in Augusta, Milledgeville, Macon, and Purysburg. In an 1828 advertisement, he offered his customers in Georgia and South Carolina "oysters, either pickled or in the shell, by the keg, barrel or otherwise." Individuals who visited Middleton's Oyster Hall found "oysters, roasted, stewed, fried or in the shell, and other relishes, served up at any hour."[102] When available, Middleton served "turtle soup and turtle" at the Oyster Hall. Turtle soup was available "everyday from 10 until 2 o'clock." Middleton also sold "Green Turtle, by the single Turtle."[103]

Although gender norms permitted the exclusion of women from most skilled trades, southerners had no problem conducting business with free women of color engaged in culinary ventures. By serving the needs of hungry customers, free women of color turned food production into an opportunity to make money outside of the systems of contractual labor or bonded servitude. Nancy, a "free negro," earned enough income to live "well" in rural 1820s Scott County, Virginia, by selling bread. Unlike some of her less fortunate neighbors, Nancy was "free from want" in regard to her ability to obtain food, clothing, and lodging.[104] In southern cities, free women of color became proprietors of boardinghouses and restaurants that served the needs of customers on the go. Amelia Shad operated the Oyster Hotel and Victualling House on French Street in Wilmington, Delaware. In addition to "oysters fried, stewed, roasted, open, or in the shell," Shad also offered "poultry ... served up in a very superior style."[105] Phillis Hill worked as a pastry cook and operated a boardinghouse for travelers in Savannah, Georgia. In an 1815 advertisement, she promised her customers "her best services and accommodation" and "that her attention to please will meet the patronage of a generous public."[106] Savannah entrepreneurs Catharine Deveaux, Sylvia Whitfield, and Leah Simpson sold turtle soup.[107] Whitfield promised her patrons "a fine Green Turtle, fresh from Nassau."[108] Araminta Webster retailed lobsters, soft-shell and hard-shell crabs, sheepshead, pickled oysters, and turtle soup to her customers in Alexandria, District of Columbia.[109] Rebecca Dwight developed a steady business selling liquors, wines, turtle soup, relishes, and steaks to the people of Charleston, South Carolina. Following Dwight's death, her daughter Caroline C. Dwight continued the family business.[110]

The early nineteenth-century South's maritime economy hinged on the aptitude and knowledge of free people of color.[111] With many of the South's major towns and cities situated near bodies of water, free people of color with knowledge of the waterways and their flora and fauna transformed bodies of water into food sources and transportation networks. A number of free men of color worked as fishermen and watermen. They gathered the fish that people ate and transported the goods that people needed and desired. Among the free people of color in Petersburg, Virginia, waterman was the third most common occupation in 1803.[112] A few free men of color became sea captains and ships' masters. Jonathan Rial was a sea captain based in Wilmington, Delaware, during the 1810s. Around the same time, London Cary owned and operated a small watercraft called the "Shark" out of Petersburg.[113] Henry Aberdeen headed voyages from Norfolk, Virginia, to places such as New York. Aberdeen's schooner transported both freight and passengers.[114]

By the early nineteenth century, white southerners, especially elite men, had developed a preference for the spa-like grooming services provided by the region's barbers of color.[115] They relied on these free men of color to shave their faces, cut their hair, and revitalize their wigs. In an 1817 advertisement, Arthur Mitchum of Natchez, Mississippi, explained to potential customers that he was "prepared with Razors kept in the best order, clean Napkins, &c." He promised that "no pains will be spared to give complete satisfaction" for customers visiting his shop supplied with "soaps of different kinds ... refined wash balls, Cologne water, Magnumbonum Razors and cases, Double head brushes, Double tooth brushes, &c."[116] At the beginning of 1821, Philip Thomas sought to attract customers to his Nashville, Tennessee, barbershop by promising to provide "at the shortest notice, Wigs, Braids, Frizettes, &C. of first elegance, and [the] latest fashions."[117] Thomas Inglis of Charleston, South Carolina, asked potential clients, "What is more to be admired than a fine head of Hair?" His shop offered "an extensive assortment of Quirk's Heads of Hair, Toupets, Curls and Frizets." Inglis guaranteed that his products were "of a superior quality, worthy the attention of the Ladies and Gentlemen of this City."[118] The work of barbers sometimes extended beyond trimming and grooming hair. Free men of color used their barbershops to sell merchandise. William Haden, another Natchez, Mississippi, barber, announced the arrival of "an assortment of elegant toys" at his shop in 1826.[119] In addition to his barbering services, Samuel Oldham offered a hodgepodge of knickknacks "at the most reduced prices," including "playing cards," "ivory snuff boxes," "security chains," and "musical monkeys," according to an advertisement that circulated in a Lexington, Kentucky, newspaper between 1829 and 1830.[120]

Barbers were highly valued by nineteenth-century southerners, and as a result, barbering became a common path to success for a cadre of free men of color. The Charleston, South Carolina, barber Thomas Inglis transformed a hustle of shaving, trimming, and fitting wigs to heads into real estate, human chattel, and other assets. Inglis's will mentioned the ownership of a house, several enslaved people, bank stocks, a "gold watch, chain and trinket," and a pew in Saint Philip's Church.[121] Born into slavery, John C. Stanly of New Bern, North Carolina, improved his fortunes and the lives of many others through the barber's trade. After working as a barber for several years, Stanly accumulated sufficient money to acquire slaves; some, such as his wife, Kitty, and children, he freed soon after their purchase, while others he used to help him build his financial empire. Like other businessmen of his era, Stanly invested in the purchase of children, whom he could buy cheap, and then raised them, trained them in his trade, and profited from their success. Boston and Brister, two of the children purchased and trained by Stanly, eventually took over his barbershop when Stanly began to shift his attention to other matters. After many years of service, Stanly freed these men but continued to hold others in bondage.[122]

In a world in which machines had yet to dominate the means of production, southerners counted on skilled artisans of color who had spent years honing their craft to perform an assortment of tasks.[123] Henry Adams, Cato Day, Edward Franklin, and Moses Liverpool were among the skilled caulkers working at the Washington Navy Yard during the first decade of the nineteenth century. Shipbuilding operations required the expertise of caulkers to transform masses of wood and metal into reliable watercraft.[124] Jethro Duncan, a "coloured man," practiced the cooper's trade in Brandywine, Delaware in the 1810s. Barrels made by men like Duncan held a range of goods for transport and storage. Meredith Chavis, "a free mulattoe," worked in his Orange County, North Carolina, community as a shoemaker and provided footwear to an otherwise barefoot populace.[125] By 1821, John Woodland, a man of "light yellow complexion," was practicing the trade of a ropemaker in the District of Columbia. The ropemaker's product was essential in every area of commerce from farming to shipping to construction.[126] Alexander Lange, "a free man of color," served the people of Baton Rouge, Louisiana, as a carpenter during the 1820s. Houses, commercial structures, boats, and outbuildings were the products of the carpenter's hands.[127] Lincoln Bourdeaux, "a free man of colour," was a well-respected wheelwright and blacksmith in Barnwell District, South Carolina, in the 1820s. The wheelwright crafted wood and metal into durable wheels, while the blacksmith produced hardware and tools.[128] John Wallace DeRosario served the people of York and James City Counties in Virginia as the local gunsmith during the early part of the century. The people in these communities only kept their weapons in working order with the attention and expertise of DeRosario.[129] Among the most successful artisans of color was Thomas Day, a cabinetmaker. Day operated a shop in Hillsborough, North Carolina, before moving his business to the nearby town of Milton by 1827. At his Milton location, Day sold "Mahogony, Walnut and Stained Furniture" along with "the most fashionable and common Bed Steads."[130] Some of his region's most affluent citizens, including Governor David S. Reid, looked to Day to furnish their homes and craft their staircases and woodwork.[131]

Although southern communities depended on the work of artisans of color to meet their various needs, customers in those communities did not value all artisans' work equally. Artisans who performed somewhat common tasks such as carpentry and shoemaking struggled alongside common laborers and domestics. David Wilson, a Washington County, Maryland, shoemaker, struggled to support his family. A veteran of the American Revolution, Wilson by the 1820s was landless and owned only a small collection of personal property, including an old horse, a cow, and a couple of hogs.[132] Artisans like Thomas Day of Milton, North Carolina, however, managed to transform their labors into financial success. At the height of his business, Day owned several enslaved workers and employed them in his shop on Milton's main street. Day's workforce also included white journeyman artisans. Day interfaced with elite whites in his community and abroad and built a strong enough relationship with them that he could consult with and depend on them for legal and political support.[133]

Whether they were elite craftsmen or artisans eking out a living, free people of color played an important role in educating the next generation by teaching their trades to apprenticed workers. Communities depended on the generational transmission of skills and knowledge in order to keep their economy in motion and their basic needs met. On June 5, 1811, Louise Lominil, a "free quarteroon woman," bound her nephew Jean Louis Moreau, who had arrived in New Orleans from Saint-Domingue, to Ferdinand Lioteau, a local cabinetmaker. Lioteau promised to teach Moreau his trade during a five-year apprenticeship. In addition, Lioteau guaranteed Moreau six months of schooling along with food and housing.[134] William Matthews of Washington in the District of Columbia took on as an apprentice Evan Harry, who came to Washington from neighboring Prince George's County, Maryland, in 1812. Under Matthews's guidance, Harry would learn the hatter's trade. Harry pledged to serve Matthews for three years in exchange for food, clothing, and other necessities.[135]

Nothing better illustrates the value white southerners placed on the work of artisans of color than their willingness to push, bend, and break the strictures of the southern racial hierarchy in order to protect their access to the expertise and skills of these often-indispensable craftsmen. Following the passage of Virginia's 1806 law requiring free persons of color to obtain a license from the county court in order to carry a firearm, thirty-two of John Wallace DeRosario's white neighbors from York County and James City County signed a petition supporting his application for a license. They described DeRosario as "a Landholder," a person of "honesty and Integrity," and, most important, "an excellent gunsmith and stocker." The petitioners feared that unless DeRosario received a license, they would be without a person to whom they could "entrust their Firelocks." DeRosario's neighbors saw him as more than a nameless free person of color. DeRosario's talent and skill kept his community functioning.[136]

The first three decades of the nineteenth century had proved to be a period of great opportunity for Andrew Noel of Wilmington, Delaware, and many other free people of color. This was the situation in spite of the developing radical proslavery and white supremacist machine working in the state capitals of the South to limit the presence and curb the influence of free persons of color. Throughout the period, free people of color built important relationships with white neighbors as well as with some whites beyond their home communities. They established businesses that brought new wealth into their families and created opportunities for people sometimes only a few years or a generation separated from human bondage. Through their work, free people of color made themselves essential to the regular operations of their communities.

By the first decades of the nineteenth century, however, the radical proslavery and white supremacist agendas had already begun to seep into southern social life. In some localities, whites were implementing segregation based on racial categorization and establishing racial hierarchy within shared social institutions, especially churches. Nevertheless, free people of color were not completely discouraged by the situation. They worked with their white neighbors when whites were able to provide for their needs. In other cases, free people of color, sometimes working with enslaved people in their communities, built separate institutions to fulfill their religious, educational, and social requirements. During this period, free people of color made major efforts to create social networks that protected them and provided a sense of, if not actual, political autonomy. These lessons would be important for free people of color and their enslaved allies in the years to come.

CHAPTER 5

Rebellion and Radicalism

During the fall of 1831, Arnold Artis, Thomas Haithcock, Berry Newsom, Isham Turner, and Exum Artis found themselves sitting before court officials in Southampton County, Virginia, facing charges for what would become the most infamous slave rebellion in U.S. history. Although not enslaved themselves, these free persons of color were engulfed in the flames of paranoia that consumed parts of the South after Nat Turner and his coconspirators executed dozens of white Southampton County residents in a brazen attempt to overthrow their enslavers. All of these individuals except Berry Newsom would survive the backlash from the Nat Turner Rebellion.[1] Nevertheless, their collective stories, along with the experiences of countless free people of color who were affected by the suspicion and violence that followed, illustrate how, in certain ways, the South was becoming an increasingly challenging environment for them.

The Nat Turner Rebellion added fuel to the fire set by proslavery radicals and white supremacists years before the outbreak of insurrection. The vast majority of Southampton County's people of color, free and enslaved, had nothing to do with the insurrection and in some cases resisted the plot. Yet, accounts of enslaved people axing, beating, and shooting to death white women, men, and children demonstrated that existing controls on people of color were not enough to keep white southerners safe. Although whites suppressed the rebellion relatively quickly, the rebellion represented the bloodiest insurrection of bondspeople against their masters in U.S. history.[2] Proslavery radicals and their flock refused to ignore this. Slavery's most ardent defenders used the postrebellion environment as an opportunity to push through legislation curbing the liberties of free people of color. Radical ideas with little chance for success under normal circumstances gained support in a political environment in which lawmakers needed to appear tough on the issue of protecting the average white citizen from the threat of rebellious slaves and their alleged potential allies, a group that included free persons of color. The rebellion became the justification for silencing ministers of color, prohibiting free people of color from carrying guns, and making the criminal justice system increasingly discriminatory.

Even as the impacts of the rebellion faded, the challenges mounted. Ideologues, lawmakers, and vigilantes persisted in their attacks on free people of color. This was not so much because of the threat of rebellion or because of a revolutionary change in the ways average white southerners thought about the free persons of color in their midst. Instead, these attacks were part of an increasing radicalization of slavery's defenders and their growing willingness to exploit and attack anyone or anything that represented a potential threat to slavery. The successes and contributions of free people of color highlighted the possibility that enslaved people could be productive members of society without the threat of an overseer's whip. Free people of color, including some formerly enslaved persons, operating as the equals of white men in politics, churches, and business exposed the fallacies behind white supremacist ideology. The truth was no ally to the lies that underpinned the radicalism of some southern lawmakers.

For the South's free people of color, the increasing radicalism of politicians and their allies created serious obstacles and threatened their liberty. Inspired by the radical agenda, white thugs pestered free persons of color in their neighborhoods and, against the greater sentiments of their fellow white community members, committed destructive and violent acts. Free people of color periodically found themselves under suspicion for aiding runaways and distributing antislavery materials, and several people landed in state penitentiaries as a result. More frequently, free persons of color ended up in jail not for assisting enslaved people but under the suspicion that they themselves were escapees from bondage. The greatest impact of the radical agenda, however, manifested in the system of discriminatory punishment. As the nation crept closer to conflict, increasing numbers of free people of color, especially poor persons, faced whipping, excessive fines, and hiring out while white neighbors who committed similar crimes met lighter punishments.[3]

Rebellion and Backlash

The Nat Turner Rebellion provided the impetus for whites in some communities to act more aggressively toward the free persons of color in their midst. In these places, especially in areas relatively close to the rebellion, white officials and vigilantes used the uprising as grounds to target free people of color. Whites subjected free persons of color to largely baseless home searches. Some county governments confiscated guns and other weapons owned by free people of color. Officials in a handful of communities jailed free people of color as well as enslaved persons suspected of aiding or plotting rebellion. Free persons of color also landed in the jails and courts for failing to provide proper documentation of their freedom and residential status. Laws that were usually not enforced in times of peace became tools of terror in times of fear. As with most public scares, the direct effects of the rebellion diminished with time. Yet the increasing influence of radical proslavery ideas and the developing ideological connection between slave escape or rebellion and the mere presence of free people of color continued to create problems.

Directly following the Turner rebellion, whites across Virginia and North Carolina used the event as an opportunity to assert their authority over free persons of color and their enslaved neighbors. Local officials deputized bands of often unruly whites to search the homes of the people of color in their communities and arrest anyone whom they deemed suspicious. These groups of white people used their short-term powers to harass persons of color, especially those who under normal circumstances were their social superiors, both economically and by reputation. Willis Augustus Hodges, a free man of color who lived in Princess Anne County, Virginia, in 1831, recalled, "Every white man that had a gun or could get one, was out armed, and a guard was kept at every public place and at every fork or cross road. Parties went from house to house and took revenge on the free people of color." On reaching Hodges's house, the patrol arrested Charles Blachford, a white schoolmaster; Eliza Nelson, "a young colored woman ... who was very light and could pass for white"; and Nat Briggs, "a boy." They also seized "all the books, papers, bibles, dresses and many other small and useful articles" from the house.[4] In Edenton, North Carolina, "people were pouring in from every quarter within twenty miles of the town." Harriet Jacobs, an enslaved woman living in Edenton, described the period immediately following the rebellion as "a grand opportunity for the low whites, who had no negroes of their own to scourge." She remembered, "The dwellings of the colored people, unless they happened to be protected by some influential white person, who was right at hand, were robbed of clothing and every thing else." When the white "marauders" reached the home of Jacobs's grandmother Molly Horniblow, a free woman of color, "They snatched at every thing within their reach. Every box, trunk, closet, and corner underwent a thorough examination." After the band finished searching the house, they "proceeded to the garden, and knocked about every bush and vine." The patrollers left Jacobs and Horniblow with minor property damage and plenty of insults but no physical harm. A number of "colored people and slaves" in Edenton and its outskirts were less fortunate. The patrollers attacked some people of color and "whipped" them "till the blood stood in puddles at their feet." They jailed others.[5] White men, especially the poor, used the post-Turner period of lawlessness to assert power and authority rarely granted to them by the slaveholding elites. Their ill-treatment of free persons of color was an expression of their power as white men in a social, political, and economic environment that commonly emphasized their lack of wealth over their masculinity or whiteness.

Free people of color across the region landed in local jails for a variety of alleged crimes following the Turner insurrection. In the most serious cases, officials imprisoned free persons of color on charges of inciting or plotting rebellion. Southampton County residents Arnold Artis, Thomas Haithcock, Berry Newsom, Isham Turner, and Exum Artis found themselves jailed for allegedly conspiring with Nat Turner.[6] Officials in Isle of Wight County, a Virginia community located directly northeast of Southampton County, arrested and indicted Davy Thomas, "a free negro man," on charges of "insurrection & rebellion or conspiring to make insurrection & rebellion."[7] While Davy Thomas languished in the Isle of Wight County jail, James Grimes, Eli Hall, Daniel Watts, and Jesse Watts, "free men of color," remained in custody under suspicion that they had "consulted, advised, and conspired with a number of free persons of colour & negroes slaves ... to induce, entice, and incite [the] said Free persons of color and negroes slaves to rebel or make insurrection" in the town of Portsmouth, Virginia.[8] Officials in other Virginia counties such as Surry, Sussex, Brunswick, Westmoreland, and Spotsylvania imprisoned people on charges of plotting or inciting rebellion but narrowed their list of suspects to members of the enslaved population.[9] Focusing on free people of color was not a natural reaction to fear brought about by the Turner rebellion but a conscious choice by leaders in select communities.

Many more free people of color were imprisoned on charges that were less serious but still personally taxing. In Virginia locales such as Isle of Wight County, Norfolk County, Princess Anne County, and Petersburg, officials and patrollers jailed and harassed free people of color who failed to produce documentation of their free status. In Richmond, Petersburg, Norfolk, and Powhatan County, the courts indicted emancipated free persons of color based on the infrequently enforced 1806 manumission restrictions that prohibited freed persons from remaining in the commonwealth without explicit permission.[10] Willis Augustus Hodges explained that in his community "the pretext for the wholesale arrest of free people of color during the days of 'Nat Turner's War,' was that they were, some of them runaways, on the eve of making in Princess Anne County, a bold blow for liberty of all the slaves in the county." He, however, viewed this justification as "a lie, pure and simple." Hodges asserted that "everyone arrested, with perhaps one or two exceptions, were well known to everyone in the county, white and black, rich and poor, bond and free."[11] These arrests on charges unrelated to the rebellion represented efforts by local whites to demonstrate their power over free persons of color. Discriminatory legislation provided white opportunists with the ability to transform a brief moment of instability and fear into a chance to improve their social positions at the expense of less fortunate community members.

In some localities, white officials resorted to less explicit measures in order to demonstrate their authority in the days following the Southampton County insurrection. Powerbrokers in Isle of Wight, King George, and Prince Edward Counties in Virginia voided previously issued gun licenses and ordered each sheriff and their posse to seize the guns of free people of color in their communities.[12] On a nine-to-six vote, the city council of Alexandria, District of Columbia, implemented new restrictions on free persons of color and enslaved people.[13] The new rules included a prohibition on "all meetings or assemblies of slaves, or of free negroes, and mulattoes, or of slaves, free negroes, and mulattoes, at any meeting or other house, either in the day or night." The council also approved restrictions that forbade any member of the targeted groups to "have in his possession, or circulate, any newspaper or other publication or any written or printed paper or book, of a seditious and evil character, calculated to excite insurrection or insubordination among the slaves or colored people."[14] These acts were soft measures by comparison to the actions taken by officials in other locations. Still, they allowed local leaders to depict themselves as serious about closing legal loopholes.

In the days and months following the insurrection, officials in Southampton County investigated numerous individuals accused of conspiring with Nat Turner. The local courts eventually absolved four of the five free persons of color entangled in the process of identifying and punishing Turner and his collaborators. Arnold Artis was the first to walk free. On September 5, 1831, after a brief examination of the evidence, the court discharged him. Thomas Haithcock, Berry Newsom, Isham Turner, and Exum Artis were not as lucky. At their initial hearings, the court determined that they should face trials and sent their cases to the county's superior court. They languished in jail for months before the Circuit Superior Court of Law and Chancery heard their cases. Berry Newsom and

Isham Turner were first to face trial during the April 1832 court session. One jury absolved Isham Turner, while those who evaluated Newsom's case found him guilty. After the cases against Turner and Newsom concluded, jurors determined that Exum Artis and Thomas Haithcock were not guilty. Following the trials, the court provided Newsom with the opportunity to present any additional evidence that might challenge his conviction. Newsom failed to produce any supplementary evidence, and the court ordered "that he be hanged by the neck until he be dead." While Newsom was the only free person of color convicted in the conspiracy, all four men who faced trial suffered greatly. In November 1832, the court removed Henry B. Vaughan from his position as the county's jailer as a result of the poor conditions under which Haithcock, Artis, Turner, Newsom, and two other prisoners were held while awaiting their trials. The court convicted Vaughan of failing to provide the prisoners with "cleanly and sufficient bed and bedding," causing them to suffer during the cold winter months. Their accommodations were so bad that they "became afflicted with a disease and Rheumatism." Some of the prisoners "could not walk without assistance." One "was unable to walk or stand" at all. Another prisoner, who is not named in the court record, "died in Jail" as a result of the cold. While the vast majority of Southampton County's free people of color escaped the reaction to Turner's insurrection unscathed, Haithcock, Artis, Turner, and Newsom found themselves entrapped in a living hell. For Berry Newsom, that hell ended only with his death.[15]

Following weeks of imprisonment in local jails, the free men of color in Isle of Wight and Norfolk Counties who faced charges of attempting to incite insurrection convinced juries of their innocence. In the Davy Thomas case, an Isle of Wight County jury heard evidence from two witnesses against the defendant: Martha Ann, an enslaved woman held by Joseph Atkinson, and George, an enslaved man in the possession of Ann Todd. Martha Ann claimed that after initiating a discussion with Thomas about the ongoing rebellion in Southampton County, Thomas claimed that "he would or intended to get his gun and take a crack at two or three white folks about here and then go to Southampton and them & they would be like brothers." George offered a similar account of a statement allegedly made by Thomas. He declared that Thomas said "he intended to get a gun and take a crack at two or three of the white people about here" and "that he would then go to Southampton and get on the back track of the negroes there & shoot some of the white people there and then join the negroes there." Although justice of the peace James C. Jordan considered the allegations against Thomas serious enough to bring him to trial, Martha Ann's and George's statements left the jury unconvinced of Thomas's guilt. The court ordered Thomas free on giving "security for his good behavior."[16] In Norfolk County, the attorney for the state brought James Grimes to trial for purportedly conspiring to incite rebellion. After hearing the evidence, the jury struggled to decide the case but ultimately concluded that Grimes was innocent. The court subsequently ordered him discharged. Failing to obtain a conviction against Grimes, the prosecutor dropped the charges against Daniel Watts, Jesse Watts, and Eli Hall. After languishing in jail for over two months, the men were finally free to return home.[17]

As days and months passed, and the initial excitement caused by the rebellion ebbed, officials dropped the charges against or liberated most of the free people of color who had been arrested for failure to produce evidence of their freedom or permission to remain in the commonwealth. Prosecutors in some jurisdictions simply dropped the charges against emancipated persons without permission to stay in Virginia. The free people of color whose charges remained were able to petition for and secure legal refuge in the state. A number of free people of color procured witnesses who could testify to their free status and paid for their registrations. The weeks following the Turner insurrection represented a peak period for registration among free people of color across Virginia. Others recovered lost registrations or secured new copies of their old registrations. In communities such as Mecklenburg County, free people of color who had never bothered to register before appeared before the court clerks in unprecedented numbers to obtain their free papers and have their registrations recorded. It cannot be determined from the surviving records of most localities whether free persons of color registered because of persecution or as a precautionary measure.[18]

In Princess Anne County, officials used the assessment of jail fees as a way to further exploit free people of color who had just scraped up the cash to pay for their free papers and registrations. During the October 1831 court session, officials ordered fifteen free persons of color "discharged from jail on paying jail fees."[19] Willis Augustus Hodges explained, "Almost all of those who did pay their jail fees, did so at a great sacrifice." He surmised that Princess Anne County officials had "arrested only the poorest of the free people of color, the object, it would seem, was to hire them out in default of non-payment." Among those who failed to pay their jail fees was Kinner Flurry, who "was sold to the highest bidder" in order to pay his fee. During his term of service, Josiah Wilson, Flurry's purchaser, had him flogged for running away to pay respects to his wife, who had died during his term of service. The injuries inflicted during the flogging ultimately led to Flurry's death.[20] Although Flurry's plight was unusual among free people of color as a whole, his death shows how far some local whites were willing to go to demonstrate their power in the aftermath of the Turner rebellion. Flurry's death also underscores the corrupt nature of the South's proslavery regime. This corruption affected the daily lives of enslaved people but was sometimes a threat to free persons as well.

The corruption of local officials following the rebellion extended beyond the abusive assessment of jail fees. In Isle of Wight County, Archibald Atkinson, an attorney for the state, prosecuted Nathaniel Young, the clerk of the court, for charging free people of color excessive amounts for their free papers and registrations in the days following the rebellion. In 1832, Young faced allegations of overcharging Harrison Pope, Amelia Pope, and Elisha Johnson for their registrations in the same court where he worked. The jurors appointed by the court ultimately convicted Young, even without hearing testimony from the victimized free persons of color, who could not legally testify against him because he was white. The court fined Young six dollars for each conviction.[21] For Young, the Turner rebellion provided an opportunity to exploit a vulnerable population and make a little cash. Young and many like him were less concerned with calming the fears of community members and more interested in using the rebellion as a chance to assert their authority. The call to protect innocent white people from potentially rebellious people of color served as a cover for insidious behavior.

In the days after the Turner insurrection, free persons of color had reason to fear for their safety and the security of their property. A minority of the South's free people of color, especially those located near the epicenter of the rebellion, confronted serious obstacles posed by bands of white marauders, calculating local politicians, and corrupt officials following the outbreak of violence in Southampton County. The insurrection further strengthened an already problematic proslavery environment, which had subjected free persons of color to legal discrimination and, in some cases, social stigmatization. Most free people of color in the South, however, experienced little direct effect, even in Virginia, where the insurrection took place. Free people of color in the western parts of the state, including Staunton, Botetourt County, Pittsylvania County, and Rockbridge County, made no rapid movements toward the local courthouses to register and obtain free papers. In Lancaster County on the Northern Neck, the first person to register after the rebellion did not apply for freedom documents until October, and only one additional person applied during the remainder of the year.[22] While whites harassed, imprisoned, and prosecuted free persons of color in some communities, whites in other parts of the region seemed more concerned with the enslaved population or other issues altogether.

As the weeks turned to months, community interest shifted elsewhere, even in the localities where whites persecuted free people of color most doggedly. The inhabitants of Richmond, though not necessarily the politicians in the state capitol, quickly turned their attention to a disease outbreak that threatened the city.[23] The rate of registrations slowed as the months passed. During the three months that followed the rebellion, ninety-eight free people of color registered with the clerk of court in Mecklenburg County, Virginia. By December, the rush to register had come to an end. A similar pattern took place in Surry County, which bordered Southampton County. From September to December 1831, 92 free persons of color registered with the court. Just 22 free people of color made a point of registering during the entire year of 1832. The clerk in Fairfax County registered 116 free people of color between September and December 1831. By comparison, 11 free people of color registered during all of 1832. The decrease in registrations was especially noticeable in Louisa County, where 18 free people of color rushed to register in September 1831 but by October, not one person approached the court clerk to register.[24] In Edenton, North Carolina, Harriet Jacobs explained, "The white citizens found that their own property was not safe from the lawless rabble they had summoned to protect them." She noted that they eventually "rallied the drunken swarm" and "drove them back into the country."[25]

A semblance of normalcy returned to areas of the region surrounding the epicenter of the Turner rebellion. Nevertheless, the behavior of white marauders, corrupt officials, and silent bystanders in the days following the insurrection signaled to some free people of color that they ought to leave the South. The outburst of a rebellion, or simply rumors of a rebellion, were enough for some white people to pursue power recklessly and ignore the most basic tenets of the law. Two years after the insurrection, a committee studying the removal of free people of color for the state of Virginia reported that "343 free negroes and mulattoes" resided in Princess Anne County according to the 1800 census enumeration. The committee further explained that "since the insurrection in Southampton County, many free negroes have removed from the county and we presume there are not at this time over 300 in the county."[26] Mrs. Coleman Freeman, who lived in North Carolina in 1831, recalled, "I came away from North Carolina in consequence of persecution. There was a rebellion among the slaves in Virginia, under Nat Turner, near where I was." She explained that the outrageous behavior of some whites in her community ultimately motivated her to leave. According to Freeman, "The white people that had no slaves would have killed the colored, but their masters put them in jail to protect them from the white people and from fears they had themselves of being killed. They came to my mother's, and threatened us—they searched for guns and ammunition: that was the first time I was ever silenced by a white man. One of them put his pistol to my breast, and said, 'If you open your head, I'll kill you in a minute!' I had told my mother to hush, as she was inquiring what their conduct meant. We were as ignorant of the rebellion as they had been." After this incident, Freeman remembered, "Then I made up my mind not to remain in that country." Freeman stayed in North Carolina long enough to sell her family's crop and then left for Ohio.[27] The white people in her community had betrayed her trust.

In day-to-day life, southern whites associated free people of color with insurrections or slave escape plots only sporadically following the suppression of the Turner insurrection. White supremacists and radical proslavery ideologues mentioned such associations as part of their fearmongering and political diatribes, but the actual instances of free people of color accused or convicted of these acts were infrequent and more decentralized. Free people of color, especially those with enslaved relatives, occasionally attracted attention from officials in the years after the Southampton County violence. Some white slaveholders also sought to disassociate their bondspeople from free people of color. Maryland slaveholder Veal Buckingham used threats to drive a wedge between his enslaved people and free persons of color. Buckingham told his bondsman Isaiah Brown that he would sell him "off to Georgia" if he executed his plan to marry Catherine Sappington, a Carroll County free woman of color.[28] John H. Jackson, who grew up in 1850s Wilmington, North Carolina, remembered that his master instructed him to "not have nothin' to do with free issue chil'en" because "they was'nt fitten to 'sociate with us."[29]

The historical record provides no evidence to suggest that the majority, or even a significant minority, of the South's free people of color were interested in helping enslaved people rebel against their masters through violent direct action. Yet from time to time, free persons of color landed in the courts for allegedly helping or attempting to aid enslaved people in their escape from bondage.[30] Free people of color in southern communities located near the free states, in particular, faced scrutiny for allegedly helping runaways. In 1839, Leonard Grimes, a "free mulatto," found himself before Loudoun County, Virginia, officials charged with leading Sophia Purcell as well as Patty, Thomas, Charles, Maria, Vincent, and Agnes Douglas, all held in bondage by Joseph Mead, into neigh-

In 1840, a Loudoun County, Virginia, jury convicted Leonard Grimes of plotting to assist several enslaved people to freedom. Grimes served two years in the state penitentiary before relocating to the North, where he continued his antislavery work. (Courtesy of the Library of Congress)

boring Fairfax County as part of a plot to guide the group to freedom. Following a trial that included testimony from white and enslaved witnesses, a Loudoun County jury convicted Grimes and sentenced him to two years in the state penitentiary. That Grimes received only two years' imprisonment reflects the influence of several testimonies presented to the court from customers and associates from the District of Columbia who attested to his superior character and work ethic.[31] A decade after the Grimes case, Abraham Brogden appeared before a court in Anne Arundel County, Maryland, charged with aiding Cinderella, an enslaved woman, in an attempted escape. Cinderella was Brogden's wife, and the impending sale of Cinderella to cover her master's debts motivated Brogden to move. Although he acted only to protect his wife and not to overthrow slavery as a whole, jurors decided to convict him, and the court sentenced Brogden to four years in the Maryland penitentiary.[32]

While officials in areas bordering the free states were on the alert for free people of color attempting to assist runaways, whites elsewhere in the region also watched for free persons of color who sought to guide enslaved acquaintances out of the land of bondage. In 1856, James Peck and Mary Gibbs, free people of color, appeared before a Davidson County, Tennessee, court on the charge of "harbouring a slave." The attorney for the state alleged that Peck and Gibbs had concealed Jack, an enslaved man, on a steamship headed from Nashville to Cincinnati, Ohio, with the purpose of helping him to freedom. Crewmen arrested Peck and Gibbs as well as Jack and placed them in a Kentucky jail ahead of their appearance in Davidson County. Before the prosecution of the case, the state offered to drop the charges against Gibbs in exchange for her testimony against Peck. Gibbs accepted the proposal and became the star witness in Peck's prosecution. Both Gibbs and Peck concurred that Jack had portrayed himself as a free man needing to return north to obtain evidence of his freedom, but they disagreed about who took the lead in concealing Jack. Gibbs pointed to Peck as the ringleader of the plot, even though she admitted to knowing that Jack was in hiding during the trip north. Elizabeth Kingsley, who claimed Jack as her slave, explained that she permitted Jack to hire himself on steamboats in exchange for part of his earnings. Although he was not free, Jack acted in ways similar to free persons, including receiving wages. A Davidson County jury ultimately convicted Peck, who was unable to muster a defense to counter Gibbs's statements. Peck appealed his conviction all the way up to the Tennessee Supreme Court, which affirmed the jurors' conclusion.[33]

In the years following the Nat Turner Rebellion, local officials on rare occasions sought to make examples of free people of color suspected of having antislavery leanings. They likely acted in this manner as an attempt to dissuade people of all backgrounds from assisting potential runaways or affirming ideas that challenged the doctrines of the proslavery agenda. On October 28, 1831, a grand jury in the District of Columbia indicted William Wormley, a free man of color, for circulating a copy of William Lloyd Garrison's *Liberator*, a newspaper that they claimed had the propensity "to inflame & excite the said free negroes & slaves to insurrection and rebellion against the white population." Wormley had acted as an agent for the *Liberator* since its founding just months before the Turner rebellion. Sherry Wilson, a "free negro," was among the first people in Maryland indicted under the laws prohibiting the circulation of seditious materials. These laws were put in place across the South in response to the increased popularity of antislavery literature such as David Walker's *Appeal* and William Lloyd Garrison's *Liberator*, which came into circulation immediately before the rebellion. In 1839, officials in Queen Anne's County, Maryland, tried and convicted Wilson for "circulating a book containing abolition doctrines."[34] The court sentenced Wilson to ten years in the state penitentiary, where he remained for nearly nine years before receiving a pardon from Governor Philip F. Thomas based on his "good behavior" and "exemplary character."[35] Following the escape of his son to Canada, Samuel Green, a "free negro" and Methodist minister, gained the attention of local officials in Dorchester County, Maryland. While conducting a search of Green's home, officers recovered a copy of Harriet Beecher Stowe's *Uncle Tom's Cabin*, a book attacked by slavery's most ardent defenders and banned by white lawmakers across the South. Following the discovery of the antislavery volume, local officials tried and convicted Green. In 1857, the local court sentenced Green to ten years in the penitentiary. Green served as an example of what could happen to people who sought to defy the proslavery regime. In the North, especially among abolitionist circles, he represented the wider repression of free persons of color in the South.[36] Although slavery was on the decline in Maryland, slavery's advocates wielded their authority to tamp down actions that threatened to accelerate further the decline of bondage in the state. They stood together with their brethren in the rest of the South as bona fide proslavery radicals.

As hard as slavery's defenders worked to make examples out of individuals like Sherry Wilson, Samuel Green, and those convicted of assisting runaway slaves, some free people of color met the challenge head on and worked against the proslavery agenda undaunted. Samuel D. Burris, a free man of color and native of Kent County, Delaware, with the assistance of other antislavery agents, escorted runaways from Delaware to

Philadelphia en route to freedom farther north. Delaware officials eventually became aware of Burris's antislavery activities and arrested him. In Dover, the court tried and convicted Burris. Unlike some of his comrades in the antislavery movement, Burris found a way to exploit the gaps in the proslavery system and escape to liberty. As in other cases of free people of color convicted of crimes in Delaware, officials attempted to hire out Burris at public auction to serve as a forced laborer. Yet instead of falling into the hands of a local master who sought to extract labor from him, Burris fell into the embrace of a white friend who bid on him and then whisked him away to freedom in Pennsylvania. From there, he continued on to California in order to avoid recapture.[37]

Radical Politics

The rebellion in Southampton County invigorated the South's proslavery radicals and white supremacists in the months following its suppression. Political extremists seized the moment to execute their political agenda and push more moderate politicians toward their cause. The legislative sessions of 1831–32 were some of the most productive for radical lawmakers and their allies. They passed numerous bills that chipped away at the liberties of free people of color across the region. At the same time, these sessions were not a complete victory for extremists. Some of their most radical ideas failed to gain traction.

In the months following the Turner insurrection, invigorated radicals sent petitions to state legislatures across the South calling for a variety of actions against the free people of color in their communities. Most of the ideas that they espoused were not new, but the Turner rebellion provided them with an opportune moment to rebrand their fanatical thoughts as rational, timely solutions. In Delaware, radicals attacked the rights of free people of color to bear and keep arms. A group of petitioners from New Castle County cited "rumours of intended insurrectionary movements among the black portion of our population" as a reason to disarm the free people of color in their state. They also attacked the rights of free people of color to assemble freely for religious purposes under the leadership of so-called "ignorant and fanatic black preachers."[38] Petitioners in Lenoir County, North Carolina, used the moment to target retailers of color who came from the neighboring town of New Bern to sell "cakes, tobacco, & spirituous liquors." They charged that the free movement of these merchants "afforded for the dissemination of seditious writings & notions among their slaves" and provided them with an opportunity to "communicate verbally the murderous plans of a Nat Turner." These Lenoir County residents asked their state legislature to give them the power to "exclude all coloured retailers" from their community or at least to tax those retailers of color who entered the county from beyond its borders.[39] The Turner rebellion provided cover for them to implement a protectionist agenda that had more to do with tax policy and economic competition than the threat of rebellion.

The South's various colonization organizations used the moment to campaign for the forced relocation of free people of color. By depicting free persons of color as threats to social stability, they presented their removal plots as logical, moderate actions designed to secure their communities. A group of Northampton County, Virginia, petitioners explained to lawmakers "that it is absolutely necessary, not only to the correct government of our slaves, but also to the peace & security of our society, that all free persons of colour should be promptly removed" from their community. They sought to enact a fund-raising scheme that would support the transport of Northampton County's "free negroes" to "Liberia in Africa."[40] Virginia legislators also received several standardized petitions asking them to "free our country" of free persons of color. The petitioners described free people of color as "a class of persons who are neither freemen nor slaves" and pronounced their presence as "incompatible with the tranquility of society." Moreover, the petitioners maintained that free people of color excited "impractible hopes in the minds of those who are even more ignorant and unreflecting—and their locomotive habits fit them for a dangerous agency in schemes, wild and visionary, but disquieting and annoying."[41]

Although these radical agendas often had little to do directly with the insurrection, the Turner rebellion proved a moderately effective tool for those hoping to reshape the law. In the months after the rebellion, Virginia lawmakers passed an assortment of new acts regulating the activities and restricting the rights of free people of color. By 1832, Virginia "free negroes" had lost the right to carry guns, preach, sell liquor, and purchase slaves other than their enslaved relatives. Lawmakers also curbed their access to trial by jury and forced alleged criminals among them to face justice before courts of oyer and terminer, the same tribunals used to try enslaved plaintiffs. The colonization lobby received an important concession from Virginia legislators who agreed to provide partial funding for their movement. Virginia lawmakers also targeted "free negroes" who distributed antislavery materials.[42]

The Virginia legislative debates that followed the Turner rebellion resulted in an incomplete victory for the political enemies of free people of color. While colonizationists secured funding from the state legislature, the more radical proponents of removal failed to gain enough support to exile the state's free persons of color. Funding colonization was a political compromise, not a symbol of complete triumph for radicals. Radicals attempted to curb the rights of free people of color to own enslaved persons and real estate but succeeded only in pushing through the restrictions on holding bondspeople. Their attempt to severely limit the movement of free people of color failed to gain support in both houses of the General Assembly. In the House of Delegates, a scheme to prohibit "any slave, free negro or mulatto" from learning "a trade or art" as an apprentice for the "encouragement and protection of white mechanics" died in committee. A proposal "prohibiting the owners of mills from employing, as millers, slaves, free negroes or mulattoes" also failed to gain support in committee.[43]

Although officials never demonstrated that the Turner plot extended beyond Virginia, lawmakers in other states capitalized on the situation. Most of the legal activity that followed in the months after the insurrection took place in the states geographically closest to the epicenter of the event. North Carolina legislators prohibited "any free negro, slave or free person of color" from preaching or exhorting "in public." They required "any free negro, mulatto or free person of color" to obtain a license in order "to hawk or peddle" within a county.[44] The North Carolina General Assembly also crafted legislation permitting local officials to hire out for up to five years "any free negro or free person of colour" who could not pay a court-assessed fine. Maryland lawmakers passed a comprehensive law targeting "free negroes and slaves." The new law restricted the movement of "free negroes" from out of state by reinforcing the prohibition on their immigration, limiting their stay in Maryland to no more than ten days, and preventing anyone from hiring them. As a result, Maryland lawmakers required resident "free negroes and mulattoes" to give local officials written notice if they planned to leave the state temporarily for more than thirty days. The Maryland act required a "free negro or mulatto" to obtain a license in order "to keep or carry a firelock of any kind, any military weapon, or any powder or lead." A "free negro or mulatto" retailer now needed a license to sell "bacon, pork, beef, mutton, corn, wheat, tobacco, rye, or oats." Maryland lawmakers also directed that religious meetings of "free negroes" or "slaves" could not take place without "a white licensed or ordained preacher or some respectable white person or persons," except in Baltimore and Annapolis, where their congregations only needed the permission of a white minister to meet after ten o'clock at night.[45] Delaware legislators came together to restrict the rights of free people of color to bear arms and practice religion freely. They required "free negroes and free mulattoes" to obtain licenses in order to possess "a gun or fowling" and excluded them from legal ownership of "any sword, pistol or other warlike instrument." Delaware's lawmakers also required the presence of "three respectable white men" at the religious services of "free negroes or free mulattoes" taking place after "ten o'clock in the night season" and prohibited any nonresident "free negro or free mulatto" from preaching or leading religious services without prior approval from a judge or justice of the peace.[46] The Tennessee legislature passed a less ambitious agenda following the Turner rebellion but imposed immigration restrictions on free people of color and closed the doors to legal migration into the state.[47]

Even though the Deep South states and territories, with the exception of Louisiana and South Carolina, had some of the smallest populations of free people of color in the region and lay hundreds of miles from the epicenter of the rebellion, their lawmakers still decided to take advantage of the moment. The Mississippi legislature pushed through some of the most extreme legislation passed after the Turner rebellion. Part of the state's 1831 legislation required "all and every free negro or mulatto" between ages sixteen and fifty "to remove and quit the state" within ninety days of the law's passage and not return "under any pretence whatsoever." The law provided an exception for "any free negro or mulatto" who applied to the county of residence "for permission to remain and reside" in Mississippi and received a license granting permission to do so. Mississippi's post–Turner rebellion legislation also included restrictions on hiring free persons of color on watercraft without papers proving their freedom and prohibited free people of color from preaching or vending merchandise.[48] The case of Mississippi suggests a link between the ability to muster support for more extreme legislation and small overall numbers of free people of color. As a part of their 1831 legislation targeting free persons of color and slaves, South Carolina's legislators passed new rules permitting courts to punish free people of color and slaves involved in civil litigation as if they were "guilty of a misdemeanor." South Carolina lawmakers also used the moment to give whites a monopoly over the production of liquor in the state by prohibiting free people of color and the enslaved from using or keeping stills. If authorities caught a free person of color distilling liquor, officers could seize that person's still and other equipment and offer it for public sale.[49] This punishment created a reliable method of transferring the property of free people of color to whites because the law prevented free persons of color from owning stills, thereby leaving whites as the only legal purchasers. In Florida Territory, lawmakers opened up the option to hire out free people of color convicted of crimes. Alabama legislators took advantage of the moment to close the state's borders and shut down all avenues of legal immigration to free persons of color, bringing the state in line with most of its neighbors.[50]

Although most southern states used the moment of the Turner insurrection to pass legislation curbing the rights of free people of color, radical lawmakers in Kentucky, Georgia, Louisiana, Missouri, and Arkansas failed to capitalize on the situation at the state level. Most of these states were far from the rebellion's epicenter, and some already had strict laws on the books that targeted free people of color. In 1830, for example, Louisiana lawmakers had passed a string of new prohibitions and regulations regarding free people of color. Georgia, too, already had a long list of extreme policies focused on free people of color. Slavery's defenders in Little Rock, Arkansas, however, demonstrated it was possible to initiate new restrictions at the local level. An ordinance approved by Mayor Matthew Cunningham on February 4, 1832, sought to limit interactions between free people of color and enslaved persons by prohibiting "any free negro or mulatto" from allowing bondspeople to assemble at that person's home to gamble or consume liquor. The ordinance specified that violators would be fined or face a prison sentence of up to twenty days.[51]

Radicals won important political victories during the early 1830s. Yet free people of color did not cower in the face of the radical political storm that followed the Turner insurrection. Free people of color acted proactively and defensively to protect their legal and social positions. In October 1831, a group of eighteen free men of color under the leadership of the Reverend Peter Spencer published an appeal to the citizens of Wilmington, Delaware, asking them to act calmly in the postrebellion environment. The men attacked the "various reports which some mischevious [sic] person or persons have circulated in regard to the coloured population" and described them as "without the least foundation." They further declared, "We have been treated by the citizens of Wilmington and its vicinity generally with kindness, for which we ought to be grateful, and it is our solemn purpose to pursue such a course of conduct as may merit a continuance of their favor and confidence; should any among us be found so wicked and blinded as to enter into plots or contrivances inimical to the present harmony, we thus solemnly pledge ourselves to our white friends & neighbors that we will be among the first to sound the alarm and unite in affecting the apprehension and suppression."[52] Spencer and his associates sought to shed light on the activities of their political enemies who used the postrebellion environment to stir up trouble and, at the same time, present themselves as peaceful, law-abiding members of the community.

Following the passage of the postrebellion restrictions in Delaware, free people of color petitioned lawmakers in Dover, protesting the discriminatory acts and calling for their immediate repeal. Although these free people of color sent several separate petitions to lawmakers, their work represented a collective effort to challenge oppression. Their petitions shared common verbiage, demonstrating their desire to speak through a single, forceful, and well-crafted message. After stating that the new legislation "operated very oppressively upon" them, they argued that the act had "a demoralizing effect upon the free People of Colour ... by placing them under suspicion—making them to feel that the eyes of the white people are continually over them." The petitioners declared that the section of the law constricting their religious practices violated "their rights of conscience" and exposed "them to all the horrors of perpetual slavery for the act of worshipping their Creator according to the dictates of their consciences."[53] These free persons of color sought to rebrand the restrictive legislation as a measure of oppression rather than an attempt to provide social protection, as contended by its proponents. The petitioners pushed lawmakers to consider to what degree they were willing to threaten the liberties of large numbers of free people in order to endorse opportunistic fearmongering.

Post-Rebellion Radicalism

In the years following the Nat Turner Rebellion, radical lawmakers made important inroads in their efforts to reshape the southern legal landscape in order to diminish the status of free people of color. Model legislation that developed in one or two states slowly became standard among southern legal codes. By the end of 1835, the laws of every state in the South excluded free people of color from the franchise. Restrictions on legal access to guns and other weapons became commonplace. White liquor lobbies successfully pushed legislators to exclude free people of color from the spirits market, granting whites a monopoly over the production and distribution of alcohol. Free people of color lost the right to sell merchandise without a license in many parts of the South. Lawmakers provided local officials with the power to hire out free people of color at public sale as punishment for a variety of offenses. Legal access to basic education became more difficult to obtain in many areas of the region.[54]

In the early 1830s, North Carolina and Tennessee remained the only states in the South wherein free men of color could vote.[55] Such a reality challenged the very essence of white supremacist logic. Both states had property qualifications attached to voting rights, which meant that it was possible for certain propertied free men of color to qualify to vote in elections in which white men who failed to meet the property qualifications could not vote. During an 1834 state constitutional convention, some Tennessee lawmakers launched a campaign to amend the election laws to enfranchise a greater number of white men while effectively excluding free men of color from voting. They sought to rearrange the political order by targeting one group of voters and simultaneously elevating another class. At the 1834 convention, several representatives offered slightly different proposals to accomplish their shared goal of disfranchisement. Representative G. W. L. Marr, who represented Weakley and Obion Counties, however, built the strongest coalition of support around his proposal. Marr's resolution restricted the franchise to "free white men of the age of twenty-one years and upwards" who were citizens and had resided within Tennessee for at least six months. In defense of his proposal, Marr contended that "free persons of color, including Mulattoes, Mustees and Indians, were not parties to our political compact, nor were they represented in the Convention which framed the evidence of the compact." Following a few small changes to the resolution, members of the convention passed Marr's proposal. The opponents of complete disfranchisement sought to make substantive amendments, including a clause permitting those free men of color who were already enfranchised to continue voting, but their efforts largely failed. The representatives, however, managed to force through a compromise that exempted free men of color from militia service and poll taxes.[56] In effect, these changes protected lawmakers from charges of promoting taxation without representation and further cemented the contrasting legal statuses and duties of white men and free men of color. By excluding them from roles that supported the common defense and welfare of the state, lawmakers denied free men of color the leverage to demand civil rights.

Following the victory for white supremacy in Tennessee, radical politicians pressed the issue of disfranchising free men of color at North Carolina's 1835 constitutional convention. The North Carolina constitutional convention was the site of the last stand for those who sought to protect the voting rights of free men of color in the South. Free men of color had exercised the franchise under the state's original constitution for nearly six decades. John D. Toomer of Cumberland County called disfranchisement "tyranny." In defense of the voting rights of the "most respectable" free men of color, Joseph J. Daniel of Halifax County cited their military service during the American Revolution. Daniel was willing to accept qualifications on the right to vote for free men of color but thought the property holders among them should retain unrestricted access to the ballot. Weldon N. Edwards of Warren County argued that as long as free men of color paid taxes, lawmakers should not strip them of the right to vote. Radical politicians such as James W. Bryan of Carteret County, former Speaker of the U.S. House of Representatives Nathaniel Macon of Warren County, and Jesse Speight of Greene County led the charge against the rights of free men of color. Using a logic similar to that expressed in the Tennessee debate, Bryan, Macon, and Speight contended that the creators of North Carolina's original constitution never intended to include free men of color among the state's citizenry. Macon declared that "free persons of color never were considered as citizens, and no one had a right to vote but a citizen." Although he recognized the participation of some free men of color in the American Revolution, Macon argued that "they have been employed to fight, but were never made citizens—they made no part of the political family." Jesse Wilson of Perquimans County deployed traditional white supremacist tropes to defend disfranchisement. Wilson suggested that free people of color had neither the "requisite intelligence nor integrity" to vote. William Gaston of Craven County made a last-ditch effort to preserve the rights of the most successful free men of color by accepting disfranchisement for all free men of color except those worth five hundred dollars or more. Others proposed slightly amended versions of Gaston's plan. Nevertheless, these moderate efforts ultimately failed. Gaston's opponents defeated his proposal on a vote of sixty-four to fifty-five. Disfranchisement passed and became part of the North Carolina constitution.[57]

Radicals successfully cornered more moderate politicians by pushing them into a debate about the final form of disfranchisement instead of continuing to fight disfranchisement at large. This tactic forced the allies of free people of color to defend them as individuals instead of as a collective and further deflected moderates' attention away from the deep-seated agendas of radical representatives. Following the convention, Jesse Speight, who backed disfranchisement, revealed that the roots of his support were not purely about the unfitness of free men of color. Instead, he explained that he voted for disfranchisement in order to improve his own political prospects. Speight argued that if you "deduct the free negro votes, . . . it was no contest at all. It is known that nearly all of them voted against me."[58] Advocating for white supremacy presented a path to power for Speight, and moderates failed to identify and attack such self-serving motives during the constitutional debates.

The disfranchisement of free men of color signaled an important shift in the power balance between radical lawmakers and more moderate voices. Nevertheless, the votes to disfranchise exposed a continuing split among white southerners in regard to free people of color. After the

North Carolina constitutional convention, the *Fayetteville Observer* reported a "general feeling of regret" among its constituents concerning disfranchisement. The newspaper stated that "there are a few, some eight or ten, of that class, in Fayetteville, who have every qualification of intelligence, respectability, usefulness, and property, to entitle them, fairly, to exercise this high privilege."[59] This reaction to disfranchisement, in many ways, was representative of the white moderate opposition to radical political moves. White moderates attempted to highlight the accomplishments and status of particular free people of color while they failed to defend the rights of free people of color more broadly. Their inability to promote broad civil rights sometimes left them exposed in debates with their more radical colleagues.

The moderate defense of free people of color continued to crumble in many parts of the South, especially in regard to the rights of free persons of color to compete on equal footing with whites in the marketplace. White business interests sought to shut out free people of color from various forms of work and trade and therefore create white monopolies. An 1836 ordinance prohibited "any free negro or mulatto" from selling or bartering an assortment of alcoholic beverages or operating "any tavern, ordinary, shop, porter-cellar, refectory or eating-house of any kind, for profit or gain," within the limits of Washington in the District of Columbia.[60] During the 1844–45 legislative session, North Carolina lawmakers brought their state in line with much of the South by granting a virtual monopoly to white liquor sellers. They prohibited "any free negro or mulatto" from selling "any ardent spirits to any person whatever." In 1846, Kentucky lawmakers followed with a similar law that banned "any free negro or mulatto" from manufacturing or selling "any whiskey, brandy, or other spiritous liquors."[61] An 1856 Florida law was among the most restrictive in the region and stated, "It shall not be lawful for any person or persons to buy or sell to any Free Negro or Mulatto in this State, without the written consent of the Guardian of such Free Negro or Mulatto." The act imposed a fine "in a sum not less than One Hundred nor more than Five Hundred Dollars" on those convicted of violating the restrictions.[62] Florida lawmakers' actions reveal a desire to place free people of color in a legal position closer to that of enslaved persons. Just as enslaved people needed permission from their masters to engage in legal trade, free persons of color now required similar approval from their white guardians.

This radical measure gained traction in the Florida legislature but not without evoking significant criticism. Even at the height of the radicals' power in the South, detractors of extremism were willing to speak out. Their critiques failed to overturn most radical victories, but their protests exposed the fractures in southern politics late into the 1850s. The degree to which free people of color appreciated support from critics of the radical agenda remains unclear. Yet the actions of some free people of color demonstrate that they were unwilling to sit idly by in order to learn whether white allies would overtake the extremists and bring a sense of moderation back to the Florida legislature. Within a year of the passage of the economic restrictions, free persons of color had left Florida or were preparing for their exit. On February 14, 1857, the *Pensacola Gazette* reported that "many" free people of color in the community were planning to relocate to Mexico.[63] Less than two months later, thirty-five free persons of color left Pensacola for Tampico, Mexico. The local newspaper reported that "it was a painful sight to see them parting from their friends and their native country to seek homes in a foreign land. They take with them the sympathy of all our citizens on account of the cause which have led them to leave us."[64]

Acts that were supposed to promote white supremacy came at a steep cost for the communities that benefited from the presence of free people of color. On the eve of the Civil War, support for the restrictions on Florida's free people of color began to break down. Early in 1861, Florida lawmakers issued an exemption to sixty-two free persons of color from Escambia County, whom they described as "natives of the State of Florida," "Spanish subjects," and "the descendants of Spanish subjects prior to the treaty of peace and amity between the King of Spain and the late government of the United States of America." Many of those exempted by lawmakers were valuable members of the Pensacola community, including landholders Emilita Garetta and her husband, John Garetta, a master mason; Tabitha Vaughan and her husband, Ambrose Vaughan, a cabinetmaker; Filomena Roberts and her husband, John S. F. Roberts, a merchant; and Rosa Ramirez and her husband, Miguel Ramirez, a plasterer.[65] After lawmakers permitted these free persons of color to conduct business without interference, protests against the 1857 law increased. Free people of color from other parts of the state, with legacies going back to the Spanish period, petitioned for exemptions. John and Cecile Kelker, along with John's kinsman Frederick Kelker, all of Santa Rosa County, lobbied lawmakers for relief from the 1857 act. They requested exemptions for themselves as well as John and Cecile's seven children.[66]

The battle between radicals and moderates over weapons access for free people of color created a patchwork of inconsistency across the South. Some legislatures followed the Virginia model and implemented broad weapons bans. In 1833, lawmakers in Florida Territory passed an act making it unlawful for "any slave, free negro, or mulatto, to keep or retain in his or their house or houses, any fire-arms whatsoever." They permitted patrollers to search homes in order to enforce the law and authorized a punishment of up to "thirty-nine lashes" for offenders.[67] In 1841, proponents of weapons restrictions in North Carolina finally overcame legislative hurdles and passed an act requiring a license for "any free Negro, Mulatto, or free Person of Colour, [who] shall wear or carry about his or her person, or keep in his or her house, any Shot gun, Musket, Rifle, Pistol, Sword, Dagger or Bowie knife."[68] Of course, laws requiring licenses were insufficient for some extremists. North Carolina radicals continued to push for broader restrictions for nearly two more decades. They did not succeed in passing a broad weapons ban until the 1860–61 legislative session.[69]

Free people of color reacted with both compliance and resistance to restrictions on their access to guns and other weapons. They frequently managed to secure the cooperation of their white neighbors in order to obtain licenses for their weapons. In 1833, Thomas Burke petitioned the court in Prince George's County, Maryland, for a gun license, arguing that "a principal means of support to himself and family is derived from his killing wild fowl."[70] He received a license with the backing of a white justice of the peace, who certified that Burke was "a sober and industrious man and a good citizen."[71] With a recommendation from three white neighbors, James Staten received a gun license in 1847 from the court in Baltimore County, Maryland. Staten explained to the court that he was a tenant on a 210-acre farm and desired to keep a weapon "for gunning for a subsistence during the game season."[72] Other free people of color simply ignored the gun registration laws and occasionally came to the attention of local authorities. In 1856, a jury in Brunswick County, North Carolina, convicted Asa Jacobs of carrying a shotgun without a license. Jacobs appealed his conviction to the state supreme court but lost his case.[73]

Though white radicals claimed many victories in the southern state legislatures during the years between the Turner rebellion and the outbreak of the Civil War, the actual impact of their laws varied greatly and free people of color reacted to them in different ways. Extremists failed to create a political environment that automatically deemed all free people of color guilty of any accusation. Moreover, they failed to transform the southern judicial systems into machines that meted out the maximum penalties to convicted free persons of color. Even when radicals successfully pushed through their agendas in the legislatures, they depended on local people to implement the law. Local people tended to do so only sporadically, which led to inconsistent enforcement of the radical agenda.

In some communities, officials were clearly aware of the presence of lawbreakers but decided to ignore them and their offenses. Courts also tended to be selective in their sentencing; they reserved the harshest punishments for certain individuals instead of imposing blind justice.[74]

In the wake of the Turner rebellion, Virginia's 1806 act requiring the removal of newly emancipated persons continued to be the prime example of a law that was subjected to sporadic and largely lax enforcement.[75] In addition, some emancipated people and their allies took advantage of the law's major loophole that allowed them to petition the state legislature or, according to a later amendment, their local county officials for permission to stay in Virginia. The legislature on rare occasions and the counties in greater numbers granted these requests. Armistead Miller petitioned for permission to remain in Fredericksburg after officials summoned him to face charges for living in the state without authorization. During the period following his manumission, Miller obtained a house and lot in the town without being harassed about his status. On receiving a petition on his behalf, local authorities approved Miller's request.[76] Although individuals like Miller eventually sought permission to reside in their home state, countless numbers of manumitted people of color remained within Virginia's borders without legal authorization. Authorities in Loudoun County repeatedly indicted free people of color for living in the state without permission only to decide later to drop the cases. In 1850, the commonwealth's attorney pressed charges against Lucy Green in Loudoun County court for remaining in Virginia for almost two years after her emancipation. Green's case remained on the court docket until 1852, when the state decided to no longer pursue the case.[77] Officials in Alexandria County used a similar approach when dealing with manumitted people who decided to reside in their jurisdiction without permission. In 1853, Betsey Williams and Lucy Kitt faced charges in the county court for remaining in the state without permission. Their cases remained active until 1855, when the prosecutor decided to drop the charges.[78] Authorities in Lynchburg openly acknowledged the presence of manumitted people living within their community without permission. In 1850, the city clerk registered and issued freedom documents to William Henry Boyd, Eleanor George, Pamelia Morgan, and Maria Dunn but noted in the registration book that each individual had "no leave to remain in the Com[monweal]th of Va."[79]

The last three decades before the Civil War represented the zenith of restrictions on marriage between different categories of people. Since the colonial period, lawmakers had sought to shape the social hierarchy by regulating marriage and sexual relations between whites and persons of color. North Carolina law had long discouraged such relationships but had not explicitly outlawed the practice. During the 1838–39 General Assembly session, lawmakers revised the state's marriage regulation. The new code declared it unlawful "for any free negro or free person of color to marry a white person" and voided all such marriages enacted after the passage of the new restrictions.[80] Following their removal to Indian Territory, marriage between Indians and outsiders became a topic of serious debate within some nations. Members of the Cherokee Nation had discouraged marriage between citizens and slaves for several years before moving to Indian Territory. In 1839, however, they expanded their regulations to prohibit all unions "between a free male or female citizen with any slave or person of color not entitled to the rights of citizenship." Displaying a particular interest in ending marriage between "colored" men and Cherokee women, the National Council required a punishment of "one hundred lashes" for "any colored male" convicted under the law but limited punishments for all others to no more than "fifty stripes."[81] In 1858, Chickasaw Nation lawmakers sought to isolate "negroes" more broadly. They declared, "All persons other than a negro is hereby prohibited from cohabiting with a negro or negroes." Violators faced a fine of twenty-five to fifty dollars.[82]

The degree of impact from discriminatory taxation varied according to the economic status of the affected free persons of color. Officials in places such as South Carolina, Georgia, and Virginia collected thousands of dollars in head taxes on free people of color. This part of the radical agenda had the greatest impact by far on free people of color with the least means. During the 1850s, South Carolina lawmakers forced each adult free person of color to pay an eight-dollar annual capitation tax, a significant sum for a poor person. An 1852 Georgia law required every free person of color between eighteen and fifty years of age to pay a five-dollar annual head tax. This was the same amount levied on professionals, including lawyers, doctors, and dentists. The Virginia tax on adult free men of color was one dollar, and even this amount was too great a burden for the poorest families. Every year, county authorities encountered free people of color who simply could not afford to pay their taxes. Virginia law directed sheriffs to hire out free people of color who were unable to pay their taxes, but this aspect of the law was infrequently enforced.[83]

Across the South, radical legislators pushed through a series of laws permitting local officials to punish convicted free people of color who were unable to pay their fines by forcing them into periods of servitude.[84] These acts laid the legal groundwork for the convict lease system that developed on a much larger scale in the years after the Civil War. Due to sporadic enforcement and the limited number of free people of color affected by them, these laws differ significantly from their postwar reincarnations. Nevertheless, as in the postwar period, these laws presented a substantial burden for impoverished free people of color in particular. The way that officials implemented them, furthermore, illustrates the corrupt nature of many local regimes. Officials in some parts of Virginia severely abused the laws permitting the hiring out of free people of color who could not pay their fines and sold the labor of free people of color at prices enormously below their value. After spending several months in a Richmond, Virginia, jail for failing to produce her free papers, officials hired out Elizabeth Brown, a "free mulatter Girl," for a period of twenty years to Moses, a waterman, who paid Brown's $72.50 jail fee.[85] When officials hired out Brown in 1843, the $72.50 that Moses paid for her labor over a twenty-year period fell well below the amount that a common laborer could have accumulated in wages in a single year, let alone twenty years. If Richmond officials had permitted Elizabeth Brown to pay off her debt in installments, she probably could have done so in a much shorter period. In 1845, Virginia lawmakers attempted to address this kind of excess and placed a two-year limit on the hiring out of free people of color convicted for failure to produce freedom papers.[86]

In North Carolina, county officials never resorted to hiring out as a primary form of punishment for free people of color. North Carolina lawmakers, however, neglected to impose caps on fines associated with certain crimes, which allowed local officials to issue excessive fines selectively in order to force free people of color, especially the poor, to work as convict laborers. James Carter, "a free man of colour," became the victim of such a practice when he and his partner Susan Privott, a white woman, were convicted of fornication and adultery in the Robeson County Superior Court. After their conviction in 1847, the court fined Privott five dollars but assessed a fifty-dollar penalty against Carter. Neither Privott nor Carter could pay the fines; even five dollars was a significant amount of money for a poor person. Officials permitted Privott, as a white person, to take an oath of insolvency, which absolved her of further responsibility for the fine. The court did not make the same option available to Carter. Instead, the court ordered the sheriff to "hire out" Carter to someone willing to pay the fee.[87] The unequal outcomes for Carter and Privott demonstrate how North Carolina lawmakers' failure to set limits on fines allowed local officials to exploit the labor of free people of color.

Officials in parts of Delaware made hiring out a standard punishment for free people of color who could not pay their fines regardless of the amount. During the early 1850s, convicted free people of color in Kent County commonly faced the prospect of hiring out if they could not gather the money needed to pay their fines and court costs. Between 1850 and 1855, the vast majority of free people of color who confronted the possibility of hiring out were those convicted of larceny. The county court also hired out individuals convicted of attempted rape, keeping a disorderly house, and assault and battery. Those free people of color who had the money to pay their fines avoided hiring out while those without the money sometimes faced years of service. In 1852, the court convicted Joseph Turner of larceny. Turner paid his fine and avoided hiring out. The sheriff, however, hired out Henry Ashwell for a term of seven years following his conviction for the identical crime during the same court term. Ashwell likely would have avoided such a fate if he had access to more money. Categorization as "white" would also have protected him from the auction block. In Kent County, the court forced white people convicted of larceny who could not pay their fines to wear a scarlet letter on their clothing, marking their status as convicted thieves.[88] This type of punishment may have been embarrassing, but it was not the equivalent of years of forced and unpaid labor.

During the expansion of public education in the South, lawmakers attempted to shut out free persons of color from tax-funded education, and radicals in some locales sought to bar them from all forms of classroom instruction, regardless of who was paying. At the 1830–31 General Assembly session, Virginia lawmakers approved a proposal to exclude free people of color from formal education. Their law criminalized "all meetings of free negroes or mulattoes, at any school-house, church, meeting-house or other place for teaching them reading or writing, either in the day or the night." The act forbade all persons, whether white or of color, from teaching at such assemblies.[89] South Carolina lawmakers banned free persons of color from operating schools as part of a larger package of acts designed to curb the liberties of all persons of color, enslaved and free, in 1835.[90] The Cherokee National Council in 1841 outlawed providing literacy education to "any free negro or negroes not of Cherokee blood."[91] In 1847, Missouri lawmakers prohibited the establishment of "any school for the instruction of negroes or mulattoes, in reading or writing."[92] When North Carolina legislators enacted a law supporting the establishment of public schools in 1841, they permitted only "white children under the age of twenty-one years" to attend these educational institutions.[93] These restrictions left countless free people of color without rudimentary math and literacy skills because they were unable to pay for their schooling or access education provided by charity organizations.

Attempts to shut out free people of color from formal education, however, proceeded with mixed results. Private educational operations in Maryland, the District of Columbia, and North Carolina continued throughout the antebellum period largely unfettered. Even in states like Virginia and Georgia, where there were strict prohibitions on the formal instruction of free people of color, educators continued to teach reading, writing, and arithmetic to hungry young minds in spite of restrictions. During the late 1850s, Joseph and Emmett Wilson, free boys of color, attended a school operated by Agnes W. Davis, a white woman who openly defied the law and taught free children of color in Petersburg, Virginia. Local officials were aware of Davis's activities but were seemingly uninterested in enforcing the law. At least into the early 1850s, white elites in Norfolk, Virginia, provided free children of color with basic education at the Christ's Church Sunday School. In 1852 and 1853, Margaret and Rosa Douglass, a white woman and her daughter, ran a school out of their home for Norfolk's free children of color. They conducted their work without interference until local officials with strong proslavery sympathies decided to make examples of them. Margaret Douglass served one month in prison for violating the state's prohibition on educating persons of color. Yet those same officials who prosecuted Margaret Douglass continued to ignore the illegal educational activities taking place at Christ's Church. In Savannah, Georgia, free people of color led the movement to educate their children within a hostile legal environment. With the assistance of her daughter Mary Jane, Mary Woodhouse, a free woman of color, provided both free and enslaved children of color with an elementary literacy education at her clandestine school in Savannah. Children who attended the school traveled with their books wrapped in paper and entered the Woodhouse premises one by one in order to confuse the prying eyes of unsympathetic whites and law enforcement. Students seeking additional instruction after completing the Woodhouses' introductory courses visited Mary Beasley, a free woman of color who also participated in underground educational efforts.[94]

Restrictions on the movements of free persons of color were only as effective as those tasked to uphold them. White southerners frequently turned a blind eye to free people of color living among them without sanction. Local officials admitted as much when they chose to register free people of color who had illegally entered their states. In 1832, the clerk of the court in Mason County, Kentucky, recorded the registers of Thomas Bowles, who was originally from Lynchburg, Virginia, and James M. Bowles, who had come from Muskingum County, Ohio, even though both men had no legal right to reside in Kentucky. The census records for 1850 and 1860 reveal the limited effect of immigration restrictions, even during the peak period of radical influence in the South. Willis Freeman, a native Virginian, moved his family into Person County, North Carolina, even though his adopted state passed immigration restrictions in 1826. The 1850 census shows that Freeman and five other free persons of color in his household were born in Virginia, including three children who were born after the passage of the immigration restrictions.[95] While many free people of color illegally resided in states without incident, others fell victim to officials' strict enforcement of the law. In 1843, authorities in Somerset County, Maryland, arrested and jailed Griffin, a "free negro man," for illegally entering the state from Accomack County, Virginia. Following an appearance in court, the authorities sent Griffin back to jail until he could pay a twenty-dollar fine plus court fees.[96] Enforcement was not necessarily a sure deterrent for free people of color set on residing in places of their choice. In 1851, Richmond County authorities charged and convicted Anderson Youngblood, "a free person of color," for residing illegally in Georgia. The court fined Youngblood one hundred dollars and ordered him hired out by the sheriff to cover the fine, which Youngblood was unable to pay.[97] Despite such harsh punishment, Youngblood remained in Georgia after his conviction. The 1860 census shows Youngblood still living in Richmond County nine years after the court ruled against him.[98]

Immigration restrictions appear to have been most successful in the Deep South, where the populations of free people of color remained relatively low. Large numbers of free people of color never resided in Georgia, Florida, Alabama, Mississippi, Arkansas, Texas, and Indian Territory. After Texans declared independence from Mexico, the authors of the 1836 Texas Constitution prohibited any "free person of African descent, either in whole or in part," from residing permanently in the Lone Star Republic "without the consent" of the republic's congress.[99] Free persons of color who participated in the movement for Texas independence, including men such as Greenberry Logan, Samuel McCulluck, Joseph Tate, William Goyens, William Ashworth, and Abner Ashworth, had to beg for permission to remain in the very republic they had helped to establish. Such a strict regime kept the number of free people of color living in Texas under one thousand throughout the pre–Civil War period.[100] The hostile legal codes of the Cherokee and Choctaw Nations limited the population of free people of color below five hundred in Indian Territory. The Choctaw Constitution of 1838 actually prohibited their immigration, and in 1840, Choctaw lawmakers expelled "all free negroes" without "Choctaw and Chickasaw blood" from their nation.

They threatened to enslave individuals who failed to follow the law and punish those who might hire or conceal "a free negro or negroes." Six years later, Choctaw lawmakers required the removal of emancipated people on receiving their freedom.[101] Cherokee leaders adopted a firm but slightly less restrictive program. They sought only to remove "free Negroes" without ties to the nation. Their 1842 law permitted individuals freed by Cherokee citizens to remain.[102] In 1858, following the separation of the Chickasaw Nation from the Choctaw Nation, the Chickasaws adopted similar restrictions to those outlined in the 1840 Choctaw law. The Chickasaw law, however, lessened the punishment for convicted "free negroes" to one year of enslavement.[103] The immigration restrictions in Mississippi were not completely effective after their initial passage in the months following the Nat Turner Rebellion, as the population of free people of color grew from 519 to 1,366 between 1830 and 1840. The trend began to reverse between 1840 and 1850, when the population of free people of color declined from 1,366 to 930 over the course of the decade. Although Louisiana boasted a population of free persons of color greater than the total number of free people of color living elsewhere in the Deep South, immigration restrictions likely affected the growth of the population. Between 1840 and 1850, the population of free people of color in Louisiana declined by nearly 8,000 souls. Even though the port city of New Orleans attracted newcomers by the boatload, the number of free people of color in the state never bounced back.[104]

Delaware's 1851 law prohibiting any "free negro or mulatto not now residing in this State" from entering carried unintended consequences that actually forced lawmakers to weaken the state's immigration restrictions. Following the law's passage, legislators received petitions complaining of the negative economic effects of the restrictions. One of the petitions declared that the act "works great injury to the white inhabitants of the State, as well as injustice to an unfortunate and degraded class of our population." The petitioners explained that "as our State improves in productiveness, population and wealth, more laborers are required" and that by keeping "colored people" out of the state, the law created "a scarcity of laborers and [an] increase of wages." They also complained of the "thousands of dollars" lost by banning the entrance of "colored people" from other states. "Steamboat and vessel owners and other citizens furnishing subsistence" to "colored people" from nearby jurisdictions could no longer depend on their important business.[105] After receiving news of the negative economic effects of the restrictions, lawmakers found themselves unable to arrive at a compromise that would have permitted free people of color to enter Delaware from all the surrounding states. Yet in 1855, they managed to pass an act permitting "free negroes and free mulattoes of sober and industrious habits, residing in the State of Maryland, to come into and reside in New Castle or Kent Counties ... for the purpose of labor."[106] New Castle County and Kent County were the sections of Delaware where slavery was weakest and consequently where free labor was most important. This law may have helped some of the state's farmers but likely failed to fill the gap for business people, such as boat operators and small merchants, who depended on free persons of color as customers. The amended law still prohibited free people of color from Philadelphia, the region's largest economic hub, from bringing their labor, and perhaps more importantly their wealth, into neighboring New Castle County.

From the 1830s up to the Civil War, the degree to which officials enforced registration laws varied across the South. Free people of color in Richmond, Virginia, faced one of the stricter enforcement regimes, which required them to carry free papers proving their status. John H. Hill, a free person of color and native of the city, explained that in Richmond, "if a man's free papers are lost, he must advertise them, and if they are not found, he can get others if he can prove he has lost them; if he can't he is liable to see trouble." Years after the Turner rebellion, Richmond officials frequently prosecuted free people of color for not possessing proof of their liberty.[107] It was common for free people of color to advertise their attempts to recover lost freedom documents in the local newspapers. In an August 12, 1852, *Richmond Dispatch* advertisement, Nancy Peters, "a free woman of color," requested the recovery of freedom documents belonging to her son Elisha, who lost them while on board a steamship. She promised a "reasonable reward" for their return.[108] Benjamin F. Fortune advertised for the restoration of his freedom certificate, which documented his liberty and ties to the "Pamunkey Indian tribe," in the November 11, 1854, edition of the same newspaper. Fortune offered a three-dollar reward on the delivery of his papers.[109] Even though the enforcement of registration laws varied, freedom papers remained an important tool for free people of color seeking to travel. Train companies required free people of color to produce documentation of their free status in order to ride. An 1853 advertisement informed patrons on the Virginia and Tennessee Railroad that "free colored persons" were "required to produce their free papers" in order to travel on the train.[110] By 1858, the New Orleans, Jackson, and Great Northern Railroad forced "free persons of color" to carry "a Pass similar to that of a Slave, signed by some respectable White Person known to the Ticket Seller in New Orleans, or the Station Agent at the Station where he enters the Train."[111]

The inability of radicals to implement and execute laws that enslaved free people of color or removed them from the southern states exposed the boundaries within which radical politicians operated on the eve of the Civil War. During the late 1850s and into the early 1860s, several southern legislatures received proposals for the enslavement and removal of their states' free people of color. Radicals had floated the idea of removal for decades, but not until the 1850s did lawmakers across the region take the idea seriously. In 1859, grand juries from the districts of Beaufort, Edgefield, Greenville, Newberry, and Kershaw petitioned the South Carolina General Assembly to legislate the removal or enslavement of the state's free persons of color. In addition to requesting the enslavement or removal of free people of color living in South Carolina at the time, the grand jury from the Edgefield District also asked that "all mulattoes born of a white woman" in the future be sold at public auction on their second birthdays."[112] In 1860, the Tennessee General Assembly received four petitions from Wilson County calling for the removal of "the entire free negro population."[113]

The supporters of enslavement and removal found adamant spokesmen in the southern assemblies. Unbound by any sense of human equality, these men were a toxic influence in discussions about the rights of free people of color. Curtis W. Jacobs of Worcester County served as the primary spokesman for the scheme to legislate enslavement and removal in the Maryland Assembly. As the vice president of the Convention of Slaveholders of the Eastern Shore, Jacobs was among the most radical advocates for slavery in his state. In a January 10, 1859, letter to the editor, Jacobs declared, "Neither in Heaven, Earth or Hell, can I find this principle of equality, upon which they [the abolitionists] prate so much, either recognized or practiced by God himself." Jacobs continued his diatribe by arguing, "The State of Maryland, and the people of Maryland have the *right* to enslave every free negro amongst us, absolutely and without condition; we have the *right* to banish every one of them from the State unconditionally."[114] In Tennessee, William H. Barksdale, a Democrat from the north central part of the state, championed the enslavement and removal cause. In reference to "free negroes," Barksdale declared that "the majority of them are idlers and do not work for an honest support, but live by pilfering the farm-yards of their neighbors. Some make their living honestly, and such a law [to remove them] would seem to operate hard upon them, but it is better that they should suffer this hardship, than for the public to suffer the inconvenience of their presence."[115] State Senator Lotte W. Humphrey from Onslow County, North Carolina, was a young attorney and rising star in the national Democratic Party who worked diligently to enslave and remove his state's free people of color. During the 1858–59 General Assembly session, Humphrey introduced a bill that required free people of color to leave the state or face enslavement. He also presented a bill that increased the penalties for free persons of color who illegally entered the state. Humphrey's fellow lawmakers quashed his proposals. Unwilling to concede defeat, he continued to champion similar bills into the early 1860s.[116]

Enslavement and removal proposals appeared before the people and their representative bodies from Maryland to Missouri and Virginia to Arkansas. Some of these proposals stalled in committee while others received a full vote. James Thomas, a free man of color of Saint Louis, Missouri, observed that "the ablest men" opposed these measures.[117] North Carolina lawmakers shot down numerous attempts to pass legislation for the enslavement and removal of free people of color. During the 1858–59 session, the Senate Judiciary Committee concluded that such a law "would be in violation of the organic law of North Carolina."[118] Although they failed to support Abraham Lincoln for president in the election of 1860, Maryland voters decided overwhelmingly against a proposal to enslave the state's free people of color. Tennessee's removal bill passed the Senate but died in the House without a full vote. Removal and enslavement bills received votes before the legislative assemblies of South Carolina and Mississippi but failed to garner enough support for passage. Florida's removal bill passed the House and the Senate but failed to gain the signature of the governor. Missouri's less rigorous bill requiring the enslavement of all free people of color who entered the state since 1847 died on the governor's desk. The governor cited concerns about the proposal's constitutionality as cause for the veto.[119]

The only group of lawmakers who successfully passed an enslavement and removal law were those in Arkansas, but they found implementing the measure much more difficult than passing it. Even though Arkansas had one of the smallest populations of free people of color in the South, the state's lawmakers failed to create a plan to turn their legislative victory into absolute removal. Radicals had created another unfunded mandate. The enslavement and removal law provided no money to assist free people of color in their forced exodus. Free persons of color were therefore left to devise and find financial backing for their relocation. By the end of 1859, some had obtained the funds to support their removal. Free people of color left behind their homes, friends, and relatives in Arkansas and found refuge in places like Ohio and Kansas Territory. Only a few free persons of color remained by the beginning of 1860.[120] The radicals could claim a small victory in Arkansas, but their broader plot to remove or enslave the South's free people of color was unsuccessful.

While radicals failed to make enslavement and removal bills into law in most of the South, they were more successful in passing legislation permitting voluntary enslavement. Most voluntary enslavement laws allowed free people of color to choose masters and become the bondspeople of those masters. Free people of color could make official their transition from freedom to slavery by petitioning state lawmakers. Between 1856 and 1860, radicals secured passage of voluntary enslavement legislation in Virginia, Maryland, Kentucky, Alabama, Mississippi, Texas, Florida, Louisiana, and Tennessee. In South Carolina and Georgia, individual free persons of color could petition to be enslaved, but there were no formal laws on the books sanctioning the practice. Historians have shown that the number of free people of color who volunteered themselves for enslavement was small and likely fewer than two hundred individuals. Scholars who have studied voluntary enslavement have concluded that free people of color who asked to be enslaved generally did so to preserve their family ties and to avoid the family separations that might occur as a result of the enforcement of state residency laws. Physical disability also encouraged them to petition to be enslaved. In 1860, Fannie Gillison, a recently emancipated woman from Fauquier County, Virginia, requested to be enslaved due to her old age. Through much of the antebellum period, officials only sporadically enforced laws requiring the removal of nonresident free people of color and recently emancipated people. When law enforcement decided to act, however, voluntary enslavement provided one method for free people of color to remain in their communities and with their families.[121]

As removal bills floundered, radical lawmakers revived and strengthened other tools for controlling the movements and actions of free people of color. Radicals in several locales succeeded in tightening their immigration laws. Louisiana's 1859 immigration act required three to twelve months' imprisonment at hard labor in the state penitentiary for free people of color convicted of entering the state and failing to leave within five days of notice. Free people of color who returned to the state after being removed faced five years' imprisonment and hard labor.[122] Kentucky legislators enacted an even tougher law. For simply entering the state, a "free negro or mulatto" faced one to five years' imprisonment. If the person came into the state with the intent of making permanent residence, the minimum sentence was six years in the penitentiary. Lawmakers required life imprisonment for an individual who returned to the state after being convicted and removed. Kentucky radicals also targeted resident free people of color. They gave officials the power to strip residency from any "free negro or mulatto" who left Kentucky to visit "any State where negro slavery is prohibited." A "free negro or mulatto" could travel to these locales only if employed on a watercraft or with court-granted permission.[123]

Public discussion of enslavement and removal provided colonizationists with an opportunity to portray themselves as moderates who offered a less extreme method of reducing the South's free population of color. Colonization aligned with the goals of radicals but also appealed to more moderate whites like William D. Valentine, a North Carolina Whig. Valentine was hardly an egalitarian, but his experience living in a community with a significant population of free people of color had led him to accept that they were "civilized and some of them enlightened." He did not support colonization because he strongly despised free people of color. In his mind, African colonization represented the "best" option for a people with an increasingly anomalous legal position.[124] Renewed calls for colonization led Virginia assemblymen to pass laws supporting the scheme in 1849, 1850, and 1853. They set aside thirty thousand dollars toward the colonization cause in 1850. Legislators also instituted a one-dollar levy on every free man of color to support colonization further. In 1855, Missouri assemblymen promised to support the colonization cause with an appropriation of three thousand dollars per year for ten years. Each person applying to leave Missouri for Liberia could receive up to sixty dollars for the trip. In 1856, Kentucky lawmakers appropriated five thousand dollars to support the migration of free people of color to Liberia. This act allowed the state to grant seventy dollars to persons above the age of two years who were willing to migrate. These laws were not particularly successful and only partially achieved their aims. In 1851, the American Colonization Society reported that the average cost of sending an individual to Liberia was fifty dollars. For the same amount, an individual could purchase ten to twenty acres of land in some parts of rural Virginia. Three years after Virginia lawmakers appropriated thirty thousand dollars toward colonization, the state had sent only 419 emigrants to Liberia. Almost two years after the passage of the Kentucky statute, a budget review requested by lawmakers revealed that only one free person of color had applied for and received funds to support her removal. The review led a group of lawmakers to advocate for a repeal of the colonization funding law. Their effort succeeded in one chamber of the General Assembly and almost passed in the other.[125]

Radical politics manifested not only in the halls of southern legislatures but also in the press. Radical media outlets routinely misrepresented free people of color in order to promote white supremacy and the proslavery agenda. They created a political litmus test out of an individual's level of opposition toward free persons of color. For newspapermen across the country, the caricature of a nameless free person of color became an important facet of the 1840 national election. On September 24, 1840, the *Edgefield Advertiser*, a Democratic-leaning South Carolina newspaper, printed an ode that associated Whig presidential candidate William Henry Harrison with the growing population of free people of color. Bringing to life an imaginary free man of color named "Jim Brown," the song began, "O! I am a free nigger, tanks be to Arter Tappin, / And to 'de ole hero' wot libs in 'log cabbin.'" The lyrics continued, "I'll vote for 'de Gineral' wot libs in 'log cabbin' / An when we gits 'de bank' wi I'll be a grabbin."[126] The songwriter tried to link Harrison's candidacy to the interests of free persons of color and northern antislavery advocates, such as Arthur Tappan. In so doing, the writer suggested that Harrison was out of step with the interests of "good white people." Interestingly, Harrison's supporters adopted a similar strategy to attack his opponent, President Martin Van Buren. The *Boon's Lick Times*, a pro-Harrison newspaper out of Fayette, Missouri, attacked Van Buren by suggesting that he was in favor of free people of color exercising the right to vote. Meanwhile, Democrats had contended that Harrison supported voting rights for free men of color. The *Boon's Lick Times* claimed that while Van Buren was active in New York state politics, he supported "letting every FREE NEGRO in New York VOTE, the same as a white man!"[127] The editors of Nashville's *Republican Banner*, S. Nye and A. A. Hall, portrayed Van Buren as a supporter of "free negro testimony" against whites.[128]

The editors of these newspapers used a careful mix of white supremacist ideology and antinorthern sentiment to attack the political opponents of their preferred candidates. Free men of color had already lost access to the franchise, and persons of color regardless of status could not testify against whites in much of the country. Nevertheless, these publications weaponized the possibility that candidates might reinstate the rights of persons of color and regard free people of color as equal to whites. The paper's chosen candidate represented white superiority while the opponent threatened to diminish the status of white men by placing them on equal footing with "free negroes." Of course, the outcome of the federal election had little to do with the position of free people of color or white men because lawmakers at the state level largely dictated those rules dealing with voting rights and courthouse decorum.

Radical newspapermen ran articles highlighting the alleged absurd or criminal behavior of free people of color to support the radical contention that free people of color, and therefore enslaved people, were not equipped for freedom. They argued that free persons of color were inherently criminal and backward. The October 29, 1856, edition of Kentucky's *Louisville Daily Courier* published "Disorderly Negro," an article that associated free men of color with the mistreatment of white women and depicted them as threats to white womanhood. The paper reported that "Robert Myer, a free nigger with a black mustache, was presented on the charge of disorderly conduct, and insulting a German girl in the house."[129] The article suggested that free men of color were so unruly that they were a threat to the lowest class of white women, European immigrants. Even in New Orleans, a community populated by some of the most accomplished free people of color in the country, proslavery newspapermen used the printed page to portray free persons of color as a degraded caste. The March 17, 1846, issue of the city's *Daily Delta* included an article titled "Gambling Niggers," which reported on the arrest and punishment of "Jimmy, Vallery, and Ben, three slaves," and "George Ridgway, a free man of color," for "gambling in a stable on St. John Street."[130] Reports such as this one depicted free people of color as the social equals of enslaved persons and suggested that they were all immoral, petty criminals. On October 11, 1854, the *New Orleans Crescent* reported on Pierre Bonny, a "free man of color," who the paper alleged had "been in the habit of expressing his ideas on the right of man and free niggers in particular, also insulting white people."[131] The *Crescent*, like so many other outlets, made a direct connection between the equality of people regardless of race and the denigration of white people.

For radical southern newspapermen, the free persons of color of their imaginations played an important role in their attacks against the North as well as their justification of the continuation of human bondage in the South. On August 29, 1850, the *Louisville Daily Courier* imagined the happenings of a so-called Free Nigger Convention held in Cazenovia, New York, and led by Frederick Douglass, a formerly enslaved man and antislavery spokesman. The paper claimed, "The no-party, no-religion, no-condition, no-union, black and white convention met in this place today, and to show their utter contempt for all white men and white things." Moreover, the paper alleged, "resolutions were adopted against the North, against the South, against Free Soil, and against almost everything and everybody."[132] The *Louisville Daily Courier* was suggesting that northern free people of color and their white allies were akin to clueless buffoons when, in reality, they represented a well-organized threat to slavery. Had the newspaper reported what actually happened at northern antislavery meetings and disseminated the actual words of Frederick

Douglass, proslavery critics would likely have accused the paper of circulating incendiary materials. Radicalism had forced the truth underground, and extremists replaced factual reporting with cheap propaganda.

In addition to newspapers, organized white labor was one of the most important purveyors of white supremacist and anti–free people of color sentiment in the South during the decades leading up to the Civil War.[133] White mechanics' groups targeted free people of color and treated them as a threat to their livelihood. Frederick Douglass, who worked alongside white mechanics employed in the shipyards of Baltimore during the 1830s, suggested that slaveholders cultivated among white mechanics ill will toward people of color. He argued that "the slaveholders, with a craftiness peculiar to themselves, by encouraging the enmity of the poor laboring white man against the blacks, succeeded in making the said white man almost as much a slave as the black slave himself." Douglass concluded that the slave masters "appealed to their pride, often denouncing emancipation as tending to place the white working man on an equality with negroes, and by this means they succeeded in drawing off the minds of the poor whites from the real fact, that by the rich slave master they were already regarded as but a single remove from equality with the slave." Despite this level of manipulation, the white mechanics only became more hostile toward free people of color as the years progressed. At Douglass's shipyard, whites assaulted people of color with whom they once worked peacefully.[134] In 1849, a group of white mechanics aggressively protested competition from people of color. They resolved, "That we regard the teaching of any Negro any branch of the mechanic arts, as prejudicial to the interest, and injurious to the morals of the laboring White man." The group also declared, "That we, whose names are hereunto annexed, will not work for any employer who shall take a Negro into his employ, for the purpose of teaching said Negro any branch of the mechanic arts."[135] White mechanics became a key constituency for radical politicians. By the 1850s, white organized labor had become important proponents for the deportation of free people of color.[136] The animosity expressed by white workers toward free people of color in the years leading up to the Civil War continued to prevent harmony between these groups in many parts of the country well into the twentieth century.[137]

Although some supporters of the radical proslavery agenda likely found common cause with white organized labor, as suggested by Douglass, white laborers' attacks on people of color did not always serve the interests of the slaveholding elite. Some white planters such as David Gavin of South Carolina detested the general class of laboring whites as much as they disliked free people of color. Gavin complained that "idle, vagrant white persons and free negroes are the only persons specially favoured by the Legislature.... The industrious white must pay all the taxes."[138] Furthermore, the extent to which white organized labor sought to exclude people of color, both free and enslaved, from the labor market created a rift between elites and the white working class. By the 1850s, white organized labor was publicly attacking all "negro" labor, free and enslaved. At a meeting in Little Rock, Arkansas, white mechanics declared their opposition to competition from "free and slave negroes." They described teaching "free negroes" the "arts of mechanic and trader" as "injurious to the southern white mechanic" and a "danger to southern interests and institutions in general." The workers refused to "instruct free and slave negroes in the mechanic arts," swore not to "employ the negro mechanic," and declared their hostility toward anyone who hired people of color over whites. Some southern newspapers amplified such sentiments. In 1858, the *Intelligencer* of Wheeling, Virginia, claimed "that white labor was degraded when brought into competition with negro labor."[139] During the same year, the editor of Tennessee's *Fayetteville Observer* declared that "to ask the Southern mechanic to continue intensively pro-slavery, while the 'institution' in one of the phases, is literally snatching the bread from his mouth, is requiring an extent of devotion to the South which is not [to] be expected from poor human nature."[140] In the South as well as the North, laboring white men sought to carve out an economic space for themselves by scapegoating people of color. They saw white preference in work, even to the detriment of slaveholders, as necessary for their survival. Of course, slaveholders were unwilling to accept such arguments.[141]

The Turner rebellion likely represented the peak of vigilante violence against free people of color in the pre–Civil War South. Yet political extremism continued to manifest from time to time in the form of vicious attacks on the persons and property of free people of color. Such incidents are much better documented for northern localities but also occurred in a few southern communities.[142] Extremists targeted free people of color through violent assaults, riots, the destruction of homes, and verbal intimidation. The Snow Riot of 1835 was one of the most significant attacks on free people of color in the years after the insurrection in Southampton County. The outburst of violence followed the outbreak of a labor dispute between white mechanics and the operators of the Washington Navy Yard. This conflict eventually spilled into the streets, and the white mechanics took out their anger on people of color. The violence and destruction began when a group of whites attacked and destroyed the establishment of Beverly Snow, a free man of color who owned a restaurant on Pennsylvania Avenue and Sixth Street. A rumor that Snow had made derogatory comments about the wives of white mechanics emboldened the mob. Snow adamantly denied the charge. Fearing for his life, Snow escaped Washington and fled to Fredericksburg, Virginia. After the assault on Snow's business, whites targeted free people of color more broadly. They plundered the homes of the district's elite free persons of color and burned and demolished the dwellings of others. The rioters partially destroyed area schools for people of color. John F. Cook, a free man of color and teacher targeted for his antislavery sympathies, escaped the mob.[143] Conflicts between whites and free people of color occurred more sporadically in North Carolina. On October 22, 1842, the *Raleigh Microcosm* reported on the case of Allen Jones, "a free negro" who "was violently forced from his house" and "so severely lynched by a mob, that for a while it was thought he would not recover." The attack on Jones was generally met with public outrage.[144] Only months earlier, a group of vigilantes styling themselves the "Raleigh Regulators" had destroyed a log schoolhouse on the edge of the state capital supported by free people of color, including Allen Jones, for their children.[145]

The negative publicity coming from radical media outlets, white organized labor, and militant vigilantes aided radical lawmakers in their attacks on free people of color and undergirded the association radicals drew between free persons of color and emancipation, northerners, labor competition, and racial equality. Collectively, the years after the Turner insurrection were the most successful period for proslavery radicals and white supremacists. Ultimately, more rational minds kept the extremists at bay, and they failed to execute the most radical parts of their agenda. Nevertheless, the laws they passed negatively affected the lives of free people of color in the South. Some free people of color became fearful and decided to leave the region altogether, especially in the last decade leading up to the Civil War. The radicals' laws also had a disproportionate effect on poor free people of color, who were often the primary victims of discriminatory punishment.

In the days, months, and years following the Nat Turner Rebellion, free people of color faced an assortment of obstacles that ranged from fear to property damage to assault. The increasing value of slave property and growing polarization around the proslavery-antislavery divide fed economic and political transformations that negatively affected free people of color. Proslavery radicals and white supremacists gradually reshaped the body politic and laws of the South in ways that made the region an increasingly difficult place to live for some free people of color.

These challenges were enough to push some free people of color to seek refuge in other regions of the country or, in some cases, other parts of the world. Beverly Snow, the initial victim of the District of Columbia's Snow Riot, left the South and resettled in Canada. After nearly losing his life to a mob in Raleigh, North Carolina, Allen Jones moved with many of his neighbors to Ohio.[146] Most free people of color remained in the South but were vexed by their white neighbors' mix of extremism and blind moderation. James Thomas of Saint Louis declared, "I like the southern people individual[l]y, but collectively, and political[l]y, 'Dam'em.'"[147] The frustration and hardship that resulted from the radicals' behavior during the post–Turner rebellion years, however, are only part of the story of the South's free people of color in the days leading up to the Civil War.

CHAPTER 6

Resisting Radicalism

Pierre Casanave was one of many entrepreneurs in mid-nineteenth century New Orleans. A free man of color and cabinetmaker by trade, he launched an embalming and undertaking business in the 1850s. In an 1856 newspaper advertisement, Casanave informed readers that he had obtained a partial interest in an embalming process and was offering funerary services. Casanave announced that "bodies embalmed by him are warranted to keep free from decomposition and can be taken to any part of the world without exhaling the slightest odor, in any season of the year." Even bodies in "an advanced state of decomposition" could be "restored to a perfect state of preservation," according to Casanave.[1] Casanave developed a reputation as Louisiana's sole practitioner of this embalming process, and he would continue to do business through the Civil War years.

Casanave was one among many free people of color in the South who offered important services to their communities and kept the southern economy in motion. Radicals sought to portray individuals like Casanave as pariahs, but free people of color demonstrated through their roles as good neighbors and vital economic participants that they were instead essential members of their communities. Historians have concluded that the economic contributions of free persons of color foiled some of the most extreme political plots against them.[2]

The radical and sometimes desperate actions of the proslavery and white supremacist coalition could have spelled calamity for the South's free people of color between 1830 and the beginning of the Civil War. Although political radicals were successful in placing legal limitations on free persons of color across the region, they never figured out how to enact their extremist vision fully. Decade after decade, the total number of free people of color in the South continued to increase, particularly in the Upper South. While some free people of color experienced declining fortunes over time, other free people of color found unprecedented success in business, in landownership, and in the creation of new community organizations. Radical politicians had effectively altered the legal codes of the South to discriminate against the greater interests of free people of color. Still, free persons of color managed to overcome some restrictions and find justice in a system not designed for their benefit. Free people of color, sometimes with the assistance of white allies, used their ingenuity to build relationships across boundaries of racial categorization, wealth, and gender; in doing so, they reinforced their position as vital members of their home communities.

Population

Although radical proslavery advocates and white supremacists gradually ramped up their attacks against the presence of free people of color in the region between 1830 and 1860, the number of free people of color in the South as a whole only increased. In 1830, the South was home to approximately 182,070 free persons of color, but by 1860 the number had swelled to approximately 262,322 people. Throughout the entire antebellum period, free people of color in the South outnumbered the population of free persons of color in the North.[3]

Lawmakers in the Deep South largely curbed the growth of free people of color in their jurisdictions. Alabama, Georgia, and South Carolina were the only Deep South states with populations of free people of color that increased steadily between 1830 and 1860, and South Carolina was the lone state among them to experience a noteworthy population increase. In South Carolina, the number of free people of color increased from 7,921 in 1830 to 9,914 in 1860. On the other hand, Alabama and Georgia experienced increases from only 1,572 to 2,690 and 2,486 to 3,500, respectively. In Florida, the population rose slightly from a negligible 844 souls to 932 people between 1830 and 1860. Between the 1830 and 1840 census enumerations, the number of free people of color in Florida actually fell from 844 to 817 before recovering to 932 in 1850. Following the U.S. acquisition from Spain, several groups of free people of color had left Florida in search of places with more favorable political climates. Louisiana residents saw the number of free people of color collapse during the period. A refuge for free people of color under Spanish rule and during the early national period, Louisiana saw the number of free persons of color reach 16,710 in 1830 and 25,502 by 1840. By 1850, however, the population declined by nearly 8,000 individuals. It recovered only by slightly less than 1,200 people between 1850 and 1860. Arkansas, Mississippi, and Texas all experienced population drops during the period, and by 1860 none of these states had more than 800 free people of color living within their boundaries. Indian Territory was home to 404 free people of color in 1860, with 277 of those persons living in the Creek Nation; 67 in the Choctaw Nation; 30 in Seminole County; 17 in the Cherokee Nation; and 13 in the Chickasaw Nation.[4] The Deep South was largely a haven for slavery and not for free persons of color. Those with strong community ties or good business connections were most likely to find sanctuary in a region designed largely for the benefit of wealthy slaveholders, shady speculators, and slick entrepreneurs.

Between 1830 and 1860, the vast majority of free people of color continued to live in the Upper South, and the states in this region took on the overwhelming growth in the South's number of free people of color. During the period, not a single state in the Upper South experienced a decrease in its population of free persons of color. By 1860, approximately 224,963 out of the South's 262,322 free people of color lived in the Upper South. The states of Maryland and Virginia each had more free people of color within their borders than the entire Deep South throughout the three decades preceding the Civil War.[5]

Slavery remained firmly entrenched in much of the Upper South as in other parts of the region. In Delaware, Maryland, and the District of Columbia, however, human bondage was gradually receding. Radicals sought to salvage slavery in these locales, but human bondage was becoming increasingly unpopular. Early in the century, Delaware's bondspeople had become a minority among persons of color, and the proportion of enslaved people among the state's population of color continued to decline. In 1860, Delaware's population included 19,829 free people of color but only 1,798 enslaved persons, making Delaware the only southern state where free people outnumbered the enslaved among the population of color. On the eve of the Civil War, slavery had nearly collapsed in Delaware's two northernmost counties, New Castle and Kent, where enslaved people numbered 203 and 254, respectively. The presence of 4 unlucky enslaved souls in Wilmington kept Delaware's largest city from becoming free from human bondage. Only Delaware's most southern county, Sussex, contained a sizable enslaved population; of the state's 1,798 bondspeople, 1,341 resided in Sussex County. Still, most people of color in Sussex County were free persons, not slaves.[6]

By 1830, the District of Columbia had joined Delaware as the only other major jurisdiction in the South in which free persons of color outnumbered bondspeople. In every subsequent decade, the number of free people of color only increased. Enumerators for the 1860 census found that 11,131 out of the District of Columbia's 14,316 people of color were free. As part of the Compromise of 1850, President Millard Fillmore and majorities in both houses of Congress ended the domestic slave trade in the District of Columbia, thereby curbing the influence of slave traders in the nation's capital and creating a more welcoming environment for free people of color. In addition, a small but strong antislavery presence in the nation's capital provided opportunities for freedom unavailable in many other parts of the South. The manumission laws in the District of Columbia, which were among the least restrictive in the region, allowed enslaved people to purchase themselves, free persons of color to emancipate enslaved relatives and associates, and white masters to liberate their bondspeople. Natural growth among free people of color along with immigration from nearby states like Virginia and Maryland only accelerated the population boom.[7]

In Maryland, the number of free people of color approached parity with the enslaved population by 1860, with the latter outnumbering the former by only 87,189 to 83,942. All of Maryland's counties except for Allegany County had populations of free people of color above 1,000 individuals. The combined area of Baltimore and Baltimore County, with 29,911 free people of color, had the largest concentration of free people of color in the entire United States. More free persons of color than enslaved people lived in nine of Maryland's twenty-one counties. All of these counties were located either on the border with the free state of Pennsylvania or on the Eastern Shore. Economic changes and a relatively strong antislavery element in the state had encouraged the decline of slavery early in the century. This climate provided greater opportunities for manumissions. Throughout most of the pre–Civil War period, Maryland's laws compared to those in most of the South were liberal in their regulations of the manumission process. Private arrangements for gradual emancipation were also more common in Maryland than in other parts of the South. Throughout the state, slaveholders incentivized cooperation from their bondspeople by promising future liberation. Term-slavery, a practice in which slaveholders issued legal emancipations to their bondspeople years before the enslaved could actually access the legal rights associated with freedom, became commonplace.[8] Providing enslaved people with opportunities to access legal freedom after set terms of service likely played an important role for masters trying to prevent their bondspeople from simply escaping across the border into free territory. For slaveholders, accepting a limited term of slave labor was preferable to trying to recapture an escaped bondsperson.

Natural increase and manumissions continued the positive growth trend for free people of color in Virginia and North Carolina between

1830 and 1860. Attempts to curb manumissions and deport free people of color to Africa failed to halt the surge. Virginians enforced manumission restrictions sporadically and only rarely expelled free people of color from the state. Some free people of color obtained permission to remain in Virginia, while others continued to live in the state without license. Only a few free people of color ventured to Liberia between 1830 and 1860. In North Carolina, the state with the South's third largest population of free people of color, growth continued largely unabated. Natural growth in areas with high concentrations of free people of color continued to push North Carolina's population numbers upward. Between 1830 and 1840, the actual population increase among free people of color in North Carolina was larger than in neighboring Virginia. Between 1840 and 1850, the population increase as a percentage of the total number of free people of color in North Carolina exceeded that of the much more populous Virginia.[9]

The inhabitants of the rapidly developing western section of the Upper South—Missouri, Kentucky, and Tennessee—witnessed a steady surge in their populations of free persons of color between 1830 and 1860. The number of free people of color in Missouri rose more than sixfold between 1830 and 1860 from 569 persons in 1830 to 3,572 by 1860. Manumissions in Saint Louis, Missouri, actually peaked during the 1840s and 1850s, the period in which radicals were offering some of their most extreme proposals concerning free people of color. Kentucky's larger population of free people of color more than doubled during the same period from 4,917 to 10,684, a population number that exceeded every Deep South state's population except that of Louisiana. The growth rate in Tennessee was less than in Missouri and Kentucky but still significant. In 1830, Tennessee was home to approximately 4,555 free people of color, and by 1860, 7,300 free persons of color resided in the state. Large concentrations of free people of color coalesced around each state's metropolitan center. By 1860, Jefferson County, Kentucky, which encompassed the city of Louisville; Saint Louis County, Missouri, which included the city of Saint Louis; and Davidson County, Tennessee, which contained the city of Nashville, all hosted populations of free people of color over 1,000 and were among the fifty local jurisdictions in the South with the largest populations of free people of color. A significant increase in manumissions from the 1830s through the 1850s helped to spur the population growth in Jefferson County. With over 2,000 free people of color, Jefferson County was among the twenty-five jurisdictions with the largest populations of free persons of color in the South.[10]

These metropolitan areas offered enslaved people greater opportunities for freedom than some of the surrounding rural areas. In places like Louisville and Saint Louis, enslaved people found work that allowed them to purchase themselves, family members, and friends. The same opportunity existed for free people of color who desired to help others on the road to freedom. Some of the areas' more well-to-do free people of color assisted those searching for an escape from bondage by providing loans to use for self-purchase and buying friends and relatives. Washington Spradling, a successful barber in Louisville, financed loans for those looking to free themselves and their families. Spradling claimed to have assisted in the liberation of thirty-three persons, some who were able to pay back their loans and others who were not. John Berry Meachum, a minister in Saint Louis, played a similar role in his community. Both men could empathize with the situation of bondspeople yearning for freedom and the liberty of their families. Spradling and Meachum were born into slavery, and after obtaining their liberty, they used their hard-won earnings to secure the freedom of their families.[11]

As their numbers continued to grow, the South's free people of color served as living, breathing challenges to radicals' portrayals of people of color as criminal, lazy, and ignorant. Whether they were formerly enslaved persons themselves or the descendants of enslaved people, free people of color living and flourishing in the South countered radical proslavery arguments that people of color were unfit for liberty and could only serve society productively as human chattel.

Serving the Community

Throughout the period from 1830 to 1860, free people of color experienced persistent challenges as they sought to remain in their home communities unmolested by vigilante violence and discriminatory legal regimes. Nevertheless, free persons of color across the South continued to serve important roles in their communities, and many of their white neighbors recognized their contributions despite the increasingly hostile political environment in parts of the South. White-owned businesses depended on free people of color to purchase their goods and services. Free people of color were also important economic actors during the period, providing their communities with skilled services and labor. Many free people of color struggled even though their labor was essential to the southern economy. Other free people of color thrived and became among the most well respected people in their communities despite their increasingly inferior legal status.

Between 1830 and 1860, the practice of segregation based on racial categorization gradually emerged in different parts of the South, primarily in the cities. Yet even in these areas, segregation appeared sporadically. As a result, free people of color continued to have a great deal of interaction with their white neighbors, even as radicals accelerated their use of incendiary rhetoric and attempted to trample the rights of free people of color. Significant interactions among free people of color, whites, and enslaved persons persisted. For generations, free people of color and whites had connected and developed a level of familiarity, notably in more rural communities.[12]

Although kind treatment was not assured for free people of color in all facets of life, especially in the late antebellum years, local officials in parts of the South offered basic provisions to their communities' most desperate souls, including free persons of color. The records of the overseers of the poor strongly demonstrate that white people were the primary beneficiaries of poor relief. Yet free people of color, with the assistance of their neighbors, were able to access funds to support themselves and their struggling families in times of need or during periods of immobility. From the 1840s through the 1860s, the trustees of the poor in Sussex County, Delaware, accepted dozens of free people of color into the local almshouse. Most of the admitted free persons of color suffered from physical disabilities, sickness, or cognitive disorders. In 1850, Risdon Nutter arrived in the poorhouse suffering from rheumatism. Having lost her sight, Leah Hamilton entered the almshouse in 1851. After the admitting official concluded that she was suffering from "insanity," the overseers received Susan Hill in 1857.[13] The overseers of the poor in Queen Anne's County, Maryland, also supported free persons of color facing unfortunate circumstances by providing shelter at the almshouse as well as by distributing rations to struggling families. During June 1847, Hester Meeds, who was about twenty-five years old at the time, became a long-term resident of the county almshouse on giving birth to her daughter Sarah. Hester and Sarah resided at the almshouse until the following November, when they disappeared from the list of residents. Hester returned to the almshouse on January 27, 1849, without Sarah and remained there through July 29, 1849, when she left for a short period. After returning on December 19, 1849, Hester continued to reside at the almshouse into July 1852, when she again departed with her son William, who was born during her stay. Hester Meeds's actions suggest that she saw the almshouse as a secure place where she could seek assistance during her most vulnerable moments. While Hester Meeds sought the shelter and benefits provided by the almshouse, other free people of color in Queen Anne's County requested public assistance to acquire such necessities as food and clothing. On several occasions during the 1850s, Nancy Emory, Emanuel Richards, Betty White, William Hemsely, and James Paca all obtained food rations from the overseers of the poor. In addition to food, most of these individuals also depended on the overseers for rations of fabric and shoes.[14]

As the nineteenth century progressed, segregated religious services became increasingly common in the South. Yet generations of operating within shared religious spaces did not break down instantly. Free people of color continued to attend churches with whites, and in many communities, shared churches were the only formal option available. Worshipping in the same churches with whites likely provided comfort and familiarity for many free persons of color. At the same time, these churches also offered free people of color protection from suspicion at a time when state laws limited the ability of free people of color to worship together without supervision from whites. Free people of color in Person County, North Carolina, proceeded to join Bethel Hill Baptist Church and attend services there throughout the antebellum years. Like many southern churches of the time, white men were the top administrators in the church and controlled most church business. Yet for free people of color, the church supplied religious community, a baseline for proper social decorum, and a space to settle disputes between neighbors outside of the courtroom. Bethel Hill provided Bird Sheppard and William Epps with the opportunity and space to reconcile after the two free men of color had a disagreement. With the support of fellow church members, Sheppard and Epps "talked the matter over and got fully satisfied with each other." In 1837, the church became a space for Drury A. Harris, a white man, and Allen Epps, a free man of color, to sort out their differences. Harris had accused Epps of "telling an untruth." After discussing their grievances with a committee of church members, the parties concluded that their conflict was based on "a misunderstanding." Both retained their memberships in the church.[15]

Many white ministers, in particular, maintained ties with free people of color in their communities, who depended on them to perform baptisms and weddings and offer religious guidance. In some parts of the South at this time, white ministers or other white officials were the only people legally sanctioned to perform such tasks. As in earlier years, members of the French-speaking population of free people of color in Louisiana commonly sought white ministers of Catholic churches to perform their weddings. In 1852, Louis Valcour Boute and Marguerite Elizabeth Plique secured the Reverend F. Masson, a white Catholic priest, to wed them in New Orleans. The Reverend P. Alexandre presided over the union of Dorsin Sabatier and Francoise Lamamiere at the church of

Notre Dame de Bon Secours of the same city in 1859.[16] During the 1850s, William T. McElroy, a white Presbyterian minister, traveled through Kentucky marrying couples and baptizing children and adults, including many free people of color. McElroy presided over the Mercer County wedding of Spy Meaux and Elizabeth Meaux, whom he described as "free negroes," on March 8, 1855. McElroy recorded in his diary that "about 50 or 60 free blacks" attended the wedding and that he and two witnesses were the only white people at the affair. This situation, however, did not seem to bother McElroy. After the ceremony, he ate dinner with the wedding party and received two dollars for his services. The next year, McElroy returned to Mercer County to join together Vance W. Meaux and Susan Mary Meaux, both free persons of color. In addition to officiating marriages, performing baptisms was part of McElroy's mission. On June 20, 1858, while presiding over his church in the town of Paris, McElroy baptized Samuel Richardson, the adopted son of Rachel Brest, a free woman of color.[17]

Some southern newspapers recognized the contributions of free people of color to their communities and sought to document the appreciation that a wide swath of the public held for these respected individuals. In an 1850 obituary for George Wells, "a free man of color" and minister of the Second Colored Baptist Church in Louisville, Kentucky, a local newspaper explained that Wells "left numerous friends, both white and black, to mourn his loss." The paper testified further that Wells's "orderly and Christian like course, caused all who knew him, to like him."[18] Following the death of James Scott, "a free negro" known throughout Tennessee and Kentucky as "Old Scott, the Fiddler," a Clarksville, Tennessee, newspaper printed a memorial that honored the life of this beloved musician. The paper explained that Scott was "one of the best fiddlers in the country, and twenty years ago was an indispensable feature at all the frolics in town and country." It went on to describe Scott as "a man of strong natural sense" who "had acquired considerable intelligence, and a very polite manner."[19]

Free people of color were important customers for white business owners who depended on them to keep their enterprises in motion. Through cash payments, trade, and barter, free people of color purchased a variety of goods from their white neighbors' businesses. In 1832, several of the customers at William O'Neale's business in Montgomery County, Maryland, were free persons of color who procured an assortment of processed and manufactured goods. William Meshires purchased cotton yarn, calico, shoes, and pantaloons from O'Neale. O'Neale received both cash and eggs in return for the goods. Milly Offutt paid cash for a pair of shoes, cotton goods, silks, and check fabric.[20] Free people of color were frequent customers at the Libertytown Store in Frederick County, Maryland. Their names appeared on nearly every page of the ledger kept by the store clerk during the late 1850s. William Key and Lidia Carter both purchased fine hats from the Libertytown Store, while Charles White, Lewis Asberry, and Upton Todd each procured such alcoholic beverages as peach brandy, old rye, and rum.[21] Between 1859 and 1860, free people of color in Nansemond County, Virginia, regularly conducted business with Augustus H. Holland, a white merchant. On multiple occasions, Morris Hare purchased foodstuffs like bacon and molasses from Augustus H. Holland. Susan Boon, Moses Boon, and William Holland all bought footwear. Latisha Howell's account with Augustus H. Holland included payments for kersey and calico fabrics, flour, fish, whiskey, and a pair of shoes. Armecy Boon purchased homespun cloth, flannel, check fabric, an apron, spool, thread, soap, and flour at Holland's store.[22]

Free people of color commonly provided business to white doctors in their communities and relied upon these individuals to prescribe medications, perform surgeries, and give care following injuries or during sickness. John T. Lewter of Hertford County, North Carolina, regularly saw free people of color as patients. They were an important part of Lewter's practice in a county where the majority of inhabitants were persons of color and approximately one in five free inhabitants was a free person of color. In 1857, Benjamin Reynolds, a free man of color, paid Lewter for medications provided for his wife and daughter. The next year, records indicate that Benjamin Reynolds paid Lewter to perform surgery on his wife, Mary, in order to remove a tumor from her breast. That same year, Willis Melton, a free man of color, called on Lewter to attend his son John, who had broken his arm. Lewter set the broken limb and received ten dollars for his work.[23] Free people of color were a much smaller part of the population in Berkeley County, Virginia. Still, James P. Carter, a white doctor in the village of Gerrardstown, depended on the county's free people of color for business. On at least eight occasions in 1857, Carter visited and provided medication to William Cole, a free man of color. Cole paid Carter between one dollar and a dollar and seventy-five cents per visit. Later that year, Samuel Wells, a "free colored" man, called on Carter to attend a childbirth for a member of his household. Carter billed Wells five dollars for his services. The next year, Carter returned to the Wells family for a visit and to administer medication to a child.[24]

Significant financial assets allowed well-to-do free people of color to draw white people into dependent relationships with them. In some cases, free people of color with substantial resources became the creditors and landlords of their white neighbors. William Johnson of Natchez, Mississippi, a successful barber, became a creditor to several white men. From the 1830s to his death in 1851, he issued loans of up to one thousand dollars to white businessmen and his barbershop patrons. Johnson also invested in real estate and rented his properties to white business owners. His buildings hosted shopkeepers, doctors, fruit sellers, and local militiamen. Some of the savviest members of this affluent group of free people of color used their financial assets as a way to assert power within a system that largely excluded them from formal politics. William Johnson donated money to political causes that he believed supported his long-term interests. In 1845, he contributed one dollar to a celebration in honor of the U.S. annexation of Texas. He did not donate because he cared deeply about Texas becoming part of the United States. Instead, Johnson sided with the most popular cause, a position likely to benefit him politically and ultimately economically in the longer term. He explained, "I am always re[a]dy for Anything. I would have Given the Same Amount of money to have fired for the Defeat of the Texas An[n]exation."[25] Writing in 1858, Cyprian Clamorgan, a Saint Louis, Missouri, barber, stated that free people of color in his community were "not idle spectators" even if they had "no voice in the elections." He explained that landlords of color often compelled their white tenants to vote according to their interests. Free persons of color also used their position as customers to pressure certain merchants who were dependent on their business. These free people of color also gained sway by offering financial contributions to favored candidates.[26] As Clamorgan made clear, the franchise was not the only path to political influence.

White organized labor ramped up attacks on free people of color and tried to exclude them from parts of the southern economy. Yet in many areas of the South, white participants found themselves economically dependent on the contributions of free people of color. The number of free people of color involved in the mechanisms of production in the South only increased over time. White business owners depended on free people of color as laborers and craftspeople. A minority of free people of color owned their own farms, however, and some produced enough goods to move beyond the confines of subsistence farming. As in past generations, the region's free people of color continued to perform an assortment of skilled trades and provided their neighbors with important work and a variety of goods.

The number of free people of color participating in the skilled trades grew in many parts of the South during the decades preceding the Civil War. Free persons of color continued to serve their communities as barbers, producers of clothing and shoes, blacksmiths, carpenters, nurses, and experts of the culinary arts. Entrepreneurial free persons of color expanded old establishments and opened new ones. Several business people of color rented stalls at the city market in Annapolis, Maryland, during the 1830s, including Benjamin Toogood, who rented a provisions bench, and Thomas Burley, who leased a fish bench. By the 1840s, Thomas Cuff of Chestertown, Maryland, had developed a regionwide reputation for a brand of corn commonly known as "Cuff corn." One local paper described Cuff's product as "a very good corn, with white flinty grain."[27] Sarah Davis ran a highly successful boardinghouse in the Creek Nation. By lodging and entertaining travelers, traders, and government agents visiting Indian Territory, Davis accumulated an estate that included a house with seven rooms, several horses, livestock, and an orchard. This was quite a fortune for a woman who was once enslaved. Antoine Labadie, a Saint Louis, Missouri, butcher, found great success by expanding his business to export cattle into the southern markets. Joseph and Richard E. Dereef of Charleston, South Carolina, transformed themselves into successful dealers and processors of wood. Labadie as well as the Dereefs were worth many thousands of dollars by 1860. Brothers Eugène and Daniel Warbourg were respected marble sculptors in New Orleans. They produced busts, statues, and tombstones. Eugène received contracts to perform work for the Saint Louis Cathedral as well as for local hotels. Government agencies depended on the labor and expertise of free people of color to execute a variety of important tasks. Free men of color played an important role in renovations to the North Carolina governor's mansion in Raleigh. Allen Jones and Henry I. Patterson, free men of color, were among the craftsmen hired to repair the executive mansion in 1836 and 1837. During the 1850s, Solomon G. Brown, a free man of color, began his tenure as an assistant at the Smithsonian Institution in the District of Columbia. His early duties at the museum included arranging and maintaining furniture and constructing cases for exhibits. Over time, his responsibilities increased to managing Smithsonian staff, greeting guests, and performing clerical work.[28]

Many of the antebellum South's export industries depended on the labor of free people of color to grow and thrive. During the period, North Carolina led the nation in the manufacture of naval stores, and free persons of color found their place in the production boom. By 1860, Wilson Jacobs, James Lacewell, and Hardy Young, all free men of color, were producing turpentine from the pine forest of Bladen County. In the same county, Ben Moore worked as a distiller. The tree resins these men and others like them collected and processed became products such as lamp fuel, lubricants, rubber, and soap. The demand for shingles and staves produced from the cypress trees of the South's swamps provided opportunities for free people of color in rural areas. The Dismal Swamp Land Company employed free people of color along with white and enslaved workers from Virginia and North Carolina to produce wooden shingles and staves for export. On several occasions, Joseph Skeeter, the company's white shingle counter, received loads of shingles from free men of color who worked in the Great Dismal Swamp. In February 1852 alone, Skeeter counted deliveries from several free men of color, including Dick and Frank Sawyer, Hardy Read, Patrick Milteer, Dick Jones, and Hardy Boyet. Free men of color who worked as shingle getters commonly employed teams of hired laborers to cut and process trees. Thomas Baker produced shingles with the assistance of a hired workforce composed of runaway slaves who lived in the swamp. The production and shipment of shingles and staves from the swamp required not only the work of the men who transformed trees into marketable goods but also the labor of boatmen, carters, ditch diggers, and repairmen. In 1843, Dick Tynes, a free man of color, received payment from the Dismal Swamp Land Company for repairs to a house owned by the company. Nearly three years later, the company compensated Tynes for eight days' work refurbishing the company's lighters. Luke Ash, a free person of color, received two dollars and fifty cents from the company for five days of work lightering wood in the swamp in 1849. On September 13, 1851, the company paid Minton Folk, a free man of color, thirty dollars for cutting a canal in the swamp.[29]

Throughout the late antebellum years, free people of color who could work in the South's fishery operations were in great demand. Fishery operators searched for and bargained with free people of color who could catch and process fish to be sold to feed the nation's growing demand for cheap, ready-to-eat fish-based products. Free persons of color who labored as watermen such as Harris Miles, Pleasant Harris, Israel Griffin, and Aaron Jonathan kept the fishery at Berkeley Plantation in Charles City County, Virginia, in motion during the 1840s.[30] In 1849, John A. Anderson helped John B. Chesson of Washington, North Carolina, recruit laborers from a nearby county to work in his fishery. Among the hired laborers were Benjamin Weaver and Jesse Reynolds, whom Anderson hired as hands, and Feraby Melton, Barsha Reynolds, Sally Butler, and Velia Bizzell, whom he recruited as fish cutters. The men working as hands received a higher wage than the women laboring as fish cutters, even though the women's work as cutters was actually in greater demand. In a letter to Chesson, Anderson revealed that he had to bargain with the women and offer them incentives in addition to their wages. The demand for workers in the fisheries by the 1850s was so great that James L. Cox and George Wareham, proprietors of a fishery on the Potomac River in Westmoreland County, Virginia, asked the state legislature to loosen restrictions on the immigration of free people of color from other states. After struggling to find hands to work in their fishery for a wage they could afford, Cox and Wareham hoped to bring in free persons of color from Maryland to work for them.[31] As business owners, they were more concerned with obtaining cheap, efficient labor than with upholding the machinations of political extremists. While the fishery operators were not egalitarians, they were unlikely to approve of some of the more extreme plans of proslavery radicals and white supremacists, such as the removal or forced enslavement of free people of color.[32]

The economic significance of certain free people of color continued to motivate white neighbors to support them in a variety of causes. These white neighbors recognized the needs fulfilled by free people of color in their communities and supported efforts to circumvent legal restrictions that affected free persons of color and those who depended on them. In 1852, five white neighbors of Hilary Croom of Wayne County supported Croom's petition for an exemption to North Carolina's immigration laws in part because he was "one of the best blacksmiths we have." Croom faced expulsion from the state after leaving North Carolina to follow his enslaved wife to Alabama and then returning with her and their children after the grace period for free persons of color traveling out of state had lapsed.[33] At the beginning of 1861, a group of seven white Virginians requested immunity from the state's residency law for James Walden, "a free negro formerly a resident of North Carolina." They pointed to Walden's work as a "fireman" on the "Stationary Engine" of the Danville Railroad as part of their rationale for seeking the exemption. The petitioners further explained that Walden was "noted for industry, honesty and faithful and assiduous attention to his business" and that "his removal would be a loss—as his place is hard to supply."[34] Lawmakers did not always react positively to the requests of community members hoping to protect valued free people of color. These petitions, nevertheless, demonstrate the real importance of free people of color in some localities of the South. They also reveal that some white people, even at the peak of extremist attacks against free persons of color, still maintained the ability to judge their neighbors of color beyond a simplistic racial hierarchy.

The range of work that free people of color performed in southern communities produced a wide variety of economic outcomes during the late antebellum years. Wealth disparities had existed among free persons of color since the colonial days. Changes within the southern and national economies, however, created unprecedented levels of wealth that caused wider gaps between the poor and the well-to-do. Most free people of color worked regularly for their subsistence but never obtained the most basic markers of wealth. The majority of the South's free persons of color remained landless and possessed limited personal property. Working as farm laborers, seamstresses, and washers, they rarely earned an income sufficient to climb out of poverty. Recently emancipated persons enjoyed important legal rights unavailable to enslaved people, but they often lacked the highly sought skills held by many artisans and therefore struggled to move far beyond the lowly conditions they experienced in slavery. The economic expansion of the late antebellum period left many free people of color behind but provided great opportunities for some. Those free persons of color who were well connected, owned farms, or practiced skilled trades stood to benefit from the boom times. While radical lawmakers attacked their legal rights, some of the South's free people of color gradually ascended up the economic ladder. On the eve of the Civil War, the number of landholding free persons of color in certain parts of the South was actually on the rise.[35]

The opportunities that granted wealth to the South's white elites often provided for the region's most prosperous free people of color. The exploitation of slave labor in plantation and business settings, land speculation, and inheritances acquired from white progenitors seeded the status of the South's elite free persons of color. Although the vast majority of southern planters were white men, the prosperity associated with the cultivation of cash crops and exploitation of enslaved laborers was not confined to them. Like their white peers, some free people of color discovered that they could reach elite status by operating their own plantations. The Deep South, where slavery was most entrenched, was home to a small minority of the South's free people of color. Nevertheless, most of the region's most successful free persons of color lived in the Deep South and benefited from the concentrations of wealth and investment found there. Eighty-eight percent of free people of color with real estate valued at five thousand dollars or more lived in the Deep South states. Louisiana's landholding free persons of color had the highest average real estate property values among free people of color living in the South in 1850 and 1860. The average was propped up by free persons of color such as Antoine Dubuclet and Zacharie Honore of Iberville Parish, Auguste Donato of Saint Landry Parish, Joseph Cavelier of Jefferson Parish, and Andrew Durnford of Plaquemines Parish, all planters with estimated property values in the tens of thousands of dollars. Landowning free persons of color in Mississippi and South Carolina were also near the top of the list.[36]

Building Institutions

Following the Nat Turner Rebellion, lawmakers in several locales across the South had attempted to restrict the growth of institutions controlled by people of color, specifically churches and schools. Despite these reactionary efforts, free people of color throughout the region, particularly in areas where they resided in large concentrations, continued to seek educational opportunities for their children, fight to retain some control over their institutions of worship, and create organizations that provided socialization and protected their welfare.

During the early 1830s, radicals in such states as Virginia, Delaware, and North Carolina used the Turner rebellion as an opportunity to push through restrictions on ministers of color and limit the right of people of color to practice their religions free from white supervision. Yet free people of color across the South, most notably in the Upper South, responded to the challenge with vigor. As a result, the last three decades before the Civil War were years of development for religious institutions operated by the South's free people of color. At the same time that their opponents ramped up efforts to strip them of their legal and political rights and denigrate their social position, free people of color made significant efforts to obtain some semblance of control over their spiritual lives and the political power embedded in the hierarchies of religious organizations.

Many free people of color and their enslaved associates sought autonomy through the creation of their own religious institutions. Throughout the antebellum period, however, numerous free people of color decided to seek a measure of power within white-dominated churches. The churches' white powerbrokers in conjunction with southern laws generally prevented free persons of color from obtaining the highest offices within these religious institutions. Nevertheless, free people of color and their enslaved brethren negotiated for control of their affairs. Some southern churches, accordingly, included separate meetings and services for people of color and whites. Other establishments permitted people of color to have their own church leaders, such as deacons and moderators, and separate church organizations. Free persons of color and enslaved people also controlled their membership by deciding who could join their churches and who should be excluded.

Churches for persons of color could be found throughout the South by 1860, especially in the Upper South. Some of these congregations included both free and enslaved members, while others had memberships composed exclusively of free people of color. Baltimore, the city with the largest population of free persons of color in the nation, hosted at least fifteen churches for persons of color in 1858. The city's people of color belonged to several denominations, including African Methodist Episcopal, Presbyterian, Protestant Episcopal, Methodist Episcopal, and Baptist. People of color in Washington, District of Columbia, could choose among nine congregations and five denominations: Wesleyan, African Methodist Episcopal, Baptist, Methodist Episcopal, and Presbyterian. Nashville, Tennessee, hosted one Baptist, one Christian, and two Methodist congregations of color. Norfolk, Virginia, had three Baptist churches and one Methodist Episcopal church for people of color. Richmond, Virginia, was the home to three "African" Baptist churches. Even some rural communities with significant populations of free people of color had separate churches for parishioners of color. In 1849, a group of free men of color purchased land from their Quaker neighbors to build a Methodist Episcopal church in rural Caroline County on Maryland's Eastern Shore. By the early 1850s, over one hundred free people of color worshipped at Pleasant Plains Baptist Church, which was for the exclusive use of free persons of color in Hertford County, North Carolina.[37]

Like previous generations of free people of color and enslaved persons, the founders of churches for people of color organized their institutions in order to increase their participation in church affairs but also in reaction to white Christians' increasing unwillingness to give them an equal voice. Numerous churches permitted whites, free people of color, and enslaved persons to share the same sanctuaries. Nevertheless, each category of people had disparate influence within their congregations. Whites could interfere in the activities of persons of color, but free people of color and enslaved persons had little to no power over their white brethren. First Baptist Church in the District of Columbia experienced two mass exoduses of members of color during the antebellum years. After dealing with discrimination from white members throughout much of the decade, a group of thirty persons of color under the leadership of William Butler and Sampson White left the church in 1839. New members of color joined First Baptist after the exodus, but members of color, both new and old, began to conduct various facets of church business separately from their white brethren. In 1857, Paul Jennings, a man formerly held in bondage by James and Dolley Madison, guided most of the church's remaining members of color out of the congregation to form a new church. This exodus left only a small group of older members of color within the mother institution. In 1841, John F. Cook led a group of the District of Columbia's people of color out of the white-run Presbyterian churches. Cook and his followers issued a statement citing the discrimination they experienced in these congregations. They complained, "From circumstances over which we have no control [we] do not enjoy in our white churches, all the privileges that we desire" and described their ability to have influence in their old churches as "feeble" and largely "destroyed."[38] The fight for self-determination and the desire to release themselves from the clutch of bigotry went hand in hand. People sought autonomy not simply as a symbol of racial pride but in reaction to race-based discrimination.

In places like the District of Columbia, Maryland, and Kentucky, free people of color successfully established religious organizations over which they maintained almost full autonomy. The African Methodist Episcopal church, from its foundations, sought to empower people of color at a time when whites challenged their rights within mixed congregations. When a group of free men of color organized the African Methodist Episcopal Church of Fredericktown in 1835, they explicitly wrote in their church charter that "none shall be eligible as trustees except freemen descendants of Africans."[39] This statement protected their church from outside influence. It also preserved the members' autonomy within a greater religious landscape in Maryland in which whites often denied free persons of color the opportunity to control church business.

Unlike members of the African Methodist Episcopal church, people of color within the South's Baptist churches maintained various degrees of affiliation with their white Christian brethren. Some of these "African" or "Colored" Baptist churches had white pastors and representatives, but the members of the First Colored Baptist Church in Louisville, Kentucky, worked hard to assert and defend their independence while still occasionally affiliating with the white Baptists in their city. Members of the First Colored Baptist Church sustained a relationship with the white-run First Baptist Church in Louisville in order to protect themselves "from molestation in times of excitement and save them from present or future laws prohibiting assemblies of slaves in certain cases." In 1844, the membership reasserted its wish to remain under the protection of a standing committee of white brethren, but only under "the expressed understanding that the existence of such a committee shall in no way whatever impair the independence and rights of the Colored Baptist Church, as a legally constituted, Regular Baptist Church."[40]

Laws that prevented people of color from pastoring their own churches without white supervision limited the autonomy of many congregations.

Still, the benefits of having their own churches in which they could serve in positions of power, such as on deacons' boards and boards of trustees, gave free people of color greater authority than they could find in most of the South's mixed congregations. In the majority of mixed congregations, whites occupied all the positions of power; meanwhile, free people of color had no opportunity to vote on the most basic matters of church business. By 1851, Charleston, South Carolina, had just two sites of public worship exclusively for people of color, and both of them were led by white men. Ministers Paul Trapier and John B. Adger presided over the Colored Episcopal Church and Colored Presbyterian Church, respectively.[41] In Lynchburg, Virginia, the white-run First Baptist Church frequently interfered in the regular operations of the African Baptist Church, a congregation of color. Members of the African Baptist Church had their own sanctuary and deacons, and they had the right to control applications for membership. Both men and women could vote as part of the approval process for applications to join the church. Yet a committee composed of white members from the First Baptist Church maintained broad oversight of the African Baptist Church's affairs. Members of the committee had the right to adjudicate disputes involving deacons of the African Baptist Church. The white oversight committee, in consultation with the larger First Baptist Church congregation, controlled the amendment process for the African Baptist Church's constitution. That constitution called for a white Baptist pastor to minister to the African Baptist Church and required that the pastor and at least two members of the oversight committee attend "every meeting for business" of the congregation of color. The pastor and committee also dictated the process of selecting delegates to represent the church at meetings of the Baptist association.[42]

During the late antebellum period, free people of color and their churches hosted a variety of events that fostered connections between congregations and their neighbors. Baptisms attracted longtime church members, new members, and individuals from outside the main church family. For several days in March 1849, John Berry Meachum, a free man of color and pastor of the First African Church in Saint Louis, Missouri, and officials for the North Colored Church of the same city, hosted baptisms at Chouteau's Pond. People of color as well as whites attended the events. Of those baptized, most were people of color, but the ministers also anointed a small number of German and Dutch converts.[43] Church fairs were an important way for free people of color and their fellow parishioners to raise funds and build connections with their neighbors. During the summer of 1854, members of Saint Louis's Second Colored

Church held a fair to build community support for their congregation and pay off the church's debts. A local paper encouraged "white faces to make them [members of the Second Colored Church] a call, not only for the luxury of eating and drinking, but of doing good."[44] In 1856, the women of the District of Columbia's Zion Wesley Church hosted a fair, which combined church affairs with a greater social activist agenda. Their advertisement for the fair promised that "every thing usual at such festivities is for sale" and contended that "no one of any color, visiting it with a proper end in view, can fail to be greatly pleased with the proof it embraces of the comfortable situation and laudable ambition of the mass of the large colored population of the federal city."[45] The women of Zion Wesley Church sought not only to raise funds but also to demonstrate the significance of people of color to the prosperity of their city in a time when radical proslavery and white supremacist voices argued for their removal.

Around their churches, free people of color built social organizations that encouraged fraternity and nurtured important connections among them as well as between them and their home communities. They created a host of benevolent organizations charged with improving their communities and fulfilling their faith obligations. The Benevolent Daughters' Society of Louisiana was a New Orleans–based organization that raised funds for the African Methodist Church during the 1850s. Elizabeth A. Parsons and Celestine Thoroughgood, both free women of color, served as the group's president and secretary, respectively.[46] In the District of Columbia, Daniel A. Payne, as a representative of the African Methodist Episcopal Church, organized a cross-denominational alliance with the ministers of the Presbyterian Church and Zion's Church. Together they operated as the city's first pastoral association for ministers of color.[47]

For many free people of color, the church was the center of political life in a region in which they had limited voice in local, state, and federal governments. Churches played an important role in adjudicating personal disputes and defining social decorum. Members of the First African Baptist Church of Richmond, Virginia, sanctioned their fellow parishioners for an assortment of violations. On August 6, 1848, the church excluded Kitty Ball, a free woman of color, and her enslaved husband, Lewis Ball, for "conjugal discord" after the two had separated and "fallen into difficulties." The church removed three free women of color from its membership for various offenses on January 7, 1850. The congregation excluded Adeline Freeman for "lying," Milly Harris for "quarreling," and Polly Johnson for committing "adultery." Even Gilbert Hunt, a well-respected free man of color and deacon of the church, incurred

Daniel A. Payne eventually rose to become a bishop in the African Methodist Episcopal church. Before reaching the peak of his career, he served as a teacher in his native city of Charleston, South Carolina, as well as in Baltimore. Payne was also active in many local organizations, including one of Baltimore's burial societies. Toward the end of his life, he published an autobiography and a history of the African Methodist Episcopal church. (Courtesy of the Smithsonian Institution)

scrutiny for an alleged violation. In 1849, a church committee launched an investigation into Hunt's attempt to influence church trustees in secret and beyond the purview of the church body. Following the investigation, the committee suspended Hunt "from the privileges of an officer" and demanded his apology. After six months, Hunt capitulated and presented the church with a written apology.[48] These cases demonstrate the efforts of church leaders and their followers to define the limits of acceptable social behavior and control the internal affairs of the church. Although Richmond's First African Baptist Church was not free from the influence of white Baptists, the church did afford its membership, both free and enslaved, greater autonomy and agency. The church as an institution also helped to vet community leaders and placed individuals on a path to greater political influence.

In the Catholic churches of the South, free people of color and whites attended services together, and the church permitted whites to stand as godparents to children of color. Beyond these basic acts, however, the Catholic Church limited the ability of free people of color and whites to interact as equals. As a result, some free people of color, who were unwilling to break off completely from the church, pushed for separate organizations under the Catholic order. The Oblate Sisters of Providence was among the earliest Catholic orders for free women of color. Father James Hector Nicholas Joubert de la Muraille, a white minister, and Elizabeth Clarisse Lange, a free woman of color and native of Saint-Domingue, established the order in Baltimore, with education as its explicit purpose. In 1842, Henriette Delille, Juilette Gaudin, and Josephine Charles, all free women of color, organized the first order for free women of color in New Orleans. This order would eventually be known as the Sisters of the Holy Family. Under Delille's leadership, these Catholic sisters established multiple asylums for women as well as for the aged and sickly. They also founded a convent.[49] By 1860, thirty persons of color had organized themselves as the Society of Saint Benedict the Moor at Saint Augustine, Florida. The members tasked themselves with promoting "morality and piety among the colored men" and encouraging religious education.[50]

Although Christianity in its various forms was the dominant religious worldview among free people of color, a small number developed religious communities around alternative ideas. By the 1850s, spiritualism, a religion in which followers believed that they could converse with the dead, developed a following among the Francophone community in Louisiana. In 1858, Henry Louis Rey, François Dubuclet, and J. B. Valmour led a group of French-speaking free persons of color in establishing the Cercle Harmonique. These individuals had encountered spiritualism in settings that included whites and people of color but decided to create a religious community of their own. Members of the Cercle Harmonique were mostly men, but a few women also joined. Their approach to religion was much more egalitarian than the Catholicism that dominated their families' pasts. They claimed to speak with the spirits of people ranging from political leaders to family members.[51]

Despite the radicals' attack on the education of people of color in the South, especially following the Nat Turner Rebellion, free people of color only amplified their demands for greater access to formal education. Education became increasingly important for the South's free people of color, just as it had for white southerners, who were more willing than ever to support public education for white children. Successful free people of color, in conjunction with religious institutions and white allies, advocated for and established schools for free children of color across the South. Free persons of color and whites tutored children of color in private homes and small schoolhouses. In the face of an increasingly hostile political environment, some of these educators reached beyond a rudimentary curriculum to provide their students with a progressive education.

Religious organizations operated by people of color played a pertinent role in the movement to educate the South's free children of color. Free people of color through their religious institutions supported schools in such locales as Baltimore, the District of Columbia, Louisville, Kentucky, and Nashville, Tennessee. In Baltimore, the African Methodist Episcopal Church operated schools for free people of color. During his tenure at the city's Bethel Church in the 1840s, Daniel A. Payne began tutoring a small group of children in response to a request from one of his parishioners. Other requests followed, and Payne soon found himself teaching approximately fifty pupils. For two years, Payne tutored Baltimore's children in English, Greek, and Latin in addition to providing religious instruction. The African Methodist Episcopal Church offered further instruction to Baltimore's children following Payne's efforts. In Louisville, the African Methodist Episcopal Church and the city's Baptist churches for people of color sponsored schools that educated the city's children of color.[52]

Free people of color found opportunities for education through the efforts of the Catholic Church. Often the exertions of free people of color within the institution pushed the church in certain locations to champion education for free persons of color. The free women of color who comprised the Oblate Sisters of Providence provided free children of color in Baltimore and the surrounding area with some of the best educational opportunities available in the region. Beginning in 1828, Father Joubert employed the Oblate Sisters of Providence to operate the School for Colored Girls in Baltimore. The school's pupils undertook coursework in English, French, mathematics, and sewing. The order and its mission, as well as the school and its curriculum, continued to grow through the antebellum years. Eventually known as the Saint Frances School for Colored Girls, the school became a favorite destination for the daughters of the region's more affluent families of color. During the 1850s, the Oblate Sisters of Providence also organized a school for boys, the Saint Frances Male School.[53]

Although religious institutions played an important role in the establishment of educational facilities for people of color, some free people of color adopted the task of educating the South's children of color independently of the churches. With community support, these free people of color assumed the educational work that southern public schools failed to provide. Between 1830 and 1860, John H. Fleet, John Thomas Johnson, Charles H. Middleton, Thomas Mason, Eliza Anne Cook, and Annie E. Washington were among the free people of color educating children in the District of Columbia. In 1855, Rufus Conrad taught the children of Nashville, Tennessee.[54] John S. Stanly of New Bern, North Carolina, educated the children of his community as well as those who traveled from other parts of the state to receive a formal education. John P. Green, a student of Stanly's during the 1850s, recalled, "As a reader, speller and penman," Stanly "was not surpassed; and in all the studies, pertaining to a thorough English education, he was the equal of the best."[55]

With the support of free people of color in their communities, a small cadre of progressive white people strove to expand educational opportunities for the South's free people of color. Primarily northerners who ventured to the South for the explicit purpose of helping people of color, these whites developed relationships with the free people of color in their adopted communities. Together, they worked to fulfill their benevolent objectives and overcome the obstacles imposed by southern lawmakers and vigilantes who attacked their efforts to educate the South's people of color, free and enslaved. At the African School in Wilmington, Delaware, J. W. Adams taught free children of color. Adams believed that "no natural obstruction" existed "to the improvement of coloured children" in Wilmington "than anywhere else or than white children provided they have in every respect an equal opportunity." During the 1830s, he provided instruction in elementary subjects such as the alphabet and basic writing skills as well as more advanced topics like arithmetic, geography, and English grammar.⁵⁶ Harriet Peck, a white Quaker woman from the North, instructed free persons of color at a school in Guilford County, North Carolina, during the late 1830s. Free people of color, both adults and children, traveled, in some cases miles, to receive lessons from Peck. She observed that many of her school's pupils were destitute, and yet they attended in spite of their struggles. Some students arrived without appropriate attire for the season, while others attended class without having anything to eat for the entire school day.⁵⁷

Myrtilla Miner, another white northern transplant, taught a slightly more advantaged group of free girls of color in the nation's capital during the late antebellum period. Miner was a woman with strong antislavery convictions who believed that women were best suited to go into the South and educate people of color. Unlike men, Miner argued, women were less likely to incite violent reactions from the proslavery vigilantes. She founded her school in the District of Columbia in 1851. Although she was based in the South, Miner provided her students with a progressive curriculum that included lessons about the antislavery cause and the accomplishments of women in history.⁵⁸ In 1852, Mary Victoria Cook, a free girl of color and one of Miner's students, completed an essay on Mary Lyon, the founder of Mount Holyoke Female Seminary, which later became Mount Holyoke College.⁵⁹ The young women at Miner's school learned to use the written word to challenge white supremacist and proslavery ideologies. Reflecting on her educational experience, Mary Brent, another of Miner's students, wrote to her teacher, "I have thought though men enslave the body yet they cannot enslave the mind and prevent it from thinking. When we have obtained our complete Education I hope we may use well the means God has given us and not desire the favour of men rather than God."⁶⁰ After reading about the possibility of providing enslaved people with a Christian education, Miner's pupil M. A. Beckett explained to her teacher: "I think the slaves need the Bible as a necessary means of salvation and we should teach them to search the scriptures as one of the commands of Christ." Challenging the many acts that prohibited enslaved people from receiving any literacy education, including learning to read the Bible, Beckett continued, "I think that no government or class of men has a right to make a law to hinder any human being from receiving and reading the Bible. Giving the Bible to any class is the best means of preparing the way for the elevation."⁶¹

Without public funding, schools for free people of color required donations and fundraisers to keep them in operation. Myrtilla Miner's school in the District of Columbia received donations from contributors across the country, including many northern antislavery activists.

Support organizations for Catholic schools such as Saint Peter's Colored School and the Saint Frances Male School in Baltimore held sales and fairs to raise money. The steamer *Relief* hosted an afternoon cruise featuring live music, supper, confectionery, and ice cream to support the Colored School on Biddle Street in the same city.[62]

Affluent free people of color played important roles in the movement to provide children of color with formal education in the antebellum period. Their financial support, in particular, was essential. Marie Couvent of New Orleans, a free woman of color and native of West Africa, made a significant donation at the time of her death to establish a school for orphaned free children of color in her city. After years of legal battles over Couvent's last testament, her executor and other advocates helped to staff and construct the Catholic Institute for Indigent Orphans, a school for girls and boys of color. François Lacroix, a free man of color and successful tailor in the city, along with other benevolent members of the community, continued to support the school and its mission. Under the leadership of Felicie Cailloux, a free woman of color and the school's first teacher, Couvent's dream to educate New Orleans's free children of color became reality. The school's students studied writing, oratory, and mathematics. In the late 1850s, they deliberated about important issues of the time, including migration to Mexico and Haiti, U.S. imperial aspirations in Central America, and racial discrimination.[63]

Although free people of color were successful in establishing schools for their children in various parts of the South, they encountered difficulties securing the advanced training offered by colleges and universities for their children. A few Native students from Indian Territory attended southern institutions of higher learning during the antebellum period, but these educational centers primarily served whites. Free persons of color with the financial means looked north and abroad to provide their youth with advanced education. The wealthy Louisiana planter Andrew Durnford sent his son Thomas to Lafayette College in Easton, Pennsylvania. John Patterson Sampson, the son of James D. Sampson, a successful Wilmington, North Carolina, businessman, graduated from Comer's College in Boston, Massachusetts, in 1856. Benjamin Kellogg Sampson, another son of James D. Sampson, attended Oberlin College in Ohio and graduated in 1860. Some of New Orleans's elite free people of color received their educations in France, including Norbert Rillieux, an inventor, and Joseph Chaumette and Louis Charles Roudanez, who both became doctors.[64]

Beyond organizing churches and supporting schools, the South's free people of color founded a variety of other organizations to fulfill their

John Patterson Sampson, a native of Wilmington, North Carolina, was the son of James D. Sampson, a successful businessman. His father's achievements provided him with the opportunity to seek advanced education, and in 1856 he graduated from Comer's College in Boston. Following his graduation, Sampson adopted many pursuits, including teaching, preaching, politics, editing, and the law. (Courtesy of the Library of Congress)

needs. Creating spaces and means for the burial of their dead was a priority for some free people of color during the decades preceding the Civil War. Free people of color living in rural areas typically buried their deceased loved ones in family cemeteries located on their own farms or those of relatives and friends. Free persons of color who lived in urban environments, however, needed more centralized locations to serve as burial grounds. Some cities provided segregated areas for the removal of the dead or permitted free people of color to bury their relatives and friends in the local potter's field.[65] In other parts of the South, free people of color adopted the task of establishing their own cemeteries; they also created burial societies to sell plots and care for the cemeteries. By 1848, a group of twenty-two free men of color and one free woman of color, Sally George, had purchased land for a burial ground in Richmond, Virginia, and organized themselves into the Union Burial Ground Society. The group coalesced in response to "feeling a deep interest in the welfare of our race and the importance of advancing in morality, and believing as we do that the formation of a society for the interment of the dead will exert its due weight of influence." William Lightfoord, James Ellis, and Benjamin Harris served as the inaugural trustees of the society. The society's constitution also provided for a president, vice president, treasurer, secretary, and nine managers.[66] In 1851, Laurel Cemetery opened to serve the needs of Baltimore's people of color and was operated by an executive committee of nine, which included many of the city's most respected free men of color, such as ministers Daniel A. Payne and Darius Stokes.[67]

As in earlier generations, free people of color living during the antebellum period established beneficial societies and fraternal organizations designed to protect their members from poverty, care for them during sickness, and provide for their burial upon death. These organizations also worked to protect the economic and political interests of their members. Free people of color in Baltimore organized several beneficial societies. The Tobias Society, organized by the city's Catholics of color, focused on securing proper burials for its members. The Brothers Immediate Society of Baltimore tasked themselves with meeting the needs of their members who fell sick and securing coffins for deceased members.[68] Under the leadership of James Y. Green and Richard G. Hazle, the well-to-do free people of color of New Bern, North Carolina, organized themselves into a society by the 1840s. Unlike societies such as the Brown Fellowship Society in Charleston, which limited membership to "brown" men, the New Bern elites admitted members of "varying shades of color."[69] The members of the New Bern group met on various occasions to discuss issues important to the common good. In an 1844 meeting, John R. Green offered a resolution in favor of remembering William Gaston, a North Carolina Supreme Court justice and politician, whom Green described as "our generous friend & kind protector."[70] Although excluded from voting after the 1835 state constitutional convention, free people of color used their association as a way to express their political views and demonstrate their support for certain political objectives.

As pressure from white organized labor increased, some beneficial organizations also served as trade guilds for people of color, protecting their interests from the gangs of ruffians who sometimes violently sought to establish white domination in certain fields of employment. In Baltimore, free men of color in the barbering, brickmaking, and caulking trades organized. The barbers unified as the Colored Barbers' Beneficial Society. Several officers led the association, including a president, vice president, secretary, assistant secretary, treasurer, stewards, and a reporting committee.[71] The Colored Caulkers' Association in Baltimore was a particularly important support group for people of color who were actively targeted by white competitors. In addition to providing assistance during conflicts with white organized labor, the Colored Caulkers' Association offered other benefits common to beneficial societies, including burial support.[72]

A small cadre of free people of color, located mostly in the Upper South, participated in formal political activity, both before and after the final disfranchisement of free men of color in the region. They worked among themselves as well as with free people of color from the northern states to protest inequality and battle against radicals' political schemes. In June 1831, free men of color from Maryland, Delaware, and Virginia joined their allies from the northern states in Philadelphia for the First Annual Convention of the People of Color. At the meeting, delegates discussed challenges to their legal oppression and the possibility of founding a college for young men of color.[73] On July 12, 1831, the Reverend Peter Spencer chaired a meeting of people of color in Wilmington, Delaware, to consider the issue of African colonization. Following addresses by prominent free men of color, including Abraham D. Shad, Junius C. Morell, Benjamin Pascal, and John P. Thompson, members of the meeting voted to condemn the colonization movement. In a resolution, they renounced "all connection with Africa" and explained that while they were "the descendants of that much afflicted country, we cannot consent to remove to any tropical climate, and thus aid in a design having for its object the total extirpation of our race from this country."[74] In July 1852, free men of color from Baltimore as well as Kent, Dorchester, Caroline,

Talbot, Harford, and Frederick Counties assembled for the Convention of the Free Colored People of Maryland, which met in Baltimore. Under the leadership of the Reverend William Tasker of Frederick County, the men discussed political and legal topics that affected free people of color in the 1850s. They considered colonization, education policy, the forced separation of children through the apprenticeship system, and discriminatory punishment. The representatives were divided in their support of African colonization, but all agreed that more needed to be done for their children in regard to education. They backed a plan to raise funds to support free schools for "poor and destitute children" and called on religious leaders to mobilize their congregations for the effort.[75]

Societies focused on promoting academic pursuits such as debating, intellectual discussion, reading, and music allowed free people of color to engage with one another over cultural and political topics. Their activities were not necessarily intended to be forms of active resistance against proslavery and white supremacist propaganda. Nonetheless, their ability to form intellectual communities challenged the fundamental principles of their political opponents, who portrayed them as docile and incompetent. Baltimore's free persons of color were leaders in organizing societies for intellectual engagement. In 1838, the Colored Musical Association, under the direction of Richard Bradford, held concerts that included instrumental and vocal performances for the public. The city hosted multiple societies focused on intellectual discussion. The Young Men's Mental Improvement Society formed to deliberate philosophical and moral queries. Some of the city's caulkers of color created the East Baltimore Mental Improvement Society, which hosted debates. The H. H. Webb Mental Improvement Society met several evenings a week to converse, share poetry, and enjoy fine music.[76] Outside of Baltimore, free people of color also found opportunities to pursue their scholarly and cultural interests. The Robertsonian Society in Frederick, Maryland, hosted debates on such questions as "Which is the greatest loss to man—the loss of his country, or the loss of his wife?" and "Which deserves the greatest honor—Columbus for the discovery of America, or Washington for preserving America?" the themes of two debates in 1858.[77]

In the South's urban centers, such as New Orleans, Baltimore, Saint Louis, and the District of Columbia, free men of color, sometimes in conjunction with enslaved persons, organized Masonic lodges.[78] In 1856, the *Evening Star*, a Washington newspaper, described the "lodges of colored Free Masons" in the district as "composed of very respectable colored men well known to our citizens." Although the white Masonic lodges of the South did not recognize these Masons, the paper reported that "at the North ... they are received in fellowship, and it is not unusual for them to visit in the white lodges."[79] Like similar fraternal organizations, the Masons regularly held meetings and socials. On June 25, 1855, the Hiram Lodge, Number 4, of Georgetown, District of Columbia, held a gala for Masons in the district. The event included a speech by John Costin of Washington, a banner presentation by Isabella Brisco, and dinner for approximately 250 guests. The local paper commented, "The whole affair was certainly a very pleasing one, and excellent order, general politeness, and beautiful fraternal feelings that characterized all present, would have done no discredit to many of their more fortunate neighbors of the present day."[80]

The temperance movement of the late antebellum period attracted the attention of a diversity of people, including free people of color. Some free persons of color joined integrated temperance societies, while others formed their own organizations to curb alcohol consumption in their communities. In 1845, the District of Columbia was home to nine temperance societies with an estimated total membership of 2,150. Most were affiliated with local churches, including the African Total Abstinence Society of Georgetown, the largest of these organizations, with approximately five hundred members.[81] By 1841, some people of color in Baltimore had organized themselves into the Colored Temperance Society, which held meetings in the Presbyterian School Room. Seven years later, one of the city's Wesleyan churches hosted a convention of Baltimore's numerous temperance organizations for people of color. Baltimore's temperance associations for people of color did not limit themselves to the issue of removing spirits from the community. They also integrated other causes into their organizational missions. Temperance societies participated in processions for the city's deceased. At an 1851 temperance meeting, Darius Stokes promoted the idea of supporting the establishment of an orphan asylum for Maryland's children of color. In addition, free people of color used the meetings as social outlets. Newspaper coverage of the 1851 meeting in which Stokes advocated for the orphans of Maryland described attendees of the event as "handsomely habited with their different badges of distinction." A band entertained them while they sampled from a table adorned with an assortment of delicacies, including beef tongue, boned turkey on a pedestal, pâté of venison, and oysters.[82]

Fighting Oppression, Defending Our Rights

The agendas of white supremacists and slavery's radical advocates caused more legal trouble for free people of color in the final decades before the

Civil War than in previous years. This onslaught of oppression, however, did not prevent the South's free people of color from trying to establish and protect their rights.

In the courts of the South, free people of color strategically asserted their freedom, their autonomy over their children, and their right to protect themselves. On some occasions, they challenged their white neighbors' abilities to treat them as inferiors by attacking the South's system of racial classification. In the 1857 *Dred Scott v. Sandford* decision, Chief Justice Roger B. Taney suggested that "persons of color ... were not included in the word citizens," contended that they could "claim none of the rights and privileges" provided by the federal Constitution, and denied that the states could gift them nationally accepted citizenship rights. Yet free people of color failed to accept Taney's statement as a true reflection of their status. With the help of white lawyers and white neighbors, free people of color acted as citizens with the basic rights outlined in their nation's founding documents. Even as the southern legal environment became more difficult to navigate, free persons of color persisted in their quest to find justice in an often-unjust system. They did not win every legal battle. Nevertheless, free people of color did find solutions in a less-than-perfect system. Scholars point to the local nature of many southern courts as an explanation for how a system clearly rigged against people of color in many ways still produced favorable outcomes for free persons of color. The courts did not need to go so far as to promote egalitarian principles in order to maintain some sense of peace and consequently support the interests of free people of color.[83]

Although their legal position in most southern states had deteriorated over the course of the century, free people of color still sought out their local and state courts for remedies. Free people of color filed lawsuits to protect their business and financial interests, settle property disputes, and protect themselves from abusive spouses. Through these lawsuits, free people of color asserted their position as legal persons under the law and challenged radical ideas that asserted that they had no legal rights. By coming into the courts to pursue litigation, they acted as citizens and by their actions defied claims that free people of color were outsiders to the body politic. Free persons of color demonstrated their ability to maneuver within southern legal systems that in many ways were structured against their interests.[84]

Free people of color pursued cases against neighbors, both white and of color, whom they charged with violating their bodies or property. After a vicious assault against him that took place in 1847, Augustin, a free man of color, sued eight of his white neighbors in Jefferson Parish, Louisiana, for $2,500 in damages. Augustin testified that the men pinned him down and beat him with "sticks about five feet long, four or five inches wide and two or three inches thick." The injuries from the beating were so severe that Augustin lay in bed "for several weeks in the most desperate condition." The local court sided with Augustin after hearing his case. The defendants appealed up to the Louisiana Supreme Court, where the justices upheld the judgment for Augustin.[85] Between 1850 and 1851, Joseph Locklear, a free man of color, filed a lawsuit to recover a debt from Charles Townsend, one of his white neighbors. After hearing from witnesses and reviewing Townsend's promissory note to Locklear promising reimbursement for twenty-three days of work and "thirteen sticks" of timber, jurors for the Superior Court of Robeson County, North Carolina, ruled in favor of Locklear.[86]

As in previous generations, free people of color continued to approach the courts in order to clarify questions about their freedom status. During the early 1830s, Benjamin Reid waged a battle for his freedom in the Louisiana courts after falling victim to South Carolina's law requiring the jailing of seamen of color. Reid, who was originally from Portsmouth, Virginia, worked as a sailor and traveled from port to port in both the North and South. During a trip to Charleston, South Carolina, Reid was jailed and eventually sent to New Orleans, where several men bought and sold him as a slave. Following more than two years in bondage, Reid's uncle Jasper Reid, who was also a sailor, discovered him in New Orleans. With his uncle's assistance, Reid sued for his freedom. At the trial, Henry William Palfrey, the white man who held Reid as a slave, denied that Reid was a free man. Jasper Reid and another free man of color, John Brady, countered Palfrey's testimony. Jasper Reid explained to the court that Mourning Reid, his sister, was Benjamin Reid's mother and that she was "born free" and "of Indian Extraction." Brady reiterated the points made by Jasper Reid and further explained that Benjamin Reid had served his uncle as an apprentice while living in Norfolk, Virginia, nearby the Reids' hometown of Portsmouth. After hearing the testimony, the court sided with Benjamin Reid.[87] In 1853, a man named Bob came before the court in Alexandria County, Virginia, to complain that J. C. McCracken had "illegally detained" him "as a slave." He explained to the court that his former mistress, Mary Anne Hutchinson of Fairfax County, had manumitted him as part of her will. Yet McCracken and his mistress's administrator, Silas Hutchinson, prevented Bob from claiming his freedom. Following the presentation of evidence, which included a copy of Mary Anne Hutchinson's will, the court sided with Bob and awarded him the cost of his case.[88]

The courts were an important tool for free people of color seeking remediation for domestic matters. In 1858, Keziah Wilson, a free woman of color, petitioned the Circuit Court of Petersburg, Virginia, for a divorce from her husband, Richard H. Wilson. A little more than a decade after her marriage, Keziah learned that her husband was in an adulterous relationship with Mary Ann Clay, a "white woman" and "an inmate and boarder at one of the most notorious houses of prostitution" in Petersburg. According to Keziah's divorce petition, Richard had abandoned his duties to his wife and children and spent what resources he could gather on Clay. Richard's relationship with his mistress ultimately led to a conflict with another man, whom Richard shot. The local court tried Richard for the shooting and sent him to the state penitentiary. Following his imprisonment, Keziah maintained, Richard's "hatred" for her only grew. She had learned from a recently discharged inmate that Richard planned to kill her and take control of their children. The Wilsons' relationship included a long history of abuse. Keziah explained that Richard "beat her with sticks, switches & cowhides, often threatened her life & twice shot at her with his pistol." He also had "driven & pursued her from the house in the night time & compelled her to fly, almost in a state of nakedness to her neighbors for protection," according to Keziah's statement. During the divorce proceedings, witnesses confirmed Keziah's claims of adultery and abuse and also provided endorsements of her fitness as a mother. After reviewing the evidence, the court decided in favor of Keziah, granted her request for a divorce, and bestowed her with full custody of her sons.[89]

Free women of color hauled partners who had gone astray into southern courts where they sought restitution and shared responsibility for the children born to them. By seeking child support from their children's fathers, free women of color not only fought for their welfare and that of their children but also pursued the interests of their communities. Women who sought support from their children's fathers attempted to keep their families financially solvent and therefore off the welfare rolls, a goal shared by local officials across the region. During an 1833 appearance before James B. Peace, a Granville County, North Carolina, constable, Anna Hawley, a "single woman of color," declared that Solomon Anderson, a "free man of colour," was the father of her daughter. Anderson appeared before the lower court of Granville County, which affirmed Hawley's claim of Anderson's paternity and required him to provide "support and maintenance" for the child.[90] In 1852, Stephen Lewis, a "Negro," posted a bond with the Sussex County, Delaware, court after the court determined that he was the father of a male child born to Emeline Johnson, a "mulatto" woman. By winning her case, Johnson gained a court-protected assurance from Lewis that he would provide for their son until the child reached seven years of age.[91]

Local and state courts constituted an essential element in the South's discriminatory legal system. Indeed, local and state officials implemented discriminatory restrictions and punishments through court actions. Still, free people of color regularly used the courts to challenge discriminatory policies and bigoted activities. They were unwilling to cede their states' judiciary systems to the cause of subjugation. In 1836, Isaac N. Carey, a free man of color and barber, battled the Corporation of Washington in the U.S. Circuit Court for the District of Columbia over a discriminatory law preventing him, as a free person of color, from receiving a business license to sell perfume in the nation's capital. After moving through the appeals process, the case reached the bench of Chief Justice William Cranch, who ruled against the Washington ordinance. Cranch explained that "although free colored persons have not the same political rights which are enjoyed by free white persons, yet they have the same civil rights, except so far as they are abridged by the general law of the land. Among those civil rights, is the right to exercise any lawful and harmless trade, business, or occupation." Cranch concluded that the laws governing Washington officials did not give them the "power" to prohibit free people of color from practicing "a trade, business, or occupation."[92] In 1843, Elkaney Cropper emerged victorious when the Virginia Supreme Court reversed a conviction against her. Cropper claimed that the justices in Accomack County had convicted her illegally in a court of oyer and terminer for allegedly stealing a shirt and a pair of socks. She and her counsel argued that the court of oyer and terminer had "no jurisdiction" in petit larceny cases concerning free persons of color and that her imprisonment for the crime was unlawful. The Virginia Supreme Court agreed with Cropper and suggested that a single justice of the peace should have heard her case given that the value of the allegedly stolen items was less than twenty dollars. Cropper and her counsel successfully exploited a loophole in the discriminatory laws of Virginia to obtain a favorable judgment.[93]

Across the South, free people of color and their white associates sought legal remedies for what they thought were injustices or cases of excessive punishment. Even into the late antebellum years, southern governors received petitions from free persons of color and their supporters requesting intervention. These petitions reveal the ability of free people of color to draw on their personal relationships with their neighbors, who were often white, in order to correct what they perceived as miscarriages of justice. Sometimes neighbors believed that the free people of color convicted or facing trial were not at fault for their alleged transgressions. Governor Thomas Watkins Ligon of Maryland received a request to stop the prosecution of Peter Bostick of Cecil County in 1857. The request, signed by Richard Grason, an attorney; Charles W. Benny, a constable; and Tobias Rudulph, explained that Bostick awaited trial for breaking Maryland's residency law, which prohibited free persons of color from leaving the state and returning without official sanction. According to the men, Bostick broke the law after receiving advice from "very respectable gentlemen" who proposed that he leave the state temporarily to escape his wife, a "negro woman" who was "a thief and a perfect termagant." Bostick's defenders promised that he bore "the character of a sober, industrious, honest and well behaved negro." After evaluating the situation, Governor Ligon intervened and quashed the prosecution.[94]

For many free persons of color, the liability associated with court-imposed fines exacerbated their financial struggles. Unable to pay these fines, free people of color pleaded their cases before their governors who they hoped might exercise pardon powers to excuse the potentially detrimental financial burden. In 1832, Kentucky governor Thomas Metcalfe received a petition from Maria Dye, a free woman of color from Mercer County, who was requesting remittance of a court-imposed fine. Dye explained to Governor Metcalfe that after selling "refreshments" at a militia muster in her community, a local magistrate had charged and fined her for illegally selling whiskey. She described herself as "a poor coloured woman with three small children, a slave for her husband, & of good character" and asked the governor to remit the fine before the sheriff arrived to seize her property in lieu of the ten dollars demanded by the court. Appended to the request were the signatures of eighteen of Dye's neighbors, including that of Charles P. Burton, commandant of the battalion that mustered before Dye's prosecution. Burton certified that he "gave leave to Maria Dye together with others to sell cakes, cider & other refreshments at the muster field," a "privilege" which "had always been allowed." Following an opportunity to review the case, Metcalfe rescinded the fine against Dye.[95] In another case, Delaware governor William H. Ross received a petition from George Matthews, a "free negro" convicted during the April 1854 term of Sussex County's Court of General Sessions for gun possession. Matthews asked the governor to remit the fine assessed against him as punishment for his conviction. He contended that he was innocent of the charge and that his conviction depended on the testimony of a sole witness, Cyrus Ward, who "was contradicted by the other witnesses in the case as to the material fact & as to the other facts in the case." Matthews's petition included a declaration from two judges present at the trial who likewise asserted that Ward's testimony was contradictory to other facts presented in the case. Seven additional men signed on to Matthews's petition. The support of the judges and citizens of Sussex County was sufficient to convince the governor to retract Matthews's fine.[96]

Free people of color and their white associates commonly pursued executive clemency in cases involving particularly harsh sentences that threatened the health of convicted persons. In 1840, North Carolina governor Edward B. Dudley pardoned Nicholas Goin, a free man of color, after receiving a petition signed by fifty-eight of Goin's Rockingham County neighbors. The petition also received the endorsement of David S. Reid, R. P. Cardwell, and George D. Boyd, elite men with broad political influence. Goin's supporters explained to the governor that a jury for the Superior Court had convicted Goin of larceny. However, the supporters claimed that the "witnesses" against him "forswore themselves" and that Goin "was not guilty." Moreover, they explained that after two months in confinement, Goin suffered from "rheumatism" and an injury to his chest that he sustained as a result of the whipping he received as part of his punishment.[97] The allies of Ann Shipley, a free woman of color from Howard County, emphasized her physical condition when they approached Maryland governor Thomas Watkins Ligon for a pardon in 1855. On the same day of Shipley's conviction for stealing a coat, the ten jurors who decided the case asked the governor to pardon her. The jurors had convicted Shipley because she admitted to the crime. After they presented their decision, however, the jurors discovered that her admission was the result of "persuasion or other undue influences, which were excluded by the court."[98] They sought clemency based on these grounds but also because of Shipley's good reputation and pregnancy at the time of the conviction. This petition, along with letters of support from other citizens of Howard County that noted Shipley's physical condition and coerced confession, persuaded Governor Ligon to grant a reprieve.[99]

Even after convictions for capital crimes, free people of color and their allies sometimes sought and received executive clemency. Seeking a pardon was the only legal means to save free people of color from death. These cases reveal the efforts of free people of color and their neighbors to preserve their lives under the most serious conditions. They also highlight the ability of southern politicians to act in favor of free people of color despite the possibility of political backlash. Although southern radicals managed to influence some aspects of the political process, instances of clemency exposed the limits of the proslavery and white supremacist agenda. In 1852, North Carolina governor David S. Reid granted a reprieve to William Boon, alias Hussey, a free man of color convicted by a Sampson County court for burglary and the attempted rape of a white woman. Several white people, including key public officials, petitioned Reid on behalf of Boon. After ruling against the appeal of Boon in the state Supreme Court, Justices Thomas Ruffin, Frederick Nash, and Richmond M. Pearson explained that they found "no error" in the process of submitting evidence in the original case. However, when considering the question that they were asked to decide, they found the evidence submitted to be inadequate. The justices described the evidence as "so very slight, inconclusive, and unsatisfactory . . . as not to authorize the conviction." Viewing Boon as "fit" for a pardon, they contended that "no human being ought . . . to lose his life upon such a bare possibility of guilt. Therefore we deem it our duty to the public justice & the cause of humanity to recommend this man to the Executive Clemency."[100] Other advocates also petitioned the governor on behalf of Boon, including state Attorney General William Eaton Jr., who offered similar supporting statements.[101]

Since the colonial period, the enforcers and potential beneficiaries of local apprenticeship programs had challenged the rights of parents of color, chiefly mothers, to retain possession of and control the labor of their children. Countless poor parents had lost their children to apprenticeships as local justices distributed them to masters who benefited from their labor. Even in this context, some free people of color strove to regain control of their children and protect them from abuse. These parents and their associates used the courts to lodge complaints and sue for custody of their children. In 1856, Rachel Turner, alias Johnson, "a free colored woman," filed a complaint in the Orphans Court of Anne Arundel County, Maryland. She explained that her daughter Becky Turner was being held by Richard A. Harwood beyond the agreed term of service. Rachel Turner also detailed that the deed of indenture required Becky to serve until March 16, 1859, under the assumption that Becky would turn eighteen on that date. Becky, however, was already eighteen, her mother contended, and therefore should be liberated from all obligations to Harwood and given her freedom dues. After receiving the petition, the court heard from Rachel Turner and Harwood and determined that Becky was indeed eighteen and had served her time. In another case before the same court in Anne Arundel County, Susan Pully, a "free negro," complained that the court had bound her four children, Jim, Mary, Julia Ann, and Charles, to John Hanshaw without her consent. Pully further declared that in the case of her children, she was "fully able to provide for their wants & necessities" and could "verify" her ability to do so. In January 1859, the court decided in favor of Pully, "annulled" the apprenticeships, and ordered Hanshaw to return the children to their mother.[102] Although Maryland law prevented free people of color from testifying against whites, Rachel Turner and Susan Pully were able to procure evidence to support their claims against Harwood and Hanshaw, both white men, and win their cases. Turner secured her daughter's independence, and Pully won custody of her children and retained their labor for the benefit of her family.[103]

During the three decades preceding the Civil War, lawmakers and court officials in states such as Virginia, South Carolina, and Mississippi permitted a minority of free people of color to assert that they identified as "Indians," "Moors," or "not negroes," which excluded them from some of the discriminatory legislation that applied to most free people of color. Under the laws of many southern states, the category "free persons of color" encompassed various people of different ancestral backgrounds, physical features, and identities. Generally, lawmakers and courts lumped together all free people of color regardless of their ancestral, physical, or personal differences. Yet the laws of some states recognized multiple subcategories under the broader category "free persons of color" and assigned to those subcategories of people different rights. Across the South, individuals used these legal loopholes to obtain protections unavailable to most free people of color. Officials in Henrico County, Virginia, processed and approved John Scott Bailey's request to be categorized as "not a Negro" in 1852.[104] Sarah M. and Frances C. Burton testified on Bailey's behalf and provided the court with a lengthy narrative describing Bailey's ancestry. While admitting that the "colour" of some of Bailey's ancestors was "not remembered," they stated that the rest of Bailey's ancestors were "white," "nearly white," or "Indian."[105] In 1860, Ellen Burckmeyer of South Carolina received certification of "Indian descent" for herself and her children, Eve, Isaac, and Henry. That same year, Margaret E. Gordon came before a notary public and certified that Burckmeyer "was of Indian descent and that she was a free person of color and so was by common report and estimation."[106]

Individuals who successfully made claims to being "Indian" or "not a Negro" and received certification as such used their categorization to protect themselves from discriminatory levies. Sally Carter of Barnwell County, South Carolina, obtained an exemption from discriminatory taxation after Frederick J. Hay provided the county with a statement of her ancestry. On June 18, 1845, Hay declared before the court that he "knew the mother of Sally Carter, that she lived a number of years on my Plantation, that she was always considered to be of Indian blood and that her appearance indicated it." Hay's statement was enough evidence for the court to provide Carter with a document stating, "Sally the bearer here of is the daughter of Sucky Carter deceased and is not subject to the Tax law of the State."[107] Officials in Norfolk County, Virginia, heard a complaint from eleven men of the Weaver, Harmon, Bracy, Bass, and Newton families, who claimed that they were "improperly charged as free negroes with the Revenue Tax of $1.00 for the year 1850." Before the 1850 tax assessment, many of the men had received certificates from the county court proclaiming them "not free negroes or mulattoes." After hearing the complaint in 1851, the court remitted the taxes against them.[108]

Declarations supporting individuals' subcategorization as "Indian" or "not a negro" were important tools for some free people of color engaged in legal actions. The way that the courts classified individuals determined the rights they possessed during prosecution or a legal dispute; in criminal cases, an individual's classification guided the types of punishment available to judges and juries. In cases in which the categorization of an individual was unclear, grand juries sometimes had to make determinations of defendants' classifications prior to the start of trials. Before the state could prosecute Robert S. Driggers of Marlboro District, South Carolina, for stealing a banknote, a grand jury needed to determine Driggers's classification. After investigating the case, the grand jurors concluded that "Robert S. Driggers is a free person of color and should not exercise the privileges of a white man, that they live in the neighborhood where said Driggers resides, and that he is not generally considered a white man but a free person of color."[109] While the grand jury's decision did not benefit Robert S. Driggers, some of his contemporaries found success in the courts of the South. In 1852, the prosecution in the case against Baylor Winn failed to prove that the defendant had "negro blood." The Jefferson County, Mississippi, court was considering the case against Winn for the murder of William Johnson, a free man of color from nearby Natchez. Yet the prosecution's inability to demonstrate that Winn had "negro blood" blocked the prosecution from presenting "negro testimony" against Winn. Eyewitnesses may have seen Winn kill Johnson, but Winn's defense of not having "negro blood" prevented the presentation of their testimony under Mississippi law.[110]

As the Civil War loomed, free people of color continued to play essential roles that held together the social fabric of many southern communities. In the face of increasing radicalism on the part of slavery's advocates, free persons of color like Pierre Casanave, New Orleans's successful undertaker, continued to stride forward. They built homes, churches, and businesses. In spite of the increasingly hostile ideas contained in southern legal codes, free people of color battled for their rights and property in southern courtrooms and regularly pushed the region's all white male judiciary to support their causes. With discrimination on the rise in southern life, free people of color sought greater autonomy by establishing more of their own churches and organizing associations, societies, and events. Working with white allies, free people of color created additional avenues to teach their children how to read, write, speak, and analyze.

On the eve of their last stand, proslavery radicals had failed to force free people of color completely to the margins of society. Many of the South's least fortunate free persons of color suffered under their brutal influence, but free people of color as a whole were far from broken as 1861 approached.

CHAPTER 7

Preserving Freedom in a Divided South

On July 5, 1854, Marietta T. Hill, a free girl of color and student at Myrtilla Miner's District of Columbia school, predicted that freedom would overcome slavery only through "blood shed." In a letter to Miner, Hill expressed "despair" following the passage of the Kansas-Nebraska Act. She asked, "Will slavery forever exist?" Slavery's supporters had cast a "dark cloud" across the country that was growing darker still. Nevertheless, Hill held out hope for better days. If people were willing to fight for change, freedom for all could become a reality.[1] By early 1861, the bloodshed so wisely predicted by young Marietta T. Hill arrived. Free people of color across the South watched and contemplated their roles in the ensuing conflict.

After decades of debate over slavery and its expansion, radical political leaders across the South pushed their neighbors into rebellion against the United States. They seized control of the governments of eleven southern states and built loyal followings and alliances with individuals in the other southern states as well as among some leaders of indigenous nations in Indian Territory. After years of pressing for radical proslavery policies, including the unbound expansion of slavery into the federal territories, southern politicians felt emboldened to take their most extreme steps: attempting to separate from the United States and waging war against the very institutions that many of their ancestors had helped to create. At the outset of the rebellion, proslavery radicals had not succeeded in executing the most virulent aspects of their agenda against free people of color. Their attempts to enslave the mass of free persons of color had largely failed. Whereas they had hoped to curb the growth of the population, the number of free people of color in the South increased during the last decade before the war began. Nevertheless, other aspects of the radical proslavery agenda were succeeding. In 1861, proslavery extremists sought to found the first country in the world explicitly dedicated to the protection of "the right of property in negro slaves."[2]

The rebellion led by proslavery southerners ripped apart the nation and divided the South. Free people of color from Texas to Virginia were trapped in a territory run by men seeking to place the "negro in his rightful place ... slavery." Radicals had used the election of Abraham Lincoln and the new president's attempt to resupply Fort Sumter as grounds to break away from the union. In Delaware, Maryland, the District of Columbia, Kentucky, and Missouri, politicians seeking to maintain power by promoting moderation kept the proslavery radicals at bay. They provided free people of color in the area with a semblance of relief by simply offering the status quo. In both sections of the South, free people of color worked to preserve the precious freedoms that they had retained in spite of decades of attacks from proslavery extremists and white supremacists.[3]

Although the threats presented by the radicals reached new heights during the conflict, free people of color responded by challenging attempts to degrade their free status. Throughout the war years, free people of color devised an assortment of strategies to protect the liberties they held most dear. In areas held by the rebels, those strategies ranged from keeping quiet and going about daily life to cooperating with forced impressment and confiscations to even making small public gestures and statements in support of the rebel cause. In a few instances, free men of color, posing as whites, enlisted in the rebel forces. Free people of color in the states and jurisdictions under the control of the federal government found greater opportunity to protect their freedom and, in some cases, fought to expand their liberty. They supported the efforts of President Abraham Lincoln and the U.S. military by sacrificing supplies and provisions, providing guidance and intelligence to U.S. troops, and sabotaging the rebel efforts. After Lincoln issued the Emancipation Proclamation, free men of color came in droves to support their country by joining the U.S. military and fighting directly against the armies of the South's proslavery regime.

When Marietta T. Hill wrote to Myrtilla Miner, she summarized concisely what was at stake: "The question is are we willing to give up our lives for freedom?"[4] By 1863, the answer to her question was clear. Thousands of free people of color and their once enslaved comrades responded with an enthusiastic, "Yes!"[5]

Life under Rebel Control

Throughout the Civil War, the rebel South shared many social, political, and economic features with its prewar antecedent. The region continued to be a discriminatory legal environment for free people of color. Yet at the same time, white southerners remained dependent on the very people whose suffering they allowed by upholding unjust laws. While these long-standing features of the region endured, the war presented an opportunity for white southerners to act in even more extreme ways. The rebels impressed free people of color to work on fortifications and other construction projects, which stripped them of the ability to determine their destiny during the war years. Rebel officials forced free people of color to labor on behalf of a government built on the premise of white supremacy, an ideology of no value to them. The rebel government confiscated untold amounts of property from free persons of color in order to supply troops who fought to uphold southern extremism. Under these circumstances, free people of color had few choices. Many capitulated, a few actively collaborated, and others resisted.

Local governments continued sporadically throughout the war years to enforce discriminatory state laws, both new and old. Virginia's 1860 law permitting the sale of convicted free persons of color into "absolute slavery" had its greatest effect during the war years. Westmoreland County officials used the law on multiple occasions in that period. In late 1861, the county court sentenced Robert Jordan and Frederick Fulcher to "sale into absolute slavery" following their convictions for aiding enslaved persons during an escape attempt. George Tate received the same sentence after a conviction for violently assaulting another man in 1863. The punishments doled out to Jordan, Fulcher, and Tate were the product of southern proslavery radicalism at its height.[6] By late 1860, officials in Warren County, Mississippi, had decided to crack down on free people of color who lived in the state without permission. In 1861, Minerva Barlow fell victim to the renewed effort. Barlow claimed that her mother was a white woman and that this fact gave her leave to remain in the state. Warren County's police board disagreed and demanded that Barlow and her son leave the state within ten days. The vestiges of radicalism in its earlier stages persisted as irritants to free persons of color. In 1861, officials in Cumberland County, North Carolina, used their state's law permitting the hiring out of free people of color who could not pay their court fines. Unable to pay a thirty-dollar fine levied against him for an assault and battery conviction, Archibald Grove found himself hired out for a five-year term. In Richmond County, Georgia, free persons of color proceeded to register under the state's old guardianship laws. Dilsey Maria Ruff and Sarah Ruff were among sixty-three individuals who received court-appointed guardians between April 1863 and January 1864.[7]

Free people of color, facing a discriminatory legal environment, sought stability during challenging times as they had done in the past. To keep food on their tables, they continued to work in the fields, on the water, in their businesses, and in other areas of the economy. Free persons of color maintained their religious faith and participated in church activities. They traveled back and forth to visit family and friends. At their homes, free people of color shared meals and conversation. Attending weddings remained a favorite pastime. Children continued to be born. Burying loved ones was among life's persistent necessities.[8]

While some aspects of life remained the same during the war, rebel efforts to impress free people of color into service represented a major shift in life for them.[9] Groups of white southerners pushed for legislation coercing free people of color to labor for the rebel cause. On November 18, 1861, a group of ninety-eight residents of Laurens District, South Carolina, complained to state legislators about "free negro men" in their community who they thought "should be pressed into the service" to labor as "cooks" and "render such other service to our soldiers as they may require of them." The petitioners proposed forcing "free negroes from the ages of sixteen to sixty" to serve.[10] The *Fayetteville Observer* circulated an article promoting the impressment of North Carolina's free men of color into rebel service after receiving a complaint about the lack of "free colored men" willing to labor as "servants, cooks, &c., to the officers and men in camp." The paper called for the impressment of free men of color "with reasonable pay."[11] At the beginning of 1862, H. W. Shaw on behalf of H. A. Wise, who was in charge of defending Roanoke Island, begged North Carolina governor Henry T. Clark to impress "free negro laborers" who could help build up the defenses on the coast. He described his current force of workers as "totally inadequate" and warned that North Carolina and parts of Virginia were in jeopardy.[12]

Southern legislatures responded to these demands and enacted laws permitting officials to draft free men of color into the rebel service as laborers, and forced workers soon composed the teams that built the fortifications and dug the trenches. Free men of color in Saint Martin Parish, Louisiana, labored under duress for the rebels. Monroe Baker remembered, "I and 62 other free colored men were seized upon or conscripted by Confederate authorities and taken to Alexandria, La. to work upon the rebel fortifications."[13] Gustavus Gaines remembered being part of a group of men forced by his local sheriff in Fauquier County, Virginia, to "throw up breastworks" near the Rappahannock River during the first year of the war.[14]

Those free people of color who avoided working on the fortifications, breastworks, and trenches did not necessarily escape compulsory labor, as the rebels pressed them to participate in a variety of other tasks. Rebel officials faced a constant need for labor and forcibly employed free people of color to do everything from constructing buildings to caring for their sick and wounded. Officials in Charlottesville, Virginia, drafted twenty-eight free men of color to assist with the construction of a hospital for wounded rebel troops.[15] The sheriff in Culpeper County, Virginia, forced Slaughter Madden to work in a rebel hospital. Madden recalled, "I was compelled under a threat by the sheriff to go to Culpeper and wait on the wounded at the hospital after the 1st battle of Manassas. He told me if I did not go I would have to take the consequence of a refusal, which I knew meant the lash."[16] Robert Carter of Fairfax County, Virginia, stated that during "the first year of the war, a rebel officer came to my place and forced me to drive a team for them." After one day of service, the rebels took Carter's teenage son as a substitute and required him to drive in his father's place.[17] The rebels forced Thomas Morgan of Johnston County, North Carolina, to care for their horses. Morgan recalled, "The Confederates pressed me and made me shoe horses for them for nothing."[18] After working on the defenses, the rebels shifted Benjamin Watts of Norfolk County, Virginia, to service work. Watts explained, "In 1861, May I think[,] I was impressed to work on the Rebel fort on Craneys Island in the Elizabeth River. There I was detailed as a waiter on the Rebel officers. I remained there about three months."[19] Mary Ann Pollard, who lived in Culpeper County, Virginia, during the war, remembered that the rebels "arrested and confined" her husband, Reuben, in the county jail for "favoring the yankees and for preaching the downfall of slavery." When the rebels finally released Reuben Pollard from jail, they sent him to work on "a magazine at Manassas." Mary Ann recalled that her husband "was an excellent carpenter and they [the rebels] compelled him to work there two or three weeks for nothing."[20]

Hiding from the rebel forces became an important strategy for free people of color seeking to maintain their autonomy and avoid impressment. Some free persons of color sought refuge in their home communities, while others trekked great distances in order to escape rebel officials. John Malvin of Fauquier County, Virginia, evaded the rebels by concealing himself in a nearby forest. Malvin recollected, "The conscript officers came after me six or seven times. I used to conceal myself in the Pines when they were around. I stayed in the Pines a great deal. My wife would give me a signal when they were gone."²¹ David Veney of Richmond County, Virginia, devised an ingenious scheme to protect his oldest sons from conscription. He explained, "I never had anything at all to do with them [the rebels]. They wanted to force the boys all over to Richmond, and my sons were of right smart size." In order to protect his sons, Veney "got them over to Maryland until the war was all ended."²² Lafayette Robinson of Huntsville, Alabama, left home in order to avoid conscription. He explained, "Part of the time I was in Ohio, partly in Tennessee."²³

Free men of color often resisted working for the rebels by running away. Throughout the war, rebel officials had a difficult time keeping their conscripted labor force under control. Although Fort Sumter in South Carolina was surrounded by water on all sides, free people of color found ways to escape. Tom Bass, a free man of color from Marlboro District, South Carolina, fled from the fort on June 2, 1864. The official in charge complained that escapes, such as the one committed by Bass, could not "be avoided as I have no place to keep these negroes."²⁴ On January 31, 1865, Edwin White, the lieutenant engineer at Fort Sumter, reported seventeen "Free Negro Conscripts" missing from his post. He explained to his superior that "most of these Negroes deserted this post before I took charge."²⁵

Some free people of color faced violent retribution after their attempts to escape the rebel service. Asserting their claims to freedom by escaping rebel impressment was a risky business, and some free people of color lost their lives as a result. In October 1861, a Wilkes County, North Carolina, mob lynched Fletcher, "a free negro" who resisted impressment. Fletcher had fled from rebel impressment agents and during a chase by those agents allegedly killed one of his pursuers. Eventually, the agents captured Fletcher and locked him in the jail at Wilkesboro, where the mob took him.²⁶ In Robeson County, North Carolina, rebels used violence and intimidation to track, capture, and punish free people of color seeking to escape forced labor. During the fall of 1864, rebels shot Sinclair Lowry during an escape attempt. Lowry was lucky; his injury was not fatal. The next year, the rebels, in search of information about deserters, attacked Wylie Oxendine, who survived the encounter and lived to tell his story. He recalled that a gang of rebels "tied him up and swore they would kill him" if he did not reveal the location of an encampment of deserters.²⁷

Bribery became an important tool for free men of color who sought to remain at home and avoid laboring for the rebels. If those free persons of color who could afford to pay bribes and could find rebel officials willing to accept money in lieu of service, they could continue to work for their own profit and protect their homes and families. Early in 1862, John Hagan, "a public officer authorized by law to procure free negroes to work on batteries and fortifications" being constructed in defense of the rebel capital, landed before a court in Richmond, Virginia, for "receiving money" in place of "labor," including forty dollars from James Evans.[28] Robert S. Brown of Charles City County, Virginia, labored under the rebels by force on multiple occasions before he decided to attempt to bribe an official to release him. Brown recalled, "I gave $500 to the sergeant who acted as foreman" at the fortifications "to let me go."[29] Alfred Fox of Loudoun County, Virginia, suggested that the rebels, in an act of extortion, forced him to pay a bribe for his release. He explained, "I think in the year 1861 when the rebel army was throwing up breastworks around Leesburg I was forced to go down there to work on the breastworks, they came after me at night and took me out of bed, I had to pay them $49.50 and was released for that sum [the] next morning."[30]

Like many enlisted men, free men of color also used medical exemptions to protect their liberty and avoid impressment. Beverly Matteaur of Appomattox County, Virginia, evaded impressment throughout the war. He recalled, "They tried to get me into the service but I would not go and got a certificate from Dr. Matteaur on account of an infirmity of one of my legs. Without this, I should have been compelled to go, the same as a slave."[31] Beverly Matteaur was not an enslaved person but clearly associated the power that rebels exercised to impress free people of color with the force that slaveholders used to control bondspeople. In another case, Richard Dabney of Dinwiddie County, Virginia, labored under the rebels for six months before running away and obtaining a medical exemption. He remembered, "In 1861 I was forced into the rebel service as a teamster. I was told I should be kept only 30 days but I was kept 6 months & then ran away. The day after I got home, a Rebel officer came for me. I refused to go with him. He drew his pistol. I told him he might shoot but I would not go. My family were starving & besides I was unfit for service. He told me to get a Doctor's certificate which I did & was not molested again till just at the end of the war."[32]

If they were unable to qualify for disability exemptions, free people of color and their white neighbors often applied for exemptions on different grounds. With white men absent due to their service in the rebel army and enslaved men away toiling on the rebel defenses, free men of color became increasingly important to their home communities. Free people of color or their white employers, consequently, petitioned rebel officials for protection from impressment. In November 1864, Jane Williams of Randolph County, North Carolina, requested an exemption for Enoch Brown, a free man of color whom she employed. Williams explained to the enrollment officer that she had "a small farm and three small children" and that her husband as well as two brothers were in the "military service of the Confederate States." Under the circumstances, she declared that without Brown's assistance she could not "keep up" her farm or "make a support for her little children."[33] The enrollment official found Williams's declaration convincing and issued Brown an exemption from service.[34]

Although many free people of color managed to avoid serving the rebel forces for a variety of reasons, the rebels still found ways to extract resources from them. Rebel troops found the produce grown on their farms along with their horses, hogs, and other animals to be valuable resources. Using force if necessary, the troops sought to obtain the provisions and supplies that they needed. Fannie Richer, who owned a plantation in Pointe Coupee Parish, Louisiana, claimed, "The Confederates took horses & other small property from me & attempted to arrest me several times but did not take me away from my place."[35] During the war, the rebels regularly seized a portion of Thomas Jefferson Hill's crops, which he grew on his farm in King William County, Virginia. Hill reported, "In 1862 & every year after the Confederates took my corn & fodder. They never paid anything for it & I never asked for any pay. It would have been of no use. It was taken by the Rebel Government."[36]

Rebel efforts to seize property were particularly vicious in Indian Territory, where free people of color sometimes lost not only their property but also their lives and their freedom.[37] Tyra Durant recalled after the war that the rebels were "robbing and murdering all the colored people they could find."[38] Free people of color, who were among this group, frequently fell victim to rebel rampages during the war. Raiders under the command of James M. McIntosh seized Clory Warrior's cattle in 1861. She lost most of her remaining possessions after deciding to leave Indian Territory for Kansas with Creek leader Opothleyahola later that year.[39] Eliza Bruner, who resided on the edge of the Arkansas River, lost her property during a rebel raid in 1863. Aware that the rebels were capturing "colored people" and sending them to Texas, Bruner fled, leaving behind her home and other property. She eventually ended up at Fort Gibson, Kansas, where she remained through the war.[40] Early in the conflict, Manuel Jefferson found himself the victim of raiders under Cherokee leader Stand Watie, a rebel ally. Jefferson lost his possessions and his freedom. While on his way to Kansas after harvesting his crops, Jefferson was captured by the rebels. The rebels seized his assets, including the corn crop, and carried Jefferson to Texas, where they sold him as a slave. He remained in Texas through the duration of the conflict. Jane Mehardy lost her children in a similar raid. The rebels kidnapped four of her children, all born free, and transported them to Texas. These abductions were not isolated incidents but reflections of a more general willingness by rebels to disregard the free status of people of color. Rebel troops under Robert E. Lee committed similar atrocities against free persons of color in Pennsylvania during the Gettysburg campaign.[41]

In the same way that some free people of color used the assistance of their white neighbors to avoid impressment, others took advantage of similar networks to protect their personal property from seizure by the rebels. Sarah Ann Black of Savannah, Georgia, in collusion with some of her white neighbors, devised an ingenious scheme to protect her property. Black explained, "6 of my cows were taken by the Confederate authorities & driven to the cattle pen to be driven across the river the next day. It was just before Sherman's army entered the city." Yet Black implemented a plan to regain her cows. She remembered, "I had a friend[,] a white lady living near me & she went to the pen and claimed the cattle as hers & they let her drive them off & I then took them & put one of them in each of my neighbors yards as each person was allowed to have one cow & when they came round afterwards they seeing only one cow in each yard left it & so I kept them from the Confederates."[42]

Even though many of their compatriots cooperated with the rebels hesitantly or resisted them outright, some free people of color decided to work with the rebels. Necessity as well as opportunism likely drove them to do business with the rebels. With the outbreak of the war, the rebel government became an important purchaser of goods for southern businesspeople, including free persons of color. Free people of color involved in a variety of occupations discovered that trading with the rebel government permitted them to sell large quantities of goods during otherwise tight economic times. Throughout the war, Matthew N. Leary Jr., a Fayetteville, North Carolina, saddler, provided the rebels with an assortment of leather goods. In 1861, the state of North Carolina paid Leary $450 for two artillery harnesses. During the same year, Leary sold the rebels $296 worth of equipment, including cartridge boxes and sword scabbards. In 1864, Leary received $52 for providing the rebels with leather straps and repairing harnesses, bridles, and other items. Richard E. Dereef, a slaveholder and the owner of a lumber factory in Charleston, South Carolina, continued to increase his wealth by conducting business with the rebel government. Between June and September 1862, Dereef sold over $1,400 worth of pine and oak to the rebels. In August 1864, he received payment from the rebels for the rental of one of his properties, which they used for storage.⁴³ Selling products and services to the rebels provided an important source of income for these businessmen, whether or not they sympathized with the cause of the rebel government.

Over the course of the war, the rebels obtained a variety of farm goods from free people of color. It is unclear whether or not these free people of color sold to the rebels by choice or through force, but they received payment in exchange for their goods, which was not always the case for farmers and planters. In 1863, Richardson Corn, a farmer from Alamance County, North Carolina, sold $132.93 worth of crops to the rebels at Danville, Virginia. The shipment of farm goods included crops used to feed horses, such as hay, oats, fodder, and shuck. Foster Chastang, a Mobile County, Alabama, farmer, sold the rebels twenty-five cords of pine wood for $375 in 1864. Maximillian Dubroca of the same community provided the rebels with wood and wool throughout the war.⁴⁴

The southern rebellion restructured the maritime economy and pushed free people of color into war-related work on the streams, riverways, and ocean. Whereas free people of color had navigated and labored on water vessels with little fanfare before the war, U.S. officials during the conflict began to consider their activities as aiding the enemy. Under the new rebel economy, however, many free people of color were faced with the choice of either working for the enemy of the federal government or starvation. Those free people of color who continued to work in the maritime industries during the war often played a vital role in the traffic of goods between the rebel states and the loyal states or foreign territories. Working alongside white mariners, these free people of color attempted to evade the federal naval blockade, which sought to choke off the rebel economy from the rest of the world and starve the rebels into submission. William Harmon, a "mulatto" man from Virginia, helped funnel goods between Virginia and Maryland by boat. By 1862, the U.S. Navy had captured Harmon twice while he was engaged in the illicit traffic.⁴⁵ Dennis Pettit and Solomon Battell, free men of color, worked on board the *Whiteman*, a blockade-running steamer. Pettit was working as a steward and Battell was the ship's cook when the U.S. Navy captured the vessel near Louisiana's Lake Pontchartrain on May 17, 1862.⁴⁶ Free people of color with years of experience on the South's waterways were important facilitators for maritime traffic during the war. The rebels depended on them to guide watercraft and manage river crossings. "A free negro" commanded the rebel sloop *Susan McPherson* before the U.S. Navy captured the vessel.⁴⁷ In 1865, David Pinn, "a free negro," assisted rebel marines across the Rappahannock River in Virginia. Federal officials failed to ascertain whether Pinn assisted the marines "voluntarily or not," but an informant suggested that the rebels paid him.[48]

Free people of color fulfilled a variety of other important war-related roles. As in the prewar period, white southerners depended on the skills and expertise of persons of color, and free people of color needed wages to sustain themselves and their families. Officials at the arsenal at Fayetteville, North Carolina, employed Thomas Lomax, a mason, to repair the barracks and other structures in 1861. In 1862, Bennett Boon earned ten dollars for digging a well for the Confederate Stable Yard in Wilmington, North Carolina. That same year, the rebels hired William Botts to work as a brakeman and fireman in Richmond, Virginia. Until September 1863, Henry Meyers worked at the Hudson Place Salt Works near Darien, Georgia. Free women of color labored as laundresses in hospitals. Ann Green washed at the General Hospital at Mount Jackson, Virginia, for two months in 1862. For four months in 1864, Martha Bragg worked in the same capacity in hospitals in Bristol, Tennessee, and Marion, Virginia.[49]

Many free people of color resisted attempts to extract their labor and seize their property and aided the rebels only under duress. Yet a small number of free persons of color actively collaborated with the rebels.[50] Their aid to the rebel cause demonstrates the diversity of ways free people of color thought about the rebellion and its impact on their futures. Some free people of color hoped the U.S. government would retake the South and saw victory by the U.S. army as the most likely path to political and social improvement. Other free persons of color hedged their bets on the existing power structure in the South. At the war's onset, limited numbers of free people of color offered their support to the rebels. A small group of free people of color in Charleston, South Carolina, promised their allegiance to the state government. The group of thirty-seven free men of color, derived from some of Charleston's most elite families of color, such as the Sasportas, Holloway, and Desverney families, alluded to a blood kinship between themselves and the architects of secession. They declared, "We are by birth citizens of South-Carolina. In our veins flows the blood of the white race—in some, half, in others, much more than half, white blood." After linking themselves to their state's power structure, the free men of color offered their support. They proclaimed, "Our attachments are with you; our hopes of safety and protection from you; our allegiance is due to South-Carolina, and in her defence, we are willing to offer up our lives, and all that is dear to us." In exchange for their support, the men asked that "our wives and children be taken care of and provided for."[51] These men publicly embraced the concept of white superiority in order to protect and possibly enhance their position in society. They were likely aware that radical proslavery advocates had drawn a connection between the presence of free people of color and the threat to slavery's continuation in the South. As a result, they attempted to separate themselves from suspicion and align themselves with the ideas of white superiority and the proslavery cause. Articulating their support for these ideas demonstrated their unwillingness to challenge the founding tenets of the Confederate States of America and the secessionist movement.

For free people of color, declarations of allegiance to the rebels were often unambiguous strategic appeals made for direct personal gain. In his 1863 petition to the Texas General Assembly, Peter Allen of Houston described himself as "born and raised in the south" and contended that "all his interests, sympathies and feelings" were "in the land of his nativity." He sought to show lawmakers that he was willing to sacrifice for the rebel cause by explaining that "for more than eight months of the past year he was attached to Terry's Regiment" and provided "good and efficient service" to the rebels at "the Battlefields of Woodsonville and Shiloh."[52] Allen made these declarations in an attempt to secure an exemption from the Texas residency law that prohibited free people of color from moving into the state. He used the special context provided by the ensuing war to complicate what might have been a much easier choice for Texas assemblymen. Allen presented himself to be more than a free man of color simply asking for clemency. He strategically represented himself as a fellow southerner, a patriot, and an asset to the rebel cause.

Free people of color showed token support for the rebels by making small donations to the troops. Those who donated tended to be people of means who could afford to give up a few textile goods or other items of limited value. During the first year of the war, Josephine Hassel, a Montgomery, Alabama, seamstress, contributed twenty pairs of "cotton flannel drawers" to the rebel troops.[53] She was the partner of a successful white planter and merchant. According to her daughter, Josephine Hassel and her family were "the only colored people in the neighborhood."[54] Charleston's elite free people of color created an organization to raise funds to support rebel troops. The association, which was chaired by Samuel Weston, Robert Howard, J. M. F. Dereef, Anthony Weston, Jacob Weston, and J. U. Dereef, worked with the Brown Fellowship Society and other groups of free persons of color to obtain donations. By September 1861, the organization had collected $450 for wounded and sick troops stationed in Virginia.[55] In 1862, a small number of free people of color were among dozens of Alamance County, North Carolina, residents who donated to the Sixth North Carolina State Troops, a rebel regiment. Sam Martin sacrificed a pair of shoes. Egbert Corn donated a quilt while Ned Corn gave two quilts. Dixon Corn provided two blankets. The Corns were all farmers and landholders.[56] Even as the rebel effort was crumbling by the end of 1864, George Shrewsbury, a wealthy free man of color, apparently saw some value still in supporting the rebel cause. In October of that year, he joined other South Carolinians in donating to a relief fund for troops imprisoned at Morris Island. With a $100 donation, Shrewsbury was among the cause's top donors.[57]

Limited numbers of free men of color offered to serve as home guards for rebel governments at the beginning of the conflict. Serving in a home guard organization permitted free people of color to ally themselves with the local power structure and challenge any suspicion regarding their loyalty. An April 27, 1861, advertisement in New Orleans's *Daily Picayune* called for "All Free Colored Persons wishing to offer their services to the Government as volunteers to serve as a Home Guard."[58] Free men of color from the city organized into a unit known as the Native Guards. While New Orleans was under rebel control, the Native Guards played a largely symbolic role by marching in local parades and participating in guard duty. Moreover, their allegiance was far from fixed. Following the fall of the city in 1862, free men of color from the Native Guards switched their allegiance to the U.S. forces and were among the first men of color to join the U.S. military during the war.[59] Arnold Bertonneau, a member of the Native Guards who later joined the U.S. forces, indicated that he and other free men of color originally allied with the rebels out of necessity. He explained that free people of color lacked "arms and ammunition or any means of self defence." Bertonneau asked, "When summoned to volunteer in the defense of the State and city against Northern invasion, situated as we were, could we do otherwise than heed the warning, and volunteer in the defence of New Orleans?"[60] Newspapers reported the establishment of smaller guard units composed of free men of color in other parts of the South, including Pensacola, Florida, and the towns of Natchitoches, Shreveport, and Baton Rouge in Louisiana.[61] In a letter to North Carolina Governor Henry T. Clark, Stephen D. Collins and Doctor F. Edmond proposed organizing similar guard units composed of "Free Mulatoes" from the Scuffletown neighborhood in Robeson County. Their proposal suggested that "so many" of this group were "willing to turn out in behalf of our homes & firesides" that they could raise "three full companies" to fight the "Yankee foe" and protect the state's coast.[62] Officials eventually moved several free men of color from Robeson County to the North Carolina coast, but not to serve as a fighting force or home guard unit. Instead, like so many other free men of color from the region, they worked as laborers.⁶³

Until the last days of the conflict, the rebel government explicitly prohibited the enlistment of people of color for regular armed service. The prohibition prevented any sizable number of free people of color from engaging in combat on behalf of the rebels. A small number of free people of color, however, slipped through the cracks of the policy and landed in the rebel combat services. They did not serve as "persons of color" but enlisted as "whites." Race-based policies depended on those charged with their enforcement to discern who was white and who was not. Yet making distinctions was not always easy, and, as a result, some people deemed "free people of color" in their home communities were able to slip past the visual inspection of rebel recruiters. In other instances, rebel recruiters may have simply enlisted men who met the visual requirements of whiteness regardless of their family history.⁶⁴ On September 2, 1861, Samuel Chavers, a man with light hair and blue eyes, defied the official policy and enlisted with the Twenty-Eighth North Carolina Infantry at Orange County, North Carolina. He fought with his unit, and, in 1862, U.S. forces captured him at Fredericksburg. Later, they returned him to the rebels during a prisoner exchange, and Chavers continued with his regiment until early 1863, when his superior discharged him for "being partly of negro descent." Despite the discharge, Chavers eventually reenlisted with the same unit and served until May 23, 1864, when he died at Jericho Ford, Virginia.⁶⁵ Small numbers of free men of color from Moore County, North Carolina, joined rebel units throughout the war. Edward and Duncan Goins signed up with the Thirtieth North Carolina Infantry at Jonesboro in 1861. While Edward served as a soldier and teamster through the conflict, Duncan succumbed to disease less than a year after his initial enlistment. Other Goins family members, including Andrew, John W., Henry, and Richard Goins, joined the Thirty-Fifth North Carolina Infantry. Andrew lost his life at Malvern Hill, Virginia, in 1862, but the other three served throughout the conflict.⁶⁶ Although a few free men of color slipped through the cracks of rebel enlistment protocols because of their appearances, the vast majority of those who fought in the war served on behalf of the United States.

Fighting for the United States

At the beginning of the war, nearly half of the South's free people of color remained in territories still under the control of the U.S. government, and, as the war ensued, this number only increased. The struggles of free people of color to maintain their freedom while living in areas under federal control differed from the toils of their brethren living under the authority of the rebels. The lack of widespread sanction for forced impressment of free men of color protected many families from the hardships experienced by free people of color living in rebel-controlled areas. Free people of color in sections loyal to the federal government did not face the difficult decision of whether to assist an emphatically proslavery regime. Still, radical proslavery politics and white supremacy threatened the liberties of free people of color throughout the South, even if they lived in loyal areas.

Like their counterparts farther south, radical politicians in the loyal southern states continued their vicious attacks on free people of color into the early war years. Through 1863, Delaware lawmakers continued to pass additional restrictions on the lives of free people of color. In 1861, they made it "unlawful to bind any free negro or mulatto child to any other free negro or mulatto" and required sheriffs to hire out any "free negro or mulatto" who was imprisoned for debt and could not discharge the debt within ten days. Two years later, radicals pushed through legislation further burdening free people of color who sought to travel out of state. Lawmakers imposed a five-day limit on "any resident free negro or free mulatto" who left the state with the intent to reenter. Those who failed to return within the set time period became nonresidents under the law.[67] Radicals in Maryland attacked free people of color as they fought abolitionists' attempts to end human bondage in the state. In an exaggerated statement, an anonymous writer for the *Frederick Union* declared in 1864 that "Maryland has at this very time nearly twice as many free negroes as any other State, and her people, like the people of other States, are heartily sick and tired of them." Attempting to instill fear in readers, the writer continued, "Are we not already sufficiently taxed for the support of free negroes in our Jails, Alms Houses and Penitentiaries.... Are we willing that our State shall become the rendezvous for 175,000 free negroes, whose labor will be brought into competition with that of the white man?"[68]

Although some Upper South radicals failed to push their states to abandon the union and join the proslavery rebellion, they remained undeterred from using discriminatory laws rooted in white supremacist and proslavery logic to infringe on the rights of free people of color. Free persons of color in the border South continued to live under discriminatory policies and contend with their enforcers. Free people of color in Maryland applied for documents to prove their free status during the war. In 1863, Kitturah Elzey requested new freedom documents from officials in Dorchester County. Approximately two years earlier, someone had broken into Elzey's chest and stolen her freedom papers while she was living in Baltimore.⁶⁹ In Jefferson County, Kentucky, free people of color planning to cross the Ohio River to work or see family and friends in Indiana had to secure permission from local officials. Just before the war, Kentucky lawmakers had threatened free people of color with jail time if they left the state and returned under any circumstances. In order to shield himself from the harsh law, William Sikes, a "free man of color," obtained the assistance of Thomas W. Gibson, a white attorney. In 1861, Gibson applied to the Jefferson County court for permission to take Sikes to Charleston, Indiana, so that he could visit his sick mother.⁷⁰ Although many of the nation's most vocal proponents of discrimination left the capital after the formation of the Confederate government, free people of color in the District of Columbia continued to struggle with segregation and exclusion during the war. Even after the abolition of slavery in the capital in 1862, discrimination persisted. Ford's Theater in Washington included a section "specially designed for colored people."⁷¹ Free people of color, regardless of their station, suffered under the enforcement of segregation on the city's streetcars. In 1864, A. T. Augusta, a free man of color and surgeon for the U.S. army, could not access the streetcars after he refused to ride on the front of the train instead of inside a train car. The conductor informed Augusta that streetcar policy did not permit "colored persons" to ride in the cars.⁷²

While they enjoyed some small victories, proslavery radicals and white supremacists were not able to dominate completely the political conversations in loyal parts of the South. The issuance of Lincoln's Emancipation Proclamation and the gradual collapse of slavery in the District of Columbia and Maryland, however, turned the tide for free people of color in federally held areas of the South. The Emancipation Proclamation allowed free men of color to serve in the U.S. military and take up arms against the proslavery rebels. The proclamation, furthermore, gave free men of color an opportunity to help crush the threat of enslavement once and for all. Slavery's demise in the District of Columbia and Maryland provided free people of color with additional capacity to defend their freedoms by removing the most extreme threats to their liberty and opening up the possibility of focusing specifically on ending discriminatory practices.⁷³

The enlistment of free people of color from across the South into the U.S. military began in 1862 and ramped up in 1863 following the issuance of the Emancipation Proclamation.⁷⁴ Free people of color living in areas under federal control enlisted at nearby military installations and recruitment centers. François Hippolyte, a cigarmaker and native of New

Orleans, joined the army in his hometown, which federal forces had recently captured. Hippolyte remembered, "I enlisted in 1862. I think in July, although I am not positive as to the month, in Co. D. 1st La. Native Guards, which was afterwards called the 73 U.S.C. Inf[antry]." After joining the Seventy-Third U.S. Colored Infantry, Hippolyte later transferred to the Seventy-Fourth U.S. Colored Infantry, another regiment mostly consisting of Louisiana residents.[75] William Boon of Nansemond County, Virginia, traveled to nearby Norfolk, Virginia, to volunteer for military service. He recalled, "I enlisted of my own free will in Co. A 2 U.S. C. V. Inf[antry] in June 1863 near Norfolk, Va.... I was stripped naked and examined by the doctors at enlistment. I was measured and pronounced a sound man."[76] Brothers Alfred and Cornelius Ridgeway of Kent County, Delaware, joined the army at the town of Smyrna. Alfred joined as a substitute, but Cornelius remembered, "I did not enlist but was drafted August 13th 1863 and served in Co. C 8th U.S. C. T. until mustered out with my command at Brownsville, Tex[as]."[77] Some free men of color traveled long distances to enlist in the U.S. army. A group of men left their homes in Cecil County, Maryland, and trekked north to Boston, where some of them joined the Fifth Massachusetts Cavalry. Charles H. Hall, a member of the Cecil County party who did not end up entering the army, recalled that a number of his group were motivated by the "$300 bounty and $200 premium" that the state promised to those who could help fill the enlistment quota.[78] On enlistment, free men of color went through basic training to prepare them for the fight ahead. After traveling from his home community in Dorchester County, Maryland, to enlist with the Fourth U.S. Colored Infantry, Nathaniel Cornish participated in drills with his unit. He recalled drilling for "two months and a half" before the army sent him to Yorktown, Virginia.[79]

Free people of color escaped from rebel-controlled territories and moved into areas held by the federal government, where they enrolled in the U.S. forces.[80] John Cornelius Nickens of Loudoun County, Virginia, labored for the rebels as a teamster for several months until he found his way to Alexandria, where a recruiter encouraged him to join the U.S. army. On June 22, 1864, he enlisted in the Fifth Massachusetts Cavalry.[81] Traveling from the outskirts of town, William and Daniel Keys arrived in Washington, North Carolina, after federal forces gained control of the area. Daniel explained, "When the war broke out and Washington, N.C. was taken by [the] Union Army, we both came together and went [to] Washington, N.C. He [William Keys] enlisted in the U.S. Army. I went [to] work in [a] blacksmith shop." During the war, William served with the Thirty-Sixth U.S. Colored Infantry.[82]

During the Civil War, most free men of color who served in the U.S. forces joined the army. Free men of color, however, were also among the thousands of persons of color who served in the U.S. Navy during the conflict. George Ash, an oysterman and native of Norfolk County, Virginia, enrolled in the navy as a landsman on the U.S.S. *Brandywine* at Fort Monroe on July 15, 1863. During his period of service, he also served on the U.S.S. *Louisiana* and U.S.S. *St. Lawrence*.[83] Jarrett Charms of Baltimore joined the naval service as a landsman on May 4, 1864. His period of enlistment included stints on the U.S.S. *Macedonian* and U.S.S. *Allegheny*.[84]

Free men of color were among the thousands of U.S. troops wounded in battles with the rebels. A shell fractured the skull of Baltimore native Hezekiah Jackson, a private with the Thirty-Ninth U.S. Colored Infantry, at Cemetery Hill on the outskirts of Petersburg, Virginia, in 1864. During the 1864 Battle of Ocean Pond in Florida, Mitchell Harmon, a native of Sussex County, Delaware, and member of the Eighth U.S. Colored Infantry, received a gunshot wound in the right thigh.[85] Alexander Shorter of Baltimore was wounded while fighting with the Fourth U.S. Colored Infantry outside of Petersburg. His comrades Lewis Miner and William E. Matthews remembered that after Shorter was shot, "he laid like a dead man for an hour or more before he was carried from the field. He was shot in the left Breast, Ball passing through the breast and coming out in the back."[86] Jarret Morgan, a native of Harford County, Maryland, lost his thumb while serving with the Fourth U.S. Colored Infantry. During a skirmish at Spring Hill, Virginia, an enemy bullet hit his hand, "cutting the thumb nearly off." After falling back, Morgan reported to the surgeons, who amputated the mangled appendage.[87]

Numerous ailments afflicted free men of color who served in the U.S. forces during the war.[88] Lack of proper clothing and shelter caused some soldiers to suffer. William H. Chew of Washington in the District of Columbia, a member of the First U.S. Colored Infantry, remembered enduring frostbite at Fort Fisher, North Carolina. Poor nutrition, lack of sanitation, and crowded conditions exposed numerous free men of color to diseases that put them out of commission during the war. As a sergeant in the Eighth U.S. Colored Heavy Artillery, Clark Barber of Jefferson County, Kentucky, remembered, "I contracted chills and fever at Victoria, Texas."[89] A serious bout of diarrhea sent George L. Linthicum of Dorchester County, Maryland, to the hospital at Fort Monroe, Virginia, while enlisted with the Fourth U.S. Colored Troops. Venereal infections also afflicted enlisted men. Jean Baptiste Madere suffered from syphilis while enlisted with the Seventy-Third U.S. Colored Infantry.[90]

Moses Hammond worked as a shoemaker in Frederick County, Maryland, before enlisting in the Fourth U.S. Colored Infantry during the Civil War. While in the army, Hammond served as an assistant hospital steward and cared for the needs of his regiment's sick and wounded. (Courtesy of the National Archives and Records Administration)

Many but not all free men of color overcame the flurry of sickness they encountered during the war. Though bullets killed thousands, disease was responsible for many more deaths. While serving as a private with the Thirty-Ninth U.S. Colored Infantry, Theophilus Bantum of Talbot County, Maryland, contracted "chronic diarrhea" and died as a result in a New York hospital on October 18, 1864.[91] Frank Lopez, a native of New Orleans who served in the Seventy-Third U.S. Colored Infantry, perished at Fort Jackson, Louisiana, on January 27, 1863, after contracting consumption.[92] On February 8, 1864, smallpox killed Mathias Cuffee of Norfolk, Virginia, a private in the First U.S. Colored Cavalry, at Camp Hamilton, Virginia.[93]

During their enlistments with the U.S. forces, free men of color engaged in a variety of tasks in addition to fighting on the battlefields. Heavy labor was one of the most common responsibilities assigned to troops of color. While stationed with the Fourteenth U.S. Colored Heavy Artillery at Fort Macon, North Carolina, Lemuel Reynolds of Hertford County, North Carolina, recalled that he and his brother Hampton Reynolds "had to cut long poles to build houses ... & had to carry them on our shoulders sometimes over a ¼ mile."[94] John Swan, a native of Charles County, Maryland, and member of the Fourth U.S. Colored Infantry, labored as part of an army detail charged with digging a canal at Dutch Gap, Virginia.[95] Free men of color also undertook other tasks while with the army. Moses Hammond, a shoemaker from Frederick County, Maryland, became an assistant hospital steward while serving with the Fourth U.S. Colored Infantry. Under the authority of the primary hospital steward, Hammond managed the health care needs of his regiment's sick and wounded.[96] Peter Reed of Kent County, Delaware, worked for the commissary as a member of the Eighth U.S. Colored Infantry. He recalled, "I was detailed to do duty for the commissary. I use[d] to do his cooking and attended to his horse and sometimes I went with the wagon with the rations."[97]

Throughout the war, injuries sustained off the field placed free men of color out of commission from their service and therefore prevented them from participating more fully in the suppression of the rebellion. Nathan Dempsey, a native of Pasquotank County, North Carolina, and member of the Thirty-Sixth U.S. Colored Infantry, was confined to the hospital at Fort Monroe, Virginia, after sustaining a serious injury. He explained, "About two weeks after our arrival at Point Lookout, I was detailed to unload a boat of ammunition when one of the men who was helping to lift a box stumbled and it threw all the weight on me and I fell with the box." The accident left Dempsey crippled for years.[98] William H. Moore of Beaufort County, North Carolina, broke his leg while serving with the Fourteenth U.S. Colored Heavy Artillery at Fort Macon, North Carolina. He recalled that during a test of the fort's guns, a "carriage ran back and hit me on my right leg and broke it. I was on duty at the time with the gun squad. We were testing the soundness of one part of the Fort. We had been firing quite a while and then the gun burst and the carriage hitting my leg broke it."[99]

Defeating the rebellion was the prime objective for free people of color serving with the U.S. forces. Yet some free people of color used their time in the military as a chance to pursue long-denied educational goals. For years, southern lawmakers had barred free persons of color from attending public schools. As a result, basic literacy skills were reserved for those with sufficient financial resources to pay for private education or individuals who learned these skills from friends who already possessed an elementary education. During the war, however, teachers set up schools in military camps and provided many people of color with their first serious chance to learn how to read and write. William Aldred Boon of Gates County, North Carolina, who served with the First U.S. Colored Cavalry, recalled, "I could not read or write when I enlisted in the Army—what I know about reading and writing and all I know about it, I learned during the war, while I was in the Army."[100] Julius Mackey, a native of Hyde County, North Carolina, and member of the Fourteenth U.S. Colored Heavy Artillery, had a similar experience. He stated, "I learned how to write after I enlisted and toward the last of my service."[101]

Although many free men of color departed their friends and family to serve in the military, they frequently attempted to maintain ties to their home communities. Writing letters to their loved ones, by their own hands or through the assistance of friends, became an important way to sustain connections and share their thoughts and feelings about the war. Nicholas Gross, a native of Baltimore and a private in the Fourth U.S. Colored Infantry, used letters to keep in regular contact with his mother and brother. He shared the good times and challenges of military service. Writing from Williamsburg, Virginia, on January 8, 1864, Gross sent holiday greetings and asked his family to tell him more about their Christmas holiday. He wrote: "Dear Henry let me no how you injoyoyed the holerday on crimas we had a quit a lively crismas heare."[102] On June 20 of the same year, Gross informed his brother of recent events that took place outside of Petersburg, Virginia. He explained that during the fighting, members of the U.S. Colored Troops sought retribution for the slaughter of surrendering soldiers by Nathan Bedford Forrest's rebel army at the Battle of Fort Pillow earlier in the year. Gross noted, "We had a hard battle at Petersburg.... We took no prisoner[.] We don them as they did our troops at fort piller [Fort Pillow]."[103] While in service with the 114th U.S. Colored Infantry, Joshua B. Doram corresponded with his father, Dennis Doram, in order to keep in contact with his family back in Danville, Kentucky. On December 23, 1864, he wrote to his father to inform him that he was in good health and to update him about the latest happenings on the battlefields. Doram shared his observation about the gradual collapse of rebel forces in his area: "The Rebbuls Are Coming in Ev[e]ry Day the Amount Is from 12 And from that to 20 A Day Coming in An Giving their self up."[104] During his enlistment and travels with the Second U.S. Colored Cavalry, John Chalk of Nansemond County, Virginia, kept his wife, Emeline, abreast of his health and general condition.

On February 11, 1865, from Richmond, Virginia, he informed Emeline, "I am well at present.... I arrived safe to the Regement and found my company at the Regement[.] We have left the anvelance train[.] We have all taken muskets in perpose to Do provost Duty in town."[105]

Free men of color tried to re-create their lives at home by bringing their families with them. When Richard Spellman decided to enlist in the 35th U.S. Colored Infantry, his wife, Mary, traveled with him from their home in Currituck County, North Carolina, to nearby Roanoke Island, where he entered the army. Mary Spellman remembered, "I went to Roanoke Isl[an]d with him he enlisted there, then went to Newbern, where the Reg[imen]t was made up I think.... I stayed at Roanoke Isl[an]d nearly three years and the Government gave me rations after my husband enlisted."[106] Sarah Bow followed her husband, Addison Bow, from their home in Elizabeth City, North Carolina, to New Bern, where he joined the Thirty-Fifth U.S. Colored Infantry. She explained, "We lived in Perquimans Co. for a year or two until the war came on then we came to Eliz[abeth] City and stayed a short time then went to New Berne N C where my husband enlisted. After my husband enlisted I stayed at Howards Camp near New Berne N C until the war ended."[107]

Though the U.S. government excluded them from combat service, free women of color found other ways to assist the federal government in crushing the rebellion. These women performed many of the essential tasks that allowed U.S. troops to focus on fighting and defeating the enemy. Jane Pepino worked for the federal government as the chief laundress at the convalescent hospital in her hometown of Saint Augustine, Florida.[108] Algae Porche nursed and housed sick U.S. troops at her home in Pointe Coupee Parish, Louisiana. Elizabeth Wingfield of Dinwiddie County, Virginia, provided federal troops with a variety of services. She recalled, "I washed for the Yankee soldiers. I fed them & took care of the sick & wounded."[109]

Service in the U.S. military provided free people of color with the opportunity to crush the most adamant supporters of their oppression, yet they still found that discrimination tainted the federal government's effort to suppress the rebellion. Fed up with experiencing discrimination while in the service of their country, several free men of color serving in the Louisiana Native Guards resigned from the army in 1863. In a letter addressed to Major General Nathaniel P. Banks, a group of sixteen men explained, "At the time we entered the army it was the expectation of ourselves and men that we would be treated as soldiers, we did not expect or demand to be past on a perfect equality in a social point of view with the whites." They did, however, "expect the priviledges and respect due to a soldier who had offered his services and his life to his government, ever ready and willing to share the common dangers of the battlefield." Yet these men received "scorn and contempt from both military and civilians." "White officers" provided them with "abrupt and ungentlemanly answers." They reported that "even our own regimental commander has abused us under the cover of his authority." The men concluded, "This treatment has sunk deep into our hearts, we did not expect it and therefore it is intolerable. We cannot serve a country in which we have no more rights and priviledges given us."[110]

Even as they encountered discrimination, free people of color generally continued to see U.S. victory as the most likely path to improving their station. Nevertheless, some free men of color struggled to persist in making the great sacrifice required of military service. Like other men participating in the conflict, some free men of color abandoned their posts and absconded from service. David Franklin, a Baltimore native and member of the Ninth U.S. Colored Infantry, appeared before a military tribunal charged with absence without leave for abandoning his post for three days in April 1865. Following a trial, the military convicted Franklin and required him "to forfeit ten dollars ($10) of his monthly pay."[111] While enlisted with the First U.S. Colored Cavalry, John Carr of Nansemond County, Virginia, landed in jail for protesting his transfer to Texas at the end of the war. Carr explained, "I was arrested on June 15, 1865 at Ft. Monroe, Va., that is gave up my arms, and was arrested while on board the 'Dudly Buck' going to Texas.... I was arrested with others for stating that I did not wish to go to Texas, believing that I should have been discharged at the close of the war, as I enlisted for three years or during the war." Following his arrest, Carr remembered, "I was court martialed at Santiago, Texas and sent to Ft. Jefferson, Fla."[112] Carr received a dishonorable discharge, and the army withheld his pay.[113]

Outside of the military, free people of color performed services essential to the effort to crush the proslavery rebellion. Free people of color served as pilots for the U.S. army and guided troops through unfamiliar territory. They were important assets to U.S. forces, who could not always depend on the loyalty of whites in territories held or formerly occupied by the rebels. Charles B. Morin of Natchitoches Parish, Louisiana, assisted federal forces passing near his community. Morin remembered that he "acted as a guide for the Union Army and piloted them by short cuts through the swamps to Cloutierville. The distance around by the main road was 19 miles and the way I took them it was about 9 miles."[114] Sylvanus T. Brown of Charles City County, Virginia, used his knowledge of the local geography around the rebel capital at Richmond to assist the U.S. war effort. He recalled, "I took a scout of the Union Army from Harrison's Landing and took him across the Chickahominy Swamp and through by the rebel camps in the night close up to Richmond to see the position of the Confederates and took him back to the same place. We were gone 5 days in all."[115]

Federal troops escaping the rebel forces sometimes depended on free people of color for provisions and information.[116] Free persons of color willingly supplied both and saved the lives of soldiers otherwise trapped in enemy territory. Elijah Popewell of Lexington County, South Carolina, aided U.S. troops who had absconded from rebel imprisonment in late 1864. He explained, "I gave rations to 2 escaped Union prisoners to last them 3 or 4 days. I secreted them (the soldiers) at my farm for several hours."[117] Within a year of the war's end, William Jacobs of Richmond County, North Carolina, assisted a U.S. soldier who had escaped from the rebels in nearby South Carolina. After traveling approximately eighteen miles, the soldier arrived at Jacobs's door "nearly starved." Jacobs sheltered the soldier and allowed him to recuperate for over a week before sending him on. Under the cover of darkness, Jacobs transported the soldier from Richmond County to Fayetteville, where he placed the man under the care of his cousins William and Edmund Chavers, who provided the soldier with a map and guided him over the neighboring Cape Fear River.[118]

Aiding the efforts of the federal government sometimes endangered free people of color who lived near supporters of the rebellion. They made great sacrifices while cooperating with federal officials and risked their bodies and property in the cause of suppressing the rebellion. After Oscar Wilson of Maryville, Tennessee, gave the U.S. forces information about enemy activities, the rebels sought retribution. In October 1863, rebel soldiers attacked Wilson's home. He recalled that during the assault, "They robbed my house and took my bed clothes, dishes, wearing clothes, and broke up and destroyed my furniture. They robbed me of everything I had and left me destitute." Following the attack, Wilson and his family escaped to Knoxville, where he eventually enlisted in the U.S. army.[119] The rebels attempted to capture and kill Sheldon Cohen of Beaufort County, South Carolina, whom they suspected of working as a spy for the federal forces. Cohen's wife, Lavinia, remembered, "My husband was very much threatened by the Rebels after they had found out that he was in the habit of going to Hilton Head," where Cohen regularly visited the federal forces. She further explained, "They came to the house several times to catch him and way laid the house at night and would have killed him if they had caught him, but he laid out in the woods and swamps and they did not get him. The Rebels took our two horses and destroyed a great deal about the place, broke open the corn house and scattered the corn, took half of our bacon and destroyed our clothing and bedding what they could not carry off."[120]

For at least one free man of color, providing U.S. officials with intelligence demanded the ultimate sacrifice. James Bowser of Nansemond County, Virginia, lost his life after the rebels learned of his support for the U.S. army. After the federal forces reached his area of Virginia, Bowser became an informant and provided the army with useful details about his community. Eventually, some white people learned of Bowser's activities and decided to seek retribution. In the middle of the night, a group of white men forced Bowser and his son from their home and took them into the woods, where the vigilantes decapitated Bowser. The mob permitted Bowser's son to live, so that he could tell the story of his father's death as a warning to others who might cooperate with U.S. forces.[121]

Free people of color surrendered untold amounts of property in support of the federal victory. As the U.S. forces traveled through the South, they required civilians, including free people of color, to forfeit their personal property to help maintain the troops. Federal forces confiscated two water vessels from William Pugh of Norfolk County, Virginia, for military purposes in 1863. Pugh explained, "When the steamer came up, the lighter was hard aground on low tide, and they ordered me to bring it to the steamer as soon as tide would permit which I did—a few days afterward this the same party came up the river on the steamer C P Smith and took my sail boat."[122] After the U.S. forces gained control of Nashville, Tennessee, they began the process of obtaining greatly needed provisions and supplies. On at least two occasions, the army confiscated property from William C. Napier of the city. During their first visit, troops confiscated Napier's hogs. He explained, "An Ohio regiment was encamped ... about one half mile from my home.... A Lieutenant from the regiment came with wagons and a squad of soldiers to my home and there put into the wagons the hogs and carried them off. The soldiers killed the hogs, threw them into the wagons and drove off with them." In a second instance, troops carried off Napier's horses from his farm on the outskirts of town. Napier stated that the soldiers "in hunting around for horses went on my place and got the horses ... 4 bays, a brown, and a roan colt and took them to their camp."[123]

The lines of the battlefield and military camps sometimes encroached onto yards and farms of free persons of color, whose homes were transformed into makeshift shelters for U.S. troops. Free people of color in Henrico County, Virginia, incurred significant losses during and after the 1862 Battle of Frayser's Farm, when their property became part of the federal encampment. Isaac Sykes explained, "My farm was part of the battlefield.... The army camped on my place & all around it." William James, Isaac Sykes's neighbor, recalled that he saw "pretty much all" of his neighbor's property seized by federal troops. He stated, "Gen[era]l McClellan's army was camped on his place nearly three days & the battle of Frasier's farm was partly fought on his place."[124] Isaac Sykes's brother Richard Sykes was also affected by the fighting. He lost an assortment of property, including livestock, crops, and lumber. The troops used his fence rails for firewood and the construction of breastworks. In addition, the army seized his home and an outbuilding. Richard Sykes remembered that "Gen[era]l McCall took my house & barn for hospitals after the fight & they were used for that purpose for seven days."[125]

As the U.S. army traveled through the South, enslaved people ran by the thousands for cover under the U.S. banner, costing slaveholders, including a small number of free people of color, millions of dollars in losses. For these free persons of color, suppression of the rebellion came at a significant financial cost. The federal presence in their communities symbolized the possibility of accessing greater political rights and privileges but also represented an immediate restructuring of their social relations with enslaved people, who were their longtime subordinates.[126] By September 1864, Clifton, an enslaved man held by the Johnsons, a free family of color from Natchez, Mississippi, had abandoned them. Catharine Geraldine Johnson, a member of the family, wrote in her diary about Clifton: "We was in hopes that he would never leave us, but turned out like everything, to be all hopes. I suppose it is no use grieving after spilt milk."[127] Following the arrival of federal forces in his neighborhood, Peter Alexander Williams absconded from the Metoyers, a family of slaveholding free people of color. He recalled, "I belonged to Mrs. John Baptiste Augustin Metoyer. I belonged to her daughter, Mrs. Christoph, but I lived on her place in Natchitoches Parish until the Yankees came through there and then I went with them as a teamster and came to this city [New Orleans]."[128] Other enslaved people held by the free Metoyer family, including John D. Metoyer, Louis Metoyer, John Metoyer, alias Lewis, and John Philip, also left Natchitoches Parish and relocated to New Orleans. Once in New Orleans, the men enlisted in the U.S. army and served with the Fourth U.S. Colored Cavalry.[129]

While the war persisted on the battlefields, many free people of color on the home front pursued numerous activities both directly and tangentially related to the conflict. Free women of color, sometimes with the help of free men of color in their communities, established soldiers' aid societies to support the troops. They formed organizations across the loyal areas of the country, including in parts of the South, dedicated to supporting enlisted men of color, who were not the primary focus of predominantly white soldiers' aid organizations. Women of color in Georgetown, District of Columbia, held a festival at the Masonic Hall on Washington Street to raise funds to support enlisted men of color. The Colored Soldiers' Aid Society worked with the larger Ladies' Union Aid Society of Saint Louis, Missouri, to care for federal troops. They gathered foodstuffs such as canned goods, preserves, and crackers along with bundle rags and handkerchiefs to send to the soldiers. In Louisiana, women of color organized themselves into the New Orleans Colored Soldiers' Aid Association under the leadership of Angelina A. Fayerweather, Mary Ann Boguille, M. A. Dunlop, Annie M. Nahar, and Carrie Satchell. These women worked with other local organizations, such as Saint James Chapel and the Young Ladies' Benevolent Association, to raise funds for the troops and other good causes. In Louisville, Kentucky, women led the effort to establish societies to assist the troops and their families. By 1864, the city's women had established the Colored Ladies Soldiers' Aid Society of Louisville. Similar organizations popped up in the city following the establishment of the ladies' society, including the Fifth Street Church Colored Soldiers' Aid Society and the Soldiers' Aid Society of the Green Street Baptist Church, which included women and men. These organizations raised money and accomplished numerous good works ranging from providing dinners for soldiers to caring for sick and wounded troops.[130]

Free people of color across federally held parts of the South dedicated their time and effort to the large number of formerly enslaved refugees who rushed to the federal lines throughout the war. The refugees often needed the most basic of necessities but also sought to obtain education and property, which their enslavers had long denied them. Free people of color raised money and worked directly with freedpeople to help them fulfill these needs and achieve these goals. In 1862, Elizabeth Keckley used her connections to establish and promote the Contraband Relief Association in the District of Columbia. As the head seamstress for First Lady Mary Todd Lincoln, she had developed relationships with many of the nation's political elites and called on her network to obtain support from individuals such as President Lincoln, Wendell Phillips, and Frederick Douglass. Through her efforts and those of other members of the association, the organization provided clothing for destitute freedpeople. Free women of color in New Orleans held numerous events for the benefit of freedpeople, especially children. In 1865, a group of women led by

Elizabeth Keckley and Mary Smith Peake were among the numerous free women of color who strived for the advancement of formerly enslaved refugees during the Civil War. Keckley used her connections to President Abraham Lincoln and First Lady Mary Todd Lincoln to help establish and fund the District of Columbia's Contraband Relief Association. Peake organized a school for freedpeople at Fort Monroe, Virginia. There, she instructed both young and old in the basics of reading and writing. (Courtesy of the Smithsonian Institution)

Louise de Mortie, Mary B. Williams, and Louise Roudanez organized a fair to support the Orphans' Industrial and Education Home for the Children of Freedmen. New Orleans's free people of color supported the Freedmen's Aid Association, an integrated organization designed to help formerly enslaved people establish farms and acquire education. Jean Baptiste Roudanez and Sidney Thezan, both free men of color, served as officers for the organization. At Fort Monroe, Virginia, Mary Smith Peake, a free woman of color, helped to organize a school for formerly enslaved refugees who sheltered behind the federal lines. At her school, Peake instructed the young and old, providing them with basic literacy skills and teaching them Christian hymns. With her assistance, people who had barely known the letters of the alphabet became apt readers.[131]

After New Orleans fell to the federal forces, free people of color took advantage of the situation and attempted to access rights that had been withheld from them under the old regime. As the home of many members of the Louisiana Native Guards, New Orleans became an important intellectual center for those looking to end race-based discrimination. As the war continued on the battlefields, Louisiana's free people of color worked to end discriminatory policies. They created media outlets to disseminate their ideas about political and social equality. *L'Union*, a weekly newspaper published by Louis Charles Roudanez and Paul Trévigne, became the public voice for the rights of Louisiana's free people of color. First printed in 1862, the paper was an early vehicle for the promotion of civil rights. Two years later, Louis Charles Roudanez, Paul Trévigne, and Jean Baptiste Roudanez established the *New Orleans Tribune*, which they published in both English and French. This paper took the place of *L'Union* as an important instrument to support voting rights and desegregation.[132] The paper's first issue attacked the discriminatory "Black Code of Louisiana" and, alluding to its archaic nature, called it "as bloody and barbarous as the laws against witchcraft."[133] Free people of color also engaged in direct political protest. In 1864, Jean Baptiste Roudanez and Arnold Bertonneau lobbied the federal government to provide voting rights to people of "African descent." That year they presented petitions to Abraham Lincoln and members of Congress on behalf of hundreds of Louisiana free men of color, including veterans of the War of 1812 and men enlisted in the war against the rebellion.[134] After presenting their petitions, Roudanez and Bertonneau met with antislavery advocates to gather support for their cause. In a speech before a large crowd in Massachusetts, Bertonneau made a broad appeal for support. He explained that he sought a reconstructed Louisiana in which "the colored citizens shall have and enjoy every civil, political and religious right that white citizens enjoy." Bertonneau demanded a full restructuring of southern society. He stated, "In order to make our State blossom and bloom as the rose, the character of the whole people must be changed. As slavery is abolished, with it must vanish every vestige of oppression. The right to vote must be secured; the doors of our public schools must be opened."[135] The work of the Roudanez brothers, Trévigne, Bertonneau, and others was one part of a long struggle for civil rights in Louisiana and across the nation.[136] The Civil War would bring freedom to millions, but the fight for equality persisted.

Marietta T. Hill's prediction proved correct. Much sacrifice, including bloodshed, was required to end the threat of slavery and liberate free persons of color from its influences. As a result, the period from 1861 to 1865 represented a time of major challenges and changes for the South's free people of color. During these years, government policy and the behavior of neighbors encouraged free persons of color to make important choices about their futures and take political and economic risks that could potentially lead to their ruin. Free people of color, largely by force but sometimes through expedient choice, became central parts of the human infrastructure in areas controlled by the rebels. Once the U.S. military began to enlist men of color and accept their assistance as guides, laborers, caretakers, and advisers, the options for the region's free people of color shifted. Free men of color who had assisted the rebels turned to the U.S. government to protect their freedom. In some cases, the federal government failed free people of color as well as former bondspeople, who experienced continued discrimination in areas under U.S. control as well as within the ranks of the military.

The suppression of the rebellion was largely to the benefit of most free people of color, who did not hold slaves and had suffered various forms of oppression under the rebel government. The collapse of the rebel government, however, left slaveholding free people of color in a desperate place. Like many white planters, they would need to find new means to support their economic livelihood. The postwar period would offer new hopes and present unforeseen challenges to the South's free people of color.

CONCLUSION

Less than five years after the end of the Civil War, media outlets across the United States were abuzz with the news of the election of the nation's first "Colored U.S. Senator." One newspaper described the election of Hiram Revels, the new senator from Mississippi, as "an act of retributive justice." The article explained that "nearly ten years ago Senator Jefferson Davis left the Senate and plunged into the red sea of rebellion in order to perpetuate the slavery of a race. Now one of that race is elevated to the position which he held and the seat he occupied. Mississippi has repudiated the ex-President of the rebellious Confederacy and elected a negro to succe[e]d him."[1] The election of Hiram Revels represented a new day in the South and a transformation in the political landscape of the United States. Revels's classification as a person of color made his ascendancy to power truly historic. Many facets of Revels's early life, moreover, help to explain why he became the first person of color to serve in the U.S. Senate.

In a short autobiographical statement composed after his term in Congress, Revels explained, "I was born in Fayetteville, North Carolina on the 27th day of September 1827. My ancestors as far back as my knowledge extends were free. So that it may be seen that from experience I knew nothing of slavery." Revels's familiarity with enslavement came from observation, not through direct experience. In many ways, his early existence differed greatly from the daily lives of the men, women, and children of his "race" held in bondage. Revels attended a school in North Carolina where he was "instructed by one able and accomplished teacher in all branches of learning" before moving to Indiana and matriculating into several institutions of higher learning, including seminary. Before the Civil War, Revels served communities in the Upper South and Midwest as a minister and educator.[2] Revels was no ordinary man when he entered Mississippi politics during Reconstruction. He was a man of color but also a man of privilege.

If we take seriously the opportunities that liberty afforded the South's free people of color before 1865, the fact that a free man of color who had never experienced slavery became the first person of color to serve in the

Born free in North Carolina, Hiram Revels rose to become the first person of color to serve in the U.S. Senate. In 1870, the Mississippi state legislature elected him to fill one of its state's Senate seats. (Courtesy of the Library of Congress)

P. B. S. Pinchback, a Civil War veteran, served as acting governor of Louisiana during Reconstruction. Before his rise to the governorship of Louisiana, Pinchback was only the second person of color to serve as the state's lieutenant governor. (Courtesy of the Library of Congress)

U.S. Senate should come as no surprise. Although free status in the antebellum period did not guarantee that every free person of color had access to education, wealth, and political position, liberty provided many of them with important advantages in the postwar period. During Reconstruction in the South, people of color who were free before the Civil War held disproportionate authority across the region relative to those who were born enslaved. They claimed political power even in parts of the South where free people of color were almost nonexistent in the antebellum years. In 1872, P. B. S. Pinchback, an antebellum free man of color originally from Georgia, became the acting governor of Louisiana. After serving as lieutenant governor of Louisiana, he assumed the governorship following the impeachment of Henry C. Warmoth. Pinchback's predecessor as lieutenant governor, Oscar Dunn, was also free before the outbreak of the Civil War; Dunn was the nation's first lieutenant governor of color. Furthermore, the first persons of color to represent southern states in the U.S. House of Representatives included several men whose free status dated back to the antebellum period. Among them were James T. Rapier of Alabama; Charles E. Nash of Louisiana; and Alonzo J. Ransier, Joseph H. Rainey, Robert C. DeLarge, and Richard H. Cain of South Carolina. Many other antebellum free men of color served in numerous government positions across the region at both state and local levels.[3]

The educational attainments of free people of color before the Civil War propelled them into other important positions in the postwar period. They played a key role in the education of the freedmen and others during and after the war. These women and men founded schools and taught the masses of people hungry for instruction after the laws of the South had excluded them from formal education during the days of slavery. Those who were free before the war also translated their education into political action through media. In New Orleans, freeborn men like Louis Charles Roudanez and Paul Trévigne helped reshape the southern media landscape. Their publications challenged the status quo and called for transformations in southern political and social life, including an end to discrimination against people of color. Educational attainment also pushed antebellum free persons of color to the forefront of many of the region's emerging religious institutions. With the collapse of slavery came an explosion in the growth of independent religious organizations and churches run exclusively by people of color.[4]

Liberty obtained in the years before the Civil War also translated into economic advantage in the postbellum period. Free people of color who owned businesses in the antebellum days often continued that work during Reconstruction. Others who were landholders before the war remained so following the end of the conflict. Some descendants of free people of color still owned and reaped the benefits from real estate originally obtained by their ancestors before the Civil War. With the development of institutions of higher learning for people of color during Reconstruction, some antebellum free persons transformed economic advantage into educational opportunities for their children. Many of the earliest graduates of these schools, such as Hampton Institute in Virginia and Shaw University in North Carolina, were people free before the war or the children of free persons of color. These early graduates, in turn, became educators, doctors, lawyers, writers, and other professionals.[5]

Some free people of color were not able to enjoy the privileges associated with wealth, education, and influence before the Civil War, and this pattern continued after the conflict as well. State laws limiting the franchise to men persisted in excluding women of all backgrounds from exercising formal political power, although historians have clearly demonstrated that women sought political influence through alternative means. Many people who were free but poor before the war remained so after 1865. For some antebellum free persons of color who were slaveholders before and during the war, emancipation brought about because of the conflict left them worse off than they had been during the days of slavery.[6]

Nevertheless, with some exceptions, antebellum freedom benefited those people of color who were able to enjoy it, often for years after the Civil War. When we conflate the experiences of free people of color and enslaved persons or those of their descendants, we obfuscate the advantages and challenges lived by both. Jim Crow policies affected the descendants of free people of color and enslaved people, but not always in equal ways. In some communities across the South, antebellum liberty was so valued by the descendants of free people of color that they largely continued to marry only among themselves well into the twentieth century. In some cases, these families still engage in endogamous marriages.[7]

The experiences of free people of color before and after the end of the Civil War provide us with many powerful insights into the significance of legal personhood, free status, and the social, economic, and political possibilities attached to these positions. At the same time, the story of the South's free people of color challenges many of our ideas about the significance of race in the history of the United States and its colonial antecedents. Many of us find understanding the South before 1865 much easier if we can simplify the social hierarchy. A South with white people on top and people of color at the bottom is much less complicated than a social landscape in which various forms of hierarchy intersect. However, we must abandon this simplified version of the South in order to comprehend more fully the historical experiences of the southern population in all its diversity. The existence of the free man of color who owned enslaved persons of color for the purpose of making a profit seems to be a historical contradiction. But instances like this make much more sense when we force ourselves to conceive of the slaveholder of color not simply as a man of color but also an investor, a businessman, and a person who valued financial gain over broad ideas about equality, fraternity, and liberty. When we acknowledge the unscrupulous character of kidnappers, both white and of color, who snatched children from their parents to sell on the open market, we can begin to appreciate the real challenges that victims of kidnapping and their allies faced. If we are able to grasp the inconsistencies between the law and everyday behavior in the pre–Civil War South, then we are capable of recognizing similar patterns in our own time, even if these parallels are difficult to face. Are we like the white parishioners who permitted political ideology to seep into their religious spaces and separate them from fellow adherents of Christ, all the while pretending that segregated religious spaces were acceptable? Do we resemble the organized laborers who petitioned for the expulsion of tradesmen of color and viewed them as economic threats while the majority of wealth remained concentrated in the hands of slaveholders? Are we like the southern moderates who bargained and compromised with political extremists and accepted the slow denigration of the rights of their neighbors, even though they knew such compromises were unjust?

We know that many of the injustices that affected the lives of free people of color continued and, in some cases, still persist in the United States. The physical separation of people of color and whites that gradually emerged in churches, theaters, and schools in the postrevolutionary South had become commonplace by the late nineteenth and early twentieth centuries. As the number of public places multiplied, segregation's presence in American life expanded, too. Proslavery radicals and white supremacists attempted to portray free people of color as a threat in order to protect their financial, social, and political interests. Likewise, political figures and media outlets have continued to politicize the mere presence of people of color in certain spaces for equally dubious reasons. Conservative politicians in the late nineteenth century rehashed and modified the tropes that radicals had used against free people of color in earlier years to delegitimize the ascendancy of former bondspeople, antebellum free persons of color, and their posterity. These partisans portrayed people of color as criminal and unfit for political power.

They encouraged their adherents to regard people of color as economic threats, even though the vast majority of wealth still rested with a small collective of white men.[8]

The persistence of the injustices that pervaded the lives of free people of color before the end of the Civil War are particularly apparent within the postwar criminal justice system. Developed in the eighteenth and nineteenth centuries, the process of targeting persons of color, especially poor people of color, has ballooned over time. The exaction of excessive criminal penalties, the transformation of convicted persons into forced laborers, and the criminalization of particular activities for people of a certain racial categorization were in their infancy when local officials targeted a handful of mostly poor free persons of color before 1865. Since that time, the imprisonment of large numbers of people, a disproportionate number of them persons of color, has created an explosion in the use of convicted persons as a source of unpaid or severely underpaid labor. Immediately following the Civil War, chain gangs composed largely of society's most disadvantaged people appeared on the plantations and roadsides of the South. Well into the twenty-first century, people convicted of even the pettiest crimes have slogged away as unpaid or underpaid laborers in factories and farms across the nation. The roots of what legal scholar Michelle Alexander termed "the new Jim Crow" can be seen in the criminal justice system of the old slave South, especially with regard to the treatment of impoverished free people of color. The radicals of the prewar South sought to use excessive criminal penalties and the system of hiring out to extract forced labor from underprivileged free people of color. In the postwar South, partisan politicians used an expanded version of the same strategy to turn disadvantaged freedpeople and their descendants into unpaid field hands and roadworkers. The pre–Civil War South differed from the Jim Crow South in important ways, but the discriminatory practices of the postwar South had deep roots in the earlier period.[9]

The postbellum South remained a place of complexities and contradictions, as it had been in the pre–Civil War period. Amid legal segregation and oppression, people of color found ways to survive and thrive by investing in their institutions, educating their people, and working skillfully with sympathetic or opportunistic whites. Even in a more rigid Jim Crow South, the intersections of racial categorization, gender, wealth, occupation, and other forms of status created an uneven experience for persons of color. These patterns have continued into the twenty-first century. Although people of color make up a disproportionate percentage of America's impoverished and imprisoned, they can also be found in the highest reaches of government, industry, business, and academia. While politicians attack immigrants of color and refuse to provide many of them with secure legal status, farmers and industrialists clamor for them to travel countless miles to work on their farms and in their processing plants.

In many ways, the ills of the pre–Civil War South are the problems of the modern United States.[10] In today's America, liberty is still contested.

ACKNOWLEDGMENTS

I would like to acknowledge the many individuals who helped bring this book into existence. Many thanks to my editor, Brandon Proia, who made the review and production of this book a nearly seamless venture. He edited the manuscript and chose two very supportive readers who helped to make this book much stronger in its content and analysis. Much gratitude to them. Additional thanks to the team at UNC Press, including Dylan White, Jay Mazzocchi, Cate Hodorowicz, Erin Granville, and Liz Orange, who helped move the project through the latter stages of the production process. Special thanks to Laura Dooley, Andrea Gross, and Liz Lundeen, who carefully read every word of the manuscript and offered thoughtful suggestions and corrections. This study would not have been possible without the assistance of archivists, librarians, and clerks at the various repositories that I visited for this project. They are the heroes of the history profession. I am grateful for the feedback provided by the following individuals who read and commented on sections of the manuscript: Mishio Yamanaka, Adam Domby, Peter Wood, and J. Charles Waldrup. Participants in the Triangle Legal History Seminar and Omohundro Institute Colloquium also offered valuable questions and critiques. I greatly appreciate the support of the colleges and history departments at the University of North Carolina at Greensboro, Virginia Tech, and the University of South Carolina. I am glad to have had many great colleagues in the history departments of these universities over the early days of my career. Special thanks to my former advisers at various stages of my career who helped me think through the intricacies of life for free people of color: Kathleen DuVal, Malinda Maynor Lowery, Theda Perdue, Holly Brewer, and Phyllis Hunter.

Last, but never least, I want to acknowledge the support of my family. My parents and siblings are always there when I need them. My paternal grandparents, both of whom passed as I finished this book, were instrumental figures in my life. My grandmother's stories about our ancestors and relatives initiated my interest in the history of free people of color. I am in debt to her for that and so much more. This book is for her.

NOTES

Abbreviations

ADAH	Alabama Department of Archives and History, Montgomery
ARCJC	Augusta-Richmond County Judicial Center, Augusta, Ga.
CCSCHS	College of Charleston South Carolina Historical Society, Charleston
CMSR	Compiled Military Service Records of Volunteer Union Soldiers Who Served with the United States Colored Troops: Infantry Organizations, National Archives and Records Administration, Washington, D.C.
CPRCBF	Confederate Papers Relating to Citizens or Business Firms, National Archives and Records Administration, Washington, D.C.
CSR	Compiled Service Records of Confederate Soldiers Who Served in Organizations from the State of North Carolina, National Archives and Records Administration, Washington, D.C.
CWP	Civil War Pensions, National Archives and Records Administration, Washington, D.C.
DHS	Delaware Historical Society, Wilmington
DPA	Delaware Public Archives, Dover
DU	Duke University Rubenstein Library, Durham, N.C.
ECU	East Carolina University Joyner Library, Greenville, N.C.
FCCA	Fredericksburg Circuit Court Archives, Fredericksburg, Va.
FHS	Filson Historical Society, Louisville, Ky.
GCQA	Guilford College Quaker Archives, Greensboro, N.C.
GU	Georgetown University Booth Family Center for Special Collections, Washington, D.C.
HSP	Historical Society of Pennsylvania, Philadelphia
JML	Jones Memorial Library, Lynchburg, Va.
KCA	Knox County Archives, Knoxville, Tenn.
KDLA	Kentucky Department of Libraries and Archives, Frankfort
KHS	Kentucky Historical Society, Frankfort
LC	Library of Congress, Washington, D.C.
LCCOHRD	Loudoun County Clerk's Office Historic Records and Deeds, Leesburg, Va.
LHC	Louisiana Historical Center, New Orleans
LSA	Louisiana State Archives, Baton Rouge
LVA	Library of Virginia, Richmond
MSA	Maryland State Archives, Annapolis
NARA	National Archives and Records Administration, Washington, D.C.
NCCC	Northampton County Circuit Court, Eastville, Va.
NOPL	New Orleans Public Library
PASP	Pennsylvania Abolition Society Papers
PC	Private Collection

{ 261 }

RSPPUNCG	Race and Slavery Petitions Project, University of North Carolina at Greensboro Jackson Library
SANC	State Archives of North Carolina, Raleigh
SCDAH	South Carolina Department of Archives and History, Columbia
SCC	Southampton County Courthouse, Courtland, Va.
SCCAC	Southern Claims Commission Approved Claims, National Archives and Records Administration, Washington, D.C.
SCL	South Caroliniana Library, Columbia
SHC	Southern Historical Collection, Chapel Hill, N.C.
SSDA	Slavery Societies Digital Archives
TSLA	Tennessee State Library and Archives, Nashville
UGA	University of Georgia Hargrett Rare Book and Manuscript Library
UM	University of Maryland Special Collections and University Archives, College Park
UNO	University of New Orleans
UofL	University of Louisville Archives and Special Collections
UVA	University of Virginia Special Collections, Charlottesville
VHS	Virginia Historical Society, Richmond

Introduction

1. Amariah Read Revolutionary War Pension, NARA; Auditor of Public Accounts Nansemond County Land Tax Books, 1804, LVA; Auditor of Public Accounts Nansemond County Land Tax Books, 1843, LVA.

2. Guild, *Black Laws of Virginia*, 131–33; Lorder B. Skeeter Deposition, July 25, 1919, Neverson Boone Pension, CWP.

3. 1830 U.S. Federal Census, Nansemond County, Virginia, 238.

4. For more on the concept of the Native ground, see DuVal, *Native Ground*.

5. For a sweeping history of the collapse of slavery in parts of the Atlantic world, see Blackburn, *Overthrow of Colonial Slavery*; Blackburn, *American Crucible*; and Davis, *Problem of Slavery in the Age of Emancipation*. For more on the end of slavery in the North, see Nash, *Forging Freedom*; Nash and Soderlund, *Freedom by Degrees*; Melish, *Disowning Slavery*; and Hodges, *Root and Branch*. For authoritative accounts of the collapse of slavery in Saint-Domingue and the French Atlantic, see James, *Black Jacobins*; Dubois, *Colony of Citizens*; Dubois, *Avengers of the New World*; and Scott, *Common Wind*. Works that have focused on the end of slavery in Britain and its colonies as well as the suppression of the slave trade include Drescher, *Econocide*; Drescher, *Mighty Experiment*; and Brown, *Moral Capital*.

6. Freehling, *Road to Disunion: Secessionists Triumphant*, xiii; Mason, *Slavery and Politics in the Early American Republic*, 7.

7. Scholars have concluded that Nat Turner's rebellion had limited to no long-term effects on the locales at the centers of their studies. For the case of Savannah, Whittington B. Johnson concluded that "Nat Turner's Revolt did not lead to a major white backlash in Savannah. Had whites become nervous about a ripple effect from the revolt surfacing in their city, blacks would have come under closer scrutiny." See Johnson, *Black Savannah*, 47. Melvin Patrick Ely uncovered a limited immediate reaction to the Turner rebellion in Prince Edward County, Virginia, and explained, "Even in the weeks following Nat Turner's rebellion, they [Free Afro-Virginians] did not find themselves beset by the kind of supercharged, security-driven atmosphere that could have made life a hell for them. A conspicuous, disfranchised minority, they still managed to carve out a

reasonably secure place for themselves and to win recognition from most of their white neighbors as law-abiding people." See Ely, *Israel on the Appomattox*, 175–86, 260–61. Martha S. Jones found that the Dred Scott decision largely did not stop free people of color from attempting to assert their rights. She contended, "Even as newspapers promoted the decision's significance, underscoring the holding that no black person was a citizen of the United States, nothing changed in Baltimore. Black residents continued to exercise rights and conduct themselves like citizens in the state court venues that had long been the primary arbiters of such questions." See Jones, *Birthright Citizens*, 14.

8. Kimberlé Crenshaw coined the term "intersectionality." See Crenshaw, "Demarginalizing the Intersection of Race and Sex"; and Crenshaw, "Mapping the Margins." Anne McClintock argued that "no social category exists in privileged isolation; each comes into being in social relation to other categories, if in uneven and contradictory ways." See McClintock, *Imperial Leather*, 8–9. Recent scholarship has focused on the importance of reputation in relationships between free people of color and their white neighbors and argued for its significance in understanding southern social dynamics. See Ely, *Israel on the Appomattox*; von Daacke, *Freedom Has a Face*; Marks, "Community Bonds in the Bayou City"; Welch, "Black Litigiousness and White Accountability"; and Welch, *Black Litigants in the Antebellum South*.

9. For more on segregation in the North, see Archer, *Jim Crow North*. During the 1950s, historian C. Vann Woodward theorized that race-based segregation was largely a product of political and social events that took place in the late nineteenth century. Since then, several scholars have revised Woodward's thesis, finding physical separation based on racial categories in the pre–Civil War South. In response, Woodward amended his thesis to incorporate evidence of segregation in pre–Civil War southern cities. The first edition of *The Strange Career of Jim Crow* appeared in 1955 and has gone through several revisions. See Woodward, *Strange Career of Jim Crow*. Richard C. Wade offered one of the earliest challenges to the Woodward thesis. See Wade, *Slavery in the Cities*. Ira Berlin offered an important revision of Woodward in the case of "free negroes." Berlin concluded that "by the eve of the Civil War, segregation had extended to almost every corner of Southern life." The findings in this book support his contentions about the increasing presence of segregation but not to the same extent. See Berlin, *Slaves without Masters*, 321–27, 383.

10. *Seventh Census*, ix; Kennedy, *Population of the United States in 1860*, 8, 18, 46, 54, 72–73, 180–81, 194, 214, 270, 286–87, 358–59, 452, 466–67, 484–86, 516–18, 588; U.S. Senate, *Preliminary Report on the Eighth Census 1860*, 136.

11. Kennedy, *Population of the United States in 1860*, 8, 46, 54, 74, 180–82, 194–95, 214, 271, 358–59, 452, 516–18, 588.

12. Schweninger, *Black Property Owners in the South*.

13. Jack D. Forbes was one of the early scholars to examine the use of racial terminology in colonial North American and the early United States. See Forbes, *Black Africans and Native Americans*.

14. For examples, see *State v. William Chavers* (1857), 7249 State v. William Chavers 50 N.C. 11 (Dec. 1857), Supreme Court Cases, SANC; and William D. Valentine Diary, vol. 12, 164–65, SHC.

15. Gross, *What Blood Won't Tell*; Sharfstein, *Invisible Line*; Hobbs, *Chosen Exile*.

16. Gross, *What Blood Won't Tell*, 1–4, 16–47. Scholars of Latin American history have found similar patterns of inconsistent racial categorization. See Fischer and O'Hara, *Imperial Subjects*; Rappaport, *Disappearing Mestizo*; and Twinam, *Purchasing Whiteness*.

17. Milteer, *North Carolina's Free People of Color*, 223–27.

18. Merrell, *Indians' New World*; Rountree and Davidson, *Eastern Shore Indians of Virginia and Maryland*; Herndon and Sekatu, "Right to a Name"; Herndon and Sekatu, "Colonizing the Children"; Mandell, *Tribe, Race, History*; Spear, *Race, Sex, and Social Order in Early New Orleans*; O'Brien, *Firsting and Lasting*; Shoemaker, *Native American Whalemen and the World*; Newell, *Brethren by Nature*. Scholars have observed similar patterns in the categorization of indigenous people in Latin America. See French, *Legalizing Identities*; and Tavárez, "Legally Indian."

19. Garrow, *Mattamuskeet Documents*; Rountree and Davidson, *Eastern Shore Indians of Virginia and Maryland*; Milteer, "From Indians to Colored People."

20. Coleman, *That the Blood Stay Pure*, 70–71; Copy of Laws of the Creek Nation, January 7, 1825, Keith M. Read Collection, UGA; *Constitution and Laws of the Choctaw Nation*; *Constitution and Laws of the Cherokee Nation*; Yarbrough, *Race and the Cherokee Nation*, 7, 39–55. For a detailed discussion of kinship, belonging, and race, see Perdue, *"Mixed Blood" Indians*.

21. Russell, *Free Negro in Virginia*; Wright, *Free Negro in Maryland*; Jackson, *Free Negro Labor and Property Holding in Virginia*; Franklin, *Free Negro in North Carolina*; Brown, *Free Negroes in the District of Columbia*; Sterkx, *Free Negro in Ante-Bellum Louisiana*; Wikramanayake, *World in Shadow*.

22. Berlin, *Slaves without Masters*, xiii.

23. Breen and Innes, *"Myne Owne Ground"*; Whitten, *Andrew Durnford*; Walker, *Free Frank*; Johnson and Roark, *Black Masters*; Koger, *Black Slaveowners*; Alexander, *Ambiguous Lives*; Warner, *Free Men in an Age of Servitude*; Johnson, *Black Savannah*; Bogger, *Free Blacks in Norfolk*; Phillips, *Freedom's Port*; Hanger, *Bounded Lives*; Landers, *Black Society in Spanish Florida*; Schafer, *Becoming Free, Remaining Free*; Gaspar and Hine, *Beyond Bondage*; Higgins, *A Stranger and a Sojourner*.

24. Ely, *Israel on the Appomattox*. For critiques of Ely, see Foner, Review of *Israel on the Appomattox*; Roark and Johnson, Review of *Israel on the Appomattox*; Phillips, Review of *Israel on the Appomattox*; and Capers, "Comment on Melvin Ely's *Israel on the Appomattox*."

25. Barfield and Marshall, *Thomas Day*; Dantas, *Black Townsmen*; Sumler-Edmond, *Secret Trust of Aspasia Cruvellier Mirault*; Harris, *Hanging of Thomas Jeremiah*; Thompson, *Exiles at Home*; Marshall and Leimenstoll, *Thomas Day*; Winch, *Clamorgans*; Dorsey, *Hirelings*; Myers, *Forging Freedom*; von Daacke, *Freedom Has a Face*; Wolf, *Almost Free*; West, *Family or Freedom*; Marotti, *Heaven's Soldiers*; Aslakson, *Making Race in the Courtroom*; McCleskey, *Road to Black Ned's Forge*; Winch, *Between Slavery and Freedom*; Maris-Wolf, *Family Bonds*; Hunter, *Bound in Wedlock*; Welch, *Black Litigants in the Antebellum South*; Jones, *Birthright Citizens*; de la Fuente and Gross, *Becoming Free*; Milteer, *North Carolina's Free People of Color*; Johnson, *Wicked Flesh*; Marks, *Black Freedom in the Age of Slavery*.

26. The scholarship about free people of color in other parts of the world is vast. Some of the important works on the topic include Cohen and Greene, *Neither Slave nor Free*; Heuman, *Between Black and White*; Landers, *Against the Odds*; Allen, *Slaves, Freedmen, and Indentured Laborers in Colonial Mauritius*; Welch and Goodridge, *"Red" and Black over White*; Vinson, *Bearing Arms for His Majesty*; King, *Blue Coat or Powdered Wig*; Newton, *Children of Africa in the Colonies*; Bennett, *Colonial Blackness*; Reid-Vazquez, *Year of the Lash*; Candlin and Pybus, *Enterprising Women*; Wheat, *Atlantic Africa and the Spanish Caribbean*; Livesay, *Children of Uncertain Fortune*; Newman, *Dark Inheritance*; Gharala, *Taxing Blackness*; Walker, *Jamaica Ladies*; and Morelli, *Free People of Color in the Spanish Atlantic*.

Chapter 1

1. Northampton County Wills Order Book 10, 1674–1679, 247, LVA; Taylor, *American Colonies*, x–xvii, 76–79, 118–57, 223–44, 246–55, 382–88. For further discussion of the conditions for free people of color like King Tony in colonial Northampton County, Virginia, see Breen and Innes, *"My Owne Grounds"*; Deal, "Constricted World"; and Deal, *Race and Class in Colonial Virginia*.

2. Taylor, *American Colonies*, xi–xii. Most historians have agreed that free people of color had a higher status than enslaved people in southern colonial societies, but they have debated the significance of the rights and privileges free people of color enjoyed in the face of the restrictions imposed by southern lawmakers. Furthermore, they have differed in their assessment concerning the degree of contrast between the free and slave statuses of persons of color. For discussions of the status of free people of color in southern colonial societies, see Kimmel, "Free Blacks in Seventeenth-Century Maryland"; Breen and Innes, "My Owne Grounds"; Sterkx, *Free Negro in Ante-Bellum Louisiana*, 13–35; Nicholls, "Passing through This Troublesome World"; Deal, "Constricted World"; Ingersoll, "Free Blacks in a Slave Society"; Davidson, *Free Blacks on the Lower Eastern Shore of Maryland*; Deal, *Race and Class in Colonial Virginia*, 207–405; Heinegg, *Free African Americans*; Berlin, *Many Thousands Gone*, 123–26, 154, 211–12; Morgan, *Slave Counterpoint*, 485–97; Landers, *Black Society in Spanish Florida*, 29–109; Jeske, "From Slave to Slave Owner"; de la Fuente and Gross, *Becoming Free*, 13–38; and Milteer, *North Carolina's Free People of Color*, 31–48.

3. Ann Laura Stoler argued that "racism is an inherent product of the colonial encounter, fundamental to an otherwise illegitimate access to property and power." See Stoler, *Carnal Knowledge and Imperial Power*, 24. Cécile Vidal made a similar argument specifically about French New Orleans. She suggested that "New Orleans was deeply shaped by racial ideas and practices from the outset and that this early implementation of a system of racial domination made it a Caribbean port city." See Vidal, *Caribbean New Orleans*, 23.

4. Patterson, *Slavery and Social Death*, 5, 105–31, 209–39. On the commodification of African people, see Smallwood, *Saltwater Slavery*. The enslavement of Native people had deep roots in the precolonial past. See Snyder, *Slavery in Indian Country*.

5. William Gooch to Alured Popple in Evans, "Question of Complexion," 414–15.

6. "State Convention," *Newbern (N.C.) Spectator*, November 20, 1835.

7. Johnson's Indenture for Mulatto Child, Northampton County Free Negro and Slave Records, (Gloucester Co.) Anne, alias Judah, illegally held as a slave, 1733, LVA.

8. Queen Anne's County Court Judgement Record, 1718–1719, 219–20, MSA.

9. Historians have shown that the enslavement and trade in Native peoples existed throughout the Western Hemisphere and in some parts of Europe. See Brooks, *Captives and Cousins*; Gallay, *Indian Slave Trade*; Gallay, *Indian Slavery in Colonial America*; Snyder, *Slavery in Indian Country*; Rushforth, *Bonds of Alliance*; Newell, *Brethren by Nature*; van Deusen, *Global Indios*; Reséndez, *Other Slavery*; Shefveland, *Anglo-Native Virginia*; and Monteiro, *Blacks of the Land*.

10. Craven County Court Minutes, vol. 10, 216, SANC.

11. Edgecombe County Court Minutes, vol. 4, 28, SANC.

12. Shyllon, *Black People in Britain*; Fisher, *Counterflows to Colonialism*, 20–49; Chater, *Untold Histories*; Allen, *European Slave Trading in the Indian Ocean*. For more on the experiences of "East Indians" or South Asians in other parts of the colonial world, see Allen, "Marie Rozette and Her World"; and Peabody, *Madeleine's Children*.

13. Proceedings of the Provincial Court, 1675–1676, 291, MSA.

14. "Ran away from the Subscriber," *Virginia Gazette* (Williamsburg), May 2, 1745.

15. James Dunn Case, PASP Series 4, Manumissions, Indentures and Other Legal Papers, Part 1, Petition of James Dunn, an East Indian boy (circa 1790s), HSP.

16. Northampton County Orders, Deeds, Wills, Etc., vol. 2, 16, NCCC.

17. Petition to ratify freedom, Judicial Records of the French Superior Council, #1735-06-04-02, LHC.

18. South Carolina Secretary of State Miscellaneous Records, vol. EE, 156–57, SCDAH.

19. South Carolina Secretary of State Miscellaneous Records, vol. II, 381, SCDAH.

20. South Carolina Secretary of State Miscellaneous Records, vol. GG, 21, SCDAH.

21. Olsberg, *Colonial Records of South Carolina*, 82, 111, 124, 149–50, 156.

22. Landers, *Black Society in Spanish Florida*, 27–30.

23. South Carolina Secretary of State Miscellaneous Records, vol. GG, 355, SCDAH.

24. Scholars have noted that colonial discriminatory laws also had a particularly negative effect on white women who crossed racial boundaries and free women of color. Regulations on sexual behavior and discriminatory laws that used racial categories to shape the social hierarchy intersected to create a host of problems for these women. See Brown, *Good Wives*, 187–211, 227–44; and Fischer, *Suspect Relations*, 122–29.

25. Hening, *Statutes at Large*, 2:170, 3:86–88.

26. Hening, 3:86–88.

27. Bacon, *Laws of Maryland at Large*, 267.

28. Clark, *State Records of North Carolina*, 23:62–66.

29. *Laws of the State of Delaware* (1797), 108–9.

30. Cooper, *Statutes at Large of South Carolina*, 20.

31. Candler, *Colonial Records of the State of Georgia*, 1:59–60.

32. *Code noir*, 3–4.

33. Sessions Docquett for October Genl Court 1725, Colonial Court Papers, Box 174, General Court-Criminal-1725, SANC; *Dom. Rex v. Cotton*, Colonial Court Papers, Box 174, General Court-Criminal-1725, SANC.

34. Order to take Hitchens into Custody & carry to Goal, Northampton County Criminal Causes, 1735–1759, 1735–39 Criminal Causes, 1738 Criminal Causes: Tamar Hitchens (late Smith), white to be jailed for marrying Edward Hitchens, mulatto, LVA.

35. Cope, *Limits of Racial Domination*; Milton and Vinson, "Counting Heads"; Morelli, *Free People of Color in the Spanish Atlantic*, 26–35. For an in-depth exploration of discriminatory taxation in New Spain, see Gharala, *Taxing Blackness*.

36. Guild, *Black Laws of Virginia*, 126, 130–31.

37. Clark, *State Records of North Carolina*, 23:106.

38. Bacon, *Laws of Maryland*, 360.

39. Candler, *Colonial Records of the State of Georgia*, 19:31.

40. For examples of tax lists, see Granville County Taxables, Box 20, SANC; and Surry County Orders, 1757–1763, 134–35, LVA. The names included Joseph Barkley, John Banks, John Banks Jr., James Barlow, John Eley, Thomas Thorn, John Deveris, William Walden, William Charity, Thomas Simon, Thomas Tann, David Walden, Thomas Wilson, and Edward Peters.

41. Petn of Sundry Inhabitants of Northampton, Edgecombe & Granville Counties, General Assembly Session Records, Box 2, Nov–Dec 1762 Lower House Papers, Certificates of election, petition not acted on Estimate of pay and allowances, SANC.

42. Petition from the Inhabitants of Granville 1771, General Assembly Session Records, Box 5, Nov–Dec 1771 Lower House Papers Petitions rejected or not acted on, SANC.

43. Guild, *Black Laws of Virginia*, 133–34.

44. Guild, 132.

45. Richard West to the Right Honorable the Lords Commissioners of Trade and Plantations in Evans, "Question of Complexion," 412–13.

46. William Gooch to Alured Popple in Evans, "Question of Complexion," 415–15.

47. Cooper, *Statutes at Large of South Carolina*, 136; Crow, *Black Experience in Revolutionary North Carolina*, 31.

48. Guild, *Black Laws of Virginia*, 25, 37, 44.

49. Bacon, *Laws of Maryland*, 269.

50. *Laws of the State of Delaware* (1797), 215.

51. Bacon, *Laws of Maryland*, 299.

52. Clark, *State Records of North Carolina*, 25:283, 445.

53. Guild, *Black Laws of Virginia*, 47.

54. Clark, *State Records of North Carolina*, 23:106–7.

55. McCord, *Statutes at Large of South Carolina*, 384, 396.

56. *Code noir*, 13–14.

57. Milteer, *North Carolina's Free People of Color*, 36–39. For a detailed exploration of sexual violence in colonial North America, see Block, *Rape and Sexual Power in Early America*.

58. Queen Anne's County Court Judgment Record, 1709–1716, 7–8, MSA.

59. Copy of the Order, Colonial Court Papers Civil and Criminal Papers, 1711–1719, Box CCR 149, 1715, SANC.

60. Baltimore County Court Minutes, vol. BB, June 1755, MSA.

61. Brown, *Good Wives*, 196–201.

62. Kent County Criminal Court Records, 1728–1734, 465, 479–82, MSA.

63. Bertie County Court Minutes, vol. 1, 74, SANC.

64. Perquimans Precinct Court Minutes, vol. 1, 21, SANC.

65. Copy of Agreement, Judicial Records of the French Superior Council, #1764-04-25-03, LHC.

66. *Laws of the State of Delaware* (1797), 208; New Castle County Court of General Sessions Docket, May 1769–May 1775, 116, DPA.

67. Somerset County Judicial Records, 1760–1763, 82, MSA.

68. Indenture James Hutt to James Voshell, Kent County Record of Deeds Apprentice Indentures N.D., 1723–1780, 1764 Indenture Hutt, James to Voshell, James, DPA.

69. Report about Free Negros & Mulattos, General Assembly Session Records, Box 1, July 1733/1733 Joint Committee Papers, SANC.

70. Guild, *Black Laws of Virginia*, 39.

71. Accomack County Orders, 1666–1670, 158–59, LVA.

72. Lancaster County Orders No. 2, 1686–1696, LVA.

73. Kent County Court Proceedings, 1676–1698, 911, MSA.

74. "A Free Negro Fellow, named Johny," *South Carolina Gazette* (Charleston), November 20, 1736.

75. Prince George's County Register of Wills Inventories, 1697–1720, 220–25, MSA.

76. Amelia County Will Book 1, 1734–1761, 45–47, 35, LVA.

77. Although sale and treatment as property are commonly associated with slave status, Orlando Patterson suggested that the sale was also associated with other forms of status. See Patterson, *Slavery and Social Death*, 21–27.

78. These rights applied to servants regardless of racial categorization. See Fischer, *Suspect Relations*, 101–2.

79. Proceedings and Acts of the General Assembly, April 1684–June 1692, 457, MSA.

80. Kent County Court Petition Record, vol. JS, 1739–1757, 136, MSA.

81. Norfolk County Minute Book 1, 1749-1753, October 19, 1750, LVA.

82. New Castle County Court of General Sessions Docket, May 1769-May 1775, 11-12, DPA.

83. *Grace Gibbs et al v Waitman Sipple et al*, Kent County Court of Chancery Case Files, Grace Gibbs et al v Waitman Sipple et al #G 1 Slavery Case, 1758-1760, DPA. Whether Gibbs was successful in recovering her children is not clear from the surviving record.

84. Cumberland County Court Minutes, vol. 1, 31-32, SANC.

85. Charles City County Order Book, 1687-1695, 263, LVA.

86. "Run away on the 21st Inst.," *Pennsylvania Gazette* (Philadelphia), January 29, 1740.

87. "Ran away on Sunday the 9th Inst.," *Virginia Gazette* (Williamsburg), March 21, 1745.

88. "Run away, the 2d of last month," *Pennsylvania Gazette* (Philadelphia), June 1, 1749; "Ran away on the 25th Day of July, 1756," *Maryland Gazette* (Annapolis), March 16, 1758.

89. Jackson Petition, Perthenia Overton a mallatto her Indentures 1755, Pasquotank County Apprentice Bonds and Records, Box 2, Apprentice Bonds and Records O, SANC. For more on unions between free people of color and enslaved people in the colonial South, see Snyder, "Marriage on the Margins."

90. *Jane Webb v. Thomas Savage*, Northampton County Chancery Causes, 1727-001 Chancery Causes: Jane Webb vs Thomas Savage, LVA; Jane Webbs Petn, Northampton County Free Negro and Slave Records, Free Negro & Slave Records: Jane Webb vs Thomas Savage, LVA. For more on Webb's life, see Deal, *Race and Class in Colonial Virginia*, 399-401.

91. Negro Toney's Petition, Pasquotank County Civil Action Papers, Box 3, 1748, SANC; Pasquotank County Court Minutes, vol. 1, July 1748, SANC.

92. Land Office Patents No. 6, 1666-1679, 39, LVA.

93. Lancaster County Deeds, Etc. No. 9, 1701-1715, 478-79, LVA; Lancaster County Deeds, Etc. No. 11, 1714-1728, 222-23, 305-8, LVA; Lancaster County Deeds and Wills No. 12, 1726-1736, 360-61, LVA; Nickens Last Will 1735, Lancaster County Wills, 1719-1749, LVA.

94. Charleston County Wills, 1747-1756, 302, SCDAH.

95. Travis to Williams Order to bind him, Norfolk County Apprentice Indentures, Box 1, Indentures of Apprenticeship- African American, 1764-1836, 1764 Oct William Travis to Till Williams, LVA.

96. Brown, *Good Wives*, 287-90; Nickens Last Will 1735, Lancaster County Wills, 1719-1749, LVA; Charleston County Wills, 1747-1756, 302, SCDAH.

97. Northampton County Wills, vol. 4, 226, NCCC; Northampton County Deeds, Wills & C., 10, NCCC.

98. Granville County Record of Wills, vol. 1, 164, 176-79, SANC; Chavis Bond to Keep Ordinary, Granville County Ordinary Bonds, Box 1, Ordinary Bonds, 1748, SANC; List of Taxables, Granville County Taxables, Box 20, 1758, SANC; List of Taxables, Granville County Taxables, Box 20, 1760-1761, SANC.

99. Charleston District, South Carolina Estate Inventories and Selected Bills of Sale, 1772-1776, 33, SCDAH.

100. An Exact List of..., Thomas Smith McDowell Papers, Box 1, 1766-1769 #2, SHC; A True List of Taxables for the year 1771 Taken Before me Archd M. Kissak, Thomas Smith McDowell Papers, Box 1, 1771 #4, SHC; A True List of Taxables for the year 1776 Taken by me Archd M. Kissak, Thomas Smith McDowell Papers, Box 1, 1776 #8, SHC.

101. Cope, *Limits of Racial Domination*, 161–62; Allen, *Slaves, Freedmen, and Indentured Laborers in Colonial Mauritius*, 89–92; King, *Blue Coat or Powered Wig*, 81–120.

102. Marly negre Engagement, Judicial Records of the French Superior Council, #1745-11-09-03, LHC.

103. Charleston County Wills, 1747–1756, 187, SCDAH; Olsberg, *Colonial Records of South Carolina*, 82, 124, 150, 375, 423; Lipscomb and Olsberg, *Colonial Records of South Carolina*, 249, 315; Lipscomb, *Colonial Records of South Carolina*, 201, 235, 287, 464, 515.

104. Agreement with Wm Hill Bricklayer for 1760, Maryland Province Archives, GTMGamms119, Box 15, 52T 1–13, GU.

105. *Milburn v. Bird*, Edenton District Records of the Superior Court, Box 26, 1772, SANC.

106. Last Will of Adam Seagrove, Records of Probate: Wills, Secretary of State Record Group, SANC.

107. Prerogative Court Wills, 1723–1726, 163–66, MSA.

108. Landers, *Black Society in Spanish Florida*, 22–23.

109. Clark, *State Records of North Carolina*, 22:370–80.

110. Archives of the Diocese of St. Augustine Marriages, 1632–1720, 151, 207, SSDA.

111. Archives of the Diocese of St. Augustine Baptisms, 1735–1763, 32, 41, SSDA.

112. *Parish Register of Saint Peter's*, 117, 134.

113. Cain and Poff, *Church of England in North Carolina*, 321–25.

Chapter 2

1. Baltimore County Court Chattel Records, 1763–1773, 208–9, 213–15, MSA.

2. Sinha, *Slave's Cause*, 9–33; Helg, *Slave No More*; *Seventh Census*, ix. For more on the expansion of liberty in the revolutionary South, see Jackson, "Manumission in Certain Virginia Cities," 278–314; Berlin, *Slaves without Masters*, 15–50; Essah, *House Divided*, 36–74; Williams, *Slavery and Freedom in Delaware*, 141–83; Phillips, *Freedom's Port*, 30–56; Whitman, *Price of Freedom*; Nicholls, "Passing through This Troublesome World"; Condon, "Manumission, Slavery and Family in the Post-Revolutionary Rural Chesapeake"; Wolf, *Race and Liberty in the New Nation*; Dantas, *Black Townsmen*, 97–125; and de la Fuente and Gross, *Becoming Free*, 84–100, 114–29. For more on emancipation in the North, see Zilversmit, *First Emancipation*; Nash, *Forging Freedom*; Nash and Soderlund, *Freedom by Degrees*; Hodges, *Slavery and Freedom in the Rural North*, 113–45; Horton and Horton, *In Hope of Liberty*; Melish, *Disowning Slavery*; Hodges, *Root and Branch*, 162–86; Dunbar, *Fragile Freedom*; and Polgar, *Standard-Bearers of Equality*.

3. Schweninger, *Appealing for Liberty*, 10–25, 70–91. For further discussion of freedom suits, see Schafer, *Becoming Free, Remaining Free*, 15–33; Aslakson, *Making Race in the Courtroom*, 153–83; and Vandervelde, *Redemption Songs*.

4. Hanger, *Bounded Lives*, 1–8, 40–81; Lachance, "1809 Immigration of Saint-Domingue Refugees to New Orleans"; Bogger, *Free Blacks in Norfolk*, 23–24; Sumler-Edmond, *Secret Trust of Aspasia Cruvellier Mirault*, 4–14; Neidenbach, "'Refugee from St. Domingue Living in This City.'"

5. *Epistle of Caution and Advice, Concerning the Buying and Keeping of Slaves*, 1–2.

6. Crawford, *Having of Negroes Is Become a Burden*, 73.

7. Grundy, "David Ferris," 18–29; Nash, *Warner Mifflin*, 98–109.

8. Carroll, "Religious Influences"; Andrews, *Methodists and Revolutionary America*, 123–54; "Constitution of the Maryland Society, for promoting the Abolition of Slavery, and the Relief of Free Negroes, and others, unlawfully held in Bondage," *Maryland*

Journal (Baltimore), December 15, 1789; "Constitution of the Chester-Town Society, for promoting the Abolition of Slavery, and the relief of Free Negroes, and others, unlawfully held in Bondage," *Delaware Gazette* (Wilmington), June 16, 1792; "Fredericksburg," *State Gazette of North-Carolina* (Edenton), July 28, 1796; Whitman, *Challenging Slavery in the Chesapeake*, 51, 63–64.

9. Quakers Petition November 29th 1780, Legislative Petitions, LVA.

10. Guild, *Black Laws of Virginia*, 47, 61; Dorsey, *General Public Statutory Law*, 336–37.

11. Martin, *Public Acts of the General Assembly of North-Carolina*, 201–2.

12. Caroline County Land Records, vol. A, 528, MSA.

13. Southampton County Deed Book 6, 1775–1787, 81–100, SCC.

14. Accomack County Deeds No. 5, 1777–1783, 334–38, LVA.

15. Mecklenburg County Deed Book 7, 624, MCC.

16. Washington County Deed Record, vol. A, 1799–1816, ADAH.

17. Charleston County Record of Wills, 1793–1800, 597–602, SCDAH.

18. New Castle County Deed Record, vol. H2, 127, DPA.

19. Sam Deed of Emancipation, Middlesex County Free Negro and Slave Records, 1764–1802, LVA.

20. Patterson, *Slavery and Social Death*, 282–84.

21. Fredericksburg City Hustings Court Will Book A, 1782–1817, 148–52, LVA.

22. Fredericksburg City Hustings Court Deed Book C, 1797–1804, 174, LVA.

23. New Hanover County Real Estate Conveyances, vol. 1, 328–29, SANC.

24. Saml. Jackson Pet. For Ichabud, Pasquotank County Records of Slaves and Free Persons of Color, Box 9, Bonds and Petitions to free slaves, 1778, 1792?, 1793–1800, SANC.

25. Harford County Court Manumissions, 53–54, MSA.

26. Absalom Ridgely to Sundry Negroes, Anne Arundel County Court Manumissions, MSA.

27. Eva Sheppard Wolf found that "in slightly more than half the manumissions by deed enacted from 1794 to 1806 emancipators freed slaves in exchange for money or good service or in accordance with a will or the terms upon which the slave had been acquired." Wolf, *Race and Liberty in the New Nation*, 63.

28. Richmond City Hustings Deeds 1, 1782–1792, 388, LVA.

29. Manumission Book A, 1780–1793, 227, PASP Series 4.1, HSP.

30. Manumission Henrietta James to Negro Jack, Baltimore County Miscellaneous Court Papers, 1792–1795, C1–22, 1794, Items 173–192, MSA.

31. South Carolina Secretary of State Miscellaneous Records, vol. SS, 47, SCDAH.

32. "Twenty Nailors," *Connecticut Courant* (Hartford), November 24, 1794; "Commonwealth of Pennsylvania," *Dunlap and Claypoole's American Daily Advertiser* (Philadelphia), September 25, 1794; "Notice," *Pittsburgh Gazette*, April 19, 1794.

33. South Carolina Secretary of State Miscellaneous Records, vol. SS, 340–41, SCDAH.

34. Pasquotank County Real Estate Conveyances, vol. N, 411–12, SANC; Sylvester to the Court Petn for Emancipation, Pasquotank County Records of Slaves and Free Persons of Color, Box 9, Bonds and petitions to free slaves, 1778, 1792?, 1793–1800, SANC; Pasquotank County Court Minutes, vol. 10, 203, SANC.

35. Manumission Deed Caesar King to his son David, PASP Series 4.4, Pennsylvania Abolition Society Manumissions and Related Materials, Both Parties to Contract Being Black, HSP.

36. Petition Jos. Mayo's Admrs, Legislative Petitions, LVA.

37. District of Columbia Fair Copies of Wills, vol. 1, 15–21, NARA. For more on Wash-

ington and the antislavery movement, see Furstenberg, "Atlantic Slavery, Atlantic Freedom," 247–86.

38. Westmoreland County Deeds and Wills 18, 1787–1794, 213, 239, 244, 291–92, LVA. For a full account of Robert Carter's manumission work, see Levy, *First Emancipator*.

39. Illegal enslavement was a problem from the colonial period through the end of slavery in the United States. For more on efforts to liberate people held illegally in the North, see Sweet, *Bodies Politic*, 228–240; and Newell, *Brethren by Nature*, 168–74, 234–36, 246–54.

40. General Court of the Western Shore Judgment Record, vol. JG 25, October 1794, 20–73, MSA.

41. *Negro Phillis v. Evan Lewis*, Kent County Slavery Material Petitions for Freedom, 1779–1799, 1796- Petition for freedom: negro Phillis vs. Lewis, Evan, DPA.

42. James Manly's Petition, Craven County Miscellaneous Records, Box 15, Petition for freedom from Colonel Levi Dawson by James Manly, Indian, 1782, SANC. For more on freedom suits based on "Indian" ancestry, see Wallenstein, *Tell the Court I Love My Wife*, 13–37.

43. *London v. Kellam*, Accomack County Chancery Causes, 1790-020 Accomack County Chancery Causes- London ~ vs John Kellam, LVA.

44. *Laws of the State of Delaware* (1797), 380–84.

45. Guild, *Black Laws of Virginia*, 58, 67–68.

46. Martin, *Public Acts of the General Assembly of North-Carolina*, 266.

47. Hanger, *Bounded Lives*, 7–8, 24–26.

48. Petition by Priest for Emancipation of Slave Who Offers Repayment of Sale, Spanish Judicial Records, #1775-04-03-01, LHC; Proceedings Instituted by Juan Santiago Mangloan, Spanish Judicial Records, #1788-08-19-03, LHC; Emancipation, Spanish Judicial Records, #1770-07-12-01, LHC.

49. Hanger, *Bounded Lives*, 27.

50. Scott, *Common Wind*, 22–23.

51. Spear, *Race, Sex, and Social Order in Early New Orleans*, 163–72. Spear suggested that although the Spanish outlawed Indian slavery, their efforts to stop the practice were piecemeal. At different points, enslaved people gained freedom based on "Indian" ancestry while others with similar backgrounds remained in bondage years after the end of Spanish rule in Louisiana. Over time, some officials sought to make obtaining freedom through claims of "Indian" ancestry more difficult.

52. Proceedings Instituted by Pedro Morsu, Spanish Judicial Records, #1790-05-04-01, LHC.

53. La India Mariana contra Franca Pomet Libre Su Libertad, Spanish Judicial Records, #1791-01-13-02, LHC.

54. Archives of the Spanish Government of West Florida, 1782–1816, vol. 1, 1782–1789, 1; Records of the Adjutant General's Office, 1780's–1917, RG 94, NARA.

55. For more on the impact of revolution and rebellion in the French colonies, see Dubois, *Colony of Citizens*; and Dubois, *Avengers of the New World*.

56. A Pass John Ferris to Negro Catherine, PASP, Manumissions, Indentures, and other Legal Papers, Part 2, Passes and passports for free blacks to travel, 1791–1794, 1797–1798, 1800–1801, 1803, 1805, 1807, 1817, 1820, and undated material, HSP.

57. Declaration of Slaves Felicite Barran Mulatresse Libre, Baltimore County Court Miscellaneous Court Papers, 1792–1795, 50206-334, 1794, Items 1–23, MSA.

58. Nicholas Cammel's Cert, Arlington County (Alexandria County) Free Negro Records, Certificates of Freedom (Registration of Free Negroes), LVA.

59. Baltimore County Court Minutes, 1787–1791, 352, MSA. Isle of France was the name given to modern-day Mauritius during the French colonial period.

60. Bill of Sale, Pierre Danl. Bidelrenoulleau to Luther Martin, Baltimore County Court Miscellaneous Court Papers, 1795–1797, 50206-347, 1795, Items 61–81, MSA; Manumission Luther Martin Esqr to Mullatto Sanette alias Sophia & Marie Francoise, Baltimore County Court Miscellaneous Court Papers, 1795–1797, 50206-349, 1795, Items 103–119, MSA.

61. South Carolina Secretary of State Miscellaneous Records, vol. 3Q, 131–32, SCDAH.

62. For more on the role of free people of color in the American Revolution, see Jackson, *Virginia Negro Soldiers and Seamen in the American Revolution*, 247–87; Jackson, *Virginia Negro Soldiers and Seamen in the Revolutionary War*; Quarles, *Negro in the American Revolution*; and Schmidt, "Black Revolutionaries."

63. Philip Savoy Revolutionary War Pension, NARA.

64. Isam Carter Revolutionary War Pension, NARA.

65. Joseph Ranger Revolutionary War Pension, NARA.

66. Solomon Bibby Revolutionary War Pension, NARA; Barnet Stewart Revolutionary War Pension, NARA; Drury Walden Revolutionary War Pension, NARA.

67. "Twenty Dollars Reward," *Virginia Gazette* (Williamsburg), August 1, 1777.

68. "Ten Dollars Reward," *North-Carolina Gazette* (Wilmington), May 1, 1778.

69. "Four Hundred and Fifty Dollars Reward," *Virginia Gazette* (Williamsburg), May 8, 1779.

70. Hanger, *Bounded Lives*, 109–34.

71. Book of Negroes, 21–24, 35–36, African Nova Scotians in the Age of Slavery and Abolition, Nova Scotia Archives. The original volume is held by the National Archives of Great Britain. These free people of color were part of a mass exodus of persons of color out of the fledgling United States following the British defeat. They resettled in various parts of the empire, including Nova Scotia, Great Britain, and the Caribbean. See Schama, *Rough Crossings*; Pybus, *Epic Journeys of Freedom*; and Curry, *Freedom and Resistance*.

72. Heads of Families at the First Census of the United States Taken in the Year 1790 North Carolina, 8; Return of the Whole Number of Persons.

73. "I Nathaniel Hobbs," *Virginia Gazette* (Williamsburg), November 13, 1778.

74. Henry Willis Statement, January 29, 1788, PASP, Manumissions, Indentures, and other Legal Papers, Part 2, Certificates of freedom, 1770–1826, HSP.

75. Last Will & Testament of Thomas Stewart dec'd, Dinwiddie County Wills, 1801–1869, LVA; A List of the Land Tax within the District of William Walls One of the Commissioners in the County of Dinwiddie for the Year 1790, Auditor of Public Accounts Dinwiddie County Land Tax Books, 1782–1814, LVA.

76. Narrative of the Physical Knowledge of James Derham a black man, PASP, Manumissions, Indentures, and other Legal Papers, Part 2, Character references for blacks, 1787, 1791–1793, 1796, 1812, 1816–1817, 1830, and undated material, HSP.

77. Banneker, *Benjamin Banneker's Pennsylvania, Delaware, Maryland and Virginia Almanack*.

78. "Just published, and to be SOLD by the Printers hereof," *Maryland Journal* (Baltimore), October 28, 1791; "Just published, and to be SOLD by the Printers hereof," *Virginia Gazette and Alexandria Advertiser*, November 10, 1791.

79. "To Mr. Benjamin Banneker," *Baltimore Evening Post*, October 13, 1792.

80. Thomas Jefferson to Marquis de Condorcet, August 30, 1791, Thomas Jefferson Papers, Series 1: General Correspondence, 1651–1827, LC. Benjamin Banneker has long

been the subject of scholarly inquiry. See Latrobe, *Memoir of Benjamin Banneker*; and Baker, "Benjamin Banneker, the Negro Mathematician and Astronomer," 99–118.

81. Case of Some Free Negroes from Geo. Churchman, PASP, Manumissions, Indentures, and other Legal Papers, Part 2, Certificates of freedom, 1770–1826, HSP.

82. Charleston County Wills, 1786–1800, 49–50, SCDAH.

83. Worcester County Register of Wills Wills, vol. JW 18, 1790–1799, 331, MSA.

84. Holly Brewer found that the percentage of free children of color in Frederick County, Virginia, increased following the conclusion of the American Revolution. She argued that at the same time "increased idealization of the bonds between children and their natural parents, particularly mothers," led to a decrease in the percentage of white children under apprenticeship. See Brewer, "Apprentice Policy in Virginia," 184. For a more in-depth discussion of apprenticeship and the evolution of ideas concerning children and consent, see Brewer, *By Birth or Consent*.

85. Baltimore County Court Minutes, 1787–1791, 185, 195, MSA.

86. Baltimore County Record of Wills Indentures, 1794–1799, 64, MSA.

87. Clark, *State Records of North Carolina*, 25:419–20.

88. Guild, *Black Laws of Virginia*, 62–63.

89. Proceeding to the execution of the will of Nanet Colet, a free negress, Spanish Judicial Records, #1797-10-16-01, LHC.

90. Vente d'Esclave par le Sr Lacour, Colonial Documents of the St. Landry Papers 1, Slave sale from Jean Baptiste Lacour of Pointe Coupee to George Bolard, free mulatto, LSA.

91. Proceeding instituted by Josef Casanova, free griffin, Spanish Judicial Records, #1797-09-20-01, LHC.

92. Mobile County Translated Records Book 1, 242–43, 249–50, ADAH; Mobile Translated Records Book 2, 2, 21, 29, 13, 73, 175, ADAH.

93. Nordmann, "Free Negroes in Mobile County, Alabama."

94. Thorpe, *Federal and State Constitutions*, 1686–701, 2787–94, 3241–48, 3812–19.

95. *Laws of the State of Delaware* (1797), xxviii–xlviii.

96. Marbury and Crawford, *Digest of the Laws of the State of Georgia*, 7.

97. Thorpe, *Federal and State Constitutions*, 3248–65.

98. Gordon S. Wood argued that following the Revolution, "politics became democratized as more Americans gained the right to vote" and characterized Americans as "so thoroughly democratic that much of the period's political activity, beginning with the Constitution, was devoted to finding means and devices to tame that democracy." Wood, *Empire of Liberty*, 3.

99. Dorsey, *General Public Statutory Law*, 335.

100. "The Printers of the Virginia Journal," *Virginia Journal* (Alexandria), March 22, 1787.

101. Thorpe, *Federal and State Constitutions*, 574, 1264–92.

102. Guild, *Black Laws of Virginia*, 61, 64, 95.

103. Marbury and Crawford, *Digest of the Laws of the State of Georgia*, 452–54, 459–61, 466–68, 473–75, 480–82.

104. Littell and Swigert, *Digest of the Statute Law of Kentucky*, 1149–50.

105. "State of South-Carolina. An Ordinance for the better ordering and governing of Negroes and other slaves, and of free Negroes, Mulattoes and Mustizoes, within the City of Charleston," *South-Carolina Weekly Gazette* (Charleston), November 20, 1783.

106. "An Ordinance For regulating the Hire of Drays, Carts, and Waggons; as also the Hire of Negro and other Slaves; and for the better ordering Free Negroes, Mulattoes, or Mestizoes; within the City of Savannah," *Georgia Gazette* (Savannah), October 7, 1790.

107. "At a meeting of the Commissioners of the town of Fayetteville at Lewis Barge's, Esq, on Saturday evening 25th of February 1797," *North Carolina Minerva and Fayetteville Advertiser*, March 4, 1797.

108. C. Vann Woodward initially theorized that segregation in public places began in the North and did not appear in the South until the late nineteenth century. The findings of scholars such as Richard C. Wade and Ira Berlin forced him to revise his thesis. Both Wade and Berlin provided evidence of exclusion and segregation in the first half of the nineteenth century. The case of Charleston suggests that race-based physical separation policies for public spaces date back at least to the late eighteenth century. See Woodward, *Strange Career of Jim Crow*; Wade, *Slavery in the Cities*, 266–73; and Berlin, *Slaves without Masters*, 321–27, 383. For Woodward's reaction to the findings of Wade, Berlin, and others, see Woodward, "*Strange Career* Critics."

109. "City Theatre, Church-Street. This Evening, November 24, Will be Presented The Comedy of the Jew," *Columbian Herald* (Charleston, S.C.), November 24, 1795.

110. "Charleston Theatre. To-morrow Evening, the 16th inst. Will Be Presented, The Tragedy of Alexander the Great: Or, the Rival Queens," *City Gazette* (Charleston, S.C.), March 15, 1796.

111. Henrico Petition, Henrico County, 1784, Legislative Petitions, LVA; Hanover Petition, Hanover County, 1784, Legislative Petitions, LVA.

112. "Presentments of the Grand Jury," *Georgia Gazette* (Savannah), October 23, 1788.

113. "Richmond July 4," *Lynchburg (Va.) and Farmer's Gazette*, July 11, 1795.

114. "Continuation of Mr. Smith's Speech on the Report of the Committee on the Memorial of the People called Quakers, begun in our paper of the 15th ult," *Georgia Gazette* (Savannah), May 13, 1790.

115. This reaction to the rebellion in Saint-Domingue was not confined to the South. For more on the reaction in the North, see Nash, *Forging Freedom*, 140–44; and Horton and Horton, *In Hope of Liberty*, 109–10.

116. "A Proclamation," *State Gazette of South Carolina* (Charleston), October 19, 1793.

117. "Charleston," *City Gazette* (Charleston, S.C.), October 9, 1793.

118. "Georgetown, (S.C.) October 10," *City Gazette* (Charleston, S.C.), October 18, 1793.

119. Presentments of Beaufort District, General Assembly Grand Jury Presentments, Box 1, General Assembly-Grand Jury Presentments, 1793, 1–9, SCDAH.

120. *Laws of North-Carolina at a General Assembly*, 10–11.

121. Marbury and Crawford, *Digest of the Laws of the State of Georgia*, 60.

122. "A Proclamation," *Georgia Gazette* (Savannah), June 15, 1798. For more on the reaction of Georgians to the revolt in Saint-Domingue, see Jennison, *Cultivating Race*, 51–65.

123. Scott, *Common Wind*, 184–86; Sterkx, *Free Negro in Ante-Bellum Louisiana*, 83–84. For more about the anxiety over the events in Saint-Domingue and the Pointe Coupee plot, see Hall, *Africans in Colonial Louisiana*, 316–74.

124. Memorial of Thomas Cole & other free men of colour in this State, Petitions to the General Assembly, SCDAH.

125. Petition of Free People, Petitions to the General Assembly, SCDAH.

126. "From a Virginia Paper to the Printer," *Providence (R.I.) Gazette*, November 3, 1792.

Chapter 3

1. Thomas Jefferson to Marquis de Condorcet, August 30, 1791, Thomas Jefferson Papers, Series 1: General Correspondence, 1651–1827, LC.

2. Thomas Jefferson to Joel Barlow, October 8, 1809, Thomas Jefferson Papers, Series 1: General Correspondence, 1651–1827, LC.

3. Scholars have long discussed Jefferson's views about people of color and the ways those ideas contrasts with his statements concerning human equality and slavery. Winthrop D. Jordan's analysis included a discussion of Jefferson's perception of Banneker. See Jordan, *White over Black*, 429–81.

4. Christina Snyder found that slavery in the Native South gradually shifted from systems that used kinship as a way to determine status to practices that embraced the importance of racial categories. By the late eighteenth century, Snyder concluded, "racial slavery as practiced by Indians grew more entrenched in the early nineteenth century as increasingly centralized Native governments protected and promoted the institution." See Snyder, *Slavery in Indian Country*, 211. Van Gosse recognized the importance of white supremacy in the pre–Civil War United States but also noted that "rather than exhibiting any long-term racial consensus, the early republic contained many orders operating at different levels or scales, ranging from the local to the national." See Gosse, "Patchwork Nation." Although Gosse offered a different interpretation of the way the "patchwork" of discrimination worked in the United States, he credited Ira Berlin for an earlier usage of the "patchwork" concept. See Berlin, *Slaves without Masters*.

5. Paul Finkelman explained that "free blacks" were a significant part of the Federalist coalition and that Jeffersonian Republicans used attacks on the voting rights of this constituency to challenge the Federalists. He also noted that "Republicans never tried to disfranchise any other identifiable group that supported the Federalists." Finkelman, *Slavery and the Founders*, 117–20. Edmund S. Morgan identified a paradoxical relationship between freedom and slavery that originated in the colonial period and continued with the foundation of the United States. He observed that "the rise of liberty and equality in America had been accompanied by the rise of slavery." Morgan identified this connection as the "central paradox of American history." Morgan, *American Slavery, American Freedom*, 4.

6. For more on the decline of slavery in the British Empire, see Brown, *Moral Capital*.

7. Most of the scholarship on the reaction of free people of color to discrimination focuses on the North or the most northern parts of the South. See Winch, *Philadelphia's Black Elite*; Rael, *Black Identity and Black Protest in the Antebellum North*; Alexander, *African or American?*; Ball, *To Live an Antislavery Life*; Kantrowitz, *More Than Freedom*; Diemer, *Politics of Black Citizenship*; Jones, *Birthright Citizens*; Jackson, *Force and Freedom*; and Bonner, *Remaking the Republic*.

8. Paul Finkelman suggested that the reaction to Haiti was at least partially partisan, with the Federalists in support of Haiti and the Jeffersonians in opposition. See Finkelman, *Slavery and the Founders*, 121–24.

9. The Remonstrance of the Mayor, Recorder, Aldermen & Comonalty of the town of Petersburg, Legislative Petitions, LVA.

10. Shepherd, *Statutes at Large of Virginia*, 3:252.

11. Russell, *Free Negro in Virginia*, 66–71.

12. *Seventh Census*, ix; Jackson, "Manumission in Certain Virginia Cities," 288–90; Katz, "African-American Freedom in Antebellum Cumberland County, Virginia"; Stevenson, *Life in Black and White*, 264; Wolf, *Race and Liberty in the New Nation*, 131; Eslinger, "Free Black Residency in Two Antebellum Virginia Counties"; Mariner, *Slave and Free on Virginia's Eastern Shore*, 40–42.

13. Richmond City Hustings Wills, Inventories, and Accounts 1, 1810–1816, 3–4, LVA.

14. John Dungie and Lucy Ann Dungie Petition, King William County, 1825, Legislative Petitions, LVA.

15. *Commonwealth v. George alias George Selby*, Accomack County Commonwealth Causes, Box 1, Sept. 1816–March 1824, LVA; *Commonwealth v. Adah Bagwell*, Accomack County Commonwealth Causes, Box 1, Sept. 1816–March 1824, LVA.

16. For a detailed account of the impact of Virginia's manumission restrictions on one family of color, see Wolf, *Almost Free*.

17. Clayton, *Compilation of the Laws of the State of Georgia*, 27, 118–19.

18. Richmond County Realty, vol. N, 325, ARCJC.

19. *Seventh Census*, ix.

20. Toulmin, *Digest of the Laws of the State of Alabama*, 632.

21. Alden and Van Hoesen, *Digest of the Laws of Mississippi*, 761; *Seventh Census*, ix.

22. Duval, *Compilation of the Public Acts of the Legislative Council of the Territory of Florida*, 228–29.

23. Jane G. Landers found that Spanish officials actively recruited people of color to Florida during the second Spanish colonial period from 1784 to 1821. The Spanish provided these free people of color with land grants and encouraged them to become productive members of society. See Landers, "Acquisition and Loss on a Spanish Frontier"; and *Seventh Census*, ix.

24. *Seventh Census*, ix; Littell and Swigert, *Digest of the Statute Law of Kentucky*, 1155; Haywood and Cobbs, *Statute Laws of the State of Tennessee*, 327–28.

25. McCord, *Statutes at Large of South Carolina*, 436–37.

26. "Complete Returns," *Republican Advocate* (Frederick, Md.), October 26, 1804; "Maryland Elections," *Republican Advocate* (Frederick, Md.), October 25, 1805; "Legislature of Maryland—House of Delegates," *Telegraphe and Daily Advertiser* (Baltimore), December 23, 1806; Dorsey, *General Public Statutory Law*, 542; *Laws of the State of Delaware* (1816), 108–10; Greiner, *Louisiana Digest*, 220.

27. Taylor, *Frontiers of Freedom*, 33–34; Middleton, *Black Laws*, 50–52.

28. Greiner, *Louisiana Digest*, 220.

29. Greiner, 221–22; Lachance, "The 1809 Immigration of Saint-Domingue Refugees to New Orleans." For a broad discussion of the movement of people from Saint-Domingue to Louisiana, see Dessens, *From Saint-Domingue to New Orleans*.

30. Hotchkiss, *Codification of the Statute Law of Georgia*, 831.

31. Alden and Van Hoesen, *Digest of the Laws of Mississippi*, 762, 767; *Laws: The Cherokee Nation, and C.*, 38–39; *Acts Passed by the General Assembly of the State of North Carolina at Its Session, Commencing on the 25th of December, 1826*, 13–16; "Laws of Florida," *Pensacola (Fla.) Gazette*, May 12, 1829.

32. "State Law," *Pendleton Messenger* (Pendleton Court House, S.C.), February 21, 1821.

33. For more on the political reaction to the alleged plot, see Ford, *Deliver Us from Evil*, 269–98.

34. Condy, *Digest of the Laws of the United States and the State of South-Carolina*, 145–48. For a detailed discussion of this act and similar laws, see Schoeppner, *Moral Contagion*.

35. Condy, *Digest of the Laws of the United States and the State of South-Carolina*, 148–49. Europeans and Americans have applied several meanings to the term "Moor." They commonly applied the term to people with origins in North Africa. See Forbes, *Black Africans and Native Americans*, 67–68. "Lascars" generally referred to groups of bound maritime laborers, especially those from India. See Fisher, *Counterflows to Colonialism*, 32–42.

36. Hotchkiss, *Codification of the Statute Law of Georgia*, 836.

37. House of Representatives, *Free Colored Seamen—Majority and Minority Reports*; Schoeppner, *Moral Contagion*, 65, 77–78, 94. Restrictions on the entrance of free

people of color into a jurisdiction were not limited to the United States. Michele Reid-Vazquez discovered the implementation of a similar restriction in Cuba following the end of slavery in Jamaica. See Reid-Vazquez, *Year of the Lash*, 71–73.

38. Enforcement of the Kentucky immigration ban was lax in Jefferson County until 1829. County officials conducted annual round ups in 1829, 1830, and 1831 before falling back to the status quo. See Jefferson County Court Orders Minutes, vols. 13–14, KDLA; Jefferson County Court Orders Minutes, vol. 15, 206–17, 404–7, 466–69, KDLA; Jefferson County Court Orders Minutes, vol. 16, 29–39, KDLA. For more on Nancy Garnes, see Mecklenburg County Order Book 21, 1821–1822, 366, LVA. William Kersey's will showed that he owned property in Virginia as well as in North Carolina. He also owned land in Tennessee, but whether he made the long trek to visit it is unclear. See Wm Cursey's Will, Warren County Wills, Box 5, William Cursey 1836, SANC. Taylor, *Frontiers of Freedom*, 34; Middleton, *Black Laws*, 60–66.

39. Shepherd, *Statutes at Large of Virginia*, 1:238; Dorsey, *General Public Statutory Law*, 508–10; Haywood and Cobbs, *Statute Laws of the State of Tennessee*, 329; Hotchkiss, *Codification of the Statute Law of Georgia*, 825; Alden and Van Hoesen, *Digest of the Laws of Mississippi*, 762; Scott, *Common Wind*, 24.

40. Petersburg City Register of Free Negroes and Mulattoes, 1794–1819, LVA.

41. Charlotte County Register of Free Negroes, 1794–1865, LVA; Goochland County Register of Free Negroes, 1804–1864, LVA; Mecklenburg County Register of Free Negroes, 1809–1841, LVA. For a detailed exploration of Virginia's registration system during its early implementation, see Nicholls, "Creating Identity," 214–33. Other historians have also commented on the effectiveness of the registration system. See Berlin, *Slaves without Masters*, 328, 317; Ely, *Israel on the Appomattox*, 251–54; and Eslinger, "Free Black Residency."

42. Baltimore County Court Certificates of Freedom, 1806–1816, MSA; Dorchester County Court Certificates of Freedom, 1806–1851, MSA; Washington County Court Certificates of Freedom and Manumissions, 1806–1834, MSA; Frederick County Court Certificates of Freedom, 1806–1827, MSA. For further discussion of the lack enforcement of Maryland's registration law, see Dorsey, *Hirelings*, 49–57.

43. "Notice is hereby Given," *Columbian Museum* (Savannah, Ga.), February 21, 1800.

44. Haywood and Cobbs, *Statute Laws of the State of Tennessee*, 329.

45. Young, "Racism in Red and Black," 492–518; James Monroe to Thomas Jefferson, February 13, 1802, Thomas Jefferson Papers, Series 1: General Correspondence, 1651–1827, LC; Thomas Jefferson to James Monroe, June 2, 1802, Thomas Jefferson Papers, Series 1: General Correspondence. 1651–1827, LC; "Colonization Society," *Maryland Gazette and Political Intelligencer* (Annapolis), February 12, 1818. Several scholars have written important works about the African colonization movement in the South. See Hall, *On Afric's Shore*; Clegg, *Price of Liberty*; Burin, *Slavery and the Peculiar Solution*; and Tyler-McGraw, *African Republic*. Some colonizationists proposed sending free people of color to Haiti as an alternative to Africa. For more on the relocation of free people of color to Haiti, see Fanning, *Caribbean Crossing*.

46. *Memorial of the American Colonization Society*, 1–8.

47. "House of Delegates," *Torch Light and Public Advertiser* (Hagerstown, Md.), March 7, 1826; "Friday, Feb. 16," *Raleigh (N.C.) Register*, February 23, 1827.

48. Dorsey, *General Public Statutory Law*, 878.

49. Although some free people of color entertained African colonization, most rejected it. Ousmane Power-Greene suggested, however, that some leaders among free people of color viewed emigration to Haiti as more appealing than removal to Africa. See Power-Greene, *Against Wind and Tide*.

50. Negroes 1826, Manumission Society Papers, Series 1, 1826 Reports, accts, ect. [sic] for the year #5, SHC.

51. Jackson, "Free Negroes of Petersburg," 372–73; "Richmond African Baptist Missionary Society," *Rhode-Island Religious Intelligencer* (Providence), May 3, 1822.

52. Vincent, *Southern Seed, Northern Soil*; LaRoche, *Geography of Resistance*; Cox, *Bone and Sinew of the Land*.

53. James Roberts to Willis Roberts, 1830, Roberts Family Papers, LC.

54. Guild, *Black Laws of Virginia*, 101.

55. List of Free Persons of Colour, who have been sentenced to transportation, &c., Governor's Office William B. Giles Executive Papers, 1827 November–1828 February, January 17, 1828, LVA; Free Negroes Sentenced to Transport, Governor's Office William B. Giles Executive Papers, 1827 November–1828 February, January 17, 1828, LVA.

56. Cobb, *Compilation of the General and Public Statutes of the State of Georgia*, 606, 620.

57. Condy, *Digest of the Laws of the United States and the State of South-Carolina*, 161.

58. Wikramanayake, *World in Shadow*, 127–28, 164; Charleston County Clerk of Court Manumissions Index A–D, 1801–1848, SCDAH.

59. Charleston County Wills, 1818–1834, 575–76, SCDAH; Myers, *Forging Freedom*, 60–70.

60. Shepherd, *Statutes at Large of Virginia*, 3:274; Morehead and Brown, *Digest of the Statute Laws of Kentucky*, 1471–72.

61. Greiner, *Louisiana Digest*, 219; Alden and Van Hoesen, *Digest of the Laws of Mississippi*, 745, 748; Duval, *Compilation of the Public Acts of the Legislative Council of the Territory of Florida*, 218, 228.

62. Cobb, *Compilation of the General and Public Statutes of the State of Georgia*, 614–15, 617.

63. Sumler-Edmond, *Secret Trust of Aspasia Cruvellier Mirault*, 1–33.

64. Cobb, *Compilation of the General and Public Statutes of the State of Georgia*, 607, 610–11.

65. Dorsey, *General Public Statutory Law*, 465.

66. *Laws of North Carolina Enacted in the Year 1821*, 41–42; "Laws of Florida," *Pensacola (Fla.) Gazette*, March 9, 1827.

67. Petition of Coloured Persons to the Legislature, General Assembly Session Records, SANC.

68. The Petition of Sundry Persons of Colour of Hertford County Praying the Repeal of An Act of Last Session Declaring Slaves Competent Witnesses Against Free Persons of Colour, General Assembly Session Records, November–December 1822, Box 4, Petitions (Miscellaneous), SANC.

69. "An Ordinance," *Savannah (Ga.) Republican*, February 5, 1811.

70. "An Ordinance," *Louisiana State Gazette* (New Orleans), December 4, 1817.

71. Guild, *Black Laws of Virginia*, 137.

72. Guild, 100.

73. Dorsey, *General Public Statutory Law*, 836–38.

74. Cobb, *Compilation of the General and Public Statutes of the State of Georgia*, 605–06.

75. Dorsey, *General Public Statutory Law*, 562, 697.

76. *Laws of the State of Delaware* (1816), 467–69.

77. "North-Carolina," *Carolina Sentinel* (New Bern, N.C.), March 10, 1827.

78. "Laws of the State of Mississippi," *Southern Galaxy* (Natchez, Miss.), April 16, 1829; Alden and Van Hoesen, *Digest of the Laws of Mississippi*, 700–701.

79. Guild, *Black Laws of Virginia*, 174–75.

80. Dorsey, *General Public Statutory Law*, 697, 808.

81. Toulmin, *Digest of the Laws of the State of Alabama*, 651; Alden and Van Hoesen, *Digest of the Laws of Mississippi*, 700–701.

82. Greiner, *Louisiana Digest*, 220.

83. Duval, *Compilation of the Public Acts of the Legislative Council of the Territory of Florida*, 220, 228.

84. Guild, *Black Laws of Virginia*, 101.

85. "Maryland Legislature," *Maryland Herald and Hager's-Town Weekly Advertiser*, September 21, 1803.

86. "An Act to Amend the Charter of Alexandria," *National Intelligencer and Washington Advertiser* (Washington, D.C.), February 29, 1804; "An Act to Amend the Charter of Georgetown," *American and Commercial Daily Advertiser* (Baltimore), July 31, 1805.

87. "An Act Extending the right of suffrage in Mississippi territory; and for other purposes," *Wilson's Knoxville (Tenn.) Gazette*, February 24, 1808.

88. Wesley, "Negro Suffrage in the Period of Constitution-Making," 143–68; *Revised Statutes of the State of Missouri*, 30–31.

89. Toulmin, *Digest of the Laws of the State of Alabama*, 638; Aikin, *Digest of the Laws of the State of Alabama*, 396; Alden and Van Hoesen, *Digest of the Laws of Mississippi*, 360; Guild, *Black Laws of Virginia*, 102.

90. *Digest of the Ordinances of the City Council Charleston*, 137–44.

91. Talbot County Trustees of the Poor Proceedings, 1792–1847, 82–83, MSA.

92. Craven County Court Minutes, vol. 26, 249, SANC.

93. "Richmond Bath," *Virginia Argus* (Richmond), July 12, 1806.

94. "Balloon," *Charleston (S.C.) Courier*, January 19, 1820.

95. Coffin, *Reminiscences of Levi Coffin*, 120–25.

96. For more on the kidnapping of free people of color, see Wilson, *Freedom at Risk*; Maddox, *Parker Sisters*; Heerman, "'Reducing Free Men to Slavery,'" 261–91; and Bell, *Stolen*.

97. "Kidnapping," *Federal Gazette* (Baltimore), June 14, 1803.

98. "Stop the Kidnappers," *Raleigh (N.C.) Minerva*, October 9, 1812; "Stop the Kidnappers," *Carolina Federal Republican* (New Bern, N.C.), October 3, 1812.

99. *Commonwealth v. William Stringer*, Isle of Wight County Commonwealth Causes Ended, Box 3, 1833, LVA.

100. Petition of Morgan Smith a Free Man of Color, Knox County Court of Pleas and Quarter Sessions Records, KCA.

101. "Stop the Kidnappers," *Arkansas Gazette* (Arkansas Post), August 29, 1832.

102. "Look out for the Kidnappers," *Delaware Gazette and State Journal* (Wilmington), March 20, 1827.

103. Abolition Society of Delaware Minute Book, 1801–1819, 12, 21, 40, HSP; "Deaths," *Daily National Intelligencer* (Washington, D.C.), January 31, 1832.

104. Elisha Tyson to Alexander McKim, May 12, 1811, U.S. House of Representatives 12th Congress, RG 233, Box 21, HR 12A-F2.7, NARA.

105. Memorial of the Representatives of the Religious Society of Friends by Gerard T. Hopkins, Clerk, Held in Baltimore in 1811, U.S. House of Representatives 12th Congress, RG 233, Box 21, HR 12A-F2.7, NARA.

106. "Laws," *Raleigh (N.C.) Register*, January 20, 1801.

107. Dorsey, *General Public Statutory Law*, 574, 658–63, 711.

108. Condy, *Digest of the Laws of the United States and the State of South-Carolina*, 145.

109. *Laws of the State of Missouri; Revised and Digested*, 283–84.

110. English, *Digest of the Statures of Arkansas*, 333.

111. *Isaac Carlisle v. James Jones and Joseph Johnson*, Court of Common Pleas, Sussex County Case Files, 1821–1821 November Term Affidavits-Transcripts, RG 4815 Case Files Petition for Freedom & Interrogatories, November 1821, DPA; *Henry West v. Joseph Johnson and Jesse Cannon*, Court of Common Pleas, Sussex County Case Files, 1821 November Term, RG 4815 Case Files #30–47 November Term 1821, DPA; *Thomas Spencer v. Joseph Johnson*, Court of Common Pleas, Sussex County Case Files, 1821 November Term, RG 4815 Case Files #15–29 November Term 1821, DPA; *Thomas Spencer v. Joseph Johnson*, Court of Common Pleas, Sussex County Case Files, 1822–1822 April Term Affidavits, Transcripts, S.C. Court of Common Pleas Case Files Interrogatories, July 1822, DPA; *Thomas Spencer v. Joseph Johnson*, Court of Common Pleas, Sussex County Case Files, 1823–1823, RG 4815 Case Files Interrogatories- Negro Tom Spencer vs. Joseph Johnson, Nov. 1823, DPA.

112. Joseph Watson to William Rawle, July 4, 1826, Pennsylvania Abolition Society Loose Correspondence, incoming: 1820–1849, 1857, 1859–1863, HSP. For more on these specific kidnappings, see Crump and Brophy, "Twenty-One Months a Slave"; Bell, *Stolen*.

113. "Kidnappers," *Maryland Gazette* (Annapolis), June 15, 1837.

114. For more on kidnappers of color, see Bell, "Counterfeit Kin."

115. "Baltimore, June 2," *Mirror of the Times, and General Advertiser* (Wilmington, Del.), June 6, 1801.

116. Execution Order for Remission of Term of Imprisonment to Isaac Tyre of Sussex County, Executive Papers, 1832, Negroes and Slavery, DPA.

117. *Commonwealth v. Granderson Cousins*, Mecklenburg County Judgments, Box 34, LVA.

Chapter 4

1. "Obituary," *American Watchman* (Wilmington, Del.), January 22, 1822; Petition of Andrew Noel, Series 1, Accession #10382002, RSPPUNCG.

2. For further discussion of southern free people of color and their social networks, see Franklin, *Free Negro in North Carolina*, 163–91; Buckley, "Unfixing Race"; Ely, *Israel on the Appomattox*, 51–106; Dorsey, *Hirelings*, 61–81, 100–117; Hudson, "'Upon This Rock'"; von Daacke, *Freedom Has a Face*, 42–74; Millward, *Finding Charity's Folk*, 41–66; Ribianszky, "'Tell Them That My Dayly Thoughts Are with Them as Though I Was amidst Them All'"; and Milteer, *North Carolina's Free People of Color*, 127–45.

3. *Seventh Census*, ix.

4. Condon, "Slave Owner's Family and Manumission in the Post-Revolutionary Chesapeake Tidewater"; Lachance, "1809 Immigration of Saint-Domingue Refugees to New Orleans."

5. An Exact List of ..., Thomas Smith McDowell Papers, Box 1, 1766–1769 #2, SHC; A True List of Taxables for the year 1771 Taken Before me Archd M. Kissak, Thomas Smith McDowell Papers, Box 1, 1771 #4, SHC; Robeson County Marriage Bonds, SANC; Granville County Marriage Bonds, SANC.

6. Brasseaux, Fontenot, and Oubre, *Creoles of Color in the Bayou County*, 24–25.

7. Adelaide Isidore Deposition December 6, 1878, Baptiste Isidore Pension File, CWP.

8. For more on unions between free people of color and enslaved people during the antebellum period, see Schweninger, "Fragile Nature of Freedom"; and Hunter, *Bound*

in Wedlock, 91-101. For an in-depth discussion of the strategies people used to liberate their relatives, see Whitman, *Price of Freedom*, 119-39.

9. District of Columbia Manumission and Emancipation Records, vol. 1, 8-9, NARA.

10. Manumission Hannah Kain to Negro Harry Pinnion, Baltimore County Court Miscellaneous Court Papers, C1-39, 1814-1815, 1814 Items 301-323, MSA. For more on the process of purchasing and manumitting kin, see Millward, *Finding Charity's Folk*, 46-51.

11. Document no. 2 Judith Hope's Papers, Richmond City Hustings Court Ended Causes, Box 131, LVA.

12. Harford County Register of Wills Wills, vol. SR 1, 1811-1832, 457-58, MSA.

13. Tilmon, *A Brief Miscellaneous Narrative of the More Early Parts of the Life of L. Tilmon*, 5-6.

14. Report of the Committee on Propositions in the Case of Britton Jones, General Assembly Session Records, November 1832-January 1833, Box 5, House Committee Reports, SANC.

15. New Hanover County Record of Wills, vol. 1, 69, SANC.

16. Worcester County Register of Wills Wills, vol. MH 27, 1822-1833, 184-86, MSA.

17. Charleston County Wills, 1818-1834, 575-76, SCDAH.

18. "Twenty Dollars Reward," *Maryland Gazette* (Annapolis), June 27, 1810.

19. "$200 Reward," *Fayetteville (N.C.) Observer*, April 26, 1827.

20. Hodes, *White Women, Black Men*, 1-9.

21. Abram Shoecraft Petition to Change Name, Orange County Civil Action Papers, Box 85, 1837, SANC; Jeremiah Shoecraft Application 15914, Eastern Cherokee Applications of the U.S. Court of Claims, 1906-1909, M1104, NARA.

22. Pasquotank County Record of Wills, vol. N, 176, SANC; *State v. Jordan Edge and Lurana Hewitt*, Pasquotank County Criminal Action Papers, Box 6, 1825, SANC.

23. Fredericksburg City Certificates and Registry of Free Negroes, 1790-1862, 136, LVA.

24. Washington County Court Certificates of Freedom and Manumission, vol. A, 1806-1834, 10, MSA.

25. For more on the exploitation of enslaved women by white men, see White, *Ar'n't I a Woman*, 34-41; and Yarbrough, "Power, Perception, and Interracial Sex."

26. Aslakson, "'Quadroon-Plaçage' Myth of Antebellum New Orleans"; Clark, *Strange History of the American Quadroon*.

27. For further discussion, see Gould, "'Chaos of Iniquity and Discord'"; Oubre and Fontenot, "Emancipation and Concubinage in Antebellum St. Landry Parish"; and Thompson, "'Mon Cher Dupré.'"

28. Mobile County Will Records, vol. 1, 115-17, 133-37, ADAH; Mobile County Will Records, vol. 2, 112-14, ADAH. For more on these families, see Nordmann, "Free Negroes in Mobile County, Alabama."

29. Orleans Parish Will Book 3, 85-86, NOPL; Orleans Parish Will Book 4, 17, NOPL.

30. Important exceptions include Mills, "Miscegenation and the Free Negro in Antebellum 'Anglo' Alabama"; Alexander, *Ambiguous Lives*; Rothman, *Notorious in the Neighborhood*; Jones, *Fathers of Conscience*; and Trent, *Secret Life of Bacon Tait*.

31. Richmond City Hustings Wills, Inventories, and Accounts 1, 1810-1816, 320-25, LVA.

32. Petition of John P. Waters of Wilkes County, General Assembly Session Records, November-December 1809, Box 3, Petitions (Miscellaneous), SANC.

33. Norfolk City Will Book 3, 1810-1820, 57-58, LVA.

34. Sylvia Jeffers Ancestry- Deposition of Mrs. Martha Taylor, Petersburg City Free Negro and Slave Records, LVA.

35. *Bouthemy et al. v. Dreux et al.*, Louisiana Supreme Court Cases, UNO.

36. *Acosta v. Robin*, f.w.c. January 1829 Docket #1668 Eastern District, Louisiana Supreme Court Cases, UNO.

37. Gates County Court Minutes, vol. 8, 128, SANC; Milteer, "Life in a Great Dismal Swamp Community," 160-61.

38. District of Columbia Fair Copies of Wills, 1817-1828, vol. 3, 256-57, NARA.

39. Jno D Barnes for mulatto Rachel Hill & c, Baltimore County Court Miscellaneous Court Papers, C1-39, 1814-1815, 1814 Items 281-300, MSA.

40. District of Columbia Manumission and Emancipation Records, vol. 1, 24, NARA.

41. An Act. Of Sale of the Estate of Moses Newsom Decd., Northampton County Estates Records, Box 152, Newsom, Moses, 1805, SANC; Moses Newsom's Last Will and Testament, Northampton County Wills, Box 32, Newsom, Moses, 1805, SANC; 1800 U.S. Federal Census, Northampton County, North Carolina; 1810 U.S. Federal Census, Northampton County, North Carolina.

42. Adam Adams Revolutionary War Pension, NARA.

43. Anthony Garns Revolutionary War Pension, NARA.

44. Landers, *Black Society in Spanish Florida*, 220-28; *Muster Rolls of the Soldiers of the War of 1812*, 7-8, 18-20, 30-31, 35-37; Milteer, *North Carolina's Free People of Color*, 56-57. For more on the role of free people of color in the conflict between the Spanish and the United States in Florida, see Marotti, *Cana Sanctuary*.

45. District of Columbia Manumission and Emancipation Records, vol. 1, 533, NARA.

46. For more on the role of free men of color in the War of 1812, see McConnell, *Negro Troops of Antebellum Louisiana*.

47. Pierre Laborissiere Deposition March 29, 1871, Pierre La Barosier Pension, War of 1812 Pensions, NARA.

48. Raynal Auguste Affidavit July 3, 1875, Raynal Auguste Pension, War of 1812 Pensions, NARA.

49. Celestine Baham Deposition December 25, 1879, Celestin Baham Pension, War of 1812 Pensions, NARA.

50. Phillips, *Freedom's Port*, 118; Sensbach, *Separate Canaan*, 156-57; Coan Baptist Church, Northumberland County, Membership Book, 1805-1923, Names of Colored Members, LVA; First Baptist Church (Washington, D.C.), Records, 1802-1845, LVA.

51. "Religious Intelligence," *General Assembly's Missionary Magazine*, September 1805; Lee, *Religious Experience and Journal of Mrs. Jarena Lee*, 3-4, 34-48.

52. Wightman, *Life of William Capers*, 124-28.

53. "An African Missionary," *Cross and Journal* (Cincinnati, Ohio), July 26, 1833; "Letter from the Southwest," *Baptist Advocate* (New York), April 2, 1842; Cathcart, *Baptist Encyclopaedia*, 718-19, 1256.

54. For more on Catholics of color, see Gould, "Parish Identities of Free Creoles of Color in Pensacola and Mobile," 1-10.

55. Basilica of the Assumption St. Peter's Baptisms, 1812-1819C, 7, 32-33, MSA.

56. Sumler-Edmond, "Free Black Life in Savannah," 127.

57. St. Louis Cathedral, New Orleans, Baptism, Slaves and Free People of Color, 1809-1809, 239, 255, 261-62, New Orleans Archdiocesan Archives.

58. South Carolina Secretary of State Miscellaneous Records, vol. 3Q, 285-86, SCDAH.

59. Richard Archer found a mishmash of discrimination and equality in religious institutions in New England. Archer, *Jim Crow North*, 9-10.

60. Wightman, *Life of William Capers*, 124-28.
61. Talbot County Court Church Charter Record, 1829-1851, 25-27, MSA.
62. Washington County Court Church Charter Record, 1803-1851, 56-57, MSA.
63. Richmond Free Persons of Colour Petition, Legislative Petitions, LVA.
64. Record of Burials Performed by the Rev'd Edward Phillips, Employed as the Missionary to the Charleston Protestant Episcopal Domestic Missionary Society and Subsequently the Minister of St. Stephen's Chapel, Guignard Street, Charleston, So. Carolina, St. Stephen's Church Records, Box 2, Records of Burials, 1822-1865, CCSCHS.
65. Whitman, *Challenging Slavery in the Chesapeake*, 93-99. People of color in Philadelphia were among the early advocates of religious self-determination. See Nash, *Forging Freedom*, 109-33.
66. "Emigration to Hayti," *Wilmington, and Delaware Register*, September 9, 1824; Petersburg City Hustings Court Deed Book 5, 1816-1818, 261-62, LVA. For more on the development of religious institutions for people of color in Baltimore, see Phillips, *Freedom's Port*, 117-44.
67. Charles City County Deed Book 6, 1816-1824, 214-15, LVA.
68. Records of Gillfield Church (Baptist), 1815-1842, LVA; *History of Elam Baptist Church*, 12-13.
69. *Rules and Regulations of the Brown Fellowship Society*, 23-27.
70. Jervey, *Robert Y. Hayne and His Times*, 68-69.
71. Payne, *Recollections of Seventy Years*, 14.
72. Petition of the Members of the African Benevolent Association of Wilmington in the State of Delaware, Series 1, Accession #10382501, RSPPUNCG.
73. Memorial of Sundry Free Cold. Persons, Series 1, Accession #10383001, RSPPUNCG.
74. "African School," *Federal Gazette* (Baltimore), October 4, 1809.
75. "African School," *Federal Gazette* (Baltimore), December 21, 1810.
76. Payne, *Recollections of Seventy Years*, 15; "Education," *Raleigh (N.C.) Register*, September 1, 1808.
77. *Special Report of the Commissioner of Education*, 195, 197-99.
78. Abolition Society of Delaware Minute Book, 1801-1819, 36, 38, HSP; *Special Report of the Commissioner of Education*, 198-99, 283.
79. "Infant Schools," *Delaware Register, or, Farmers', Manufacturers' and Mechanics' Advocate* (Wilmington), April 4, 1829.
80. "For the Delaware Journal," *Delaware Journal* (Wilmington), April 7, 1829.
81. Offley, *Narrative of the Life and Labors of the Rev. G. W. Offley*, 3-4, 6, 9-12.
82. Seth Rockman argued that "at a moment of great entrepreneurial energy and social mobility, prosperity came to Americans who could best assemble, deploy, and exploit the physical labor of others. The early republic's economy opened up new possibilities for some Americans precisely because it closed down opportunities for others." See Rockman, *Scraping By*, 2-3.
83. John Butler's Conditions for the Year 1826, Maryland Province Archives, GTMGamms119, Box 15, 52T 1-13, GU.
84. Landers, "Acquisition and Loss on a Spanish Frontier," 94; Whitten, *Andrew Durnford*, 14-16.
85. "Negro Men Laborers wanted," *Louisiana State Gazette* (New Orleans), October 9, 1826.
86. List of People of Colour in Petersburg 1803, Petersburg City Free Negro and Slave Records, LVA.
87. Nancy Adams to Thomas Hyde 11 Octo 1803, RG 21 Records of the District Courts

of the United States Indentures for Apprenticeships, 1801–1893, Box 1, RG21 Entry 128 1803 Nancy Adams to Thomas Hyde, NARA.

88. "Wanted," *Louisiana State Gazette* (New Orleans), July 15, 1824.

89. District of Columbia Manumission and Emancipation Records, RG 21, vol. 1, 75–76, NARA.

90. "Wanted Immediatly," *Columbian Museum* (Savannah, Ga.), October 13, 1804.

91. "Wet Nurse," *New Orleans Argus*, October 9, 1828.

92. List of People of Colour in Petersburg 1803, Petersburg City Free Negro and Slave Records, LVA.

93. Delano, *Washington Directory*, 82.

94. Johnson, *Ante-Bellum North Carolina*, 758; A List of Taxable Property within the Corporation of Fredericksburg for the Year 1811, ID 322-26, CC-TX-P-1811, FCCA; "Memorial of the Free People of Colour," *Baltimore Gazette and Daily Advertiser*, December 14, 1826; "To the Editor of the Liberator," *Liberator* (Boston), August 13, 1831.

95. List of People of Colour in Petersburg 1803, Petersburg City Free Negro and Slave Records, LVA.

96. *Matchett's Baltimore Director*, 39, 247.

97. "Louis Cornie & Co.," *Louisiana State Gazette* (New Orleans), December 12, 1821.

98. Maryland Penitentiary Prisoner Record, 1811–1840, 17, 19, MSA; "Maryland State Penitentiary."

99. "Wanted," *American and Commercial Daily Advertiser* (Baltimore), June 3, 1814.

100. "Porter, Ale, and Cider," *Easton (Md.) Gazette*, March 15, 1819.

101. "Joseph Chain, Hair-Dresser," *Easton (Md.) Gazette*, April 21, 1821; "Joseph Chain, Hair-Dresser," *Easton (Md.) Gazette*, February 2, 1822. For more on Joseph Chain, see Dorsey, *Hirelings*, 39–41, 44, 109–10, 113–14, 116–17.

102. "Oysters! Oysters!," *Georgian* (Savannah), November 13, 1828.

103. "Turtle Soup and Turtle," *Georgian* (Savannah), January 4, 1828.

104. A list of Free Negroes North District 1822, Scott County Free Negro and Slave Records, LVA.

105. "Amelia Shad's Oyster Hotel and Victualling House," *American Watchman* (Wilmington, Del.), December 16, 1825.

106. "Notice," *Columbian Museum* (Savannah, Ga.), May 8, 1815.

107. "Turtle soup," *Savannah (Ga.) Republican*, January 31, 1811; "Turtle Soup," *Columbian Museum* (Savannah, Ga.), April 29, 1817; "This day a fine Turtle Soup will," *Columbian Museum* (Savannah, Ga.), October 28, 1817. For more about free women of color in Savannah and their roles in the local economy, see Johnson, "Free African-American Women in Savannah."

108. "Turtle soup," *Savannah (Ga.) Republican*, January 31, 1811.

109. "Turtle Soup, & c.," *Alexandria (Va.) Gazette*, June 13, 1821.

110. "Turtle Soup," *Southern Patriot* (Charleston, S.C.), November 13, 1822; "Rebecca Dwight," *City Gazette* (Charleston, S.C.), February 8, 1823; "Rebecca Dwight," *Southern Patriot* (Charleston, S.C.), February 23, 1825; "Race Course," *City Gazette* (Charleston, S.C.), February 23, 1827.

111. W. Jeffrey Bolster estimated that "by 1803 black men (mostly free) filled about 18 percent of American seamen's jobs." See Bolster, *Black Jacks*, 6. For more on free people of color, particularly people of indigenous ancestry, in the maritime industries, see Shoemaker, *Native American Whalemen and the World*.

112. List of People of Colour in Petersburg 1803, Petersburg City Free Negro and Slave Records, LVA.

113. Petersburg City Hustings Court Will Book 2, 149, LVA.

114. "For New-York," *Norfolk (Va.) Gazette and Publick Ledger*, December 12, 1804.

115. For more about people of color in the barber's trade, see Bristol, *Knights of the Razor*; and Mills, *Cutting along the Color Line*.

116. "Arthur Mitchum, Barber," *Mississippi Free Trader* (Natchez), August 10, 1817.

117. "Philip Thomas, Barber and Hair Dresser," *Nashville (Tenn.) Whig*, February 28, 1821.

118. "Wigs and Toupets," *Charleston (S.C.) Courier*, October 23, 1829.

119. "William Haden, Barber and Hair Dresser," *Statesman and Gazette* (Natchez, Miss.), October 21, 1826.

120. "S. Oldham, Barber & Hair-Dresser," *Reporter* (Lexington, Ky.), January 20, 1830; "Left at the subscriber's booth," *Reporter* (Lexington, Ky.), November 3, 1827.

121. Charleston County Wills Book H, 145, SCDAH.

122. Jno. C. Stanly's Bond for the Emancipation of Kitty His Wife & Two Children, Craven County Slaves and Free Negroes, Box 10, Petitions for emancipations of slaves, petitions for freedom and bonds for emancipated slaves, 1800–1809, SANC; John C. Stanly Petition for Emancipation, Craven County Slaves and Free Negroes, Box 10, Petitions for emancipations of slaves, petitions for freedom and bonds for emancipated slaves, 1822–1829, SANC. For more on John C. Stanly, see Schweninger, "John Carruthers Stanly."

123. For more on artisans of color in the South, see Franklin, "James Boon, Free Negro Artisan," 150–80; Barnes, *Artisan Workers in the Upper South*, 127–58; and Bishir, *Crafting Lives*.

124. Josiah Fox to John Cassin, April 25, 1808, Letters Received by the Secretary of the Navy from Captains ("Captains' Letters"), M125, April 1–June 28, 1808, NARA.

125. "110 Dollars Reward," *Hillsborough (N.C.) Recorder*, December 19, 1821.

126. District of Columbia Manumission and Emancipation Records, RG 21, vol. 1, 9, NARA.

127. "$30 Reward," *Baton Rouge (La.) Gazette*, December 21, 1822.

128. Barnwell County Manumission Book, 25, Barnwell County Clerk of Court Manumission Book, 1806–1845, SCDAH.

129. Petition Jno. W. deRozareo to keep firearm & c., York County Free Negro and Slave Records, Free Negro and Slave Records, LVA.

130. "Thomas Day, Cabinet Maker," *Milton Gazette and Roanoke (Va.) Advertiser*, March 1, 1827.

131. Butler, *Papers of David Settle Reid*, 2:122, 255, 257.

132. David Wilson Revolutionary War Pension, NARA.

133. Barfield and Marshall, *Thomas Day*; Marshall and Leimenstoll, *Thomas Day*.

134. New Orleans Indentures, 1809–1814, 12, NOPL.

135. William Matthews to Evan Harry, RG 21 Records of the District Courts of the United States Indentures for Apprenticeships, 1801–1893, Box 1, RG21 Entry 128 1812 William Matthew to Evan Harry, NARA.

136. Petition Jno. W. deRozareo to keep firearm & c., York County Free Negro and Slave Records, Free Negro and Slave Records, LVA.

Chapter 5

1. Southampton County Minute Book, 1830–1835, 93, 105–8, 120, LVA; Southampton County Circuit Superior Court Law and Chancery Book, 1831–1841, 5, 17, 19–22, 24–25, 28–29, SCC; *Commonwealth v. Arnold Artis*, Southampton County Judgments, Box 93, Judgments, 1831 [Nat Turner Insurrection] Commonwealth Cases 1–29, Case 17, LVA; *Commonwealth v. Thomas Haithcock*, Southampton County Judgments, Box

93, Judgments, 1831 [Nat Turner Insurrection] Commonwealth Cases 1–29, Case 29, LVA; *Commonwealth v. Berry Newsom*, Southampton County Judgments, Box 93, Judgments, 1831 [Nat Turner Insurrection] Commonwealth Cases 30–50, Case 34, LVA; *Commonwealth v. Exum Artis*, Southampton County Judgments, Box 93, Judgments, 1831 [Nat Turner Insurrection] Commonwealth Cases 30–50, Case 36, LVA; *Commonwealth v. Isham Turner*, Southampton County Judgments, Box 93, Judgments, 1831 [Nat Turner Insurrection] Commonwealth Cases 30–50, Case 47, LVA. For a full account of the Turner Rebellion, see Allmendinger, *Nat Turner and the Rising in Southampton County*; and Breen, *Land Shall Be Deluged in Blood*.

2. Breen, *Land Shall Be Deluged in Blood*, 5–7, 37–87.

3. For a discussion of contrasting punishments, see Malka, *Men of Mobtown*, 176–86.

4. Gatewood, *Free Man of Color*, 25. Hodges referred to the "young colored woman" who lived with his family as "Eliza Nelson." Yet in the Princess Anne County court records, she appears as "Louisa Nelson." See Princess Anne County Minute Book 29, 1830–1832, 187, LVA.

5. Brent [Jacobs], *Incidents in the Life of a Slave Girl*, 97–102. For more details about the characters in Jacob's narrative, see Yellin, *Harriet Jacobs*.

6. *Commonwealth v. Arnold Artis*, Southampton County Judgments, Box 93, Judgments, 1831 [Nat Turner Insurrection] Commonwealth Cases 1–29, Case 17, LVA; *Commonwealth v. Thomas Haithcock*, Southampton County Judgments, Box 93, Judgments, 1831 [Nat Turner Insurrection] Commonwealth Cases 1–29, Case 29, LVA; *Commonwealth v. Berry Newsom*, Southampton County Judgments, Box 93, Judgments, 1831 [Nat Turner Insurrection] Commonwealth Cases 30–50, Case 34, LVA; *Commonwealth v. Exum Artis*, Southampton County Judgments, Box 93, Judgments, 1831 [Nat Turner Insurrection] Commonwealth Cases 30–50, Case 36, LVA; *Commonwealth v. Isham Turner*, Southampton County Judgments, Box 93, Judgments, 1831 [Nat Turner Insurrection] Commonwealth Cases 30–50, Case 47, LVA.

7. Isle of Wight Order Book, 1830–1834, 24, LVA.

8. Norfolk County Minute Book 22, 1830–1832, 229, LVA.

9. Surry County Orders, 1829–1833, 310–15, LVA; Sussex County Order Book, 1827–1835, 248–56, LVA; Brunswick County Order Book 33, 1829–1832, 333–35, LVA; Westmoreland County Orders, 1831–1835, 14–15, LVA; Spotsylvania County Minute Book, 1829–1832, 328–29, 334, 336–37, LVA. For an account of the trials of enslaved people that took place after the rebellion, see Brophy, "Nat Turner Trials."

10. *Commonwealth v. Anne Oliver*, Richmond City Hustings Court Ended Causes, Box 132, LVA; *Commonwealth v. James Cosby*, Richmond City Hustings Court Ended Causes, Box 132, LVA; Norfolk County Minute Book 22, 1830–1832, 240, 249, LVA; Powhatan County Order Book 22, 1831–1833, 109, LVA.

11. Gatewood, *Free Man of Color*, 27.

12. King George County Order Book 12, 1827–1833, 560–61, LVA; Prince Edward County County Court Orders No. 22, 1828–1832, 525. For further discussion of events in Prince Edward County following the rebellion, see Ely, *Israel on the Appomattox*, 175–86.

13. Alexandria City Council Minute Book 6, October 19, 1831, 1830–1845, LVA.

14. "In Council, October 19, 1831," *Alexandria (Va.) Gazette*, October 26, 1831.

15. Southampton County Minute Book, 1830–1835, 93, 105–8, 120, LVA; Southampton County Circuit Superior Court Law and Chancery Book, 1831–1841, 5, 17, 19–22, 24–25, 28–29, 58–59, SCC.

16. *Commonwealth v. Davy Thomas*, Isle of Wight County Commonwealth Causes Ended, Box 3, 1831, LVA.

17. Norfolk County Order Book, 1831–1834, Circuit Superior Court of Law and Chancery, 23–24, 27, LVA.
18. Mecklenburg County Register of Free Negroes, 54–103, LVA.
19. Princess Anne County Minute Book 29, 1830–1832, 186, LVA.
20. Gatewood, *Free Man of Color*, 26–28.
21. *Commonwealth v. Nathaniel Young*, Isle of Wight County Commonwealth Causes Ended, Box 3, 1832, LVA.
22. Staunton City Register of Free Negroes and Mulattoes, 1810–1864, LVA; Rockbridge County Register of Free Negroes, 1831–1860, LVA; Lancaster County Register of Free Negroes, 1803–1860, LVA.
23. Richmond City Hustings Court Minutes 11, 1831–1835, 62, 72–73, LVA.
24. Mecklenburg County Register of Free Negroes, 54–103, LVA; Surry County Register of Free Negroes, 176–232, LVA; Fairfax County Register of Free Negroes, LVA; Abercrombie, Free Blacks of Louisa County, 37–41.
25. Brent [Jacobs], *Incidents in the Life of a Slave Girl*, 101.
26. Princess Anne Report of the County Court to the Board of Commissioners for Transporting Free Persons, Auditor of Public Accounts Entry 757 Reports of Free Negroes, 1833–1836, Reports of Free Negroes & Mulattoes 1833 P-Y, LVA.
27. Drew, *Refugee*, 330–33.
28. Catherine C. Hammond Deposition December 21, 1911, Lloyd Hammond Pension File, CWP.
29. "Memories of Uncle Jackson," A Folk History of Slavery in the United States from Interviews with Former Slaves, 1936–1938, 11:3, Federal Writers' Project of the Works Progress Administration.
30. For further discussion of runaways assisted by free persons of color, see Franklin and Schweninger, *Runaway Slaves*, 69–71, 109–11, 130.
31. *Commonwealth v. Leonard Grimes*, Free Blacks Criminal Papers, 1839-019, LCCOHRD; "The final trial of Leonard Grimes," *Alexandria (Va.) Gazette*, March 17, 1840. Following his imprisonment, Grimes relocated to Boston, Massachusetts, where he served as a Baptist minister and continued his antislavery work. In 1854, he sought to protect Anthony Burns, a member of his congregation, who faced trial under the national Fugitive Slave Act of 1850. For more on Grimes and his connection to the Burns case, see Von Frank, *Trials of Anthony Burns*.
32. Petition and Papers in the Case of Abraham Brogden, Secretary of State Pardon Papers, 1851, Box 48, Folder 28 Abraham Brogden, MSA.
33. *State v. James Peck*, Tennessee Supreme Court Cases, TSLA.
34. Petition of Citizens of Queen Anne's County, Secretary of State Pardon Papers, 1839–1841, Box 42, Folder 27 Sherry Wilson, free negro, MSA.
35. Secretary of State Pardon Record, 1845–1865, 30, MSA.
36. Still, *Underground Railroad*, 246–50. For more on Samuel Green, see Blondo, "Samuel Green."
37. Still, *Underground Railroad*, 715–19, 746–47.
38. Negro Petition, Series 1, Accession #10383201, RSPPUNCG.
39. Memorial of Sundry Inhabitants of the County of Lenoir, General Assembly Session Records, November 1831–January 1832, Box 6, Petitions (Concerning Slaves), SANC.
40. Petition Concerning the Free Negroes of Northampton County, 1831, Legislative Petitions, LVA.
41. A Memorial of Many Citizens of the County of Amelia Calling the Attention of the General Assembly to the Subject of the Removal of the Free Negroes, Dec. 7, 1831, Legis-

lative Petitions, LVA; Goochland Memorial Concerning Free Negroes, Dec. 15, 1831, Legislative Petitions, LVA; Petition of the Citizens of James City County on the subject of free negroes & c., Legislative Petitions, LVA; Nansemond Dec. 22nd 1831, Legislative Petitions, LVA; Powhatan County A Memorial & Petition to the General Assembly of Virginia Relative to the Free People of Colour in Virginia, Dec. 23, 1831, Legislative Petitions, LVA; Westmoreland Dec. 8th 1831, 1831, Legislative Petitions, LVA; York Dec. 12th 1831, 1831, Legislative Petitions, LVA.

42. Guild, *Black Laws of Virginia*, 106–8.

43. *Journal of the House of Delegates of the Commonwealth of Virginia*, 16, 19, 21, 84, 90, 93, 95, 106, Bill No. 18.

44. *Acts Passed by the General Assembly of the State of North Carolina, at the Session of 1831-32*, 7, 10–11, 24.

45. Dorsey, *Laws of Maryland*, 1068–73.

46. *Laws of the State of Delaware* (1841), 208–10.

47. "An Act concerning free persons of color and for other purposes," *Southern Statesman* (Jackson, Miss.), December 31, 1831.

48. Alden and Van Hoesen, *Digest of the Laws of Mississippi*, 769–71.

49. McCord, *Statutes at Large of South Carolina*, 467–68.

50. "Laws of Alabama," *Democrat* (Huntsville, Ala.), February 9, 1832.

51. "Ordinances," *Arkansas Times and Advocate* (Little Rock), February 8, 1832.

52. "To the Citizens of Wilmington," *Delaware Gazette and American Watchman* (Wilmington), October 11, 1831.

53. To the Honorable, the Senate and House of Representative of the State of Delaware in General Assembly, Series 1, Accession #10383301–10383304, 10383306, 10383307, RSPPUNCG.

54. Guild, *Black Laws of Virginia*, 175–76.

55. Free men of color could still vote in the northern states of Maine, Massachusetts, New Hampshire, New York, Pennsylvania, and Vermont at the beginning of the 1830s. In New York, free men of color needed $250 in property in order to vote. Lawmakers in Pennsylvania disfranchised free men of color in 1838. See Wesley, "Negro Suffrage in the Period of Constitution-Making," 162–63, 166. For more on the disfranchisement of free men of color in Pennsylvania, see Malone, *Between Freedom and Bondage*, 57–99; and Wood, "'Sacrifice on the Altar of Slavery.'"

56. *Journal of the Convention of the State of Tennessee*, 19, 107, 208–10, 214–15, 398.

57. *Proceedings and Debates of the Convention of North-Carolina*, 3–4, 17, 60–81, 351–57. For more on the disfranchisement debate in North Carolina, see Franklin, *Free Negro in North Carolina*, 108–20; and Ford, *Deliver Us from Evil*, 418–45.

58. "The Hon. Jesse Speight," *Greensboro (N.C.) Patriot*, November 11, 1835.

59. "Convention Question," *Raleigh (N.C.) Register-Weekly*, April 21, 1835.

60. Snethen, *Black Code of the District of Columbia*, 45–46.

61. *Acts of the General Assembly of the Commonwealth of Kentucky Passed at December Session, 1845*, 54–56.

62. "Pensacola," *Pensacola (Fla.) Gazette*, February 28, 1857.

63. "Colonization," *Pensacola (Fla.) Gazette*, February 14, 1857.

64. "The Exodus," *Pensacola (Fla.) Gazette*, April 4, 1857. For further discussion of the exodus of free people of color from Florida, see Barr and Hargis, "Voluntary Exile of Free Negroes of Pensacola," 3–14; and Gould, "Free Creoles of Color of the Antebellum Gulf Ports."

65. *Acts and Resolutions Adopted by the General Assembly of Florida*, 214–15; 1860 U.S. Federal Census, City of Pensacola, Escambia County, Florida, 11, 23, 31–32. Al-

though the 1861 act claimed that those exempted were natives of Florida, some were born in other places according to the 1860 U.S. Federal Census, including Auguste Sevalier or Auguste Chevalier, a native of Africa; Ambrose Vaughan, a native of Virginia; and Tabitha Vaughan, who was born in Mississippi.

66. Petition of John Kelker, Fred Kelker, & Cecil Kelker, Series 1, Accession #10586101, RSPPUNCG.

67. Duval, *Compilation of the Public Acts of the Legislative Council of the Territory of Florida*, 65.

68. *Laws of the State of North Carolina Passed by the General Assembly at the Session of 1840-41*, 61-62.

69. *Public Laws of the State of North Carolina Passed by the General Assembly at Its Session of 1860-61*, 68.

70. Thomas Burk a coloured man License to keep a Gun, Prince George's County Circuit Court Court Papers, Blacks, 1799-1851, Petition by Thomas Burke, freeman, for license to keep gun, MSA.

71. J. H. Boteter Statement, Prince George's County Circuit Court Court Papers, Blacks, 1799-1851, Petition by Thomas Burke, freeman, for license to keep gun, MSA.

72. Petition of James Staten for permission to carry and keep a gun, Baltimore County Court Miscellaneous Court Papers, 1847, C1-108, Items 495-541, MSA.

73. *State v. Asa Jacobs*, 7195, Supreme Court Cases, SANC.

74. Some local studies have identified similar patterns between discriminatory legislation and enforcement. See Jackson, "Free Negroes of Petersburg," 371; Ely, *Israel on the Appomattox*, 225-83; and Rohrs, "Free Black Experience in Antebellum Wilmington."

75. Luther P. Jackson found that manumission rates returned to pre-1806 levels by 1820. See Jackson, "Manumission in Certain Virginia Cities," 290.

76. Guild, *Black Laws of Virginia*, 111; Petition of Armistead Miller, ID 467-277, CC-HU-R-1841, FCCA.

77. *Commonwealth v. Dickson*, Criminal Papers, 1833-30; *Commonwealth v. Rozell's Dick*, Criminal Papers, 1834-028; *Commonwealth v. William Arnett*, Criminal Papers, 1834-031; *Commonwealth v. Judy Bolen*, Criminal Papers, 1835-034; *Commonwealth v. Hannah Bolen*, Criminal Papers, 1835-035; *Commonwealth v. Titus Brown*, Criminal Papers, 1835-036; *Commonwealth v. Ned Bask*, Criminal Papers, 1835-039; *Commonwealth v. Joseph Trammell*, Criminal Papers, 1837-033; *Commonwealth v. Daniel Coats*, Criminal Papers, 1837-036; *Commonwealth v. Susan Briant alias Bryan*, Criminal Papers, 1844-022; *Commonwealth v. Lee Bryant*, Criminal Papers, 1845-029; *Commonwealth v. George Field*, Criminal Papers, 1848-009; *Commonwealth v. Harriet Craven*, Criminal Papers, 1848-014; *Commonwealth v. Ralph Perry*, Criminal Papers, 1849-002; *Commonwealth v. Lewis Jackson*, Criminal Papers, 1849-002; *Commonwealth v. James Davis*, Criminal Papers, 1850-022; *Commonwealth v. Lucy Green*, Criminal Papers, 1852-019; *Commonwealth v. Aaron Davis*, Criminal Papers, 1852-20; *Commonwealth v. David Brooks*, Criminal Papers, 1856-016; *Commonwealth v. Henry Douglas*, Criminal Papers, 1860-018 (all in LOCOHRD).

78. *Commonwealth v. Betsey Williams*, Arlington County Court Records: Criminal, Judgements, Tax and Fiscal Records, Box 3, LVA; *Commonwealth v. Lucy Kitt*, Arlington County Court Records: Criminal, Judgements, Tax and Fiscal Records, Box 3, LVA.

79. Lynchburg City Free Negro Register, 1843-1865, 56-57, LVA. At least some of these people continued to reside in Lynchburg until at least 1860. See 1860 U.S. Federal Census, Lynchburg, Campbell County, Virginia, 70.

80. *Laws of the State of North Carolina, Passed by the General Assembly, at the Session of 1838-'39*, 33.

81. Yarbrough, *Race in the Cherokee Nation*, 39–73; *Constitution and Laws of the Cherokee Nation*, 19.

82. *Constitution, Laws, and Treaties of the Chickasaws*, 96.

83. Guild, *Black Laws of Virginia*, 139; Cobb, *Compilation of the General and Public Statutes of the State of Georgia*, 659; Auditor of Public Accounts Delinquent Free Negro Taxpayers Lists, LVA.

84. *Acts Passed by the General Assembly of the State of North Carolina, at the Session of 1831-32*, 10–11; *Laws of the State of Delaware* (1841), 209–10, 306; Dorsey, *General Public Statutory Law*, 1068, 1196, 1281; Guild, *Black Laws of Virginia*, 106, 137.

85. Frantel, *Richmond, Virginia Uncovered*, 103; Register, 1841–1846, Richmond (Va.) City Sergeant Papers, Section 1, VHS.

86. Guild, *Black Laws of Virginia*, 87.

87. Robeson County Superior Court Minutes, vol. 1, Fall 1847, SANC.

88. Kent County Court of General Sessions Session Docket, April 1848–April 1859, DPA.

89. Tate, *Digest of the Laws of Virginia*, 850.

90. McCord, *Statutes at Large of South Carolina*, 468–70.

91. *Constitution and Laws of the Cherokee Nation*, 55–56.

92. *Laws of the State of Missouri, Passed at the First Session of the Fourteenth General Assembly*, 103.

93. *Laws of the State of North Carolina, Passed by the General Assembly, at the Session of 1840-41*, 11–19.

94. *Wilson v. Wilson*, Petersburg Chancery Causes, LVA; 1860 U.S. Federal Census, Centre Ward, Petersburg, Virginia, 311; Douglass, *Personal Narrative of Mrs. Margaret Douglass*; Taylor, *Reminiscences of My Life in Camp*, 5–6. For further discussion of educational efforts in Savannah, see Johnson, *Black Savannah*, 126–30. Enforcement of education restrictions were also limited in St. Louis, Missouri. See Bellamy, "Free Blacks in Antebellum Missouri," 198–226; and Winch, *Clamorgans*, 176–77.

95. Mason County Order Book, Book L, 1827–1832, 500–501, KDLA.

96. *Levin P. Bowland v. Negro Griffin*, Somerset County Register of Wills Miscellaneous Papers, 1829–1853, MSA.

97. Richmond County Minutes Inferior Court, 1849–1868, 38–39, ARCJC.

98. 1860 U.S. Federal Census, 1st Ward City of Augusta, Richmond County, Georgia, 9.

99. *Laws of the Republic of Texas*, 1:19.

100. Petition of Greenberry Logan, Series 1, Accession #11583702, RSPPUNCG; Petition of Samuel McCulluck, Series 1, Accession #11583703, RSPPUNCG; Petition of Joseph Tate, Series 1, Accession #11583904, RSPPUNCG; Petition of Wm Goyens, Series 1, Accession #11583803, RSPPUNCG; Petition of Wm Goyens, Series 1, Accession #11584002, RSPPUNCG; Petition of Citizens of Jefferson County, Series 1, Accession #11584014, RSPPUNCG.

101. U.S. Senate, *Preliminary Report on the Eighth Census, 1860*, 136; "1838 October Choctaw Nation Constitution"; *Constitution and Laws of the Choctaw Nation*, 12, 32–33, 61.

102. *Constitution and Laws of the Cherokee Nation*, 71.

103. *Constitution, Laws, and Treaties of the Chickasaws*, 115.

104. *Seventh Census*, ix; Kennedy, *Population of the United States in 1860*, 8, 18, 54, 72–73, 194, 270, 452, 484–86.

105. Petition of Caleb Heald & 38 Others, Series 1, Accession #10385303, RSPPUNCG.

106. *Laws of the State of Delaware* (1859), 281.

107. Blassingame, *Slave Testimony*, 427.

108. "Lost, On Board the Steamer Roanoke," *Richmond (Va.) Dispatch*, August 12, 1852.

109. "Three Dollars Reward," *Richmond (Va.) Dispatch*, November 11, 1854.

110. "The Following Rates," *Lynchburg Daily Virginian*, May 24, 1853.

111. "New Orleans, Jackson and Great Northern Railroad," *Daily Picayune* (New Orleans), December 15, 1858.

112. Presentment of the Grand Jury for Edgefield District at Fall Term 1859, General Assembly Grand Jury Presentments, Box 8, #s 28-32, SCDAH.

113. Legislative Petitions Roll 21, 1859-1865, Wilson County 37-1860, TSLA.

114. "Convention of Slaveholders of the Eastern Shore," *Cecil Whig* (Elkton, Md.), November 20, 1858; Jacobs, *Free Negro Question in Maryland*, 1, 4, 6.

115. "Speech of Wm. H. Barksdale, on the bill for the expulsion of free persons of color from this state," *Nashville (Tenn.) Union and American*, December 7, 1859; "Election Returns," *Nashville (Tenn.) Patriot*, August 8, 1859.

116. "Important Bills," *North Carolina Standard*, November 23, 1858; Report of Com on Judiciary, General Assembly Session Records, November 1858-February 1859, Box 9, Senate Committee Reports, SANC; *Journal of the Senate of the General Assembly of the State of North-Carolina at Its Session of 1860-'61*, 3, 77, 145-46; "The National Executive Committee of the Democratic Party," *Daily Exchange* (Baltimore), June 25, 1860. In 1860, Humphrey served as the secretary of the National Executive Committee of the Democratic Party.

117. Schweninger, *From Tennessee Slave to St. Louis Entrepreneur*, 155.

118. Report of Com on Judiciary, General Assembly Session Records, November 1858-February 1859, Senate Committee Reports, SANC.

119. "The Legislature—Twenty-Fifth Week," *Memphis (Tenn.) Daily Appeal*, March 27, 1860; "Free Negroes," *Keowee Courier* (Pickens Court House, S.C.), December 15, 1860; Freehling, *Road to Disunion: Secessionists Triumphant*, 185-201; "The Florida Legislature," *New York Herald*, December 29, 1859; "The Florida Free Negro Bill," *Arkansas True Democrat* (Little Rock), February 1, 1860; "The Free Negro Bill," *Glasgow (Mo.) Weekly Times*, March 15, 1860; "The Governor's Veto of the Free Negro Bill," *Weekly West* (St. Joseph, Mo.), March 24, 1860. For more on the debate in Tennessee, see Atkins, "Party Politics and the Debate over the Tennessee Free Negro Bill," 245-78.

120. "Expulsion of Free Negroes from Arkansas," *New-York Tribune*, January 7, 1860; "An Act to Remove Free Negroes and Mulattoes from This State," *Arkansas State Gazette and Democrat* (Little Rock), March 5, 1859.

121. West, *Family or Freedom*, 2-3; *Acts of the General Assembly of Virginia, Passed in 1855-6*, 37-38; *Public Acts of the State of Tennessee, Passed at the First Session of the Thirty-Second General Assembly*, 55-56; *Acts Passed by the Fourth Legislature of the State of Louisiana*, 214-15; *Acts of the Seventh Biennial Session, of the General Assembly of Alabama*, 63-64; *Acts of the General Assembly of the Commonwealth of Kentucky Passed at the Session Which Was Begun and Held in the City of Frankfort, on Monday, the Fifth Day of December, 1859*, 128-30; *Public Acts of the State of Tennessee, Passed at the First Session of the Thirty-Third General Assembly*, 117; Schafer, *Becoming Free, Remaining Free*, 145-62; Maris-Wolf, *Family Bonds*, 21-22; Gillison, Fanny Petition for Leave to Choose Owner, Fauquier County Chancery Causes, 1860-083, LVA.

122. *Acts Passed by the Fourth Legislature of the State of Louisiana*, 70-72.

123. *Acts of the General Assembly of the Commonwealth of Kentucky, Passed at the Session Which Was Begun and Held in the City of Frankfort, on Monday, the Fifth Day of December, 1859*, 128-31.

124. William D. Valentine Diary, vol. 12, 163–65, SHC.

125. Guild, *Black Laws of Virginia*, 119; *Local Laws and Private Acts of the State of Missouri*, 367; *Journal of the Senate of the Commonwealth of Kentucky*, 148, 173, 184, 512–13, 533–34; *African Repository*, 70; Auditor of Public Accounts Nansemond County Land Tax Books, 1850, LVA; Tyler-McGraw, *African Republic*, 58.

126. "A Song," *Edgefield (S.C.) Advertiser*, September 24, 1840.

127. "Free Negro Voters," *Boon's Lick Times* (Fayette, N.C.), April 4, 1840.

128. "Hooe's Case—Free Negro Testimony," *Tennessean* (Nashville), July 7, 1840.

129. "Disorderly Negro," *Louisville (Ky.) Daily Courier*, October 29, 1856.

130. "Gambling Niggers," *Daily Delta* (New Orleans), March 17, 1846.

131. "One of the Niggers," *New Orleans Crescent*, October 11, 1854.

132. "Free Nigger Convention," *Louisville (Ky.) Daily Courier*, August 29, 1850.

133. David R. Roediger argued that "working class formation and the systematic development of a sense of whiteness went hand in hand for the US white working class" and highlighted the significance of the contrast white workers drew between themselves and persons of color, both enslaved and free. See Roediger, *Wages of Whiteness*, 1–15.

134. Douglass, *Life and Times of Frederick Douglass*, 222–32.

135. "Negro Mechanics," *Eastern Carolina Republican* (New Bern, N.C.), January 31, 1849.

136. "Mechanics' Meeting," *Carolina Watchman* (Salisbury, N.C.), December 19, 1850.

137. Laurie, *Artisans into Workers*, 61–63, 108–9; Barnes, *Artisan Workers in the Upper South*, 106–13.

138. David Gavin Diary, 156, SHC.

139. "At a meeting of the Mechanics' Institute," *Gazette and Democrat* (Little Rock, Ark.), September 25, 1858.

140. "Is it Right to Teach Negroes the Mechanic Arts?," *Fayetteville (N.C.) Observer*, August 12, 1858.

141. Tommy L. Bogger discovered that the slaveholders in Virginia pushed back against white mechanics, especially in regard to their opposition to enslaved workers. The slaveholders rejected losing the power to train their bondspeople however they saw fit. See Bogger, *Free Blacks in Norfolk*, 75–78. Eric Foner found that prejudice against people of color was an important part of free labor ideology for many midcentury northerners. See Foner, *Free Soil, Free Labor, Free Men*, 261–300.

142. Through the 1800s, riots took place in several northern states, including Massachusetts, New York, Ohio, Pennsylvania, and Rhode Island. See Curry, *Free Black in Urban America*, 96–111; Sweet, *Bodies Politic*, 353–97; Taylor, *Frontiers of Freedom*, 50–79; and Archer, *Jim Crow North*, 14–16, 83–87.

143. "Beverly Snow," *Daily National Intelligencer* (Washington, D.C.), October 27, 1835; *Special Report of the Commissioner of Education*, 201.

144. "A Mob," *Raleigh (N.C.) Microcosm*, October 22, 1842.

145. Hamilton, *Papers of Thomas Ruffin*, 2:205–6.

146. *Special Report of the Commissioner of Education*, 201; "Stop the Runaway," *Raleigh (N.C.) Register*, March 7, 1843; Bigglestone, *They Stopped in Oberlin*, 122–24.

147. Schweninger, *From Tennessee Slave to St. Louis Entrepreneur*, 155.

Chapter 6

1. "Embalming the Dead," *Daily Crescent* (New Orleans), April 22, 1856. While Casanave claimed to use a superior embalming process, he was not the only undertaker in New Orleans. According to an 1858 city directory, Casanave was one of twenty undertakers in New Orleans. See *A. Mygatt & Co.'s New Orleans Business Directory*, 229–30.

2. "Pierre Casanave," *New Orleans Tribune*, December 27, 1864; "Editorial Paragraphs," *New Orleans Crescent*, December 9, 1866; Fields, *Slavery and Freedom on the Middle Ground*, 71; Barnes, *Artisan Workers in the Upper South*, 128.

3. *Seventh Census*, ix; Kennedy, *Population of the United States in 1860*, 8, 18, 46, 54, 72–73, 180–81, 194, 214, 270, 286–87, 358–59, 452, 466–67, 484–86, 516–18; U.S. Senate, *Preliminary Report on the Eighth Census, 1860*, 136. The figure for 1860 includes the populations of the southern states, the District of Columbia, and Indian Territory.

4. *Seventh Census*, ix; Kennedy, *Population of the United States in 1860*, 8, 18, 54, 72–73, 194, 270, 452, 484–86; U.S. Senate, *Preliminary Report on the Eighth Census, 1860*, 136. More than 130 free people of color left Florida for Cuba in 1821. This migration was followed by additional exoduses to Cuba, Haiti, and Mexico. See Landers, *Atlantic Creoles in the Age of Revolutions*, 167–68.

5. *Seventh Census*, ix; Kennedy, *Population of the United States in 1860*, 8, 18, 46, 54, 72–73, 180–81, 194, 214, 270, 286–87, 358–59, 452, 466–67, 484–86, 516–18, 588.

6. *Seventh Census*, ix; Kennedy, *Population of the United States in 1860*, 46.

7. *Seventh Census*, ix; Kennedy, *Population of the United States in 1860*, 588; District of Columbia Manumission and Emancipation Records, vols. 1–4, NARA. For more about the antislavery network in the District of Columbia, see Russell, "Underground Railroad Activists in Washington, D.C.," 28–49; and Harrold, *Subversives*.

8. Kennedy, *Population of the United States in 1860*, 214; Fields, *Slavery and Freedom on the Middle Ground*, 4–6, 30–31.

9. *Seventh Census*, ix; Kennedy, *Population of the United States in 1860*, 358–59, 516–18; Tyler-McGraw, *African Republic*, 39–61.

10. *Seventh Census*, ix; Kennedy, *Population of the United States in 1860*, 180–81, 286–87, 466–67; Moore and Zapalac, "Emancipations"; Hudson, "In Pursuit of Freedom."

11. Troxler, *Slavery in Missouri*, 206–27; Blassingame, *Slave Testimony*, 385–86; Bellamy, "Free Blacks in Antebellum Missouri."

12. Ely, *Israel on the Appomattox*, x, 5–15; Milteer, *North Carolina's Free People of Color*, 87–96.

13. Pauper Lists of Sussex County Trustees of Poor January 1, 1850–February 13, 1879, 98–99, 118–19, 154–55, DPA.

14. Queen Anne's County Trustees of the Poor Almshouse Accounts, 1847–1859, MSA.

15. Bethel Hill Baptist Church Woodsdale, NC Person County Roll and Minute Book, March 5, 1837, March 4, 1837, April 1, 1837, SANC.

16. Margaret Boute Declaration, June 9, 1877, Louis Boute Pension File, CWP; Margaret Elizabeth Boute Deposition, May 27, 1884, Louis Boute Pension File, CWP.

17. William Thomas McElroy Journal, 1852–1868, 1889, 1901–1905, 64, 81, 102, FHS.

18. "Died," *Morning Courier* (Louisville, Ky.), July 23, 1850.

19. "James Scott," *Clarksville (Tenn.) Chronicle*, January 4, 1861.

20. William O'Neale Account Book 1822, 28, 57, DU.

21. Libertytown Store Ledger, 1859–1861, 26, 36, 44, Abraham Jones Papers, UM.

22. Morris Hare Account, Augustus H. Holland Papers, PC; Susan Boon Account, Augustus H. Holland Papers, PC; Moses Boon Account, Augustus H. Holland Papers, PC; William Holland Account, Augustus H. Holland Papers, PC; Latisha Howell Account, Augustus H. Holland Papers, PC.

23. J. T. Lewter Ledger 1, 8, 117, J. T. Lewter Papers, Murfreesboro Historical Association Collection, ECU.

24. James P. Carter Ledger, 1852–1860, 71, 84, Vallie Burgess Carter Papers, DU.

25. Hogan and Davis, *William Johnson's Natchez*, 30–34, 519.

26. Clamorgan, *Colored Aristocracy of St. Louis*, 47-48.

27. "Early Corn," *Sun* (Baltimore), September 5, 1843; "New Corn Meal," *Cecil Whig* (Elkton, Md.), September 8, 1849.

28. No 113 Sarah Davis, RG75, Records of the Bureau of Indian Affairs Records Relating to Civil War Claims of Loyal Indians Records Relating to Loyal Creek Claims, 1869-70, Box 2, Claim #113 Sarah Davis, NARA; Senate, Letter from the Secretary of the Interior, Transmitting, In response to Senate resolution of June 6, 1888, papers relating to certain claims of the Creek Indians, 50th Cong., 1st sess., 1888; Clamorgan, *Colored Aristocracy of St. Louis*, 56; 1860 U.S. Federal Census, 4th Ward of the City of St. Louis, St. Louis County, Missouri, 46; 1860 U.S. Federal Census, Ward 7 City of Charleston, Charleston District, South Carolina, 31; 1860 U.S. Federal Census, Ward 5 City of Charleston, Charleston District, South Carolina, 78; Desdunes, *Our People and Our History*, 69-71; State of North Carolina for Repairs Gov' House 1837, Governors Papers, GP 88.1, Governor's Mansion Expenses, receipts, 1837-1839, SANC; His Excellency E. B. Dudley to Allen Jones, Governors Papers, GP 88.1, Governor's Mansion Expenses, receipts, 1837-1839, SANC; "Solomon Brown: First African American Employee at the Smithsonian Institution."

29. Perry, "Naval-Stores Industry in the Old South"; 1860 U.S. Federal Census, Bladen County, North Carolina, 93-94. For more on the naval stores industry, see Outland, *Tapping the Pines*. Shingle Bill February 7, 1852, Dismal Swamp Land Company Records, DU; Claim of Thomas Baker 5087, SCCAC; Dick of Tynes Amt. $20 May 1, 1843, Dismal Swamp Land Company Records, Box 3, Letters and Papers, 1841-1843, DU; Dick Tynes Amt. $8.00 October 30, 1846, Dismal Swamp Land Company Records, Box 4, Letters and Papers, 1846, DU; Ely of Winslow, Luke Ash, & Tom Oshields Amt. $7.00 December 1, 1849, Dismal Swamp Land Company Records, Box 4, Letters and Papers, 1849-1850, DU; Minton of Folk Amt. $30.00, September 13, 1851, Dismal Swamp Land Company Records, Box 4, Letters and Papers, 1851, DU. For further discussion of the communities around the Great Dismal Swamp, see Kirby, *Poquosin*, 126-216; Milteer, "Life in a Great Dismal Swamp Community"; Sayers, *Desolate Place for a Defiant People*; and Nevius, *City of Refuge*. For more on canal construction, see Cecelski, *Waterman's Song*, 103-17.

30. Ledger for Berkeley Plantation, Berkeley Plantation and Fishery Ledger, UVA.

31. J. A. Anderson to Chesson and Armstead, John B. Chesson Papers, Box 1, Chesson Papers Miscellaneous, SANC; Petition of James L. Cox and George Wareham of Westmoreland County, Legislative Petitions, LVA.

32. For more on the role of people of color in the fishing industry, see Cecelski, *Waterman's Song*, 83-102.

33. Hilary Croom to the Legislature 1852, General Assembly Session Records, October-December 1852, Box 8, Petitions, SANC.

34. James Walden A Free Negro Petition to the General Assembly, 1861, Legislative Petitions, LVA.

35. Franklin, *Free Negro in North Carolina*, 130-62; Jackson, "Virginia Free Negro Farmer and Property Owner," 390-439; Jackson, *Free Negro Labor and Property Holding in Virginia*, 102-70; Provine, "Economic Position of the Free Blacks in the District of Columbia"; Milteer, *North Carolina's Free People of Color*, 146-93.

36. 1850 U.S. Federal Census, Iberville Parish, Louisiana, 328; 1860 U.S. Federal Census, Opelousas, St. Landry Parish, Louisiana, 226; 1860 U.S. Federal Census, Jefferson Parish, Louisiana, 155; 1850 U.S. Federal Census, Plaquemines Parish, Louisiana, 279; Schweninger, *Black Property Owners in the South*, 287-90. For more about these

elite free people of color, see Davis and Hogan, *Barber of Natchez*; Whitten, *Andrew Durnford*; Johnson and Roark, *Black Masters*; and Koger, *Black Slaveowners*.

37. *Woods' Baltimore Directory for 1858-'59*, 538-40; "Church Directory," *Daily National Intelligencer* (Washington, D.C.), May 20, 1856; Campbell, *Nashville Business Directory*, 28; Caroline County Court Land Records, vol. Y, 203-4, MSA; *Minutes of the Forty-Seventh Annual Session of the Chowan Baptist Association*, 8-9.

38. First Baptist Church (Washington, D.C.), Records, 1802-1845, LVA; First Baptist Church (Washington, D.C.), Records, 1845-1886, LVA; Jennings, *Colored Man's Reminiscences of James Madison*; Taylor, *Slave in the White House*; Record of the Proceedings of Presbyterian Churches in the District of Columbia in October 1841, Carter G. Woodson Collection, Series 11, Additional Manuscripts: Presbyterian Church D. C. Proceedings 1841, LC.

39. Frederick County Circuit Court Church Charters, 1808-1880, 78-80, MSA. The organizers of the church included Jeffery Gulden, Samuel Groce, Joseph Gray, John L. Armstrong, William R. Gains, Levi Fisher, and Samuel Thorns.

40. Fifth Street Baptist Church Minutes, Book 1, 9, 41-42, UofL.

41. *Directory of the City of Charleston, for the Year 1852*, 165; 1850 U.S. Federal Census, Parish of St. Philip and St. Michaels, Charleston, South Carolina, 151, 170.

42. First Baptist Church of Lynchburg, Virginia Minutes, Book 2, 30-31, JML.

43. "Baptizing," *Western Watchman* (St. Louis, Mo.), March 22, 1849.

44. "Fair at the Second Colored Church," *Western Watchman* (St. Louis, Mo.), July 13, 1854.

45. "The Fair," *Evening Star* (Washington, D.C.), May 13, 1856.

46. "Fair," *Daily Picayune* (New Orleans), January 1, 1858.

47. Payne, *Recollections of Seventy Years*, 75.

48. First African Baptist Church, Richmond Minutes, 1841-1859, Book 1, 131-32, 146-47, 149-50, 162, LVA.

49. Morrow, *Persons of Color and Religious at the Same Time*, 1-2; Banks, "Contradiction in Antebellum Baltimore"; Gould, "Henriette Delille."

50. *Metropolitan Catholic Almanac*, 79.

51. Clark, *Luminous Brotherhood*, 1-16, 22-34. See also Bell, *Revolution, Romanticism, and the Afro-Creole Protest*; and Daggett, *Spiritualism in Nineteenth-Century New Orleans*.

52. Payne, *Recollections of Seventy Years*, 78-79; Weeden, *Weeden's History of the Colored People of Louisville*, 30-31.

53. Banks, "Contradiction in Antebellum Baltimore," 132-63.

54. Campbell, *Nashville Business Directory*, 31.

55. Green, *Fact Stranger Than Fiction*, 42.

56. J W Adams Report of State of School, Schools Collection, African School Society (Manuscripts) Folder 5, DHS.

57. Harriet Peck to Isaac Peck, March 1, 1839, Peck Family Papers, GCQA.

58. Wormley, "Myrtilla Miner," 440-57; Daniel, "Myrtilla Miner," 30-45; Null, "Myrtilla Miner's 'School for Colored Girls,'" 254-68.

59. Mary Victoria Cook to Myrtilla Miner, June 21, 1852, Myrtilla Miner Papers, Education/School Essays & Drawings by Students, 1852-54, LC.

60. Mary Brent to Myrtilla Miner, May 14, 1853, Myrtilla Miner Papers, Education/School Essays & Drawings by Students, 1852-54, LC.

61. M. A. Beckett to Myrtilla Miner, July 12, 1854, Myrtilla Miner Papers, Education/School Essays & Drawings by Students, 1852-54, LC.

62. "There Will Be a Sale of Useful and Fancy Articles," *Sun* (Baltimore), January 8, 1848; "The Fair at St. Alphonsus Hall," *Sun* (Baltimore), January 20, 1848; "Fair—For the Benefit of the St. Frances' Male School (Colored)," *Sun* (Baltimore), December 22, 1853; "Afternoon Excursion," *Sun* (Baltimore), September 3, 1849.

63. Desdunes, *Our People and Our History*, 97–108. For more on Couvent and Catholic Institute, see Mitchell, "'Good and Delicious Country,'" 123–44; and Neidenbach, "Life and Legacy of Marie Couvent."

64. Snyder, *Great Crossings*, 283–86; Whitten, *Andrew Durnford*, 102–18; "Youngsters of Yesterday," *Asbury Park (N.J.) Press*, April 21, 1926; *Annual Catalogue of the Officers and Students of Oberlin College for the College Year 1858-59*, 8; *Quinquennial Catalogue of Oberlin College*, 83, "Death of Joseph E. Sampson," *Wilmington (N.C.) Morning Star*, August 4, 1897; Desdunes, *Our People and Our History*, 73–77; 1850 U.S. Federal Census, 3rd Ward 1st Mun. New Orleans, Orleans Parish, Louisiana, 113; "Death of Dr. Louis Charles Roudanez," *Daily Picayune* (New Orleans), March 12, 1890; "Norbert Rillieux," *Daily Picayune* (New Orleans), October 28, 1894.

65. Delaney and Rhodes, *Free Blacks of Lynchburg*, 52–60.

66. Constitution of the Union Burial Ground Society, Organization Records Collection, Union Burial Ground Society Constitution 22 January 1848, LVA.

67. "Laurel Cemetery," *Sun* (Baltimore), October 18, 1851. Original members of the executive committee included Daniel A. Payne, George A. Hackett, William Bishop, James H. Davis, Samuel Wilson, Cornelius Thomson, James Morris, Daniel Kobourn, and Darius Stokes.

68. *Metropolitan Catholic Almanac*, 58; "Colored Beneficial Society," *Sun* (Baltimore), March 16, 1844.

69. Drago, *Initiative, Paternalism, and Race Relations*, 16; Green, *Fact Stranger Than Fiction*, 43–44.

70. James Y. Green and Richard G. Hazel to Alexander F. Gaston, February 29, 1844, William Gaston Papers, Box 6, Folder 90, SHC.

71. "The Anniversary of the First Colored Barbers' Beneficial Society," *Sun* (Baltimore), July 16, 1846. In 1846, the society's officers included Joseph Lewis, John A. Jones, Edward Pindle, Isaac Scott, and John H. G. Toomey.

72. "Funeral," *Sun* (Baltimore), October 24, 1848.

73. "Minutes and Proceedings of the First Annual Convention of the People of Color," *Liberator* (Boston), October 22, 1831.

74. "Public Meeting," *Delaware Gazette and State Journal* (Wilmington), August 12, 1831.

75. "Progress in Maryland," *National Era* (Washington, D.C.), August 12, 1852.

76. "The Condition of the Colored Population of the City of Baltimore," *Emancipator*, May 24, 1838; Douglass, *Life and Times of Frederick Douglass*, 231; "Discussions," *Sun* (Baltimore), October 25, 1845.

77. "Ho! For Another Grand Debate," *Examiner* (Frederick, Md.), February 17, 1858.

78. "Recorder Fabre's Court," *Daily Delta* (New Orleans), February 22, 1857; "Masonic Celebration," *Sun* (Baltimore), February 11, 1858; "Excursion of Colored Masons," *St. Louis (Mo.) Globe-Democrat*, August 10, 1859; "Colored Masons," *Evening Star* (Washington, D.C.), November 15, 1856.

79. "Colored Masons," *Evening Star* (Washington, D.C.), November 15, 1856.

80. "Georgetown Correspondence," *Evening Star* (Washington, D.C.), June 26, 1855.

81. "To the Editor of the Washingtonian," *Washingtonian* (Washington, D.C.), June 21, 1845.

82. "Colored Temperance Demonstration," *Sun* (Baltimore), February 24, 1851.

83. Jones, *Birthright Citizens*, 128–45; Edwards, *People and Their Peace*, 5, 81–82.

84. Ely, *Israel on the Appomattox*, 225–83; Edwards, *People and Their Peace*, 5, 81–82; Welch, *Black Litigants in the Antebellum South*, 10–15; Milteer, *North Carolina's Free People of Color*, 171–93.

85. *Augustin v. Peter Abel, & als.*, Louisiana Supreme Court Cases, UNO.

86. *Joseph Locklear v. Charles Townsend*, Robeson County Civil Action Papers, Box 7, 1851, SANC; 1850 U.S. Federal Census, Southern Division, Robeson County, North Carolina, 358.

87. *Reed v. Palfrey*, Louisiana Supreme Court Records, UNO.

88. Negro Bob's Petition, Arlington County Chancery Causes, Petition of Bob vs. Admr. of Mary Anne Hutchinson, 1854-046, LVA.

89. *Wilson v. Wilson*, Petersburg Chancery Causes, LVA. For more on divorce in the antebellum South, see Buckley, *Great Catastrophe of My Life*; and Schweninger, *Families in Crisis in the Old South*.

90. *Anna Hawley v. Solomon Anderson*, Granville County Bastardy Bonds, Box 3, 1832–1833, SANC.

91. Bond Stephen Lewis to the State of Delaware, Sussex County Trustees of the Poor Bastardy Bonds, 1845–1919, Folder 7, DPA.

92. Cranch, *Reports of Cases Civil and Criminal in the United States Circuit Court of the District of Columbia*, 13–23.

93. Robinson, *Reports of Cases Decided in the Supreme Court of Appeals*, 842–44.

94. Benny, Grason, and Rudulph to T. Watkins Ligon, February 2, 1857, Secretary of State Pardon Papers, 1857, Folder 31, MSA.

95. Petition of Maria Dye, Office of Governor, Governor Thomas Metcalfe, Petitions for Remission, Box 2, Folder 46, KDLA.

96. Petition of George Matthews, Executive Papers, 1851–1859, Executive Papers 1854 Petitions, DPA.

97. Petition N. Goin Rockingham, Governors Papers, GP 94, Correspondence, Petitions, etc., December 1, 1840–December 31, 1840, SANC.

98. Petition for Pardon of Ann Shipley Colored Howard Co. Larceny, Secretary of State Pardon Papers, 1855, Folder 39, MSA; Transcript, Secretary of State Pardon Papers, 1855, Folder 39, MSA.

99. George W. Nabb to Governor T. W. Ligon, October 17, 1855, Secretary of State Pardon Papers, 1855, Folder 39, MSA; William H. Worthington to Governor Ligon, October 12, 1855, Secretary of State Pardon Papers, 1855, Folder 39, MSA; John S. Tyson to T. Watkins Ligon, September 22, 1855, Secretary of State Pardon Papers, 1855, Folder 39, MSA.

100. Hon. Thomas Ruffin, Hon. F. Nash, Hon. R. M. Pearson for Pardon of Boon, Governors Papers, GP 131, Correspondence, Petitions, etc., July 1, 1852–July 31, 1852, SANC.

101. William Eaton, Jr. Attorney General Pardon of William Boon, Governors Papers, GP 131, Correspondence, Petitions, etc., July 1, 1852–July 31, 1852, SANC.

102. Anne Arundel County Register of Wills Petitions and Orders, 1851–1860, 299–300, 569, MSA.

103. For more on the apprenticeship of free people of color in the antebellum South, see Rohrs, "Training in an 'Art, Trade, Mystery, and Employment.'" Studies that also deal specifically with the rights of parents and apprentices include Bynum, *Unruly Women*, 99–103; Zipf, *Labor of Innocents*, 8–39; Jones, *Birthright Citizens*, 119–27; and Milteer, *North Carolina's Free People of Color*, 148–58.

104. Application of John Scott Bailey for certificate that he is not a negro, Henrico County Free Negro Records, LVA.

105. Affidavit of the Misses Burton, Henrico County Free Negro Records, LVA.

106. Secretary of State Miscellaneous Records, vol. 6I, 662, SCDAH.

107. Barnwell County Clerk of Court Manumissions Book, 1806–1845, 27, SCDAH.

108. Norfolk Co Remitted Taxes on Free Negroes, Auditor of Public Accounts Delinquent Free Negro Taxpayers Lists, 1850–1852, Delinquent Free Negro Taxpayer Lists (I-N), LVA; Norfolk County Minute Book 24, 27–28, 43–44, LVA; Norfolk County Minute Book 30, 237, 267, LVA. The complainants included Robert Newton, Lafayette Weaver, Andrew Bass Sr., Edward Harmon, William Newton, Allen Newton, James Newton, Benjamin Newton, Wesley Weaver, William Bass, and Randall Bracy.

109. The State vs. R. S. Driggers Aff. of Color, Marlboro County Mixed Provenance Papers Ca. 1800–ca. 1860, SCDAH.

110. "Court in Fayette," *Mississippi Free Trader* (Natchez), May 5, 1852. In their study of Johnson's life, Edward Adams Davis and William Ransom Hogan concluded that the murder was the conclusion of a long feud between Johnson and Winn. See Davis and Hogan, *Barber of Natchez*, 262–72.

Chapter 7

1. Marietta T. Hill to Myrtilla Miner, July 5, 1854, Myrtilla Miner Papers, Education/ School Essays & Drawings by Students, 1852–54, LC.

2. Holt, *Fate of the Their Country*; McPherson, *Battle Cry of Freedom*, 234–307, 404–5; Richardson, *Compilation of the Messages and Papers of the Confederacy including the Diplomatic Correspondence, 1861–1865*, 1:43.

3. While border state politicians kept their states in the union, Barbara Jeanne Fields suggested that they created a serious problem for the federal government. She described the "so-called moderates" in the border South as "parasitic upon an unstable balance between two polities and two social systems between whom, in the end, there could be no compromise." See Fields, *Slavery and Freedom on the Middle Ground*, 90–91.

4. Marietta T. Hill to Myrtilla Miner, July 5, 1854, Myrtilla Miner Papers, Education/ School Essays & Drawings by Students, 1852–54, LC.

5. The experience of free people of color in the Civil War South is still largely an understudied area in the historical literature. Most historians who have investigated free people of color in the South have constrained their studies to the prewar period. For more on southern free people of color during the war, see Nelson, "Legislative Control of the Southern Free Negro," 28–46; Mills, "Patriotism Frustrated," 437–51; Koger, *Black Slaveowners*, 187–99; Medford, "'I Was Always a Union Man,'" 1–16; Ely, *Israel on the Appomattox*, 402–17; Mills, *Forgotten People*, 257–75; Latimore, *Role of Southern Free Blacks during the Civil War Era*; and Milteer, *North Carolina's Free People of Color*, 194–214.

6. Guild, *Black Laws of Virginia*, 121; Westmoreland County Orders, 1860–1867, 100–110, 158–59, LVA.

7. "Board of Police Proceedings," *Vicksburg (Miss.) Whig*, January 16, 1861; Cumberland County Court Minutes, vol. 40, 182, SANC; Letters of Guardianship Colored Apr. 6, 1863–Jan. 23, 1864, ARCJC. Warren County officials ordered the arrest of Anna Lindsey after she failed to leave Vicksburg in November 1860. See "Here in Contravention of Law," *Vicksburg (Miss.) Whig*, November 21, 1860. For more on the efforts to remove free people of color from Vicksburg, see Morris, *Becoming Southern*, 175–77.

8. "James Scott," *Clarksville (Tenn.) Chronicle*, January 4, 1861; "Church Services," *Richmond (Va.) Dispatch*, February 2, 1861; Record of Marriages, St. Stephen's Church Records, CCSCHS; Register of Baptisms, St. Stephens's Church Records, CCSCHS; Record of Burials, St. Stephen's Church Records, CCSCHS.

9. Scholars who have studied the impressment of people of color have acknowledged the presence of free people of color in the rebel labor force but have largely focused their studies on enslaved persons. See Nelson, "Confederate Slave Impressment Legislation"; Martinez, *Confederate Slave Impressment in the Upper South*; and Woodward, *Marching Masters*, 55–79.

10. The Petition of Sundry Citizens of Laurens Dist. Praying the Passage of a Law Compelling Free Persons of Color to Go Into the Service of the Confederacy as Cooks & To Render Such Other Service As May Be Required of Them, Petitions to the General Assembly, SCDAH.

11. "Camp Servants," *Fayetteville (N.C.) Observer*, April 7, 1862.

12. H. M. Shaw to H. T. Clark, January 10, 1862, Governors Papers, GP 157, Correspondence: January 1862, SANC.

13. Claim of Monroe Baker 16195, SCCAC. The Southern Claims Commission records are a key source for this chapter. For a detailed analysis of the ways free people of color constructed evidence of their loyalty to the United States through their testimonies to the commission, see Lee, *Claiming the Union*, 113–32.

14. Claim of Gustavus Gaines 17485, SCCAC.

15. List of Free Negroes in the Employ of Government at Charlottesville, Va., Albemarle County Court Records Military and Pension, 1785–1919, Box 1, 1861 (Aug) Military & Pension: Free Negroes Requisitioned for Militia, LVA.

16. Claim of Slaughter Madden 13673, SCCAC.

17. Claim of Robert Carter 20350, SCCAC.

18. Claim of Thomas Morgan 504, SCCAC.

19. Claim of Benjamin Watts 521, SCCAC. Watts's testimony is partially confirmed by another primary source. See Free negroes list of for military service 1861, Norfolk County Free Negro and Slave Records, Box 2, 1861–1862, LVA.

20. Claim of Estate of Reuben Pollard dec'd 14687, SCCAC.

21. Claim of John Malvin 19834, SCCAC.

22. Claim of David Veney 41879, SCCAC.

23. Claim of John Robinson and son 2754, SCCAC.

24. R. L. Singletary to Provost Marshall June 2, 1864, Confederate States of America, Army, Corps of Engineers Papers, Oct 1861–1865, May 1960, n.d., 19 Feb.–20 Jul 1864, SCL.

25. Edward L. White to William H. Echols, January 31, 1865, Confederate States of America, Army, Corps of Engineers Papers, Oct 1861–1865, May 1960, n.d., 4 Jan. 1865–[1865] & 1960, SCL.

26. "A White Man Murdered By a Free Negro—The Murderer Hung," *Raleigh (N.C.) Register*, October 16, 1861.

27. Calvin Lowry Sworn Statement, Records of the Field Offices for the State of North Carolina, Bureau of Refugees, Freedmen, and Abandoned Lands, NARA; Vol. 149 N.C. Complaints and Disposition Lumberton, N.C., Records of the Field Offices for the State of North Carolina, Bureau of Refugees, Freedmen, and Abandoned Lands, NARA.

28. Richmond City Hustings Court Minutes 27, 1860–1862, 410–11, LVA.

29. Claim of Robert S. Brown 6138, SCCAC.

30. Claim of Alfred Fox 36931, SCCAC.

31. Claim of Beverly Matteaur 48759, SCCAC.

32. Claim of Robert Dabney 20408, SCCAC.

33. Jane Williams Petition, Confederate States of America Bureau of Conscription, 7th North Carolina Congressional District Records, 1862–1865, Box 2, November 1864 #25, SHC.

34. Enoch Brown Application for Detail by Mrs. Jane Williams, Confederate States of America Bureau of Conscription, 7th North Carolina Congressional District Records, 1862–1865, Box 2, vol. 1 #34, SHC.

35. Claim of Fannie Richer 4548, SCCAC.

36. Claim of Thomas J. Hill 12407, SCCAC.

37. For more on the Civil War in Indian Territory, see Hauptman, *Between Two Fires*; White and White, *Now the Wolf Has Come*; Warde, *When the Wolf Came*; Smith, "Nations Colliding," 279–319; and Clampitt, *Civil War and Reconstruction in Indian Territory*.

38. No 179 Tyra Durant, RG75, Records of the Bureau of Indian Affairs Records Relating to Civil War Claims of Loyal Indians Records Relating to Loyal Creek Claims, 1869–70, Box 2, Claim #179 Tyra Durant, NARA.

39. No 164 Clory Warrior, RG75, Records of the Bureau of Indian Affairs Records Relating to Civil War Claims of Loyal Indians Records Relating to Loyal Creek Claims, 1869–70, Box 2, Claim #164 Glory Worrior (Warrior), NARA.

40. No 162 Eliza Bruner, RG75, Records of the Bureau of Indian Affairs Records Relating to Civil War Claims of Loyal Indians Records Relating to Loyal Creek Claims, 1869–70, Box 2, Claim #162 Eliza Bruner, NARA.

41. No 194 Manuel Jefferson, RG75, Records of the Bureau of Indian Affairs Records Relating to Civil War Claims of Loyal Indians Records Relating to Loyal Creek Claims, 1869–70, Box 2, Claim #194 Manuel Jefferson, NARA; No 126 Jane Mehardy, RG75, Records of the Bureau of Indian Affairs Records Relating to Civil War Claims of Loyal Indians Records Relating to Loyal Creek Claims, 1869–70, Box 2, Claim #126 Jane Mehardy, NARA; Smith, *On the Edge of Freedom*, 188–91.

42. Claim of Sarah Ann Black 18222, SCCAC.

43. M. N. Leary, CPRCBF; R. E. Dereef, CPRCBF.

44. Richardson Corn, CPRCBF; Foster Chastang, CPRCBF; M. Dubroca, CPRCBF.

45. *Official Records of the Union and Confederate Navies*, 5:179.

46. *Official Records of the Union and Confederate Navies*, 18:450–52.

47. *Official Records of the Union and Confederate Navies*, 13:426.

48. *Official Records of the Union and Confederate Navies*, 5:537–38.

49. Return of Hired Men employed at North Carolina Arsenal, for the month of August, 1861, Governors Papers, GP 153, Correspondence: August 21–31, 1861, SANC; Bennett Boon, CPRCBF; William Botts, CPRCBF; *Official Records of the Union and Confederate Navies*, 14:669–70; Ann Green, Unfiled Papers and Slips Belonging in Confederate Compiled Service Records, NARA; Martha Bragg, CPRCBF. Thomas Lomax appeared in the original document as "Thomas Lomack."

50. For further discussion of cooperation between free people of color and the rebels, see Jordan, *Black Confederates and Afro-Yankees*, 201–31.

51. "To Thomas J. Gantt, Esq.," Broadsides, leaflets, and pamphlets from America and Europe, Printed Ephemera Collection, Portfolio 173, Folder 14, LC.

52. Peter Allen Petition, Series 1, Accession #11586302, RSPPUNCG.

53. "Josephine Hassel," *Natchez (Miss.) Daily Courier*, October 11, 1861.

54. Interview with Betty Johnson, Federal Writers' Project: Slave Narrative Project, vol. 2, Arkansas, Jackson-Lynch, LC.

55. "Colored Residents," *Charleston (S.C.) Courier*, September 3, 1861.

56. "Donations," *Semi-Weekly Standard* (Raleigh, N.C.), December 9, 1862; 1860 U.S. Federal Census Agricultural Schedule, Alamance County, North Carolina, 17–20, Francis T. Hawks Papers, SHC.

57. "The Following," *Charleston (S.C.) Mercury*, October 3, 1864.

58. "All Free Colored Persons," *Daily Picayune* (New Orleans), April 27, 1861.

59. "The Parade This Morning," *Daily Picayune* (New Orleans), November 23, 1861; "Headquarters 1st Division La. V. Troops," *New Orleans Crescent*, January 25, 1862; "Headquarters Department of the Gulf," *Daily Picayune* (New Orleans), August 24, 1862; Berry, "Negro Troops in Blue and Gray," 165–90; Hollandsworth, *Louisiana Native Guards*, 1–11.

60. "Dinner to Citizens of Louisiana," *Liberator* (Boston), April 15, 1864.

61. "Capt. H. B. Favrot," *Baton Rouge (La.) Tri-Weekly Gazette and Comet*, April 27, 1861; "Free Colored Men," *Shreveport (La.) Daily News*, May 7, 1861; "Louisiana," *Daily Picayune* (New Orleans), May 22, 1861; "The free colored people of Pensacola," *Daily Delta* (New Orleans), July 4, 1861; Mills, "Patriotism Frustrated." In his work about the myth of "black Confederates," Kevin M. Levin explored how neo-Confederates as well as a small number of academics have mischaracterized members of the Native Guards as soldiers in an attempt to prove the existence of "black Confederates." Neo-Confederates have cited the existence of the Native Guards as a way to substantiate their claims of mass support of the Confederacy by enslaved persons and free people of color. Levin, *Searching for Black Confederates*, 45–46, 135–36, 171–73.

62. Stephen D. Collins and Doctor F. Edmond to Henry T. Clark, March 12, 1862, Governors Papers, GP 157, Correspondence: March 1862, SANC.

63. Claim of Hugh Oxendine 21330, SCCAC; Claim of Solomon Oxendine 21329, SCCAC.

64. For additional examples of free people of color who enlisted or attempted to enlist as whites, see Milteer, *North Carolina's Free People of Color*, 205–6, 226; and Domby, *False Cause*, 136–37. For more on the construction of the concept of the "Black Confederate," see Levin, *Searching for Black Confederates*; and Domby, *False Cause*, 132–59.

65. Samuel Chavers Service Record, CSR.

66. Duncan Goins Service Record, CSR; Edward Goins Service Record, CSR; Andrew Goins Service Record, CSR; John W. Goins Service Record, CSR; Henry Goins Service Record, CSR; Richard Goins Service Record, CSR. The enumerators categorized the Goinses as "mulatto" in the 1850 and 1860 censuses. See 1850 U.S. Federal Census, Moore County, North Carolina, 217; and 1860 U.S. Federal Census, Moore County, North Carolina, 46, 72, 74.

67. "An Act in Relation to Free Negroes and Mulattoes," *Messenger* (Georgetown, D.C.), April 8, 1863.

68. "Remember This," *Aegis and Intelligencer* (Bel Air, Md.), March 25, 1864.

69. Dorchester County Circuit Court Certificates of Freedom, 1851–1864, 39, MSA.

70. Jefferson County Court Orders Minutes, vol. 23, 356, KDLA.

71. "Ford's New Theater," *Evening Star* (Washington, D.C.), February 16, 1864.

72. "Lingering Relics of Slavery in the District," *National Republican* (Washington, D.C.), February 12, 1864. Augusta was also involved in an earlier incident in Baltimore. See Diemer, *Politics of Black Citizenship*, 191.

73. Kurtz, "Emancipation in the Federal City"; Fields, *Slavery and Freedom on the Middle Ground*, 128–37; Oakes, *Freedom National*, 340–92.

74. Several scholars have explored the experiences of people of color in the U.S. military during the war. Most of the studies focus on the experiences of formerly enslaved persons, discuss the situations of free people of color and formerly enslaved people together, or investigate the conditions for free people of color from the North. See McPherson, *Negro's Civil War*, 161–239; Cornish, *Sable Arm*; Glatthaar, *Forged in Battle*; Berlin, Reidy, and Rowland, *Freedom's Soldiers*; Smith, *Black Soldiers in Blue*; Wilson, *Campfires of Freedom*; Reid, *Freedom for Themselves*; Bryant, *36th Infantry*

United States Colored Troops in the Civil War; Luke and Smith, *Soldiering for Freedom*; Reid, *African Canadians in Union Blue*; Spurgeon, *Soldiers in the Army of Freedom*; Egerton, *Thunder at the Gates*; and Mezurek, *For Their Own Cause*.

75. Francois Hippolyte Deposition April 18, 1894, Francois Hypolite Pension File, CWP. Hippolyte's service record suggests that he actually enlisted in the 73rd U.S. Colored Infantry in September 1862 instead of July 1862. See Francois Hippolyte Service Record, CMSR.

76. William Boon Deposition August 25, 1902, William Boone Pension File, CWP.

77. Cornelius Ridgeway Deposition July 18, 1889, Cornelius Ridgeway Pension File, CWP; Cornelius Ridgeway Service Record, CMSR; Alfred Ridgeway Service Record, CMSR; Sarah Coker to G. E. Becker October 12, 1886, Alfred Ridgeway Pension File, CWP.

78. Charles H. Hall Deposition September 25, 1897, David J. Herod Pension File, CWP. Hall claimed that thirty-seven men traveled to Boston. William E. LaRue, another member of the Cecil County party, stated that thirty-nine men left for Boston. Alexander Bond, however, testified that only twenty-two men made the trip. See William E. LaRue Deposition September 24, 1897, David J. Herod Pension File, CWP; and Alexander Bond Deposition September 24, 1897, David J. Herod Pension File, CWP.

79. Nathaniel Cornish Deposition December 15, 1884, Nathaniel Cornish Pension File, CWP.

80. For more on the movement of free people of color into territories held by the federal government, see Silkenat, *Driven from Home*, 19–20.

81. John Nickens Deposition January 28, 1908, John Nickens Pension File, CWP.

82. Daniel Keys Affidavit November 11, 1902, William Keys Pension File, CWP.

83. George Ash Affidavit October 1, 1897, George Ash Pension File, Civil War Navy Pensions, NARA; Declaration for Pension, George Ash Pension File, Civil War Navy Pensions, NARA.

84. Jarrett Charms Deposition June 7, 1894, Jarrett Charms Pension File, Civil War Navy Pensions, NARA; Pension Certificate of Rachel Charms, Jarrett Charms Pension File, Civil War Navy Pensions, NARA.

85. Hezekiah Jackson Service Record, CMSR; Deposition of Mitchell Harmon, Mitchell Harmon Pension File, CWP; Mitchell Harmon Service Record, CMSR.

86. Lewis Miner and William E. Matthew Affidavit November 20, 1869, Andrew Short Pension File, CWP.

87. Jarrett Morgan Affidavit September 26, 1887, Jarrett Morgan Pension File, CWP.

88. For more on the health of soldiers of color, see Humphreys, *Intensely Human*.

89. Clark Barber Affidavit November 14, 1889, Clark Barber Pension File, CWP; Clark Barber's service record includes mention of his sickness but does not specify the ailment. See Clark Barber Service Record, CMSR.

90. George L. Linthicum Service Record, CMSR; Jean Baptiste Madere Service Record, CMSR.

91. Faust, *This Republic of Suffering*, 4; Theophilus Bantum Pension File, CWP.

92. Frank Lopez Service Record, CMSR.

93. Mathias Cuffy Service Record, CMSR.

94. Lemuel Reynolds Affidavit May 18, 1896, Hampton Reynolds Pension File, CWP.

95. Form of Declaration for an Invalid Army Pension, John Swan Pension File, CWP; John Swann Deposition August 14, 1871, John Swan Pension File, CWP; John Swan Service Record, CMSR.

96. George G. Odiorne Letter May 7, 1866, Moses Hammond Pension File, CWP; George W. Arnold Affidavit May 2, 1892, Moses Hammond Pension File, CWP.

97. Peter Reed Deposition January 22, 1897, Peter Reed Pension File, CWP.
98. Nathan Dempsey Deposition September 28, 1874, Nathan Dempsey Pension File, CWP; Nathan Dempsey Service Record, CMSR.
99. William H. Moore Deposition November 6, 1889, William H. Moore Pension File, CWP.
100. William Aldred Boon Deposition, William A. Boon Pension File, CWP.
101. Julius McKay Deposition July 8, 1896, Julius Mackey Pension File, CWP. Mackey's name is sometime misspelled "McKay" throughout his pension record.
102. Nicholas Gross to Mother and Henry, January 8, 1864, Nicholas Gross Pension File, CWP.
103. Nicholas Gross to Brother, June 20, 1864, Nicholas Gross Pension File, CWP.
104. Joshua B. Doram to Denis Doram, December 23, 1864, Doram-Row Family Collection, MSS 21, KHS.
105. John Chalk to Emerline Chalk, February 11, 1865, John Chalk Pension File, CWP.
106. Mary Spellman Deposition April 21, 1909, Richard Spellman Pension File, CWP.
107. Sarah Bow Deposition February 21, 1885, Addison Bow Pension File, CWP.
108. Claim of George Pepino by his widow Jane 14735, SCCAC.
109. Claim of Elizabeth Wingfield 20410, SCCAC.
110. Colored Officers of 3 La. N. G. to N. P. Banks February 19, 1863, Leon G. Forstall Service Record, CMSR.
111. David Franklin Service Record, CMSR.
112. John Carr Deposition April 13, 1894, John Carr Pension File, CWP.
113. John Carr Service Record, CMSR.
114. Claim of Charles B. Morin Admr. of Suzette Morin 20897, SCCAC.
115. Claim of Sylvanus T. Brown 7724, SCCAC.
116. For more on the escapes of U.S. troops, see Foote, *Yankee Plague*.
117. Claim of Elijah Popewell 37072, SCCAC.
118. Claim of William Jacobs 301, SCCAC.
119. Claim of Oscar Wilson 18236, SCCAC.
120. Claim of Shelden Cohen by Lavinia Cohen his widow 9370, SCCAC.
121. Perdue, Barden, and Phillips, *Weevils in the Wheat*, 259–60.
122. Claim of William Pugh 527, SCCAC.
123. Claim of William C. Napier 8612, SCCAC.
124. Claim of Isaac Sykes 12429, SCCAC.
125. Claim of Richard Sykes 12430, SCCAC.
126. Books that discuss the impacts of the war and emancipation on slaveholders of color include Koger, *Black Slaveowners*, 187–99; and Mills, *Forgotten People*, 257–75. The number of works focused on enslaved persons who freed themselves during the war are part of a growing field in Civil War studies. See Downs, *Sick from Freedom*; Manning, *Troubled Refuge*; and Taylor, *Embattled Freedom*.
127. Gould, *Chained to the Rock of Adversity*, 72.
128. Peter Alexander Williams Deposition July 29, 1903, John Metoyer Pension File, CWP.
129. John B. Metoyer Deposition July 28, 1903, John Metoyer Pension File, CWP.
130. "Notice," *Evening Star* (Washington, D.C.), June 8, 1864; "Rooms Ladies' Union Aid Society," *Daily Missouri Republican* (St. Louis), March 29, 1864; "Concert," *New Orleans Tribune*, May 27, 1865; "A Card," *New Orleans Tribune*, June 7, 1865; "The Soule Asylum," *New Orleans Tribune*, December 23, 1865; "Colored Soldiers' Aid Society of the Fifth Street Baptist Church," *Louisville (Ky.) Daily Union Press*, January 7, 1865; "The Fifth Street Church Colored Soldiers Aid Society," *Louisville (Ky.) Daily Union*

Press, January 9, 1865; "Colored Soldiers' Aid Society," *Louisville (Ky.) Daily Union Press*, January 17, 1865; "General Chetlain to the Colored Ladies Soldiers' Aid Society," *Louisville (Ky.) Daily Union Press*, January 30, 1865; "Wm. J. H. Cook," *Louisville (Ky.) Daily Union Press*, March 18, 1865; Green Street Baptist Church Minutes, vol. 1, 99, 103–4, UofL.

131. Keckley, *Behind the Scenes*, 112–16; "New Items," *Daily National Republican* (Washington, D.C.), November 13, 1862; "The Contrabands Not a Burden on the Government," *National Republican* (Washington, D.C.), October 31, 1862; "A Fair for the Benefit of the Orphans of Freedmen," *Black Republican* (New Orleans), April 15, 1865; "Officers of the Freedmen's Aid Association, of the City of New Orleans," *New Orleans Tribune*, May 9, 1865; Lockwood, *Mary S. Peake*, 30–38. For more on the role of free people of color in assisting refugees, see Masur, *Example for All the Land*, 31–34.

132. Desdunes, *Our People and Our History*, 132–38; "Death of Dr. Louis Charles Roudanez," *Daily Picayune* (New Orleans), March 12, 1890; "Jean B. Roudanez," *Daily Picayune* (New Orleans), December 2, 1895.

133. "Is the Black Code Still in Force," *New Orleans Tribune*, July 21, 1864.

134. "Petition of the Free Colored Citizens of Louisiana," *Liberator* (Boston), April 1, 1864; Petition of Natives of Louisiana and citizens of the United States of African descent praying that all citizens of Louisiana of African descent born free before the rebellion may be admitted to the rights and privileges of Electors, RG 46, SEN3A-H19, NARA; Petition of Citizens of Louisiana of African descent praying that the right of suffrage may be granted to all the Natives of Louisiana of African descent, RG 46, SEN3A-H19, NARA.

135. "Dinner to Citizens of Louisiana," *Liberator* (Boston), April 15, 1864.

136. For more on the postwar civil rights struggle in New Orleans, see Yamanaka, "'Separation Is Not Equality.'"

Conclusion

1. "The Colored U.S. Senator," *Harrisburg (Pa.) Telegraph*, January 27, 1870.

2. Autobiography of Hiram R. Revels, Carter G. Woodson Collection, Series 11, Revels, Hiram R. Autobiography, LC.

3. Du Bois, *Black Reconstruction*, 461–63; Foner, *Freedom's Lawmakers*, xv–xviii, 35–36, 61, 67–68, 158, 171–72, 174–78. For more on James T. Rapier's career, see Schweninger, *James T. Rapier and Reconstruction*.

4. Desdunes, *Our People and Our History*, 66–68; Hahn, *Nation under Our Feet*, 230–34.

5. Kenzer, *Enterprising Southerners*, xiii–xiv, 12–15, 43–45; *Twenty-Two Years' Work of the Hampton Normal and Agricultural Institute*; Frazier, *Negro Family in the United States*, 493–96; *General Catalogue of the Officers and Students of Shaw University*.

6. Mills, *Forgotten People*, 273–75.

7. Dodge, "Free Negro of North Carolina," 30; Harrell, "Gates County to 1860," 66.

8. Woodward, *Strange Career of Jim Crow*, 67–109; Foner, *Reconstruction*, 368–72, 587–601; Ayers, *Promise of the New South*, 136–46, 153–59.

9. Michelle Alexander has termed the system of mass incarceration in the United States, in which people of color are disproportionately imprisoned, the "New Jim Crow." See Alexander, *New Jim Crow*.

10. Schultz, *Rural Face of White Supremacy*, 1–11; Semega, Kollar, Creamer, and Mohanty, *Income and Poverty in the United States*; Lee, *America for Americans*, 13–14, 149–62.

BIBLIOGRAPHY

Manuscript Collections

Annapolis, Md.
    Maryland State Archives
        Anne Arundel County Court Manumissions
        Anne Arundel County Register of Wills Petitions and Orders
        Baltimore County Court Certificates of Freedom
        Baltimore County Court Chattel Records
        Baltimore County Court Minutes
        Baltimore County Court Miscellaneous Court Papers
        Baltimore County Record of Wills Indentures
        Basilica of the Assumption St. Peter's Baptisms
        Caroline County Court Land Records
        Dorchester County Circuit Court Certificates of Freedom
        Dorchester County Court Certificates of Freedom
        Frederick County Circuit Court Church Charters
        Frederick County Court Certificates of Freedom
        General Court of the Western Shore Judgment Record
        Harford County Court Manumissions
        Harford County Register of Wills Wills
        Kent County Court Petition Records
        Kent County Court Proceedings
        Kent County Criminal Court Records
        Maryland Penitentiary Prisoner Record
        Prerogative Court Wills
        Prince George's County Circuit Court Court Papers, Blacks
        Prince George's County Register of Wills Inventories
        Proceedings of the Provincial Court
        Queen Anne's County Court Judgment Record
        Queen Anne's County Trustees of the Poor Almshouse Accounts
        Secretary of State Pardon Papers
        Secretary of State Pardon Record
        Somerset County Judicial Records
        Somerset County Register of Wills Miscellaneous Papers
        Talbot County Court Church Charter Record
        Talbot County Trustees of the Poor Proceedings
        Washington County Court Certificates of Freedom and Manumission
        Washington County Court Church Charter Record
        Worcester County Register of Wills
Athens, Ga.
    University of Georgia Hargrett Rare Book and Manuscript Library
        Keith M. Read Collection

Augusta, Ga.
    Augusta–Richmond County Judicial Center
        Richmond County Minutes Inferior Court
        Richmond County Realty
Baton Rouge, La.
    Louisiana State Archives
        Colonial Documents of the St. Landry Papers
Burlington, N.C.
    Private collection
        Augustus H. Holland Papers
Chapel Hill, N.C.
    Southern Historical Collection
        Confederate States of America Bureau of Conscription, 7th North Carolina
            Congressional District Records
        William Gaston Papers
        David Gavin Diary
        Francis T. Hawks Papers
        Manumission Society Papers
        Thomas Smith McDowell Papers
        William D. Valentine Diary
Charleston, S.C.
    College of Charleston South Carolina Historical Society
        St. Stephen's Church Records
Charlottesville, Va.
    University of Virginia Special Collections
        Berkeley Plantation and Fishery Ledger
College Park, Md.
    University of Maryland Special Collections and University Archives
        Abraham Jones Papers
Columbia, S.C.
    South Carolina Department of Archives and History
        Barnwell County Clerk of Court Manumissions Book
        Charleston County Clerk of Court Manumissions Index
        Charleston County Wills
        General Assembly Grand Jury Presentments
        Marlboro County Mixed Provenance Papers
        Petitions to the General Assembly
        South Carolina Estate Inventories and Selected Bills of Sale
        South Carolina Secretary of State Miscellaneous Records
    South Caroliniana Library
        Confederate States of America, Army, Corps of Engineers Papers
Courtland, Va.
    Southampton County Courthouse
        Southampton County Circuit Superior Court Law and Chancery Books
        Southampton County Deed Books
Dover, Del.
    Delaware Public Archives
        Court of Common Pleas, Sussex County Case Files
        Executive Papers
        Kent County Court of Chancery Case Files

  Kent County Court of General Sessions Session Dockets
  Kent County Record of Deeds Apprentice Indentures
  Kent County Slavery Material Petitions for Freedom
  New Castle County Court of General Sessions Dockets
  New Castle County Deed Records
  Pauper Lists of Sussex County Trustees of Poor
  Sussex County Trustees of the Poor Bastardy Bonds
Durham, N.C.
 Duke University Rubenstein Library
  Vallie Burgess Carter Papers
  Dismal Swamp Land Company Records
  William O'Neale Account Book
Eastville, Va.
 Northampton County Circuit Court
  Northampton County Deeds, Wills & C.
  Northampton County Orders, Deeds, Wills, Etc.
  Northampton County Wills
Frankfort, Ky.
 Kentucky Department of Libraries and Archives
  Jefferson County Court Orders Minutes
  Mason County Order Books
  Office of Governor, Governor Thomas Metcalfe, Petitions for Remission
 Kentucky Historical Society
  Doram-Row Family Collection
Fredericksburg, Va.
 Fredericksburg Circuit Court Archives
  Free Negro/Slave Records
Greensboro, N.C.
 University of North Carolina at Greensboro Jackson Library
  Race and Slavery Petitions Project
 Guilford College Quaker Archives
  Peck Family Papers
Greenville, N.C.
 East Carolina University Joyner Library
  J. T. Lewter Papers
Halifax, N.S.
 Nova Scotia Archives
  Book of Negroes, African Nova Scotians in the Age of Slavery and Abolition
Knoxville, Tenn.
 Knox County Archives
  Knox County Court of Pleas and Quarter Sessions Records
Leesburg, Va.
 Loudoun County Clerk's Office Historic Records and Deeds
  Criminal Papers
  Free Blacks Criminal Papers
Louisville, Ky.
 University of Louisville Archives and Special Collections
  Fifth Street Baptist Church Minutes
 Filson Historical Society
  William Thomas McElroy Journal

Lynchburg, Va.
  Jones Memorial Library
    First Baptist Church of Lynchburg, Virginia, Minutes

Montgomery, Ala.
  Alabama Department of Archives and History
    Mobile County Translated Records
    Mobile County Will Records

Nashville, Tenn.
  Slavery Societies Digital Archive–Vanderbilt University
    Archives of the Diocese of St. Augustine Baptisms
    Archives of the Diocese of St. Augustine Marriages
  Tennessee State Library and Archives
    Legislative Petitions
    Tennessee Supreme Court Cases

New Orleans, La.
  Louisiana Historical Center
    Judicial Records of the French Superior Council
    Spanish Judicial Records
  New Orleans Archdiocesan Archives
    St. Louis Cathedral, New Orleans, Baptism, Slaves and Free People of Color
  New Orleans Public Library
    New Orleans Indentures
    Orleans Parish Will Books
  University of New Orleans
    Louisiana Supreme Court Cases

Philadelphia, Pa.
  Historical Society of Pennsylvania
    Abolition Society of Delaware Minute Book
    Pennsylvania Abolition Society Papers

Raleigh, N.C.
  State Archives of North Carolina
    Bertie County Court Minutes
    Bethel Hill Baptist Church Woodsdale, N.C., Person County Roll and Minute Book
    John B. Chesson Papers
    Colonial Court Papers Civil and Criminal Papers
    Craven County Court Minutes
    Craven County Miscellaneous Records
    Craven County Slaves and Free Negroes
    Cumberland County Court Minutes
    Edenton District Records of the Superior Court
    Edgecombe County Court Minutes
    Gates County Court Minutes
    General Assembly Session Records
    Governors Papers
    Granville County Bastardy Bonds
    Granville County Marriage Bonds
    Granville County Ordinary Bonds
    Granville County Record of Wills
    Granville County Taxables

        New Hanover County Real Estate Conveyances
        New Hanover County Record of Wills
        Northampton County Estates Records
        Northampton County Wills
        Orange County Civil Action Papers
        Pasquotank County Apprentice Bonds and Records
        Pasquotank County Civil Action Papers
        Pasquotank County Court Minutes
        Pasquotank County Criminal Action Papers
        Pasquotank County Real Estate Conveyances
        Pasquotank County Records of Slaves and Free Persons of Color
        Pasquotank County Record of Wills
        Perquimans Precinct Court Minutes
        Records of Probate: Wills, Secretary of State Record Group
        Robeson County Civil Action Papers
        Robeson County Marriage Bonds
        Robeson County Superior Court Minutes
        Warren County Wills
Richmond, Va.
    Library of Virginia
        Accomack County Chancery Causes
        Accomack County Commonwealth Causes
        Accomack County Orders
        Albemarle County Court Records Military and Pension
        Alexandria City Council Minute Books
        Amelia County Will Books
        Arlington County Chancery Causes
        Arlington County (Alexandria County) Free Negro Records
        Auditor of Public Accounts Delinquent Free Negro Taxpayers Lists
        Auditor of Public Accounts Dinwiddie County Land Tax Books
        Auditor of Public Accounts Nansemond County Land Tax Books
        Auditor of Public Accounts Reports of Free Negroes
        Brunswick County Order Books
        Charles City County Deed Books
        Charles City County Order Books
        Charlotte County Register of Free Negroes
        Coan Baptist Church, Northumberland County, Membership Book
        Dinwiddie County Wills
        Fauquier County Chancery Causes
        First African Baptist Church, Richmond, Minutes
        First Baptist Church (Washington, D.C.), Records
        Fredericksburg City Certificates and Registry of Free Negroes
        Fredericksburg City Hustings Court Deed Books
        Fredericksburg City Hustings Court Will Books
        Goochland County Register of Free Negroes
        Governor's Office William B. Giles Executive Papers
        Henrico County Free Negro Records
        Isle of Wight County Commonwealth Causes Ended
        Isle of Wight County Order Books
        King George County Order Books

  Lancaster County Deeds, Etc.
  Lancaster County Deeds and Wills
  Lancaster County Orders
  Lancaster County Register of Free Negroes
  Lancaster County Wills
  Land Office Patents
  Legislative Petitions
  Mecklenburg County Judgments
  Mecklenburg County Order Books
  Mecklenburg County Register of Free Negroes
  Middlesex County Free Negro and Slave Records
  Norfolk City Will Books
  Norfolk County Apprentice Indentures
  Norfolk County Free Negro and Slave Records
  Norfolk County Minute Books
  Norfolk County Order Books
  Northampton County Chancery Causes
  Northampton County Criminal Causes
  Northampton County Free Negro and Slave Records
  Northampton County Wills Order Books
  Organization Records Collection
  Petersburg City Chancery Causes
  Petersburg City Free Negro and Slave Records
  Petersburg City Hustings Court Deed Books
  Petersburg City Register of Free Negroes and Mulattoes
  Powhatan County Order Books
  Prince Edward County County Court Orders
  Princess Anne County Minute Books
  Records of Gillfield Church (Baptist)
  Richmond City Hustings Court Ended Causes
  Richmond City Hustings Wills, Inventories, and Accounts
  Rockbridge County Register of Free Negroes
  Scott County Free Negro and Slave Records
  Southampton County Judgments
  Southampton County Minute Books
  Spotsylvania County Minute Books
  Staunton City Register of Free Negroes and Mulattoes
  Surry County Orders
  Sussex County Order Books
  Westmoreland County Orders
  York County Free Negro and Slave Records
 Virginia Historical Society
  Richmond (Va.) City Sergeant Papers
Washington, D.C.
 Georgetown University Booth Family Center for Special Collections
  Maryland Province Archives
 Library of Congress
  Federal Writers' Project: Slave Narrative Project
  Thomas Jefferson Papers
  Myrtilla Miner Papers

    Printed Ephemera Collection
    Roberts Family Papers
    Carter G. Woodson Papers
 National Archives and Records Administration
    Archives of the Spanish Government of West Florida
    Civil War Pensions
    Civil War Navy Pensions
    Compiled Military Service Records of Volunteer Union Soldiers Who Served with the United States Colored Troops
    Compiled Service Records of Confederate Soldiers Who Served in Organizations from the State of North Carolina
    Confederate Papers relating to Citizens or Business Firms
    District of Columbia Fair Copies of Wills
    District of Columbia Manumission and Emancipation Records
    Eastern Cherokee Applications of the U.S. Court of Claims
    Letters Received by the Secretary of the Navy from Captains
    Records of the Bureau of Indian Affairs Records relating to Civil War Claims of Loyal Indians Records Relating to Loyal Creek Claims
    Records of the District Courts of the United States Indentures for Apprenticeships
    Records of the Field Offices for the State of North Carolina, Bureau of Refugees, Freedmen, and Abandoned Lands
    Records of the United States House of Representatives
    Records of the United States Senate
    Revolutionary War Pensions
    Southern Claims Commission Approved Claims
    Unfiled Papers and Slips Belonging in Confederate Compiled Service Records
    United States Federal Census
    War of 1812 Pensions
Wilmington, Del.
    Delaware Historical Society
        Schools Collection

Newspapers

Aegis and Intelligencer (Bel Air, Md.)
Alexandria (Va.) Gazette
American and Commercial Daily Advertiser (Baltimore)
American Watchman (Wilmington, Del.)
Arkansas Gazette (Arkansas Post)
Arkansas Times and Advocate (Little Rock)
Arkansas State Gazette and Democrat (Little Rock)
Arkansas True Democrat (Little Rock)
Asbury Park (N.J.) Press
Baltimore Evening Post
Baltimore Gazette and Daily Advertiser
Baptist Advocate (New York)
Baton Rouge (La.) Gazette
Baton Rouge (La.) Tri-Weekly Gazette and Comet
Black Republican (New Orleans)
Boon's Lick Times (Fayette, N.C.)

Carolina Federal Republican (New Bern, N.C.)
Carolina Sentinel (New Bern, N.C.)
Carolina Watchman (Salisbury, N.C.)
Cecil Whig (Elkton, Md.)
Charleston (S.C.) Courier
Charleston (S.C.) Mercury
City Gazette (Charleston, S.C.)
Clarksville (Tenn.) Chronicle
Columbian Herald (Charleston, S.C.)
Columbian Museum (Savannah, Ga.)
Connecticut Courant (Hartford)
Cross and Journal (Cincinnati, Ohio)
Daily Crescent (New Orleans)
Daily Delta (New Orleans)
Daily Exchange (Baltimore)
Daily Missouri Republican (St. Louis)
Daily National Intelligencer (Washington, D.C.)
Daily National Republican (Washington, D.C.)
Daily Picayune (New Orleans)
Delaware Gazette (Wilmington)
Delaware Gazette and American Watchman (Wilmington)
Delaware Gazette and State Journal (Wilmington)
Delaware Journal (Wilmington)
Delaware Register, or, Farmers', Manufacturers' and Mechanics' Advocate (Wilmington)
Democrat (Huntsville, Ala.)
Dunlap and Claypoole's American Daily Advertiser (Philadelphia)
Eastern Carolina Republican (New Bern, N.C.)
Easton (Md.) Gazette
Edgefield (S.C.) Advertiser
Evening Star (Washington, D.C.)
Examiner (Frederick, Md.)
Fayetteville (N.C.) Observer
Federal Gazette (Baltimore)
Gazette and Democrat (Little Rock, Ark.)
Georgia Gazette (Savannah)
Georgian (Savannah)
Glasgow (Mo.) Weekly Times
Greensboro (N.C.) Patriot
Harrisburg (Pa.) Telegraph
Hillsborough (N.C.) Recorder
Liberator (Boston)
Louisiana State Gazette (New Orleans)
Louisville (Ky.) Daily Courier
Louisville (Ky.) Daily Union Press
Lynchburg (Va.) and Farmer's Gazette
Lynchburg Daily Virginian
Keowee Courier (Pickens Court House, S.C.)
Maryland Gazette (Annapolis)
Maryland Gazette and Political Intelligencer (Annapolis)

Maryland Herald and Hager's-Town Weekly Advertiser
Maryland Journal (Baltimore)
Memphis (Tenn.) Daily Appeal
Messenger (Georgetown, D.C.)
Milton (N.C.) Gazette and Roanoke Advertiser
Mirror of the Times, and General Advertiser (Wilmington, Del.)
Mississippi Free Trader (Natchez)
Morning Courier (Louisville, Ky.)
Nashville (Tenn.) Patriot
Nashville (Tenn.) Union and American
Nashville (Tenn.) Whig
Natchez (Miss.) Daily Courier
National Era (Washington, D.C.)
National Intelligencer and Washington Advertiser (Washington, D.C.)
National Republican (Washington, D.C.)
Newbern (N.C.) Spectator
New Orleans Argus
New Orleans Crescent
New Orleans Tribune
New York Herald
New-York Tribune
Norfolk (Va.) Gazette and Publick Ledger
North-Carolina Gazette (Wilmington)
Pendleton Messenger (Pendleton Court House, S.C.)
Pennsylvania Gazette (Philadelphia)
Pensacola (Fla.) Gazette
Providence (R.I.) Gazette
Raleigh (N.C.) Microcosm
Raleigh (N.C.) Minerva
Raleigh (N.C.) Register
Reporter (Lexington, Ky.)
Republican Advocate (Frederick, Md.)
Rhode-Island Religious Intelligencer (Providence)
Richmond (Va.) Dispatch
St. Louis (Mo.) Globe-Democrat
Savannah (Ga.) Republican
Semi-Weekly Standard (Raleigh, N.C.)
Shreveport (La.) Daily News
South Carolina Gazette (Charleston)
South-Carolina Weekly Gazette (Charleston)
Southern Galaxy (Natchez, Miss.)
Southern Patriot (Charleston, D.C.)
Southern Statesman (Jackson, Miss.)
State Gazette of North-Carolina (Edenton)
State Gazette of South Carolina (Charleston)
Statesman and Gazette (Natchez, Miss.)
Sun (Baltimore)
Telegraphe and Daily Advertiser (Baltimore)
Tennessean (Nashville)
Torch Light and Public Advertiser (Hagerstown, Md.)

Vicksburg (Miss.) Whig
Virginia Argus (Richmond)
Virginia Gazette (Williamsburg)
Virginia Gazette and Alexandria Advertiser
Virginia Journal (Alexandria)
Washingtonian (Washington, D.C.)
Weekly West (St. Joseph, Mo.)
Western Watchman (St. Louis, Mo.)
Wilmington, and Delaware Register
Wilmington (N.C.) Morning Star
Wilson's Knoxville (Tenn.) Gazette

Published Primary Sources

A. Mygatt & Co.'s New Orleans Business Directory. New Orleans: A. Mygatt, 1858.
Abercrombie, Janice, ed. *Free Blacks of Louisa County, Virginia*. Athens, Ga.: Iberian, 1994.
The Acts and Resolutions Adopted by the General Assembly of Florida, at Its Tenth Session, Begun and Held at the Capitol, in the City of Tallahassee, on Monday, November 26, 1860. Tallahassee: Dyke and Carlisle, 1861.
Acts of the General Assembly of the Commonwealth of Kentucky Passed at December Session, 1845. Frankfort: A. G. Hodges, 1846.
Acts of the General Assembly of the Commonwealth of Kentucky Passed at the Session Which Was Begun and Held in the City of Frankfort, on Monday, the Fifth Day of December, 1859, and Ended on Monday, the Fifth Day of March, 1860. Frankfort: J. B. Major, 1860.
Acts of the General Assembly of Virginia, Passed in 1855-6, in the Eightieth Year of the Commonwealth. Richmond: William F. Ritchie, 1856.
Acts of the Seventh Biennial Session, of the General Assembly of Alabama, Held in the City of Montgomery, Commencing on the Second Monday in November, 1859. Montgomery: Shorter and Reid, 1860.
Acts Passed by the Fourth Legislature of the State of Louisiana, at Its Second Session, Held and Begun in the City of Baton Rouge, on the 17th of January, 1859. Baton Rouge: J. M. Taylor, 1859.
Acts Passed by the General Assembly of the State of North Carolina at Its Session, Commencing on the 25th of December, 1826. Raleigh: Lawrence and Lemay, 1827.
Acts Passed by the General Assembly of the State of North Carolina, at the Session of 1831-32. Raleigh: Lawrence and Lemay, 1832.
The African Repository. Vol. 27. Washington, D.C.: C. Alexander, 1851.
Aikin, John G., ed. *A Digest of the Laws of the State of Alabama: Containing All the Statues of a Public and General Nature, in Force at the Close of the Session of the General Assembly, in January, 1833*. Philadelphia: Alexander Towar, 1833.
Alden, T. J. Fox, and J. A. Van Hoesen, eds. *Digest of the Laws of Mississippi, Comprising All the Laws of a General Nature, including the Acts of the Session of 1839*. New York: Alexander S. Gould, 1839.
Annual Catalogue of the Officers and Students of Oberlin College for the College Year 1858-59. Oberlin, Ohio: Evangelist Office, 1858.
Bacon, Thomas. *Laws of Maryland at Large, with Proper Indexes: Now First Collected into One Compleat Body, and Published from the Original Acts and Records, Remaining in the Secretary's-Office of the Said Province: Together with Notes and Other Matters, Relative to the Constitution Thereof, Extracted from the Provincial*

Records: To Which Is Prefixed, the Charter, with an English Translation. Annapolis: Jonas Green, 1765.

Banneker, Benjamin. *Benjamin Banneker's Pennsylvania, Delaware, Maryland and Virginia Almanack and Ephemeris for the Year of Our Lord, 1792*. Baltimore: William Goddard and James Angell, 1791.

Blassingame, John W., ed. *Slave Testimony: Two Centuries of Letters, Speeches, Interviews, and Autobiographies*. Baton Rouge: Louisiana State University Press, 1977.

Brent, Linda [Harriet Jacobs]. *Incidents in the Life of a Slave Girl*. Boston, 1861.

Butler, Lindley S., ed. *The Papers of David Settle Reid*. 2 vols. Raleigh, N.C.: Division of Archives and History, 1997.

Cain, Robert J., and Jan-Michael Poff, eds. *The Church of England in North Carolina: Documents, 1742–1763*. Raleigh: North Carolina Office of Archives and History, 2007.

Campbell, John C., ed. *Nashville Business Directory*. Nashville, Tenn.: John C. Campbell, 1855.

Candler, Allen D., ed. *The Colonial Records of the State of Georgia, Volume XIX, Part I: Statutes, Colonial and Revolutionary, 1768 to 1773*. Atlanta: Charles P. Byrd, 1911.

Cathcart, William, ed. *Baptist Encyclopaedia: A Dictionary of the Doctrines, Ordinances, Usages, Confessions of Faith. Sufferings, Labors, and Successes, and of the General History of the Baptist Denomination in All Lands with Numerous Biographical Sketches of Distinguished American and Foreign Baptists, and a Supplement*. Philadelphia: Louis H. Everts, 1883.

Clamorgan, Cyprian. *The Colored Aristocracy of St. Louis*. Edited by Julie Winch. Columbia: University of Missouri Press, 1999.

Clark, Walter, ed. *The State Records of North Carolina*. 16 vols. Goldsboro, N.C.: Nash Brothers, 1895–1907.

Clayton, Augustin Smith, ed. *A Compilation of the Laws of the State of Georgia, Passed by the Legislature since the Political Year 1800, to the Year 1810, Inclusive*. Augusta: Adams and Duyckink, 1812.

Le Code noir, ou Édit du roy, servant de règlement pour le gouvernement et l'administration de la justice, police, discipline et le commerce des esclaves nègres, dans la province et colonie de la Loüisianne. Paris: De l'Imprimerie Royale, 1727.

Coffin, Levi. *Reminiscences of Levi Coffin, the Reputed President of the Underground Railroad*. 2nd ed. Cincinnati, Ohio: Robert Clark, 1880.

Condy, Thomas D., ed. *A Digest of the Laws of the United States and the State of South-Carolina*. Charleston: A. E. Miller, 1830.

The Constitution and Laws of the Cherokee Nation: Passed at Tahlequah, Cherokee Nation, 1839–51. Tahlequah: Cherokee Nation, 1852.

The Constitution and Laws of the Choctaw Nation. Park Hill, Choctaw Nation: Mission Press, 1847.

Constitution, Laws, and Treaties of the Chickasaws. Tishomingo City, Okla.: E. J. Foster, 1860.

Cooper, Thomas, ed. *Statutes at Large of South Carolina*. Vol. 3, *Containing the Acts from 1716, Exclusive, to 1752, Inclusive*. Columbia: A. S. Johnston, 1838.

Cranch, William. *Reports of Cases Civil and Criminal in the United States Circuit Court of the District of Columbia from 1801 to 1841 in Six Volumes*. Vol. 5, *1836 to 1841*. Washington, D.C.: William M. Morrison, 1852.

Delano, Judah. *Washington Directory, Showing the Name, Occupation, and Residence of Each Head of a Family and Person in Business the Names of the Members of Congress, and Where They Board; Together with Other Useful Information.* Washington, D.C.: William Duncan, 1822.

Desdunes, Rodolphe Lucien. *Our People and Our History: Fifty Creole Portraits.* Translated by Sister Dorothea Olga McCants. Baton Rouge: Louisiana State University Press, 2001.

Digest of the Ordinances of the City Council Charleston, from the Year 1783 to July 1818. Charleston, S.C.: Archibald E. Miller, 1818.

Directory of the City of Charleston, for the Year 1852. Charleston, S.C.: Edward C. Councell, 1851.

Douglass, Frederick. *Life and Times of Frederick Douglass Written by Himself.* Hartford, Conn.: Park, 1882.

Douglass, Margaret. *The Personal Narrative of Mrs. Margaret Douglass, a Southern Woman, Who Was Imprisoned for One Month in the Common Jail of Norfolk, under the Laws of Virginia, for the Crime of Teaching Free Colored Children to Read.* Boston: John P. Jewett, 1854.

Drew, Benjamin, ed. *The Refugee: Or the Narratives of Fugitive Slaves in Canada Related by Themselves, with an Account of the History and Condition of the Colored Population of Upper Canada.* Boston: John P. Jewett, 1856.

Duval, John P., ed. *Compilation of the Public Acts of the Legislative Council of the Territory of Florida, Passed prior to 1840.* Tallahassee: Samuel S. Simley, 1839.

"1838 October Choctaw Nation Constitution." Choctaw Nation. https://www.choctaw nation.com/sites/default/files/2015/09/29/1838constitution_original.pdf.

English, E. H., ed. *A Digest of the Statures of Arkansas: Embracing All Laws of a General and Permanent Character in Force at the Close of the Session of the General Assembly of 1846; Together with Notes of the Decisions of the Supreme Court upon the Statutes.* Little Rock: Reardon and Garritt, 1848.

An Epistle of Caution and Advice, Concerning the Buying and Keeping of Slaves. Philadelphia: James Chattin, 1754.

Frantel, Nancy C., ed. *Richmond, Virginia Uncovered: The Records of Slaves and Free Blacks Listed in the City Sergeant Jail Register, 1841–1846.* Westminster, Md.: Heritage Books, 2010.

General Catalogue of the Officers and Students of Shaw University, 1875–1882. Raleigh, N.C.: Edwards, Broughton, 1882.

Green, John P. *Fact Stranger Than Fiction: Seventy-Five Years of a Busy Life with Reminiscences of Many Great and Good Men and Women.* Cleveland, Ohio: Riehl, 1920.

Greiner, Meinrad, ed. *The Louisiana Digest, Embracing the Laws of the Legislature of a General Nature, Enacted from the Year 1804 to 1841, Inclusive, and in Force at This Last Period.* New Orleans, La.: Benjamin Levy, 1841.

Guild, June Purcell, ed. *Black Laws of Virginia.* Richmond: Whittet and Shepperson, 1936.

Hamilton, J. G. deRoulhac, ed. *The Papers of Thomas Ruffin.* Vol. 2. Raleigh, N.C.: Edwards and Broughton, 1918.

Haywood, John, and Robert L. Cobbs, eds. *The Statute Laws of the State of Tennessee, of a Public and General Nature; Revised and Digested.* Knoxville: F. S. Heiskell, 1831.

Heads of Families at the First Census of the United States Taken in the Year 1790 North Carolina. Washington, D.C.: Government Printing Office, 1908.

Hening, William Waller, ed. *The Statutes at Large; Being a Collection of All the Laws of Virginia from the First Session of the Legislature, in the Year 1619.* New York: R. and W. and G. Bartow, 1823.

Hogan, William Ransom, and Edwin Adams Davis, eds. *William Johnson's Natchez: The Ante-Bellum Diary of a Free Negro.* Baton Rouge: Louisiana State University Press, 1951.

Hotchkiss, William A., ed. *A Codification of the Statute Law of Georgia including the English Statutes of Force: In Four Parts, to Which Is Prefixed a Collection of State Papers, of English, American, and State Origin; Together with an Appendix, and Index, and also a Collection of Legal Forms, in Use in Georgia.* Augusta, Ga.: Charles E. Grenville, 1848.

Jacobs, C. W. *The Free Negro Question in Maryland.* Baltimore: John W. Woods, 1859.

Jennings, Paul. *A Colored Man's Reminiscences of James Madison.* Brooklyn, N.Y.: George C. Beadle, 1865.

Jervey, Theodore D. *Robert Y. Hayne and His Times.* New York: Macmillan, 1909.

Journal of the Convention of the State of Tennessee Convened for the Purpose of Revising and Amending the Constitution Thereof Held in Nashville. Nashville: W. Hasell Hunt, 1834.

Journal of the House of Delegates of the Commonwealth of Virginia, Begun and Held at the Capitol, in the City of Richmond, on Monday, the Fifth Day of December, One Thousand Eight Hundred and Thirty-One. Richmond: Thomas Ritchie, 1831.

Journal of the Senate of the Commonwealth of Kentucky, Begun and Held in the Town of Frankfort, on Monday, the Seventh Day of December, in the Year of Our Lord, 1857, and of the Commonwealth, the Sixty-Sixth. Frankfort: A. G. Hodges, 1857.

Journal of the Senate of the General Assembly of the State of North-Carolina at Its Session of 1860–'61. Raleigh: John Spelman, 1861.

Keckley, Elizabeth. *Behind the Scenes.* New York: G. W. Carleton, 1868.

Kennedy, Joseph C. G., ed. *Population of the United States in 1860: Compiled from the Original Returns of the Eighth Census, under the Direction of the Secretary of the Interior.* Washington, D.C.: Government Printing Office, 1864.

Latrobe, John H. B. *Memoir of Benjamin Banneker, Read before the Maryland Historical Society, at the Monthly Meeting, May 1, 1845.* Baltimore: John D. Toy, 1845.

Laws: The Cherokee Nation, and C. 1825.

Laws of North-Carolina at a General Assembly, Begun and Held at the City of Raleigh, on the Second Day of November, the Year of Our Lord One Thousand Seven Hundred and Ninety-Five, and in the Twentieth Year of American Independence: Being the First Session of the Said Assembly. Edenton: Hodge and Wills, 1796.

The Laws of North Carolina Enacted in the Year 1821. Raleigh: Thomas Henderson, 1822.

Laws of the Republic of Texas. 2 vols. Houston: Office of the Telegraph, 1838.

Laws of the State of Delaware, from the Fourteenth Day of October, One Thousand Seven Hundred, to the Eighteenth Day of August, One Thousand Seven Hundred and Ninety-Seven. Vol. 1. New Castle: Samuel and John Adams, 1797.

Laws of the State of Delaware, from the Seventh Day of January, One Thousand Eight Hundred and Six, to the Third Day of February, One Thousand Eight Hundred and Thirteen. Wilmington: M. Bradford and R. Porter, 1816.

Laws of the State of Delaware, from the Sixteenth Day of January, One Thousand Eight Hundred and Thirty, to the Thirteenth Day of February, One Thousand Eight Hundred and Thirty-Five. Dover: S. Kimmey, 1841.

Laws of the State of Delaware, Passed at a Session of the General Assembly, Commenced and Held at Dover, on Tuesday, the Second Day of January, in the Year of Our Lord One Thousand Eight Hundred and Fifty-Five, and of the Independence of the United States the Seventy-Ninth. Dover: William Sharp, 1859.

Laws of the State of Missouri, Passed at the First Session of the Fourteenth General Assembly, Begun and Held at the City of Jefferson, Monday, the Sixteenth Day of November, Eighteen Hundred and Forty-Six, and Ended on Tuesday, the Sixteenth Day of February, Eighteen Hundred and Forty-Seven. Jefferson: James Lusk, 1847.
Laws of the State of Missouri; Revised and Digested by the Authority of the General Assembly. St. Louis: E. Charless, 1825.
Laws of the State of North Carolina, Passed by the General Assembly, at the Session of 1838–'39. Raleigh: J. Gales and Son, 1839.
Laws of the State of North Carolina, Passed by the General Assembly, at the Session of 1840–41. Raleigh: W. R. Gales, 1841.
Lee, Jarena. *Religious Experience and Journal of Mrs. Jarena Lee, Giving an Account of Her Call to Preach the Gospel.* Philadelphia: Jarena Lee, 1849.
Lipscomb, Terry W., ed. *The Colonial Records of South Carolina: The Journal of the Commons House of Assembly, November 21, 1753–September 6, 1754.* Columbia: University of South Carolina Press, 1983.
Lipscomb, Terry W., and R. Nicholas Olsberg, eds. *The Colonial Records of South Carolina: The Journal of the Commons House of Assembly, November 14, 1751–October 7, 1752.* Columbia: University of South Carolina Press, 1977.
Littell, William, and Jacob Swigert, eds. *A Digest of the Statute Law of Kentucky: Being a Collection of All the Acts of the General Assembly, of a Public and Permanent Nature, the Commencement of the Government to May Session 1822.* Frankfort: Kendall and Russell, 1822.
Local Laws and Private Acts of the State of Missouri, Passed at the Adjourned Session of the Eighteenth General Assembly, Begun and Held at the City of Jefferson, on Monday, the Fifth Day of November, Eighteen Hundred and Fifty Five. Jefferson: James Lusk, 1856.
Lockwood, Lewis C. *Mary S. Peake, the Colored Teacher at Fortress Monroe.* Boston: American Tract Society, 1863.
Marbury, Horatio, and William H. Crawford, eds. *Digest of the Laws of the State of Georgia, from Its Settlement as a British Province, in 1755, to the Session of the General Assembly in 1800, Inclusive.* Savannah: Seymour, Woolhopter, and Stebbins, 1802.
Martin, Francois Xavier, ed. *The Public Acts of the General Assembly of North-Carolina.* Vol. 1, *Containing the Acts from 1715 to 1790.* New Bern: Martin and Ogden, 1804.
Matchett's Baltimore Director, Corrected up to June 1829. Baltimore, 1829.
McCord, David J., ed. *The Statutes at Large of South Carolina.* Columbia: A. S. Johnston, 1840.
The Memorial of the American Colonization Society. Washington, D.C.: Way and Gideon, 1826.
The Metropolitan Catholic Almanac, and Laity's Directory for the United States, Canada, and the British Provinces, 1861. Baltimore: John Murphy, 1860.
Minutes of the Forty-Seventh Annual Session of the Chowan Baptist Association, Held with the Church at Meherrin, Hertford County, N.C., May 12–15, 1853. Raleigh: Recorder Office, 1853.
Morehead, C. S., and Mason Brown, eds. *A Digest of the Statute Laws of Kentucky of a Public and Permanent Nature, from the Commencement of the Government to the Session of the Legislature, Ending on the 24th February, 1834.* Frankfort: Albert G. Hodges, 1834.
Muster Rolls of the Soldiers of the War of 1812: Detached from the Militia of North Carolina in 1812 and 1814. Raleigh: Charles C. Raboteau, 1851.

Official Records of the Union and Confederate Navies in the War of the Rebellion, Series I. 27 vols. Washington, D.C.: Government Printing Office, 1894–1917.

Offley, G. W. *A Narrative of the Life and Labors of the Rev. G. W. Offley, a Colored Man, Local Preacher and Missionary*. Hartford, Conn., 1859.

Olsberg, R. Nicholas, ed. *The Colonial Records of South Carolina: The Journal of the Commons House of Assembly, 23 April 1750–31 August 1751*. Columbia: University of South Carolina Press, 1974.

Parish Register of Saint Peter's, New Kent County, Va., from 1680 to 1787. Richmond: William Ellis Jones, 1904.

Payne, Daniel Alexander. *Recollections of Seventy Years*. Nashville, Tenn.: A. M. E. Sunday School Union, 1888.

Perdue, Charles L., Jr., Thomas E. Barden, and Robert K. Phillips, eds. *Weevils in the Wheat: Interviews with Virginia Ex-Slaves*. Charlottesville: University of Virginia Press, 1976.

Proceedings and Debates of the Convention of North-Carolina, Called to Amend the Constitution of the State, Which Assembled at Raleigh, June 2, 1835. Raleigh: Joseph Gales and Son, 1836.

Public Acts of the State of Tennessee, Passed at the First Session of the Thirty-Second General Assembly, for the Years 1857–8. Nashville: G. C. Torbett, 1858.

Public Acts of the State of Tennessee, Passed at the First Session of the Thirty-Third General Assembly for the Years 1859–60. Nashville: E. G. Eastman, 1860.

Public Laws of the State of North Carolina Passed by the General Assembly at Its Session of 1860–61. Raleigh: John Spelman, 1861.

Quinquennial Catalogue of Oberlin College. Oberlin, Ohio: News Printing, 1900.

Return of the Whole Number of Persons within the Several Districts of the United States, according to "An Act Providing for the Second Census or Enumeration of the Inhabitants of the United States." Passed February the twenty eighth, one thousand eight hundred. 1801.

The Revised Statutes of the State of Missouri, Revised and Digested by the Thirteenth General Assembly, during the Session of Eighteen Hundred and Forty-Four and Eighteen Hundred and Forty-Five; To Which Are Prefixed the Constitutions of the United States and of the State of Missouri, and the Act of Congress Authorizing the People of Missouri Territory to Form a State Government, and the Ordinance of the Convention of the People of Missouri, by Their Representatives, Declaring the Assent of the People of Missouri to the Conditions and Provisions of the Said Act of Congress; With an Appendix. St. Louis: J. W. Dougherty, 1845.

Richardson, James D., ed. *A Compilation of the Messages and Papers of the Confederacy including the Diplomatic Correspondence, 1861–1865*. Vol. 1. Nashville, Tenn.: United States Publishing, 1905.

Robinson, Conway, ed. *Reports of Cases Decided in the Supreme Court of Appeals and in the General Court, of Virginia*. Vol. 2, *From April 1, 1843, to April 1, 1844*. Richmond: Shepherd and Colin, 1844.

Rules and Regulations of the Brown Fellowship Society Established at Charleston, S.C., 1st November, 1790. Charleston: J. B. Nixon, 1844.

Semega, Jessica, Melissa Kollar, John Creamer, and Abinash Mohanty. *Income and Poverty in the United States, 2018*. Washington, D.C.: Government Printing Office, 2019.

The Seventh Census of the United States: 1850. Washington, D.C.: Robert Armstrong, 1853.

Shepherd, Samuel, ed. *The Statutes at Large of Virginia, from October Session 1792,* to December Session 1806, Inclusive, in Three Volumes, (New Series) Being a Continuation of Hening. Richmond: Samuel Shepherd, 1835–36.

Snethen, Worthington G., ed. *The Black Code of the District of Columbia in Force September 1st, 1848.* New York: William Harned and John Street, 1848.

Special Report of the Commissioner of Education on the Condition and Improvement of Public Schools in the District of Columbia. Washington, D.C.: Government Printing Office, 1871.

Still, William. *The Underground Railroad.* Philadelphia: Porter and Coates, 1872.

Tate, Joseph, ed. *Digest of the Laws of Virginia, Which Are of a Permanent Character and General Operation; Illustrated by Judicial Decisions: To Which Is Added, an Index of the Names of the Cases in the Virginia Reporters.* Richmond: Smith and Palmer, 1841.

Taylor, Susie King. *Reminiscences of My Life in Camp with the 33d United States Colored Troops Late 1st S.C. Volunteers.* Boston: Susie King Taylor, 1902.

Thorpe, Francis Newton, ed. *The Federal and State Constitutions, Colonial Charters, and Other Organic Laws of the States, Territories, and Colonies Now or Heretofore Forming the United States of America.* Washington, D.C.: Government Printing Office, 1909.

Tilmon, Levin. *A Brief Miscellaneous Narrative of the More Early Parts of the Life of L. Tilmon, Pastor of a Colored Methodist Congregational Church in the City of New York.* Jersey City, N.J.: W. W. and L. A. Press, 1853.

Toulmin, Harry, ed. *A Digest of the Laws of the State of Alabama: Containing the Statutes and Resolutions in Force at the End of the General Assembly in January, 1823.* Cahawba: Ginn and Curtis, 1823.

Twenty-Two Years' Work of the Hampton Normal and Agricultural Institute at Hampton, Virginia. Hampton: Normal School Press, 1893.

United States House of Representatives. *Free Colored Seamen—Majority and Minority Reports.* 27th Cong., 3rd sess., 1843.

United States Senate. *Preliminary Report on the Eighth Census, 1860.* 37th Cong., 2nd sess., 1862.

Weeden, H. C. *Weeden's History of the Colored People of Louisville.* Louisville, Ky.: H. C. Weeden, 1897.

Wightman, William M. *Life of William Capers, D.D., One of the Bishops of the Methodist Episcopal Church, South; Including an Autobiography.* Nashville, Tenn.: J. B. M'Ferrin, 1858.

Woods' Baltimore Directory for 1858–'59. Baltimore: John W. Woods, 1858.

Published Secondary Sources

Alexander, Adele Logan. *Ambiguous Lives: Free Women of Color in Rural Georgia, 1789–1879.* Fayetteville: University of Arkansas Press, 1991.

Alexander, Leslie M. *African or American? Black Identity and Political Activism in New York City, 1784–1861.* Urbana: University of Illinois Press, 2008.

Alexander, Michelle. *The New Jim Crow: Mass Incarceration in the Age of Colorblindness.* Rev. ed. New York: New Press, 2012.

Allen, Richard B. *European Slave Trading in the Indian Ocean, 1500–1850.* Athens: Ohio University Press, 2014.

———. "Free Women of Colour and Socio-Economic Marginality in Mauritius, 1767–1830." *Slavery and Abolition* 26 (August 2005): 181–97.

———. "Marie Rozette and Her World: Class, Ethnicity, Gender, and Race in Late

Eighteenth- and Early Nineteenth-Century Mauritius." *Journal of Social History* 45 (Winter 2011): 345-65.

———. *Slaves, Freedmen, and Indentured Laborers in Colonial Mauritius*. New York: Cambridge University Press, 1999.

Allmendinger, David F., Jr. *Nat Turner and the Rising in Southampton County*. Baltimore: Johns Hopkins University Press, 2014.

Anderson, Benedict. *Imagined Communities: Reflections on the Origin and Spread of Nationalism*. Rev. ed. New York: Verso, 1991.

Andrews, Dee E. *The Methodists and Revolutionary America, 1760-1800: The Shaping of an Evangelical Culture*. Princeton, N.J.: Princeton University Press, 2000.

Archer, Richard. *Jim Crow North: The Struggle for Equal Rights in Antebellum New England*. New York: Oxford University Press, 2017.

Aslakson, Kenneth R. *Making Race in the Courtroom: The Legal Construction of Three Races in Early New Orleans*. New York: New York University Press, 2014.

———. "The 'Quadroon-Plaçage' Myth of Antebellum New Orleans: Anglo-American (Mis)Interpretations of a French-Caribbean Phenomenon." *Journal of Social History* 45 (Spring 2012): 709-32.

Atkins, Jonathan M. "Party Politics and the Debate over the Tennessee Free Negro Bill, 1859-1860." *Journal of Southern History* 71 (May 2005): 245-78.

Ayers, Edward L. *The Promise of the New South: Life after Reconstruction*. New York: Oxford University Press, 1992.

Baker, Henry E. "Benjamin Banneker, the Negro Mathematician and Astronomer." *Journal of Negro History* 3 (April 1918): 99-118.

Ball, Erica L. *To Live an Antislavery Life: Personal Politics and the Antebellum Black Middle Class*. Athens: University of Georgia Press, 2012.

Banks, Willa Young. "A Contradiction in Antebellum Baltimore: A Competitive School for Girls of 'Color' within a Slave State." *Maryland Historical Magazine* 99 (Summer 2004): 132-63.

Barfield, Rodney D., and Patricia M. Marshall. *Thomas Day: African American Furniture Maker*. Raleigh: North Carolina Office of Archives and History, 2005.

Barnes, L. Diane. *Artisan Workers in the Upper South: Petersburg, Virginia, 1820-1865*. Baton Rouge: Louisiana State University Press, 2008.

Barr, Ruth B., and Modeste Hargis. "The Voluntary Exile of Free Negroes of Pensacola." *Florida Historical Quarterly* 17 (July 1938): 3-14.

Baumgartner, Kabria. *In Pursuit of Knowledge: Black Women and Educational Activism in Antebellum America*. New York: New York University Press, 2019.

Bell, Caryn Cossé. *Revolution, Romanticism, and the Afro-Creole Protest Tradition in Louisiana, 1718-1868*. Baton Rouge: Louisiana State University Press, 1997.

Bell, Richard. "Counterfeit Kin: Kidnappers of Color, the Reverse Underground Railroad, and the Origins of Practical Abolition." *Journal of the Early Republic* 38 (Summer 2018): 199-230.

———. *Stolen: Five Free Boys Kidnapped into Slavery and Their Astonishing Odyssey Home*. New York: Simon and Schuster, 2019.

Bellamy, Donnie D. "Free Blacks in Antebellum Missouri, 1820-1860." *Missouri Historical Review* 67 (January 1973): 198-226.

Bendler, Bruce. "Securing One of the Blessings of Liberty: Black Families in Lower New Castle County, 1790-1850." *Delaware History* 25 (Fall-Winter 1993-94): 237-52.

Bennett, Herman L. *Colonial Blackness: A History of Afro-Mexico*. Bloomington: Indiana University Press, 2009.

Berlin, Ira. *Many Thousands Gone: The First Two Centuries of Slavery in North America*. Cambridge, Mass.: Belknap Press of Harvard University Press, 1998.

———. *Slaves without Masters: The Free Negro in the Antebellum South*. New York: New Press, 1974.

Berlin, Ira, Joseph P. Reidy, and Leslie S. Rowland, eds. *Freedom's Soldiers: The Black Military Experience in the Civil War*. New York: Cambridge University Press, 1998.

Berry, Brewton. *Almost White*. New York: Macmillan, 1963.

Berry, Mary F. "Negro Troops in Blue and Gray: The Louisiana Native Guards, 1861–1863." *Louisiana History* 8 (Spring 1967): 165–90.

Biggleston, William E. *They Stopped in Oberlin: Black Residents and Visitors of the Nineteenth Century*. Rev. ed. Oberlin, Ohio: Oberlin College, 2002.

Bishir, Catherine W. *Crafting Lives: African American Artisans in New Bern, North Carolina, 1770–1900*. Chapel Hill: University of North Carolina Press, 2013.

Blackburn, Robin. *The American Crucible: Slavery, Emancipation and Human Rights*. London: Verso, 2011.

———. *The Overthrow of Colonial Slavery, 1776–1848*. London: Verso, 1988.

Block, Sharon. *Rape and Sexual Power in Early America*. Chapel Hill: University of North Carolina Press, 2006.

Blondo, Richard Albert. "Samuel Green: A Black Life in Antebellum Maryland." M.A. thesis, University of Maryland, 1988.

Bolster, W. Jeffrey. *Black Jacks: African American Seamen in the Age of Sail*. Cambridge, Mass.: Harvard University Press, 1997.

Bonner, Christopher James. *Remaking the Republic: Black Politics and the Creation of American Citizenship*. Philadelphia: University of Pennsylvania Press, 2020.

Brana-Shute, Rosemary, and Randy J. Sparks, eds. *Paths to Freedom: Manumission in the Atlantic World*. Columbia: University of South Carolina Press, 2009.

Brasseaux, Carl A., Keith P. Fontenot, and Claude F. Oubre. *Creoles of Color in the Bayou County*. Jackson: University Press of Mississippi, 1994.

Breen, Patrick H. *The Land Shall Be Deluged in Blood: A New History of the Nat Turner Revolt*. New York: Oxford University Press, 2015.

Breen, T. H., and Stephen Innes. *"Myne Owne Ground": Race and Freedom on Virginia's Eastern Shore, 1640–1676*. New York: Oxford University Press, 1980.

Brewer, Holly. "Apprentice Policy in Virginia: From Patriarchal to Republic Policies of Social Welfare." In *Children Bound to Labor: The Pauper Apprentice System in Early America*, edited by Ruth Wallis Herndon and John E. Murray, 183–98. Ithaca, N.Y.: Cornell University Press, 2009.

———. *By Birth or Consent: Children, Law, and the Anglo-American Revolution in Authority*. Chapel Hill: University of North Carolina Press, 2005.

Bristol, Douglas Walter, Jr. *Knights of the Razor: Black Barbers in Slavery and Freedom*. Baltimore: Johns Hopkins University Press, 2009.

Brooks, James F. *Captives and Cousins: Slavery, Kinship, and Community in the Southwest Borderlands*. Chapel Hill: University of North Carolina Press, 2002.

———, ed. *Confounding the Color Line: The Indian-Black Experience in North America*. Lincoln: University of Nebraska Press, 2002.

Brophy, Alfred L. "The Nat Turner Trials." *North Carolina Law Review* 91 (2013): 1818–80.

Broussard, Joyce Linda. *Stepping Lively in Place: The Not-Married Women of Civil-War-Era Natchez, Mississippi*. Athens: University of Georgia Press, 2016.

Brown, Christopher Leslie. *Moral Capital: Foundations of British Abolitionism*. Chapel Hill: University of North Carolina Press, 2006.

Brown, Kathleen M. *Good Wives, Nasty Wenches, and Anxious Patriarchs: Gender, Race, and Power in Colonial Virginia*. Chapel Hill: University of North Carolina Press, 1996.

Brown, Letitia Woods. *Free Negroes in the District of Columbia, 1790–1846*. New York: Oxford University Press, 1972.

Brubaker, Rogers. *Ethnicity without Groups*. Cambridge, Mass.: Harvard University Press, 2004.

Brubaker, Rogers, Margit Feischmidt, Jon Fox, and Liana Grancea. *Nationalist Politics and Everyday Ethnicity in a Transylvanian Town*. Princeton, N.J.: Princeton University Press, 2006.

Brubaker, Rogers, Mara Loveman, and Peter Stamatov. "Ethnicity as Cognition." *Theory and Society* 33 (2004): 31–64.

Bryant, James K. *The 36th Infantry United States Colored Troops in the Civil War: A History and Roster*. Jefferson, N.C.: McFarland, 2012.

Buchanan, Thomas C. *Black Life on the Mississippi: Slaves, Free Blacks, and the Western Steamboat World*. Chapel Hill: University of North Carolina Press, 2004.

Buckley, Thomas E. *The Great Catastrophe of My Life: Divorce in the Old Dominion*. Chapel Hill: University of North Carolina Press, 2002.

———. "Unfixing Race: Class, Power, and Identity in an Interracial Family." *Virginia Magazine of History and Biography* 102 (July 1994): 349–80.

Burin, Eric. *Slavery and the Peculiar Solution: A History of the American Colonization Society*. Gainesville: University Press of Florida, 2005.

Burton, Orville Vernon. *In My Father's House Are Many Mansions: Family and Community in Edgefield, South Carolina*. Chapel Hill: University of North Carolina Press, 1985.

Butler, Reginald Dennin. "Evolution of a Rural Free Black Community: Goochland County, Virginia, 1728–1832." Ph.D. diss., Johns Hopkins University, 1989.

Bynum, Victoria E. *The Free State of Jones: Mississippi's Longest Civil War*. Chapel Hill: University of North Carolina Press, 2001.

———. *Unruly Women: The Politics of Social and Sexual Control in the Old South*. Chapel Hill: University of North Carolina Press, 1992.

Byrd, William L., III. *Against the Peace and Dignity of the State: North Carolina Laws Regarding Slaves, Free Persons of Color, and Indians*. Westminster, Md.: Heritage Books, 2004.

Calloway, Colin G., ed. *After King Philip's War: Presence and Persistence in Indian New England*. Hanover, N.H.: University Press of New England, 1997.

Calloway, Colin G., and Neal Salisbury, eds. *Reinterpreting New England Indians and the Colonial Experience*. Boston: Colonial Society of Massachusetts, 2003.

Campbell, James M. *Slavery on Trial: Race, Class, and Criminal Justice in Antebellum Richmond, Virginia*. Gainesville: University Press of Florida, 2007.

Candlin, Kit, and Cassandra Pybus. *Enterprising Women: Gender, Race, and Power in the Revolutionary Atlantic*. Athens: University of Georgia Press, 2015.

Capers, Corey. "A Comment on Melvin Ely's *Israel on the Appomattox*." *Labor: Studies in Working-Class History of the Americas* 6 (2009): 23–26.

Carr, Lois Green, Philip D. Morgan, and Jean B. Russo, eds. *Colonial Chesapeake Society*. Chapel Hill: University of North Carolina Press, 1988.

Carroll, Kenneth L. "Religious Influences on the Manumission of Slaves in Caroline, Dorchester, and Talbot Counties." *Maryland Historical Magazine* 56 (June 1961): 176–97.

Cecelski, David S. *The Fire of Freedom: Abraham Galloway and the Slaves' Civil War.* Chapel Hill: University of North Carolina Press, 2012.

———. *The Waterman's Song: Slavery and Freedom in Maritime North Carolina.* Chapel Hill: University of North Carolina Press, 2001.

Chater, Kathy. "Black People in England, 1660–1807." *Parliamentary History* 26 (2007): 66–83.

Chestnutt, Charles W. "The Free Colored People of North Carolina." *Southern Workman* 31 (1902): 136–41.

Childs, Matt D. *The 1812 Aponte Rebellion in Cuba and the Struggle against Atlantic Slavery.* Chapel Hill: University of North Carolina Press, 2006.

Clark, Emily. *Masterless Mistresses: The New Orleans Ursulines and the Development of a New World Society, 1727–1834.* Chapel Hill: University of North Carolina, 2007.

———. *The Strange History of the American Quadroon: Free Women of Color in the Revolutionary Atlantic World.* Chapel Hill: University of North Carolina Press, 2013.

Clark, Emily Suzanne. *A Luminous Brotherhood: Afro-Creole Spiritualism in Nineteenth-Century New Orleans.* Chapel Hill: University of North Carolina Press, 2016.

Clampitt, Bradley R., ed. *The Civil War and Reconstruction in Indian Territory.* Lincoln: University of Nebraska Press, 2015.

Clegg, Claude A., III. *The Price of Liberty: African Americans and the Making of Liberia.* Chapel Hill: University of North Carolina Press, 2004.

Clinton, Catherine, and Michele Gillespie, eds. *The Devil's Lane: Sex and Race in the Early South.* New York: Oxford University Press, 1997.

Cohen, David W., and Jack P. Greene, eds. *Neither Slave nor Free: The Freedmen of African Descent in the Slave Societies of the New World.* Baltimore: Johns Hopkins University Press, 1972.

Coleman, Arica L. *That the Blood Stay Pure: African Americans, Native Americans, and the Predicament of Race and Identity in Virginia.* Bloomington: Indiana University Press, 2013.

Condon, John Joseph, Jr. "Manumission, Slavery, and Family in the Post-Revolutionary Rural Chesapeake: Anne Arundel County, Maryland, 1781–1831." Ph.D. diss., University of Minnesota, 2001.

Condon, Sean. "The Slave Owner's Family and Manumission in the Post-Revolutionary Chesapeake Tidewater: Evidence from Anne Arundel County Wills, 1790–1820." In *Paths to Freedom: Manumission in the Atlantic World*, edited by Rosemary Brana-Shute and Randy J. Sparks, 339–61. Columbia: University of South Carolina Press, 2009.

Cope, R. Douglas. *The Limits of Racial Domination: Plebeian Society in Colonial Mexico City, 1660–1720.* Madison: University of Wisconsin Press, 1994.

Cordon, John Joseph, Jr. "Manumission, Slavery and Family in the Post-Revolutionary Rural Chesapeake: Anne Arundel County, Maryland, 1781–1831." Ph.D. diss., University of Minnesota, 2001.

Cornish, Dudley Taylor. *The Sable Arm: Negro Troops in the Union Army, 1861–1865.* New York: W. W. Norton, 1966.

Cox, Anna-Lisa. *The Bone and Sinew of the Land: America's Forgotten Black Pioneers and the Struggle for Equality.* New York: PublicAffairs, 2018.

Crawford, Michael J. *The Having of Negroes Is Become a Burden: The Quaker Struggle to Free Slaves in Revolutionary North Carolina.* Gainesville: University Press of Florida, 2010.

Crenshaw, Kimberlé. "Demarginalizing the Intersection of Race and Sex: A Black Feminist Critique of Antidiscrimination Doctrine, Feminist Theory and Antiracist Politics." *University of Chicago Legal Forum* (1989): 139–68.

———. "Mapping the Margins: Intersectionality, Identity Politics, and Violence against Women of Color." *Stanford Law Review* 43 (July 1991): 1241–1300.

Crow, Jeffrey J. *The Black Experience in Revolutionary North Carolina.* Raleigh: North Carolina Division of Archives and History, 1977.

Crump, Judson E., and Alfred L. Brophy. "Twenty-One Months a Slave: Cornelius Sinclair's Odyssey." *Mississippi Law Journal* 86 (2017): 457–512.

Curry, Christopher. *Freedom and Resistance: A Social History of Black Loyalists in the Bahamas.* Gainesville: University Press of Florida, 2017.

Curry, Leonard P. *The Free Black in Urban America, 1800–1850: The Shadow of the Dream.* Chicago: University of Chicago Press, 1981.

Daggett, Melissa. *Spiritualism in Nineteenth-Century New Orleans: The Life and Times of Henry Louis Rey.* Jackson: University Press of Mississippi, 2017.

Dangerfield, David W. "Hard Rows to Hoe: Free Black Farmers in Antebellum South Carolina." Ph.D. diss., University of South Carolina, 2014.

Daniel, Sadie. "Myrtilla Miner: Pioneer in Teacher Education for Negro Women." *Journal of Negro History* 34 (January 1949): 30–45.

Dantas, Mariana L. R. *Black Townsmen: Urban Slavery and Freedom in the Eighteenth-Century Americas.* New York: Palgrave MacMillan, 2008.

Davidson, Thomas E. *Free Blacks on the Lower Eastern Shore of Maryland: The Colonial Period, 1662 to 1775.* Crownsville: Maryland Historical and Cultural Publications, 1991.

Davis, David Brion. *Inhuman Bondage: The Rise and Fall of Slavery in the New World.* New York: Oxford University Press, 2006.

———. *The Problem of Slavery in the Age of Emancipation.* New York: Alfred A. Knopf, 2014.

Davis, Edward Adams, and William Ransom Hogan. *The Barber of Natchez.* Baton Rouge: Louisiana State University Press, 1954.

Daynes, Sarah, and Orville Lee. *Desire for Race.* New York: Cambridge University Press, 2008.

Deal, Douglas. "A Constricted World: Free Blacks on Virginia's Eastern Shore, 1680–1750." In *Colonial Chesapeake Society,* edited by Lois Green Carr, Philip D. Morgan, and Jean B. Russo, 275–305. Chapel Hill: University of North Carolina Press, 1988.

Deal, J. Douglas. *Race and Class in Colonial Virginia: Indians, Englishmen, and Africans on the Eastern Shore during the Seventeenth Century.* New York: Garland, 1993.

de la Fuente, Alejandro, and Ariela J. Gross. *Becoming Free, Becoming Black: Race, Freedom, and Law in Cuba, Virginia, and Louisiana.* New York: Cambridge University Press, 2020.

Delaney, Ted, and Phillip Wayne Rhodes. *Free Blacks of Lynchburg, Virginia, 1805–1865.* Lynchburg, Va.: Warwick House, 2001.

Dessens, Nathalie. *From Saint-Dominque to New Orleans: Migration and Influences.* Gainesville: University Press of Florida, 2007.

Diemer, Andrew K. *The Politics of Black Citizenship: Free African Americans in the Mid-Atlantic Borderland, 1817–1863.* Athens: University of Georgia Press, 2016.

Dodge, David. "The Free Negro of North Carolina." *Atlantic Monthly* (January 1886): 20–30.

Domby, Adam H. *The False Cause: Fraud, Fabrication, and White Supremacy in Confederate Memory*. Charlottesville: University of Virginia Press, 2020.

Dominguez, Virginia R. *White by Definition: Social Classification in Creole Louisiana*. New Brunswick, N.J.: Rutgers University Press, 1986.

Dormon, James H., ed. *Creoles of Color of the Gulf South*. Knoxville: University of Tennessee Press, 1996.

Dorsey, Jennifer Hull. *Hirelings: African American Workers and Free Labor in Early Maryland*. Ithaca, N.Y.: Cornell University Press, 2011.

Downs, Jim. *Sick from Freedom: African-American Illness and Suffering during the Civil War and Reconstruction*. New York: Oxford University Press, 2012.

Drago, Edmund L. *Black Politicians and Reconstruction in Georgia: A Splendid Failure*. Baton Rouge: Louisiana State University Press, 1982.

———. *Initiative, Paternalism, and Race Relations: Charleston's Avery Normal Institute*. Athens: University of Georgia Press, 1990.

Drescher, Seymour. *Econocide: British Slavery in the Era of Abolition*. Pittsburgh: University of Pittsburgh Press, 1977.

———. *The Mighty Experiment: Free Labor versus Slavery in British Emancipation*. New York: Oxford University Press, 2002.

Dubois, Laurent. *Avengers of the New World: The Story of the Haitian Revolution*. Cambridge, Mass.: Belknap Press of Harvard University Press, 2004.

———. *A Colony of Citizens: Revolution and Slave Emancipation in the French Caribbean, 1787–1804*. Chapel Hill: University of North Carolina Press, 2004.

Du Bois, W. E. B. *Black Reconstruction*. New York: Harcourt, Brace, 1935.

Dunbar, Erica Armstrong. *A Fragile Freedom: African American Women and Emancipation in the Antebellum City*. New Haven, Conn.: Yale University Press, 2008.

DuVal, Kathleen. *The Native Ground: Indians and Colonists in the Heart of the Continent*. Philadelphia: University of Pennsylvania Press, 2006.

Edwards, Laura F. *The People and Their Peace: Legal Culture and the Transformation of Inequality in the Post-Revolutionary South*. Chapel Hill: University of North Carolina Press, 2009.

Egerton, Douglas R. *Thunder at the Gates: The Black Civil War Regiments That Redeemed America*. New York: Basic Books, 2016.

Ely, Melvin Patrick. *Israel on the Appomattox: A Southern Experiment in Black Freedom from the 1790s through the Civil War*. New York: Alfred A. Knopf, 2004.

Eslinger, Ellen. "Free Black Residency in Two Antebellum Virginia Counties: How the Laws Functioned." *Journal of Southern History* 79 (May 2013): 261–98.

Essah, Patience. *A House Divided: Slavery and Emancipation in Delaware, 1638–1865*. Charlottesville: University Press of Virginia, 1996.

Evans, Emory G., ed. "A Question of Complexion: Documents Concerning the Negro and the Franchise in Eighteenth-Century Virginia." *Virginia Magazine of History and Biography* 7 (October 1963): 411–15.

Evans, W. A. "Free Negroes in Monroe County during Slavery." *Journal of Mississippi History* 3 (January 1941): 37–43.

Evans, William McKee. *To Die Game: The Story of the Lowry Band, Indian Guerrillas of Reconstruction*. Baton Rouge: Louisiana State University Press, 1971.

Fanning, Sara. *Caribbean Crossing: African Americans and the Haitian Emigration Movement*. New York: New York University Press, 2015.

Faust, Drew Gilpin. *This Republic of Suffering: Death and the American Civil War*. New York: Alfred A. Knopf, 2008.

Fede, Andrew. *Roadblocks to Freedom: Slavery and Manumission in the United States South*. New Orleans, La.: Quid Pro Books, 2011.

Ferrer, Ada. *Freedom's Mirror: Cuba and Haiti in the Age of Revolution*. New York: Cambridge University Press, 2014.

Fields, Barbara Jeanne. "'Origins of the New South' and the Negro Question." *Journal of Southern History* 67 (2001): 811–26.

———. *Slavery and Freedom on the Middle Ground: Maryland during the Nineteenth Century*. New Haven, Conn.: Yale University Press, 1985.

———. "Slavery, Race and Ideology in the United States of America." *New Left Review* (May–June 1990): 95–118.

Finkelman, Paul. *Slavery and the Founders: Race and Liberty in the Age of Jefferson*. Armonk, N.Y.: M. E. Sharpe, 2001.

Fischer, Kirsten. *Suspect Relations: Sex, Race, and Resistance in Colonial North Carolina*. Ithaca, N.Y.: Cornell University Press, 2002.

Fisher, Andrew B., and Matthew D. O'Hara, eds. *Imperial Subjects: Race and Identity in Colonial Latin America*. Durham, N.C.: Duke University Press, 2009.

Fisher, Michael H. *Counterflows to Colonialism: Indian Travellers and Settlers in Britain, 1600-1857*. Delhi: Permanent Black, 2004.

Foner, Eric. *Freedom's Lawmakers: A Directory of Black Officeholders during Reconstruction*. Rev. ed. Baton Rouge: Louisiana State University Press, 1996.

———. *Free Soil, Free Labor, Free Men: The Ideology of the Republican Party before the Civil War*. New York: Oxford University Press, 1970.

———. *Reconstruction: America's Unfinished Revolution, 1863-1877*. New York: Harper and Row, 1988.

———. Review of *Israel on the Appomattox: A Southern Experiment in Black Freedom From the 1790s Through the Civil War*, by Melvin Patrick Ely. *Los Angeles Times Book Review*, September 12, 2004.

Foote, Lorien. *The Yankee Plague: Escaped Union Prisoners and the Collapse of the Confederacy*. Chapel Hill: University of North Carolina Press, 2016.

Forbes, Jack D. *Black Africans and Native Americans: Color, Race and Caste in the Evolution of Red-Black Peoples*. New York: Basil Blackwell, 1988.

Ford, Lacy K. *Deliver Us from Evil: The Slavery Question in the Old South*. New York: Oxford University Press, 2009.

Ford, Lisa. *Settler Sovereignty: Jurisdiction and Indigenous People in America and Australia, 1788-1836*. Cambridge, Mass.: Harvard University Press, 2010.

Franklin, John Hope. *The Free Negro in North Carolina, 1790-1860*. Chapel Hill: University of North Carolina Press, 1943.

———. "James Boon, Free Negro Artisan." *Journal of Negro History* 30 (April 1945): 150–80.

Franklin, John Hope, and Loren Schweninger. *In Search of the Promised Land: A Slave Family in the Old South*. New York. Oxford University Press, 2006.

———. *Runaway Slaves: Rebels on the Plantation*. New York: Oxford University Press, 1999.

Frazier, E. Franklin. *The Free Negro Family: A Study of Family Origins before the Civil War*. Nashville, Tenn.: Fisk University Press, 1932.

———. *The Negro Family in the United States*. Chicago: University of Chicago Press, 1939.

Freehling, William W. *The Road to Disunion: Secessionists at Bay, 1776-1854*. New York: Oxford University Press, 1990.

Freehling, William W. *The Road to Disunion: Secessionists Triumphant, 1854-1861*. New York: Oxford University Press, 2007.

French, Jan Hoffman. *Legalizing Identities: Becoming Black or Indian in Brazil's Northeast*. Chapel Hill: University of North Carolina Press, 2009.

Furstenberg, François. "Atlantic Slavery, Atlantic Freedom: George Washington, Slavery, and Transatlantic Abolitionist Networks." *William and Mary Quarterly*, 3rd ser., 68 (April 2011): 247–86.

Gallay, Alan, ed. *Indian Slavery in Colonial America*. Lincoln: University of Nebraska Press, 2009.

———. *The Indian Slave Trade: The Rise of the English Empire in the American South, 1670-1717*. New Haven, Conn.: Yale University Press, 2002.

Gardner, Bettye. "Ante-Bellum Black Education in Baltimore." *Maryland Historical Magazine* 71 (Fall 1976): 360–66.

Garrow, Patrick H. *The Mattamuskeet Documents: A Study in Social History*. Raleigh, N.C.: Division of Archives and History, 1995.

Gaspar, David Barry, and Darlene Clark Hine, eds. *Beyond Bondage: Free Women of Color in the Americas*. Urbana: University of Illinois Press, 2004.

Gatewood, Willard B., Jr., ed. *Free Man of Color: The Autobiography of Willis Augustus Hodges*. Knoxville: University of Tennessee Press, 1982.

Gehman, Mary. *The Free People of Color of New Orleans: An Introduction*. Donaldsonville, La.: Dville Press, 2017.

Gharala, Norah L. A. *Taxing Blackness: Free Afromexican Tribute in Bourbon New Spain*. Tuscaloosa: University of Alabama Press, 2019.

Gillmer, Jason. *Slavery and Freedom in Texas: Stories from the Courtroom, 1821-1871*. Athens: University of Georgia Press, 2017.

Glatthaar, Joseph T. *Forged in Battle: The Civil War Alliance of Black Soldiers and White Officers*. Baton Rouge: Louisiana State University Press, 1990.

Gosse, Van. "Patchwork Nation: Racial Orders and Disorder in the United States, 1790-1860." *Journal of the Early Republic* 40 (Spring 2020): 45–81.

Gosse, Van, and David Waldstreicher, eds. *Revolutions and Reconstructions: Black Politics in the Long Nineteenth Century*. Philadelphia: University of Pennsylvania Press, 2020.

Gould, Virginia Meacham, ed. *Chained to the Rock of Adversity: To Be Free, Black, and Female in the Old South*. Athens: University of Georgia Press, 1998.

———. "'A Chaos of Iniquity and Discord': Slave and Free Women of Color in the Spanish Ports of New Orleans, Mobile, and Pensacola." In *The Devil's Lane: Sex and Race in the Early South*, edited by Catherine Clinton and Michele Gillespie, 232–46. New York: Oxford University Press, 1997.

———. "The Free Creoles of Color of the Antebellum Gulf Ports of Mobile and Pensacola: A Struggle for the Middle Ground." In *Creoles of Color of the Gulf South*, edited by James H. Dormon, 28–50. Knoxville: University of Tennessee Press, 1996.

———. "Henriette Delille, Free Women of Color, and Catholicism in Antebellum New Orleans, 1727-1852." In *Beyond Bondage: Free Women of Color in the Americas*, edited by David Barry Gaspar and Darlene Clark Hine, 271–85. Urbana: University of Illinois Press, 2004.

———. "In Full Enjoyment of Their Liberty: The Free Women of Color of the Gulf Ports of New Orleans, Mobile, and Pensacola, 1769-1860." Ph.D. diss., Emory University, 1991.

———. "The Parish Identities of Free Creoles of Color in Pensacola and Mobile, 1698-1860." *U.S. Catholic Historian* 14 (Summer 1996): 1–10.

Gross, Ariela J. *What Blood Won't Tell: A History of Race on Trial in America*. Cambridge, Mass.: Harvard University Press, 2008.
Grundy, Martha Paxson. "David Ferris: Arguments against Quaker Slaveholding." *Quaker History* 103 (Fall 2014): 18–29.
Gutman, Herbert G. *The Black Family in Slavery and Freedom, 1750–1925*. New York: Vintage Books, 1976.
Hahn, Steven. *A Nation under Our Feet: Black Political Struggles in the Rural South from Slavery to the Great Migration*. Cambridge, Mass.: Belknap Press of Harvard University Press, 2003.
Hall, Gwendolyn Midlo. *Africans in Colonial Louisiana: The Development of Afro-Creole Culture in the Eighteenth Century*. Baton Rouge: Louisiana State University Press, 1992.
Hall, Richard L. *On Afric's Shore: A History of Maryland in Liberia, 1834–1857*. Baltimore: Maryland Historical Society, 2003.
Hanger, Kimberly S. *Bounded Lives, Bounded Places: Free Black Society in Colonial New Orleans, 1769–1803*. Durham, N.C.: Duke University Press, 1997.
Harmon, Alexandra. *Indians in the Making: Ethnic Relations and Indian Identities around Puget Sound*. Berkeley: University of California Press, 1998.
Harrell, Isaac S. "Gates County to 1860." *Historical Papers of the Trinity College Historical Society* 12 (1916): 56–106.
Harris, J. William. *The Hanging of Thomas Jeremiah: A Free Black Man's Encounter with Liberty*. New Haven: Yale University Press, 2009.
Harris, Leslie M., and Daina Ramey Berry, eds. *Slavery and Freedom in Savannah*. Athens: University of Georgia Press, 2014.
Harrold, Stanley. *Subversives: Antislavery Community in Washington, D.C., 1828–1865*. Baton Rouge: Louisiana State University Press, 2003.
Hauptman, Laurence H. *Between Two Fires: American Indians in the Civil War*. New York: Free Press, 1995.
Heerman, M. Scott. "'Reducing Free Men to Slavery': Black Kidnapping, the 'Slave Power,' and the Politics of Abolition in Antebellum Illinois, 1830–1860." *Journal of the Early Republic* 38 (Summer 2018): 261–91.
Heinegg, Paul. *Free African Americans of Virginia, North Carolina, South Carolina, Maryland and Delaware*. http://www.freeafricanamericans.com.
Helg, Aline. *Slave No More: Self-Liberation before Abolitionism in the Americas*. Translated by Lara Vergnaud. Chapel Hill: University of North Carolina, 2019.
Hensley, Alexia Jones, and Patrick McCawley. *The Many Faces of Slavery*. Columbia: South Carolina Department of Archives and History, 1999.
Hepburn, Sharon A. Roger. *Crossing the Border: A Free Black Community in Canada*. Urbana: University of Illinois Press, 2007.
Herndon, Ruth Wallis. *Unwelcome Americans: Living on the Margin in Early New England*. Philadelphia: University of Pennsylvania Press, 2001.
Herndon, Ruth Wallis, and John E. Murray, eds. *Children Bound to Labor: The Pauper Apprentice System in Early America*. Ithaca, N.Y.: Cornell University Press, 2009.
Herndon, Ruth Wallis, and Ella Wilcox Sekatau. "Colonizing the Children: Indian Youngsters in Servitude in Early Rhode Island." In *Reinterpreting New England Indians and the Colonial Experience*, edited by Colin G. Calloway and Neal Salisbury, 137–73. Boston: Colonial Society of Massachusetts, 2003.
———. "The Right to a Name: The Narragansett People and Rhode Island Officials in the Revolutionary Era." In *After King Philip's War: Presence and Persistence*

in Indian New England, edited by Colin G. Calloway, 114–43. Hanover, N.H.: University Press of New England, 1997.

Heuman, Gad J. *Between Black and White: Race, Politics, and the Free Coloreds in Jamaica, 1792–1865*. Westport, Conn.: Greenwood, 1981.

Higginbotham, A. Leon, Jr. *In the Matter of Color: Race and the American Legal Process: The Colonial Period*. New York: Oxford University Press, 1978.

Higgins, Billy D. *A Stranger and a Sojourner: Peter Caulder, Free Black Frontiersman in Antebellum Arkansas*. Fayetteville: University of Arkansas Press, 2004.

History of Elam Baptist Church, Charles City Co., Va. Richmond, Va.: Reformer Electric Print, 1910.

Hobbs, Allyson. *A Chosen Exile: A History of Racial Passing in American Life*. Cambridge, Mass.: Harvard University Press, 2014.

Hodes, Martha. *White Women, Black Men: Illicit Sex in the Nineteenth-Century South*. New Haven, Conn.: Yale University Press, 1997.

Hodges, Graham Russell. *Slavery and Freedom in the Rural North: African Americans in Monmouth County, New Jersey, 1665–1865*. Madison: Madison House, 1997.

———. *Root and Branch: African Americans in New York and East Jersey*. Chapel Hill: University of North Carolina Press, 1999.

Holmes, Jack D. L. "The Role of Blacks in Spanish Alabama: The Mobile District, 1780–1813." *Alabama Historical Quarterly* 37 (Spring 1975): 5–18.

Holt, Michael F. *The Fate of Their County: Politicians, Slavery Extension, and the Coming of the Civil War*. New York: Hill and Wang, 2004.

Holt, Thomas C. *The Problem of Race in the Twenty-First Century*. Cambridge, Mass.: Harvard University Press, 2000.

Horton, James Oliver. *Free People of Color: Inside the African American Community*. Washington, D.C.: Smithsonian Institution Press, 1993.

Horton, James Oliver, and Lois E. Horton. *In Hope of Liberty: Culture, Community, and Protest among Northern Free Blacks, 1700–1860*. New York: Oxford University Press, 1997.

Hudson, J. Blaine. "In Pursuit of Freedom: Slave Law and Emancipation in Louisville and Jefferson County, Kentucky." *Filson History Quarterly* 76 (Summer 2002): 287–325.

———. "'Upon This Rock'—The Free African American Community of Antebellum Louisville, Kentucky." *Register of the Kentucky Historical Society* 109 (Summer/Autumn 2011): 295–326.

Humphreys, Margaret. *Intensely Human: The Health of the Black Soldier in the American Civil War*. Baltimore: Johns Hopkins University Press, 2008.

Hunter, Tera W. *Bound in Wedlock: Slave and Free Black Marriage in the Nineteenth Century*. Cambridge, Mass.: Belknap Press of Harvard University Press, 2017.

Hyde, Samuel C., Jr., ed. *Plain Folk of the South Revisited*. Baton Rouge: Louisiana State University Press, 1997.

Ingersoll, Thomas N. "Free Blacks in a Slave Society: New Orleans, 1718–1812." *William and Mary Quarterly*, 3rd ser., 48 (April 1991): 173–200.

Jackson, Kellie Carter. *Force and Freedom: Black Abolitionists and the Politics of Violence*. Philadelphia: University of Pennsylvania Press, 2019.

Jackson, Luther P. "Free Negroes of Petersburg." *Journal of Negro History* 12 (July 1927): 372–73.

———. *Free Negro Labor and Property Holding in Virginia, 1830–1860*. New York: D. Appleton-Century, 1942.

―――. "Manumission in Certain Virginia Cities." *Journal of Negro History* 15 (July 1930): 278–314.

―――. "The Virginia Free Negro Farmer and Property Owner, 1830–1860." *Journal of Negro History* 24 (October 1939): 390–439.

―――. *Virginia Negro Soldiers and Seamen in the Revolutionary War.* Norfolk, Va.: Guide Quality Press, 1944.

Jacobs, Margaret D. *White Mother to a Dark Race: Settler Colonialism, Maternalism, and the Removal of Indigenous Children in the American West and Australia, 1880–1940.* Lincoln: University of Nebraska Press, 2009.

James, C. L. R. *The Black Jacobins: Toussaint L'Ouverture and the San Domingo Revolution.* London: Secker and Warburg, 1938.

Jeffrey, Thomas E. *State Parties and National Politics: North Carolina, 1815–1861.* Athens: University of Georgia Press, 1989.

Jennison, Watson W. *Cultivating Race: The Expansion of Slavery in Georgia, 1750–1860.* Lexington: University Press of Kentucky, 2012.

Jeske, Mary Clement. "From Slave to Slave Owner: The Life of Robert Pearle of Maryland." *Maryland Historical Magazine* 103 (Spring 2008): 4–25.

Johnson, Guion Griffis. *Ante-Bellum North Carolina: Social History.* Chapel Hill: University of North Carolina, 1937.

Johnson, Jessica Marie. *Wicked Flesh: Black Women, Intimacy, and Freedom in the Atlantic World.* Philadelphia: University of Pennsylvania Press, 2020.

Johnson, Michael P., and James L. Roark. *Black Masters: A Free Family of Color in the Old South.* New York: W. W. Norton, 1984.

―――. *No Chariot Let Down: Charleston's Free People of Color on the Eve of the Civil War.* Chapel Hill: University of North Carolina Press, 1984.

Johnson, Whittington B. *Black Savannah, 1788–1864.* Fayetteville: University of Arkansas Press, 1996.

―――. "Free African-American Women in Savannah, 1800–1860: Affluence and Autonomy amid Adversity." *Georgia Historical Quarterly* 76 (Summer 1992): 260–83.

Johnston, James Hugo. *Race Relations in Virginia and Miscegenation in the South, 1776–1860.* Amherst: University of Massachusetts Press, 1970.

Jones, Bernie D. *Fathers of Conscience: Mixed-Race Inheritance in the Antebellum South.* Athens: University of Georgia Press, 2009.

Jones, Martha S. *Birthright Citizens: A History of Race and Rights in Antebellum America.* New York: Cambridge University Press, 2018.

Jordan, Ervin L. *Black Confederates and Afro-Yankees in Civil War Virginia.* Charlottesville: University Press of Virginia, 1995.

Jordan, Winthrop D. *White over Black: American Attitudes toward the Negro, 1550–1812.* Chapel Hill: University of North Carolina Press, 1968.

Kantrowitz, Stephen. *More Than Freedom: Fighting for Black Citizenship in a White Republic, 1829–1889.* New York: Penguin Press, 2012.

Katz, Ellen D. "African-American Freedom in Antebellum Cumberland County, Virginia." *Chicago-Kent Law Review* 70 (1995): 927–92.

Katzew, Ilona, and Susan Deans-Smith, eds. *Race and Classification: The Case of Mexican America.* Stanford, Calif.: Stanford University Press, 2009.

Kein, Sybil, ed. *Creole: The History and Legacy of Louisiana's Free People of Color.* Baton Rouge: Louisiana State University Press, 2000.

Kennedy, N. Brent, and Robyn Vaughan Kennedy. *The Melungeons: The Resurrection of a Proud People.* Rev. ed. Macon, Ga.: Mercer University Press, 1997.

Kennington, Kelly M. *In the Shadow of Dred Scott: St. Louis Freedom Suits and the Legal Culture of Slavery in Antebellum America*. Athens: University of Georgia Press, 2017.

Kenzer, Robert C. *Enterprising Southerners: Black Economic Success in North Carolina, 1865–1915*. Charlottesville: University Press of Virginia, 1997.

———. *Kinship and Neighborhood in a Southern Community: Orange County, North Carolina, 1849–1881*. Knoxville: University of Tennessee Press, 1987.

"Kidnapping of Free People of Color." National Archives Education Updates. November 12, 2013. https://education.blogs.archives.gov/2013/11/12/kidnapping-of-free-people-of-color/.

Kimmel, Ross M. "Free Blacks in Seventeenth-Century Maryland." *Maryland Historical Magazine* 71 (Spring 1976): 19–25.

King, Stewart R. *Blue Coat or Powdered Wig: Free People of Color in Pre-Revolutionary Saint Domingue*. Athens: University of Georgia Press, 2001.

Kirby, Jack Temple. *Poquosin: A Study of Rural Landscape and Society*. Chapel Hill: University of North Carolina Press, 1995.

Koger, Larry. *Black Slaveowners: Free Black Slave Masters in South Carolina, 1790–1860*. Columbia: University of South Carolina Press, 1985.

Kurtz, Michael J. "Emancipation in the Federal City." *Civil War History* 24 (September 1978): 250–67.

Lachance, Paul F. "The 1809 Immigration of Saint-Domingue Refugees to New Orleans: Reception, Integration and Impact." *Louisiana History* 29 (Spring 1988): 109–41.

———. "The Formation of a Three-Caste Society: Evidence from Wills in Antebellum New Orleans." *Social Science History* 18 (Summer 1994): 211–42.

Landers, Jane G. "Acquisition and Loss on a Spanish Frontier: The Free Black Homesteaders of Florida, 1784–1821." In *Against the Odds: Free Blacks in the Slave Societies of the Americas*, edited by Jane G. Landers, 85–101. New York: Frank Cass, 1996.

———, ed. *Against the Odds: Free Blacks in the Slave Societies of the Americas*. New York: Frank Cass, 1996.

———. *Atlantic Creoles in the Age of Revolutions*. Cambridge, Mass.: Harvard University Press, 2010.

———. *Black Society in Spanish Florida*. Urbana: University of Illinois Press, 1999.

LaRoche, Cheryl Janifer. *Free Black Communities and the Underground Railroad: The Geography of Resistance*. Urbana: University of Illinois Press, 2014.

Latimore, Carey H. *The Role of Southern Free Blacks during the Civil War Era: The Life of Free African Americans in Richmond, Virginia, 1850 to 1876*. Lewiston, N.Y.: Edwin Mellen Press, 2015.

Laurie, Bruce. *Artisans into Workers: Labor in Nineteenth-Century America*. New York: Hill and Wang, 1989.

La Vere, David. *The Tuscarora War: Indians, Settlers, and the Fight for the Carolina Colonies*. Chapel Hill: University of North Carolina, 2013.

Lee, Erika. *America for Americans: A History of Xenophobia in the United States*. New York: Basic Books, 2019.

Lee, Susanna Michele. *Claiming the Union: Citizenship in the Post–Civil War South*. New York: Cambridge University Press, 2014.

Levin, Kevin M. *Searching for Black Confederates: The Civil War's Most Persistent Myth*. Chapel Hill: University of North Carolina Press, 2019.

Levy, Andrew. *The First Emancipator: Slavery, Religion, and the Quiet Revolution of Robert Carter*. New York: Random House, 2005.

Link, William A., David Brown, Brian Ward, and Martyn Bone. *Creating Citizenship in the Nineteenth-Century South*. Gainesville: University Press of Florida, 2013.
Littlefield, Daniel F., and Mary Ann Littlefield. "The Beams Family: Free Blacks in Indian Territory." *Journal of Negro History* 61 (January 1976): 16–35.
Litwack, Leon F. *North of Slavery: The Negro in the Free States, 1790–1860*. Chicago: University of Chicago Press, 1961.
Livesay, Daniel. *Children of Uncertain Fortune: Mixed-Race Jamaicans in Britain and the Atlantic Family, 1733–1833*. Chapel Hill: University of North Carolina Press, 2018.
Loveman, Mara. "Is 'Race' Essential?" *American Sociological Review* 64 (December 1999): 891–98.
———. *National Colors: Racial Classification and the State in Latin America*. New York: Oxford University Press, 2014.
Lowery, Malinda Maynor. *Lumbee Indians in the Jim Crow South: Race, Identity, and the Making of a Nation*. Chapel Hill: University of North Carolina Press, 2010.
Lubet, Steven. *The "Colored Hero" of Harper's Ferry: John Anthony Copeland and the War against Slavery*. New York: Cambridge University Press, 2015.
Lucas, Marion B. *A History of Blacks in Kentucky from Slavery to Segregation, 1760–1891*. 2nd ed. Frankfort: Kentucky Historical Society, 2003.
Luke, Bob, and John David Smith. *Soldiering for Freedom: How the Union Army Recruited, Trained, and Deployed the U.S. Colored Troops*. Baltimore: Johns Hopkins University Press, 2014.
Madden, T. O., Jr. *We Were Always Free: The Maddens of Culpeper County, Virginia: A 200-Year Family History*. New York: W. W. Norton, 1992.
Maddox, Lucy. *The Parker Sisters: A Border Kidnapping*. Philadelphia: Temple University Press, 2016.
Malka, Adam. *The Men of Mobtown: Policing Baltimore in the Age of Slavery and Emancipation*. Chapel Hill: University of North Carolina Press, 2018.
Malone, Christopher. *Between Freedom and Bondage: Race, Party, and Voting Rights in the Antebellum North*. New York: Routledge, 2008.
Mandell, Daniel R. *Tribe, Race, History: Native Americans in Southern New England, 1780–1880*. Baltimore: Johns Hopkins University Press, 2008.
Manning, Chandra. *Troubled Refuge: Struggling for Freedom in the Civil War*. New York: Alfred A. Knopf, 2016.
Mariner, Kirk. *Slave and Free on Virginia's Eastern Shore*. Onancock, Va.: Miona Publications, 2014.
Maris-Wolf, Ted. *Family Bonds: Free Blacks and Re-Enslavement Law in Antebellum Virginia*. Chapel Hill: University of North Carolina Press, 2015.
Marks, John Garrison. *Black Freedom in the Age of Slavery: Race, Status, and Identity in the Urban Americas*. Columbia: University of South Carolina Press, 2020.
———. "Community Bonds in the Bayou City: Free Blacks and Local Reputation in Early Houston." *Southwestern Historical Quarterly* 117 (January 2014): 266–82.
Marotti, Frank. *The Cana Sanctuary: History, Diplomacy, and Black Catholic Marriage in Antebellum St. Augustine Florida*. Tuscaloosa: University of Alabama Press, 2012.
———. *Heaven's Soldiers: Free People of Color and the Spanish Legacy in Antebellum Florida*. Tuscaloosa: University of Alabama Press, 2013.
Marshall, Patricia Phillips, and Jo Ramsay Leimenstoll. *Thomas Day: Master Craftsman and Free Man of Color*. Chapel Hill: University of North Carolina Press, 2010.

Martinez, Jaime Amanda. *Confederate Slave Impressment in the Upper South*. Chapel Hill: University of North Carolina Press, 2013.

"Maryland State Penitentiary." Archives of Maryland. https://msa.maryland.gov/megafile/msa/speccol/sc5400/sc5496/030900/030976/html/030976bio.html.

Mason, Matthew. *Slavery and Politics in the Early American Republic*. Chapel Hill: University of North Carolina Press, 2006.

Masur, Kate. *An Example for All the Land: Emancipation and the Struggle over Equality in Washington, D.C.* Chapel Hill: University of North Carolina Press, 2010.

McCleskey, Turk. *The Road to Black Ned's Forge: A Story of Race, Sex, and Trade on the Colonial American Frontier*. Charlottesville: University of Virginia Press, 2014.

McClintock, Anne. *Imperial Leather: Race, Gender and Sexuality in the Colonial Contest*. New York: Routledge, 1995.

McConnell, Roland C. *Negro Troops of Antebellum Louisiana: A History of the Battalion of Free Men of Color*. Baton Rouge: Louisiana State University Press, 1968.

McKinley, Michelle A. *Fractional Freedoms: Slavery, Intimacy, and Legal Mobilization in Colonial Lima, 1600-1700*. New York: Cambridge University Press, 2016.

McPherson, James M. *Battle Cry of Freedom: The Civil War Era*. New York: Oxford University Press, 1988.

———. *The Negro's Civil War: How American Negroes Felt and Acted during the War for the Union*. Ne York: Pantheon Books, 1965.

Medford, Edna Greene. "'I Was Always a Union Man': The Dilemma of Free Blacks in Confederate Virginia." *Slavery and Abolition* 15 (December 1994): 1-16.

Melish, Joanne Pope. *Disowning Slavery: Gradual Emancipation and "Race" in New England, 1780-1860*. Ithaca, N.Y.: Cornell University Press, 1998.

Merrell, James H. *The Indians' New World: Catawbas and Their Neighbors from European Contact through the Era of Removal*. Chapel Hill: University of North Carolina Press, 1989.

Mezurek, Kelly D. *For Their Own Cause: The 27th United States Colored Troops*. Kent, Ohio: Kent State University Press, 2016.

Middleton, Stephen. *The Black Laws: Race and the Legal Process in Early Ohio*. Athens: Ohio University Press, 2005.

Mills, Gary B. *The Forgotten People: Cane River's Creoles of Color*. Baton Rouge: Louisiana State University Press, 1977.

———. *The Forgotten People: Cane River's Creoles of Color*. Edited and revised by Elizabeth Shown Mills. Baton Rouge: Louisiana State University Press, 2013.

———. "Miscegenation and the Free Negro in Antebellum 'Anglo' Alabama: A Reexamination of Southern Race Relations." *Journal of American History* 68 (June 1981): 16-34.

———. "Patriotism Frustrated: The Native Guards of Confederate Natchitoches." *Louisiana History* 18 (Autumn 1977): 437-51.

Mills, Quincy T. *Cutting along the Color Line: Black Barbers and Barber Shops in America*. Philadelphia: University of Pennsylvania Press, 2013.

Millward, Jessica. *Finding Charity's Folks: Enslaved and Free Black Women in Maryland*. Athens: University of Georgia Press, 2015.

Milteer, Warren E., Jr. "From Indians to Colored People: The Problem of Racial Categories and the Persistence of the Chowans in North Carolina." *North Carolina Historical Review* 93 (January 2016): 28-57.

———. "Life in a Great Dismal Swamp Community: Free People of Color in Pre–Civil War Gates County, North Carolina." *North Carolina Historical Review* 91 (April 2014): 144–70.

———. *North Carolina's Free People of Color, 1715-1885*. Baton Rouge: Louisiana State University Press, 2020.

———. "The Strategies of Forbidden Love: Family across Racial Boundaries in Nineteenth-Century North Carolina." *Journal of Social History* 47 (Spring 2014): 612–26.

Milton, Cynthia E., and Ben Vinson III. "Counting Heads: Race and Non-Native Tribute Policy in Colonial Spanish America." *Journal of Colonialism and Colonial History* 3, no. 3 (2002), doi:10.1353/cch.2002.0056.

Mitchell, Mary Niall. "'A Good and Delicious Country': Free Children of Color and How They Learned to Imagine the Atlantic World in Nineteenth-Century Louisiana." *History of Education Quarterly* 40 (Summer 2000): 123–44.

Monteiro, John M. *Blacks of the Land: Indian Slavery, Settler Society, and the Portuguese Colonial Enterprise in South America*. Translated by James Woodard and Barbara Weinstein. New York: Cambridge University Press, 2018.

Moore, Bob, and Kris Zapalac. "Emancipations." National Park Service. https://www.nps.gov/jeff/learn/historyculture/upload/EMANCIPATIONS.pdf.

Morelli, Federica. *Free People of Color in the Spanish Atlantic: Race and Citizenship, 1780-1850*. New York: Routledge, 2020.

Morgan, Edmund S. *American Slavery, American Freedom: The Ordeal of Colonial Virginia*. New York: W. W. Norton, 1975.

Morgan, Philip D. *Slave Counterpoint: Black Culture in the Eighteenth-Century Chesapeake and Lowcountry*. Chapel Hill: University of North Carolina Press, 1998.

Morris, Christopher. *Becoming Southern: The Evolution of a Way of Life, Warren County and Vicksburg, Mississippi, 1770-1860*. New York: Oxford University Press, 1995.

Morrow, Diane Batts. *Persons of Color and Religious at the Same Time: The Oblate Sisters of Providence, 1828-1860*. Chapel Hill: University of North Carolina Press, 2002.

Myers, Amrita Chakrabarti. *Forging Freedom: Black Women and the Pursuit of Liberty in Antebellum Charleston*. Chapel Hill: University of North Carolina Press, 2011.

Nash, Gary B. *Forging Freedom: The Formation of Philadelphia's Black Community, 1720-1840*. Cambridge, Mass.: Harvard University Press, 1988.

———. *Warner Mifflin: Unflinching Quaker Abolitionist*. Philadelphia: University of Pennsylvania Press, 2017.

Nash, Gary B., and Jean R. Soderlund. *Freedom by Degrees: Emancipation in Pennsylvania and Its Aftermath*. New York: Oxford University Press, 1991.

Neidenbach, Elizabeth Clark. "The Life and Legacy of Marie Couvent: Social Networks, Property Ownership, and the Making of a Free People of Color Community in New Orleans." Ph.D. diss., College of William and Mary, 2015.

———. "'Refugee from St. Domingue Living in This City': The Geography of Social Networks in Testaments of Refugee Free Women of Color in New Orleans." *Journal of Urban History* 42 (2016): 841–62.

Nelson, Bernard H. "Confederate Slave Impressment Legislation, 1861–1865." *Journal of Negro History* 31 (October 1946): 392–410.

———. "Legislative Control of the Southern Free Negro, 1861–1865." *Catholic Historical Review* 32 (April 1946): 28–46.

Nevius, Marcus P. *City of Refuge: Slavery and Petit Marronage in the Great Dismal Swamp, 1763–1856*. Athens: University of Georgia Press, 2020.
Newell, Margaret Ellen. *Brethren by Nature: New England Indians, Colonists, and the Origins of American Slavery*. Ithaca, N.Y.: Cornell University Press, 2015.
Newman, Brooke N. *A Dark Inheritance: Blood, Race, and Sex in Colonial Jamaica*. New Haven, Conn.: Yale University Press, 2018.
Newton, Melanie J. *The Children of Africa in the Colonies: Free People of Color in Barbados in the Age of Emancipation*. Baton Rouge: Louisiana State University Press, 2008.
Nicholls, Michael L. "Creating Identity: Free Blacks and the Law." *Slavery and Abolition* 35 (2014): 214–33.
———. "Passing through This Troublesome World: Free Blacks in the Early Southside." *Virginia Magazine of History and Biography* 92 (January 1984): 50–70.
———. "Strangers Setting among Us: The Sources and Challenge of the Urban Free Black Population of Early Virginia." *Virginia Magazine of History and Biography* 108 (2000): 155–79.
Nordmann, Christopher Andrew. "Free Negroes in Mobile County, Alabama." Ph.D. diss., University of Alabama, 1990.
Null, Druscilla J. "Myrtilla Miner's 'School for Colored Girls': A Mirror on Antebellum Washington." *Records of the Columbia Historical Society, Washington, D.C.* 52 (1989): 254–68.
Oakes, James. *Freedom National: The Destruction of Slavery in the United States, 1861–1865*. New York: W. W. Norton, 2013.
O'Brien, Jean. *Dispossession by Degrees: Indian Land and Identity in Natick, Massachusetts, 1650–1790*. New York: Cambridge University Press, 1997.
———. *Firsting and Lasting: Writing Indians Out of Existence in New England*. Minneapolis: University of Minnesota Press, 2010.
Oubre, Claude F., and Keith P. Fontenot. "Emancipation and Concubinage in Antebellum St. Landry Parish." *Louisiana History* 42 (Autumn 2001): 419–37.
Outland, Robert B., III. *Tapping the Pines: The Naval Stores Industry in the American South*. Baton Rouge: Louisiana State University Press, 2004.
Painter, Nell Irvin. *Southern History across the Color Line*. Chapel Hill: University of North Carolina Press, 2002.
Patterson, Orlando. *Slavery and Social Death: A Comparative Study*. Cambridge, Mass.: Harvard University Press, 1982.
Peabody, Sue. *Madeleine's Children: Family, Freedom, Secrets, and Lies in France's Indian Ocean Colonies*. New York: Oxford University Press, 2017.
Perdue, Theda. *"Mixed Blood" Indians: Racial Construction in the Early South*. Athens: University of Georgia Press, 2003.
Perry, Percival. "The Naval-Stores Industry in the Old South, 1790–1860." *Journal of Southern History* 34 (November 1968): 509–26.
Phillips, Christopher. *Freedom's Port: The African American Community of Baltimore, 1790–1860*. Urbana: University of Illinois Press, 1997.
———. Review of *Israel on the Appomattox: A Southern Experiment in Black Freedom from the 1790s through the Civil War*, by Melvin Patrick Ely. *Journal of American History* (December 2005): 978–79.
Polgar, Paul J. *Standard-Bearers of Equality: America's First Abolition Movement*. Chapel Hill: University of North Carolina Press, 2019.
Power-Greene, Ousmane K. *Against Wind and Tide: The African American Struggle against the Colonization*. New York: New York University Press, 2014.

Provine, Dorothy. "The Economic Position of the Free Blacks in the District of Columbia, 1800–1860." *Journal of Negro History* 58 (January 1973): 61–72.
Pybus, Cassandra. *Epic Journeys of Freedom: Runaway Slaves of the American Revolution and Their Global Quest for Liberty.* Boston: Beacon Press, 2006.
Quarles, Benjamin. *The Negro in the American Revolution.* Chapel Hill: University of North Carolina Press, 1961.
Raboteau, Albert J. *Canaan Land: A Religious History of African Americans.* New York: Oxford University Press, 2001.
Rael, Patrick. *Black Identity and Black Protest in the Antebellum North.* Chapel Hill: University of North Carolina Press, 2002.
Rappaport, Joanne. *The Disappearing Mestizo: Configuring Difference in the Colonial New Kingdom of Granada.* Durham, N.C.: Duke University Press, 2014.
Reid, Richard M. *African Canadians in Union Blue: Volunteering for the Cause in the Civil War.* Vancouver: University of British Columbia Press, 2014.
———. *Freedom for Themselves: North Carolina's Black Soldiers in the Civil War Era.* Chapel Hill: University of North Carolina Press, 2008.
Reid-Vazquez, Michele. *The Year of the Lash: Free People of Color in Cuba and the Nineteenth-Century Atlantic World.* Athens: University of Georgia Press, 2011.
Reséndez, Andrés. *The Other Slavery: The Uncovering Story of Indian Enslavement in America.* Boston: Houghton Mifflin Harcourt, 2016.
Ribianszky, Nik. "'Tell Them That My Dayly Thoughts Are with Them as Though I Was amidst Them All': Friendship among Property-Owning Free People of Color in Nineteenth-Century Natchez, Mississippi." *Journal of Social History* 50 (Summer 2017): 701–19.
Roark, James L., and Michael P. Johnson. Review of *Israel on the Appomattox: A Southern Experiment in Black Freedom from the 1790s through the Civil War*, by Melvin Patrick Ely. *Virginia Magazine of History and Biography* 112 (2004): 428–29.
Rockman, Seth. *Scraping By: Wage Labor, Slavery, and Survival in Early Baltimore.* Baltimore: Johns Hopkins University Press, 2009.
Roediger, David R. *The Wages of Whiteness: Race and the Making of the American Working Class.* London: Verso, 1991.
Rohr, Nancy M. *Free People of Color in Madison County, Alabama.* Huntsville, Ala.: Huntsville History Collection, 2015.
Rohrs, Richard C. "The Free Black Experience in Antebellum Wilmington, North Carolina: Refining Generalizations about Race Relations." *Journal of Southern History* 78 (August 2012): 613–38.
———. "Training in an 'Art, Trade, Mystery and Employment': Opportunity or Exploration of Free Black Apprentices in New Hanover County, North Carolina, 1820–1859?" *North Carolina Historical Review* 90 (April 2013): 127–48.
Rothman, Joshua D. *Notorious in the Neighborhood: Sex and Families across the Color Line in Virginia, 1787–1861.* Chapel Hill: University of North Carolina Press, 2003.
Rountree, Helen C. *Pocahontas's People: The Powhatan Indians of Virginia through Four Centuries.* Norman: University of Oklahoma Press, 1990.
Rountree, Helen C., and Thomas E. Davidson. *Eastern Shore Indians of Virginia and Maryland.* Charlottesville: University Press of Virginia, 1997.
Rushforth, Brett. *Bonds of Alliance: Indigenous and Atlantic Slaveries in New France.* Chapel Hill: University of North Carolina Press, 2012.
Russell, Hilary. "Underground Railroad Activists in Washington, D.C." *Washington History* 13 (Fall/Winter 2001–2): 28–49.

Russell, John Henderson. *The Free Negro in Virginia, 1619-1865*. Baltimore: Johns Hopkins University Press, 1913.

Saunt, Claudio. *Black, White, and Indian: Race and the Unmaking of an American Family*. Oxford: Oxford University Press, 2005.

Sayers, Daniel O. *A Desolate Place for a Defiant People: The Archaeology of Maroons, Indigenous Americans, and Enslaved Laborers in the Great Dismal Swamp*. Gainesville: University Press of Florida, 2014.

Schafer, Judith Kelleher. *Becoming Free, Remaining Free: Manumission and Enslavement in New Orleans, 1846-1862*. Baton Rouge: Louisiana State University Press, 2003.

Schama, Simon. *Rough Crossings: Britain, the Slaves, and the American Revolution*. New York: HarperCollins, 2006.

Schmidt, Ashley K. "Black Revolutionaries: African-American Revolutionary War Pensioners in the Early Republic, 1780-1850." Ph.D. diss., Tulane University, 2018.

Schoeppner, Michael A. *Moral Contagion: Black Atlantic Sailors, Citizenship, and Diplomacy in Antebellum America*. New York: Cambridge University Press, 2019.

Schultz, Mark. *The Rural Face of White Supremacy: Beyond Jim Crow*. Urbana: University of Illinois Press, 2005.

Schweninger, Loren. *Appealing for Liberty: Freedom Suits in the South* (New York: Oxford University Press, 2018.

———. *Black Property Owners in the South, 1790-1915*. Urbana: University of Illinois Press, 1990.

———. *Families in Crisis in the Old South: Divorce, Slavery, and the Law*. Chapel Hill: University of North Carolina Press, 2012.

———. "The Fragile Nature of Freedom: Free Women of Color in the U. S. South." In *Beyond Bondage*, edited by David Barry Gaspar and Darlene Clark Hine, 106-24. Urbana: University of Illinois Press, 2004.

———, ed. *From Tennessee Slave to St. Louis Entrepreneur: The Autobiography of James Thomas*. Columbia: University of Missouri Press, 1984.

———. *James T. Rapier and Reconstruction*. Chicago: University of Chicago Press, 1978.

———. "John Carruthers Stanly and the Anomaly of Black Slaveholding." *North Carolina Historical Review* 67 (April 1990): 159-92.

Scott, Julius S. *The Common Wind: Afro-American Currents in the Age of the Haitian Revolution*. New York: Verso, 2018.

Scott, Rebecca J. and Jean M. Hébrard. *Freedom Papers: An Atlantic Odyssey in the Age of Emancipation*. Cambridge, Mass.: Harvard University Press, 2012.

Sensbach, Jon F. *A Separate Canaan: The Making of an Afro-Moravian World in North Carolina, 1763-1840*. Chapel Hill: University of North Carolina Press, 1998.

Sharfstein, Daniel J. *The Invisible Line: Three American Families and the Secret Journey from Black to White*. New York: Penguin Press, 2011.

Sharp, John. "Washington Navy Yard 1808 Reduction in Force." Washington D.C. Genealogy Trails. June 27, 2008. http://www.genealogytrails.com/washdc/WNY/wny1808rif.html.

Shefveland, Kristalyn Marie. *Anglo-Native Virginia: Trade, Conversion, and Indian Slavery in the Old Dominion, 1646-1722*. Athens: University of Georgia Press, 2016.

Shoemaker, Nancy. *Native American Whalemen and the World: Indigenous Encounters and the Contingency of Race*. Chapel Hill: University of North Carolina Press, 2015.

Shyllon, Folarin. *Black People in Britain, 1555–1833*. London: Oxford University Press, 1977.

Silkenat, David. *Driven from Home: North Carolina's Civil War Refugee Crisis*. Athens: University of Georgia Press, 2016.

Sinha, Manisha. *The Slave's Cause: A History of Abolition*. New Haven, Conn.: Yale University Press, 2016.

Smallwood, Stephanie E. *Saltwater Slavery: A Middle Passage from Africa to American Diaspora*. Cambridge, Mass.: Harvard University Press, 2007.

Smith, David G. *On the Edge of Freedom: The Fugitive Slave Issue in South Central Pennsylvania, 1820–1870*. New York: Fordham University Press, 2013.

Smith, John David. *Black Soldiers in Blue: African American Troops in the Civil War Era*. Chapel Hill: University of North Carolina Press, 2002.

Smith, Troy. "Nations Colliding: The Civil War Comes to Indian Territory." *Civil War History* 59 (September 2013): 279–319.

Snyder, Christina. *Great Crossings: Indians, Settlers, and Slaves in the Age of Jackson*. New York: Oxford University Press, 2017.

———. *Slavery in Indian Country: The Changing Face of Captivity in Early America*. Cambridge, Mass.: Harvard University Press, 2010.

Snyder, Terri L. "Marriage on the Margins: Free Wives, Enslaved Husbands, and the Law in Early Virginia." *Law and History Review* 30 (February 2012): 141–71.

"Solomon Brown: First African American Employee at the Smithsonian Institution." Smithsonian Institution Archives. https://siarchives.si.edu/history/featured-topics/stories/solomon-brown-first-african-american-employee-smithsonian-institution.

Spear, Jennifer M. *Race, Sex, and Social Order in Early New Orleans*. Baltimore: Johns Hopkins University Press, 2009.

Spurgeon, Ian Michael. *Soldiers in the Army of Freedom: The 1st Kansas Colored, the Civil War's First African American Combat Unit*. Norman: University of Oklahoma Press, 2014.

Sterkx, H. E. *The Free Negro in Ante-Bellum Louisiana*. Rutherford, N.J.: Fairleigh Dickinson University Press, 1972.

Stevenson, Brenda E. *Life in Black and White: Family and Community in the Slave South*. New York: Oxford University Press, 1996.

Stewart, Whitney Nell. "Fashioning Frenchness: Gens de Couleur Libres and the Cultural Struggle for Power in Antebellum New Orleans." *Journal of Social History* 51 (Spring 2018): 526–56.

Stewart, Whitney Nell, and John Garrison Marks, eds. *Race and Nation in the Age of Emancipations*. Athens: University of Georgia Press, 2018.

Stoler, Ann Laura. *Carnal Knowledge and Imperial Power: Race and the Intimate in Colonial Rule*. Rev. ed. Berkley: University of California Press, 2010.

Sumler-Edmond, Janice L. "Free Black Life in Savannah." In *Slavery and Freedom in Savannah*, edited by Leslie M. Harris and Daina Ramey Berry, 124–39. Athens: University of Georgia Press, 2014.

———. *The Secret Trust of Aspasia Cruvellier Mirault: The Life and Trials of a Free Woman of Color in Antebellum Georgia*. Fayetteville: University of Arkansas Press, 2008.

Sweet, John Wood. *Bodies Politic: Negotiating Race in the American North, 1730–1830*. Baltimore: Johns Hopkins University Press, 2003.

Tansey, Richard. "Out-of-State Free Blacks in Late Antebellum New Orleans." *Louisiana History* 22 (Autumn 1981): 369–86.

Tavárez, David. "Legally Indian: Inquisitorial Readings of Indigenous Identity in New Spain." In *Imperial Subjects: Race and Identity in Colonial Latin America*, edited by Andrew B. Fischer and Matthew D. O'Hara, 81–100. Durham, N.C.: Duke University Press, 2009.

Taylor, Alan. *American Colonies*. New York: Viking Penguin, 2001.

———. *American Revolutions: A Continental History, 1750–1804*. New York: W. W. Norton, 2016.

Taylor, Amy Murrell. *Embattled Freedom: Journeys through the Civil War's Slave Refugee Camps*. Chapel Hill: University of North Carolina Press, 2018.

Taylor, Elizabeth Dowling. *A Slave in the White House: Paul Jennings and the Madisons*. New York: St. Martin's Press, 2012.

Taylor, Nikki M. *Frontiers of Freedom: Cincinnati's Black Community, 1802–1868*. Athens: Ohio University Press, 2005.

Thompson, Shirley Elizabeth. *Exiles at Home: The Struggle to Become American in Creole New Orleans*. Cambridge, Mass.: Harvard University Press, 2009.

———. "'Mon Cher Dupré': Interracial Marriage, Property, and Affect in Antebellum New Orleans." *Louisiana History* 58 (Spring 2017): 217–36.

Trent, Hank. *The Secret Life of Bacon Tait, a White Slave Trader Married to a Free Woman of Color*. Baton Rouge: Louisiana State University Press, 2017.

Troxler, Harrison Anthony. *Slavery in Missouri, 1804–1865*. Baltimore: Johns Hopkins University Press, 1914.

Twinam, Ann. *Purchasing Whiteness: Pardos, Mulattos, and the Quest for Social Mobility in the Spanish Indies*. Stanford, Calif.: Stanford University Press, 2015.

Twitty, Anne. *Before Dred Scott: Slavery and Legal Culture in the American Confluence, 1787–1857*. New York: Cambridge University Press, 2016.

Tyler-McGraw, Marie. *An African Republic: Black and White Virginians in the Making of Liberia*. Chapel Hill: University of North Carolina Press, 2007.

Ulentin, Anne. "Shades of Grey: Slaveholding Free Women of Color in Antebellum New Orleans, 1800–1840." Ph.D. diss., Louisiana State University, 2012.

Vandervelde, Lea. *Redemption Songs: Suing for Freedom before Dred Scott*. New York: Oxford University Press, 2014.

van Deusen, Nancy E. *Global Indios: The Indigenous Struggle for Justice in Sixteenth-Century Spain*. Durham, N.C.: Duke University Press, 2015.

Vaughn, Curtis L. "Freedom Is Not Enough: African Americans in Antebellum Fairfax County." Ph.D. diss., George Mason University, 2014.

Vidal, Cécile. *Caribbean New Orleans: Empire, Race, and the Making of a Slave Society*. Chapel Hill: University of North Carolina Press, 2019.

Vincent, Stephen A. *Southern Seed, Northern Soil: African-American Farm Communities in the Midwest, 1765–1900*. Bloomington: Indiana University Press, 1999.

Vinson, Ben, III. *Bearing Arms for His Majesty: The Free-Colored Militia in Colonial Mexico*. Stanford, Calif.: Stanford University Press, 2001.

von Daacke, Kirt. *Freedom Has a Face: Race, Identity, and Community in Jefferson's Virginia*. Charlottesville: University of Virginia Press, 2012.

Von Frank, Albert J. *The Trials of Anthony Burns: Freedom and Slavery in Emerson's Boston*. Cambridge, Mass.: Harvard University Press, 1998.

Wade, Richard C. *Slavery in the Cities: The South, 1820–1860*. New York: Oxford University Press, 1964.

Walker, Christine. *Jamaica Ladies: Female Slaveholders and the Creation of Britain's Atlantic Empire*. Chapel Hill: University of North Carolina Press, 2020.

Walker, Juliet E. K. *Free Frank: A Black Pioneer on the Antebellum Frontier*. Lexington: University of Kentucky Press, 1983.
Wallenstein, Peter. *Tell the Court I Love My Wife: Race, Marriage, and Law—An American History*. New York: Palgrave Macmillan, 2002.
Wanhalla, Angela. *In/Visible Sight: The Mixed-Descent Families of Southern New Zealand*. Wellington, New Zealand: Athabasca University Press, 2010.
Warde, Mary Jane. *When the Wolf Came: The Civil War and the Indian Territory*. Fayetteville: University of Arkansas Press, 2013.
Warner, Lee H. *Free Men in an Age of Servitude: Three Generations of a Black Family*. Lexington: University Press of Kentucky, 1992.
Watson, Alan D. *Society in Colonial North Carolina*. Rev. ed. Raleigh: Office of Archives and History, 1996.
Welch, Kimberly M. *Black Litigants in the Antebellum South*. Chapel Hill: University of North Carolina Press, 2018.
———. "Black Litigiousness and White Accountability: Free Blacks and the Rhetoric of Reputation in the Antebellum Natchez District." *Journal of the Civil War Era* 5 (September 2015): 372–98.
Welch, Pedro L. V., and Richard A. Goodridge. *"Red" and Black over White: Free Coloured Women in Pre-Emancipation Barbados*. Bridgetown, Barbados: Carib Research and Publications, 2000.
Wesley, Charles H. "Negro Suffrage in the Period of Constitution-Making, 1787–1865." *Journal of Negro History* 32 (April 1947): 143–68.
West, Emily. *Family or Freedom: People of Color in the Antebellum South*. Lexington: University Press of Kentucky, 2012.
Wheat, David. *Atlantic Africa and the Spanish Caribbean, 1570–1640*. Chapel Hill: University of North Carolina Press, 2016.
Wheeler, Roxann. *The Complexion of Race: Categories of Difference in Eighteenth-Century British Culture*. Philadelphia: University of Pennsylvania Press, 2000.
White, Christine Schultz, and Benton R. White. *Now the Wolf Has Come: The Creek Nation in the Civil War*. College Station: Texas A&M University Press, 1996.
White, Deborah Gray. *Ar'n't I a Woman? Female Slaves in the Plantation South*. New York: W. W. Norton, 1985.
Whitman, T. Stephen. *Challenging Slavery in the Chesapeake: Black and White Resistance to Human Bondage, 1775–1865*. Baltimore: Maryland Historical Society, 2007.
———. *The Price of Freedom: Slavery and Manumission in Baltimore and Early National Maryland*. Lexington: University Press of Kentucky, 1997.
Whitten, David O. *Andrew Durnford: A Black Sugar Planter in the Antebellum South*. Natchitoches, La.: Northwestern State University Press, 1981.
Wikramanayake, Marina. *A World in Shadow: The Free Black in Antebellum South Carolina*. Columbia: University of South Carolina Press, 1973.
Wilkinson, A. B. *Blurring the Lines of Race and Freedom: Mulattoes and Mixed Bloods in English Colonial America*. Chapel Hill: University of North Carolina Press, 2020.
Williams, William H. *Slavery and Freedom in Delaware, 1639–1865*. Wilmington, Del.: Scholarly Resources, 1996.
Williamson, Joel. *New People: Miscegenation and Mulattoes in the United States*. New York: Free Press, 1980.
Wilson, Carol. *Freedom at Risk: The Kidnapping of Free Blacks in America, 1780–1865*. Lexington: University Press of Kentucky, 1994.

Wilson, Kathleen. *The Island Race: Englishness, Empire and Gender in the Eighteenth Century*. London: Routledge, 2003.

———, ed. *A New Imperial History: Culture, Identity and Modernity in Britain and the Empire, 1660–1840*. Cambridge: Cambridge University Press, 2004.

Wilson, Keith P. *Campfires of Freedom: The Camp Life of Black Soldiers during the Civil War*. Kent, Ohio: Kent State University Press, 2002.

Winch, Julie. *Between Slavery and Freedom: Free People of Color in America from Settlement to the Civil War*. Lanham, Md.: Rowman and Littlefield, 2014.

———. *The Clamorgans: One Family's History of Race in America*. New York: Hill and Wang, 2011.

———. *Philadelphia's Black Elite: Activism, Accommodation, and the Struggle for Autonomy, 1787–1848*. Philadelphia: Temple University Press, 1988.

Wolf, Eva Sheppard. *Almost Free: A Story about Family and Race in Antebellum Virginia*. Athens: University of Georgia Press, 2012.

———. *Race and Liberty in the New Nation: Emancipation in Virginia from the Revolution to Nat Turner's Rebellion*. Baton Rouge: Louisiana State University Press, 2006.

Wood, Gordon S. *Empire of Liberty: A History of the Early Republic, 1789–1815*. New York: Oxford University Press, 2009.

Wood, Nicholas. "'A Sacrifice on the Altar of Slavery': Doughface Politics and Black Disfranchisement in Pennsylvania, 1837–1838." *Journal of the Early Republic* 32 (Spring 2011): 75–106.

Woodward, C. Vann. "*Strange Career* Critics: Long May They Persevere." *Journal of American History* 75 (December 1988): 857–68.

———. *The Strange Career of Jim Crow: A Commemorative Edition*. New York: Oxford University Press, 2002.

Woodward, Colin Edward. *Marching Masters: Slavery, Race, and the Confederate Army during the Civil War*. Charlottesville: University of Virginia Press, 2014.

Wormley, G. Smith. "Myrtilla Miner." *Journal of Negro History* 5 (October 1920): 448–57.

Wright, James M. *The Free Negro in Maryland, 1634–1860*. New York: Columbia University Press, 1921.

Yamanaka, Mishio. "'Separation Is Not Equality': The Racial Desegregation Movement of Creoles of Color in New Orleans, 1862–1900." Ph.D. diss., University of North Carolina at Chapel Hill, 2018.

Yarbrough, Fay A. "Power, Perception, and Interracial Sex: Former Slaves Recall a Multiracial South." *Journal of Southern History* 71 (August 2005): 559–88.

———. *Race and the Cherokee Nation*. Philadelphia: University of Pennsylvania Press, 2008.

Yellin, Jean Fagan. *Harriet Jacobs, a Life: The Remarkable Adventures of the Woman Who Wrote Incidents in the Life of a Slave Girl*. New York: Basic Civitas Books, 2004.

Young, Mary. "Racism in Red and Black: Indians and Other Free People of Color in Georgia Law, Politics, and Removal Policy." *Georgia Historical Quarterly* 73 (Fall 1989): 492–518.

Zipf, Karin L. *Labor of Innocents: Forced Apprenticeship in North Carolina, 1715–1919*. Baton Rouge: Louisiana State University Press, 2005.

GENERAL INDEX

abolitionists, 3, 39–41, 71, 148–50, 203, 248; backlash to, 169, 234–35; societies of, 40, 98–99, 196
Accomack County, Va., 7, 17, 28, 42, 47, 74, 116, 166, 213
Africa, 2, 8, 13–14, 16, 47, 51, 204; colonization of, 84–85, 151, 172, 183, 207–8; Congo, 35, 51, 120; Liberia, 84–86, 151, 172, 183
Alabama, 7, 112, 192, 225, 229, 231, 253; laws of, 75, 81, 95, 153–54, 171; population of, 166, 180; slavery in, 101, 109. *See also specific towns and counties*
Alamance County, N.C., 229, 231–32
Alexandria, D.C. *See* District of Columbia
Alexandria, La., 223
Alexandria, Va., 57, 236
Alexandria County, Va., 161, 211
Amelia County, Va., 28
Annapolis, Md., 152, 190
Anne Arundel County, Md., 44, 46, 52, 110, 148, 216
Appomattox County, Va., 226
apprenticeship, 14–15, 25–32, 57–58, 78, 92–93, 115, 129, 135, 152, 208, 211, 216–17
Arkansas, 7, 98, 166, 176, 180–81; laws of, 100, 154, 170–71
Atlanta, Ga., 7
Augusta, Ga., 89, 110–11, 131

Baltimore, Md., 7–8, 37–38, 44, 110, 175, 235, 237, 242; churches in, 120, 122, 152, 195; economy in, 130–31; education in, 124, 200–202, 204; illicit slave trade in, 99, 101; immigration to, 51, 63; population of, 182; social organizations in, 206–9
Baltimore County, Md., 26, 58, 83, 108, 116, 160, 182

Barnwell County, S.C., 217
Barnwell District, S.C., 134
Bath County, N.C., 27
Baton Rouge, La., 134, 232
Beaufort County, N.C., 239
Beaufort County, S.C., 243
Beaufort District, S.C., 64, 169
Bertie County, N.C., 26, 109
Bertie Precinct, N.C., 27
Bladen County, N.C., 33, 106, 190
Boonville, Mo., 98
Botetourt County, Va., 144
Brandywine, Del., 134
Bristol, Va., 230
Brown Fellowship Society, 122–23, 206, 231
Brownsville, Tex., 236
Brunswick County, N.C., 160
Brunswick County, Va., 53, 140
Buckingham County, Va., 98

Canada, 149, 178; Nova Scotia, 54
Caroline County, Md., 41, 108, 195
Carroll County, Md., 146
Carteret County, N.C., 157
Cecil County, Md., 45, 57, 214, 236
Charles City County, Va., 30, 122, 191, 226, 242
Charles County, Md., 34, 117, 128, 239
Charleston, Ind., 235
Charleston, S.C., 7–8, 28, 38, 42, 45, 52, 211; churches in, 88, 121, 197; commerce in, 130–33, 196, 228; discriminatory regulations in, 61–64; education in, 124, 126; population of, 55, 75; segregation in, 6, 95–96, 122; social organizations in, 124, 206, 230–31
Charlotte County, Va., 82–83
Charlottesville, Va., 224
Chatham County, Ga., 62, 89

{ 343 }

Cherokee Nation, 9, 78, 162, 164, 166–67, 181
Chestertown, Md., 40, 190
Chi Nation, 50
Chickasaw Nation, 9, 162, 167, 181
Choctaw Nation, 9, 166–67, 181
Chowan people, 9
Civil War, 220–49; atrocities during, 227–28; battles of, 224, 233, 237, 240, 245; free people of color collaborating with rebels, 228–33; free people of color resisting rebels, 224–28, 243–44; rebel impressment of free people of color, 223–27; soldiers' aid societies, 246; U.S. military service of free people of color, 235–42
Clear Spring, Md., 121
Code Noir, 21, 24
Colleton County, S.C., 17, 33, 57
courts, 1–2, 4, 41, 74, 98–102, 113–15, 222–23; during the late antebellum period, 209–18; during the Turner Rebellion, 137, 139–145; testimony in, 90–91, 172. *See also* apprenticeship; freedom suits; registration
Craven County, N.C., 16, 47, 96–98, 157
Craven County, S.C., 17
Creek Nation, 9, 181, 190
Cuba, 50, 65, 78, 106
Cumberland County, N.C., 30, 156, 222
Cumberland County, Va., 45
Currituck County, N.C., 241
Currituck Precinct, N.C., 25, 34

Danville, Ky., 240
Danville, Va., 229
Darien, Ga., 89, 230
Davidson County, Tenn., 117, 148, 183
Deep South: illicit slave trade in, 98, 102; population of, 7, 54–55, 105, 153, 166–67, 180–81, 183; wealth accumulation in, 8, 11, 193. *See also specific states, towns, and counties*
Delaware, 6–7, 52, 104–5, 118, 122, 124, 126–28; antislavery activism in, 39–40; during the Civil War, 221, 234, 236–37, 239; colonization movement in, 84, 207; commerce in, 131–32, 134; discriminatory laws of, 20, 23, 60–61, 163–64; education in, 202–3; illicit slave trade in, 98–102; immigration to, 51, 77, 167–68; justice system in, 212–14; liberation in, 43–44, 47, 76; population of, 54–55, 181; poverty in, 92, 185; reaction to the Turner Rebellion in, 152–55, 194; servitude in, 27, 29–30, 48; slavery in, 149–50. *See also specific towns and counties*
Dinwiddie County, Va., 55, 226, 241
discrimination: in the courts, 2, 23–24, 90–91, 213; in criminal punishment, 12, 20, 61, 93, 143–44, 152, 162–64; in legislation, 61–62, 82–83, 144–45; in taxation, 21–22, 61, 66, 91, 150–51, 162, 217–18. *See also* guardianship; parental rights; registration; segregation; voting rights
District of Columbia, 108, 115–17, 148, 190, 220–21, 237; antislavery activities in, 149; churches in, 118, 121, 195–96, 198; commerce in, 129–30, 132, 134–35; economic competition in, 8, 176–77; education in, 126, 165, 201–3; immigration to, 51; laws of, 94, 141, 158, 213; population of, 6–7, 76, 181–82; riot in, 176–78; segregation in, 235; social organizations in, 208–9, 246
Dorchester County, Md., 83, 149, 207, 234, 236–37
Dover, Del., 40, 44, 150, 155

East Indians, 16, 28, 47, 53, 120
Easton, Md., 131
Easton, Pa., 204
Edenton, N.C., 21, 47, 139–40, 145
Edgecombe County, N.C., 16, 22
Edgefield District, S.C., 169
education, 124–27, 200–204, 250, 253–54; through apprenticeship, 27–28, 93; exclusion of free people of color from, 164–65; of freedpeople, 246–47; fundraising for, 204, 208; medical training, 55; in the military, 239–40
Elbert County, Ga., 74
Elizabeth City, N.C., 241
Elkton, Md., 101
employment, 33–34, 127–35, 189–92; competition between people of color

and whites, 95, 175–77, 207; on waterways, 95, 192, 229
enslaved people, 12–24, 28–39, 41–51, 55, 57–66, 208, 214; during the Civil War, 245–47; in courts, 90–91; education of, 164–65, 203; labor competition with, 174–76; laws concerning, 73–79, 93, 159, 162; rebellion of, 117–18. *See also* manumission; slavery
Escambia County, Fla., 159

Fairfax County, Va., 145, 148, 211, 224
family, 13, 54, 166, 188, 216–17; endogamy, 106–7; family bonds during the Civil War, 235, 240–41; family business, 132; with free and enslaved members, 31, 45, 85, 88, 107–11, 171, 184, 214; histories of, 46–47, 218; with members of color and white, 1–2, 5, 25–26, 30, 111–16, 231. *See also* marriage
Fauquier County, Va., 171, 223–24
Fayette, Mo., 173
Fayetteville, N.C., 62, 120–21, 158, 223, 228, 230, 243, 250
Federalist Party, 70, 77, 94, 275n5
Florida, 5, 17–18, 33–34, 50, 117, 237, 241; laws of, 75–76, 78, 81, 89–90, 93, 153, 158–59, 170–71; population of, 7, 180; West Florida, 50, 59. *See also specific towns and counties*
Fort Fisher, N.C., 237
Fort Macon, N.C., 239
Fort Monroe, Va., 237, 239, 247
Fort Sumter, S.C., 221, 225
Franklin County, N.C., 52
Frederick, Md., 94, 208
Frederick County, Md., 30, 83, 188, 208, 239
Frederick County, Va., 7
Fredericksburg, Va., 43, 130, 161, 177, 233
freedom suits, 29–30, 46–50, 211

Gates County, N.C., 115
gender, 2, 5, 14, 33, 92, 115; discrimination based on, 19–24, 60, 66, 121; gendered labor, 27, 127, 131–32
Georgetown, D.C. *See* District of Columbia

Georgetown, S.C., 63, 64
Georgia, 7, 53, 146, 180, 253; discriminatory laws of, 20–21, 60–65, 87–90, 92, 154, 162, 165–66, 171, 222–23; manumission in, 17–18, 42, 74–75; population of, 54–55; registration laws of, 82–83; seamen's law of, 78, 80; slave traders from, 97, 102. *See also specific towns and counties*
Gingaskin people, 9
Gloucester County, Va., 15
Goochland County, Va., 45, 83
Granville County, N.C., 7, 22, 33–34, 106, 117, 212
Great Dismal Swamp, 191
Greene County, N.C., 157
Greenville District, S.C., 169
guardianship, 87–90, 158, 222–23
Guilford County, N.C., 96, 203

Hagerstown, Md., 94, 131
Haiti, 71, 73, 103, 204; Haitian Revolution, 63, 72–73, 104, 106. *See also* Hispaniola; Saint-Domingue
Halifax, N.C., 53
Halifax County, N.C., 7, 117, 128, 156
Hampton Institute, 254
Hanover County, Va., 62, 72
Harford County, Md., 44, 108, 208, 237
healthcare: during the Civil War, 237–39; practitioners of, 33, 55, 129–30, 188, 226
Henrico County, Va., 45, 53, 62, 72, 217, 244
Hertford County, N.C., 7, 90–91, 117, 188, 195, 239
Hispaniola, 51, 77. *See also* Haiti; Saint-Domingue
Hyde County, N.C., 240

Iberville Parish, La., 193
Illinois, 27, 85
immigration: from the Caribbean, 51, 63–65, 105–6; from Europe, 16, 113, 174; and port cities, 80–81; restrictions on, 24, 63–65, 76–81, 102–3, 109, 152–54, 165–67, 171, 192; from South Asia, 16
Indian Territory, 7, 162, 166, 181, 190, 204, 220, 227

GENERAL INDEX { 345

Indians, 19, 47, 162; ancestry, 16, 47, 168, 211; discrimination against, 21–24, 61, 90; exemption from discrimination for, 78–80; manumission of, 17, 50; as a racial category, 8–10, 217–18; as servants, 26, 28–30. *See also* East Indians; indigenous nations
Indiana, 81, 85, 96, 235, 250
indigenous nations, 9–10, 220. *See also names of specific nations*
Isle of France, 51
Isle of Wight County, Va., 7, 98, 140–42, 144

James City County, Va., 7, 31, 134–35
Jefferson County, Ky., 81, 183, 235, 237
Jefferson County, Miss., 218
Jefferson Parish, La., 193, 210–11
Jim Crow, 6, 254–56
Johnston County, N.C., 98, 224

Kansas, 170, 227
Kent County, Del., 27, 30, 40, 47, 149, 164, 168, 236, 239
Kent County, Md., 26, 28–29
Kentucky, 94, 133, 148, 187, 196, 201, 214; during the Civil War, 221, 235, 237, 240, 246; immigration restrictions of, 77, 81, 165, 171–72; laws of, 61, 7689, 95, 154, 158; newspapers of, 174; population of, 6–7, 183. *See also specific towns and counties*
Kershaw District, S.C., 169
kidnapping, 97–102, 227–28
King George County, Va., 141
King William County, Va., 74, 227

Lancaster County, Va., 28, 31, 144
Lenoir County, N.C., 150
Lexington, Ky., 133
Lexington County, S.C., 243
Little Rock, Ark., 154, 176
Liverpool, England, 16
Louisa County, Va., 145
Louisiana, 5–8, 52–54, 106–7, 113; during the Civil War, 223, 227, 229, 232, 236, 238, 241–42, 246–48; commerce in, 33, 134, 179, 193; discriminatory laws of, 20–21, 81, 93, 95, 99, 114–15, 154, 167, 171; education in, 204; justice system in, 210–11; liberation in, 17, 24, 38, 49–50; population of, 105, 180; during Reconstruction, 253; religious institutions in, 120–21, 186, 198, 200–201; slavery in, 59, 65, 128, 245; during the War of 1812, 117. *See also* Orleans Territory *and specific towns and counties*
Louisiana Purchase, 105. *See also* Louisiana
Loudoun County, Va., 146–48, 161, 226, 236
Louisville, Ky., 7, 81, 174, 183–84, 187, 196, 201, 246
Lunenburg County, Va., 129
Lynchburg, Va., 161, 165, 197

Macon, Ga., 131
manumission, 15–18, 38–50, 62, 67, 69, 105, 182–83; and family, 107–8; restrictions on, 24, 72–77, 88, 110, 140, 161
Marion, Va., 230
Marlboro District, S.C., 218, 225
marriage: and the church, 35, 186; divorce, 212; between free people of color, 106–7, 254; intermarriage, 19–21, 161–62; and women's rights, 32
Martinique, 51
Maryland, 6–7, 10, 15–16, 18, , 108–12, 116–24, 168–71, 195–96; during the Civil War, 221, 225, 229, 234–40; colonization movement in, 84–85; commerce in, 34, 128, 130–31, 134–35, 187–88, 190, 192; discriminatory laws of, 21, 23, 60, 82–83, 90, 92–94, 152, 160; education in, 127; election laws of, 60; illicit slave trade in, 97, 99–102; immigration to, 51, 77, 166; justice system in, 214–17; liberation in, 37, 40–41, 44–47; political and social organizations in, 207–9; population of, 54, 76, 105, 181–82; poverty in, 185; segregation in, 95–96; servitude in, 20, 57–58, 25–30; slavery in, 146, 148–49. *See also specific towns and counties*
Maryville, Tenn., 243

Mattamuskeet people, 9
Mecklenburg County, Va., 42, 45, 72, 81, 83, 102, 143, 145
Mercer County, Ky., 187, 214
Mexico, 159, 166, 204
Michigan, 85
Milton, N.C., 134
Mississippi, 7–8, 217–18, 245, 250; commerce in, 132–33, 189, 194; discriminatory laws of, 81–82, 89, 93–95, 153; enslavement and removal in, 153, 170–71, 222; illicit slave trade in, 99, 101; immigration restrictions of, 78; population of, 75, 166–67, 180. *See also specific towns and counties*
Missouri, 6–7, 98, 129, 173, 183, 189–90, 197–98, 246; laws of, 76, 100, 154, 164, 170, 221. *See also specific towns and counties*
Mobile, Ala., 7, 53, 59, 121
Mobile County, Ala., 112, 229
Montgomery, Ala., 231

Nansemond County, Va., 1, 7, 21, 98, 188, 236, 240, 242, 244
Nashville, Tenn., 133, 148, 173, 183, 195, 201–2, 244
Natchez, Miss., 7, 132–33, 189, 218, 245
Natchitoches, La., 232
Natchitoches Parish, La., 242, 245
New Bern, N.C., 53, 133, 150, 202, 206, 241
New Castle, Del., 124
New Castle County, Del., 27, 29–30, 43, 99, 150, 168, 181
New Hanover County, N.C., 43, 109
New Kent County, Va., 35
New Orleans, 7–8, 17, 53, 103, 113–15, 208, 211; during the Civil War, 232, 238, 245–48; commerce in, 27, 55, 59, 129–30, 135, 179, 190; discriminatory ordinances of, 91; education in, 204, 247; immigration to, 38, 77–78, 167; political newspapers in, 174, 248, 253; public transportation in, 168; religious institutions in, 121, 186, 198, 200; under the Spanish, 49–50; during the War of 1812, 117–18
Newberry District, S.C., 169

Norfolk, Va., 38, 53, 63, 114, 132, 140, 165, 195, 211, 236, 238
Norfolk County, Va., 7, 29, 32, 140, 142–43, 218, 224, 237, 244
North Carolina, 15–16, 33–35, 52–54, 96–100, 111, 113–12, 115–18, 177–78, 202–7; antislavery activism in, 39–40; during the Civil War, 224–33, 236–37, 239–41, 243; colonization movement in, 85, 172; commerce in, 128, 130, 133–34, 188, 190–92; discriminatory laws of, 20–27, 41, 47–49, 60, 90–94, 162–66, 169–70, 222–23; disfranchisement in, 155–58; education in, 126, 250, 254; immigration to, 64, 78, 81; justice system in, 211–12, 215–16; manumission in, 43, 45, 76; population of, 6–7, 105–6, 182–83; reaction to the Turner Rebellion in, 139–40, 145–46, 150–52; religious institutions in, 120, 186, 194–95; servitude in, 30–31, 58; weapons restrictions in, 160. *See also specific towns and counties*
Northampton County, N.C., 22, 34, 85, 116–17
Northampton County, Va., 13, 21, 31–32, 151
Northumberland County, Va., 52, 118
Northwest Territory, 71, 85
Nottoway people, 10
Nova Scotia, 54

Obion County, Tenn., 156
Ohio, 77, 85, 146, 148, 165, 170, 178, 204, 225, 244
Onslow County, N.C., 169
Orange County, N.C., 134, 233
Orleans Territory, 77–78, 89, 93. *See also Louisiana*

Pamunkey people, 10, 168
parental rights, 19–20, 58, 92–93
Paris, Ky., 187
Pasquotank County, N.C., 7, 31, 43, 45, 111, 239
Patrick County, Va., 96
Pensacola, Fla., 7, 53, 159, 232
Perquimans County, N.C., 39, 157, 241

Perquimans Precinct, N.C., 26–27
Person County, N.C., 166, 186
Petersburg, Va., 7, 72–73, 85, 103, 114, 122, 165; during the Civil War, 237, 240; domestic violence in, 212; employment in, 128–30, 132; registration in, 82–83, 140
Pittsylvania County, Va., 144
Plaquemines Parish, La., 128, 193
Pointe Coupee Parish, La., 33, 227, 241
politics: Democratic Party, 169–70, 173; Jeffersonian Republican Party, 70, 93–94, 102; proslavery, 3, 62, 70–76, 79, 82, 88, 91–97, 150–78, 220–21; Whig Party, 172–73
Portsmouth, Va., 140, 211
Prince Edward County, Va., 141
Prince George's County, Md., 28, 135, 160
Princess Anne County, Va., 139–41, 143, 145

Quakers, 39–40, 42–43, 85, 195, 203
Queen Anne's County, Md., 15, 25, 127, 149, 185–86

racial categories, 8–10, 79–80, 217–18
railroad, 168, 192
Raleigh, N.C., 126, 177–78, 190
Reconstruction, 250–54
registration, 61–62, 82–83, 144–45
religion: African Methodist Episcopal, 88, 118–20, 130, 195–96, 198, 201; Anglican, 35; baptism, 35, 197; Baptist, 118, 120, 122, 187, 195–96, 197–98, 200; Catholic, 35, 120–21, 186, 200–202, 204, 206; free people of color as congregants and clergy, 118–23, 194–202; Episcopal, 118, 121–22, 197; Methodist, 40, 118, 120, 122; Methodist Episcopal, 121, 195; Moravian, 118; Nicholites, 40; Presbyterian, 118, 120, 187, 195–96, 209; discrimination within, 121–22, 195–97; Society of Friends, 120; Spiritualism, 200–201; Wesleyan, 209; Zion, 122. *See also* Quakers
Revolutionary War, 1, 52–54, 116–17
Richmond, Va., 7, 63, 113, 145; churches in, 121–22, 195, 198, 200; during the Civil War, 225–26, 230, 241–43; law enforcement in, 163, 168; manumission in, 44, 74, 108, 140; organizations in, 85, 206; segregation in, 96, 121–22
Richmond County, Ga., 75, 89, 166, 222
Richmond County, N.C., 243
Richmond County, Va., 225
Roanoke Island, N.C., 223, 241
Robeson County, N.C., 7, 106, 117, 163, 211, 225, 232–33
Rockbridge County, Va., 144

Saint Augustine, Fla., 18, 33–35, 117, 128, 200, 241
Saint-Domingue, 3, 38, 51, 63–65, 71, 76–78, 104, 113, 135, 200. *See also* Haiti; Hispaniola
Saint Landry Parish, La., 7, 59, 106, 193
Saint Louis, Mo., 7, 170, 178, 183–84, 189–90, 197, 208, 246
Saint Louis County, Mo., 183
Saint Martin Parish, La., 223
Saint Mary's County, Md., 29, 77
Saline County, Mo., 98
Sampson County, N.C., 216
Santa Rosa County, Fla., 159
Savannah, Ga., 16, 18, 28, 89, 121, 228; commerce in, 129, 131–32; discrimination in, 61–65, 83, 91; education in, 165; immigration to, 38, 51; population of, 7, 55; during the Revolutionary War, 52
Scott County, Va., 131
segregation, 5–6, 12, 184–86; activism against, 248; in cemeteries, 95, 122, 206; during the Jim Crow era, 255–56; in the military, 34, 53; in public spaces, 96, 235
Seminole Nation, 9, 181
Seven Years' War, 38, 49, 50
Shaw University, 254
Shreveport, La., 232
slavery: escape from, 110–11, 146–50; slaveholding by free people of color, 32–33, 51, 89, 108, 110, 121, 128, 133–34, 193–94, 245; slave trade, 39, 97–102, 108, 182. *See also* enslaved people; manumission
Smithsonian Institution, 190
Snow Riot, 176–78

social organizations for free people of color, 122–24, 126, 204, 206–9
Somerset County, Md., 27, 47, 166
South Carolina, 28, 52, 95–97, 175, 197, 230, 243, 253; commerce in, 8, 228, 131–34, 190, 194; discriminatory laws of, 20, 23, 60–61, 63–66, 153, 162, 164, 169–71; elite free people of color in, 32–33; guardianship laws of, 87–88, 110; immigration and travel to, 77–81, 211; kidnapping laws of, 100; manumission in, 17, 24, 42, 45, 57, 75; politics in, 173; population of, 7, 54–55, 75, 180; racial categorization in, 217–18; rebel impressment in, 223, 225. *See also specific towns and counties*
Southampton County, Va., 7, 41, 137, 140–42, 144–46, 150, 176
Spanish Empire, 11, 13–15, 38, 59, 65, 159, 180; manumission in, 17–18, 49–50; military service in, 5–6, 34, 117, 52–54; religion in, 35; taxation in, 21
Staunton, Va., 144
Surry County, Va., 7, 22, 53, 140, 145
Sussex County, Del., 98, 100–102, 181, 185, 212, 214–15, 237
Sussex County, Va., 140

Talbot County, Md., 95–96, 121, 208, 238
Tappahannock, Va., 54
Tennessee, 6, 71, 94, 98, 117, 133, 187; during the Civil War, 225, 230, 243–44; commerce in, 133; discriminatory laws of, 82–83, 92, 169–71; disfranchisement in, 155–56; economic competition in, 176; immigration to, 153; manumission laws of, 76; population of, 183; slavery in, 148. *See also specific towns and counties*
Texas, 7, 180, 189, 227–28, 231, 237, 242; laws of, 166, 171
Turner Rebellion, 5, 137–155, 167, 194, 262n7
Tuscaloosa, Ala., 101

Upper South, 41, 60, 75, 194–95, 207, 234, 250; illicit slave trade in, 98–99, 102; population of, 6–8, 54, 105, 179, 181, 183. *See also specific states, towns, and counties*

violence: assault, 29, 93, 99, 101, 164, 175, 177, 210–11, 222; domestic violence, 212; lynching, 177, 225; murder, 87, 101, 218, 227, 244; rape, 25, 87, 164, 216; rioting, 176–78
Virginia, 1–2, 13, 40, 55, 57, 126, 176–77, 206–7; antislavery activism in, 40; churches in, 35, 118, 121–22, 195, 197–98; during the Civil War, 222–27, 229–31, 233, 236–44, 247; colonization movement in, 84–85, 172; commerce in, 95, 116, 128–32, 134–35, 188, 191–92; courts in, 211–13; discriminatory laws of, 19–24, 28–32, 76–77, 87, 89, 91–93, 161–66, 170–71, 222; disfranchisement in, 60; education in, 254; illegal enslavement in, 47–48, 98, 102, 211; immigration and travel to, 81; manumission in, 17, 41, 42–46, 62, 72–74, 108; population of, 6–7, 54, 105–6, 181–83; racial categorization in, 10, 217–18; registration of freedom in, 61, 82–83, 168; during the Revolutionary War, 52–54; segregation in, 96; servitude in, 15–16, 58; slavery in, 147–48; during the Turner Rebellion, 137, 139–46, 151–52. *See also specific towns and counties*
voting rights, 22–23, 60–61, 93–95, 121, 155–58, 173, 207, 248, 275n5

War of 1812, 111, 117–18
Warren County, Miss., 222
Warren County, N.C., 156–57
Washington, D.C. *See* District of Columbia
Washington County, Md., 83, 112, 134
Washington, N.C., 191, 236
Washington Navy Yard, 133, 176
Wayne County, N.C., 98, 130, 192
Weakley County, Tenn., 156
weapons: confiscation of, 139, 141, 146; regulation of, 88–89, 135, 151, 159–60
Westmoreland County, Va., 46, 140, 192, 222
Wilkes County, N.C., 113, 225
Williamsburg, Va., 30, 240

Williamson County, Tenn., 98
Wilmington, Del., 51, 101, 103–4, 135, 154, 181; antislavery activism in, 39–40, 99; churches in, 122; commerce in, 128–29, 131–32; education in, 126–27, 202; illicit slave trade in, 101; organizations in, 7, 124, 207
Wilmington, N.C., 146, 204, 230
Wilson County, Tenn., 117, 169
Worcester County, Md., 57, 109, 169

York County, Va., 134–35
Yorktown, Va., 1, 52, 236

INDEX OF NAMES

Aberdeen, Henry, 132
Acosta, Antoine, 114–15
Adams, Abraham, 95–96
Adams, Adam, 117
Adams, Fanny, 95–96
Adams, Henry, 133
Adams, John, 126
Adams, J. W., 202
Adams, Nancy, 129
Adger, John B., 197
Agustina, 35
Alexander, 26–27
Allen, Charles, 54
Allen, Peter, 231
Ames, 57
Anderson, Alexander, 29
Anderson, John, 130
Anderson, John A., 191
Anderson, Joseph, 94
Anderson, Solomon, 212
Andry, Euphrosine, 59
Angelica, 59
Ann, 42
Anthony, Monroe, 130
Arada, Virginia, 51
Armitage, Dorcas, 43
Armstrong, Comfort (daughter), 110
Armstrong, Comfort (mother), 109
Armstrong, Ebben, 109
Armstrong, Elijah, 110
Armstrong, Elizabeth, 109
Armstrong, Hannah, 109
Armstrong, Harry, 109
Armstrong, Jacob (father), 109
Armstrong, Jacob (son), 109
Armwood, Jemima, 110–11
Arthur, 28
Artis, Arnold, 137, 140–41
Artis, Exum, 137, 140–42
Asberry, Lewis, 188
Ash, George, 237

Ash, Luke, 191
Ashwell, Henry, 164
Ashworth, Abner, 166
Ashworth, William, 166
Atkinson, Archibald, 144
Atkinson, Joseph, 142
Augusta, A. T., 235
Auguste, Raynal, 117–18
Augustin, 210–11
Azou, 51

Bacus, Nicolas, 53
Bagwell, Adah, 74
Baham, Celestin, 118
Bailey, John Scott, 217
Bailly, Pedro, 65
Baker, Monroe, 223
Bales, Rachel, 111
Ball, Kitty, 198
Ball, Lewis, 198
Bampfield, George, 124
Banks, Nathaniel P., 241
Banneker, Benjamin, 55–57, 67, 69
Bantom, Thomas, 16
Bantum, Theophilus, 238
Barber, Clark, 237
Barksdale, William H., 169
Barlow, Joel, 69
Barlow, Minerva, 222
Barnes, John D., 116
Barnette, 114
Barran, Felicite, 51
Bass, Tom, 225
Battell, Solomon, 229
Beasley, Mary, 165
Beaty, Archibald, 108
Beckett, M. A., 203
Bedon, George, 124
Beens, Scipio, 126
Bell, George, 126
Ben (enslaved), 174

{ 351 }

Ben (freed), 17
Benny, Charles W., 214
Benoit, Jean, 27
Benoit, Louis, 65
Bertonneau, Arnold, 232, 248
Betty, 75
Bibby, Solomon, 52–53
Billing, Mary, 126
Billy, 18
Binah, 47
Bird, Aaron, 34
Bishop, Hannibal, 124
Bizzell, Velia, 191
Blachford, Charles, 139
Black, Sarah Ann, 228
Blades, Thomas, 41
Blamyer, William, 45
Blandin, Anne Marie, 113
Bob (of Hutchinson), 211
Bob (of Leggitt), 42
Bob (of Weedon), 43
Boguille, Mary Ann, 246
Bolard, George, 59
Bond, James, 17
Bonneau, Thomas S., 124, 126
Bonny, Pierre, 174
Boon (alias Hussey), William, 216
Boon, Armecy, 188
Boon, Bennett, 230
Boon, Moses, 188
Boon, Susan, 188
Boon, William, 236
Boon, William Aldred, 240
Bostick, Peter, 214
Boston, 133
Botts, William, 230
Bouligni, Antonio, 121
Bourdeaux, Lincoln, 134
Boute, Louis Valcour, 186
Bouthemy, Cyprian, 114
Bouthemy, Florentine, 114
Bouthemy, Pierre, 114
Bow, Addison, 241
Bow, Sarah, 241
Bowles, James M., 165
Bowles, Thomas, 165
Bowser, James, 244
Boyd, George D., 215
Boyd, Henry, 122
Boyd, William Henry, 161

Boyet, Hardy, 191
Bradford, Richard (Md.), 208
Bradford, Richard (Va.), 30
Brady, John (N.C.), 115
Brady, John (Va.), 211
Bragg, Martha, 230
Brent, Mary, 203
Brest, Rachel, 187
Briggs, Nat, 139
Brisco, Isabella, 209
Brister, 133
Brister, Susan, 130
Brogden, Abraham, 148
Brosse, Julia de la, 59
Broutin, Narcissus, 113
Brown, Abraham, 122
Brown, Cornelius, 122
Brown, Dixon, Jr., 122
Brown, Elizabeth, 163
Brown, Enoch, 227
Brown, Hugh, 45
Brown, Isaiah, 146
Brown, James, 122
Brown, John, 122
Brown, Mary, 45
Brown, Robert S., 226
Brown, Solomon G., 190
Brown, Susanna, 122
Brown, Sylvanus T., 242
Bruner, Eliza, 227
Brunetta, 43
Bryan, James W., 157
Buchanan, Mary, 114
Buckingham, Veal, 146
Bulloch, W. B., 91
Burckmeyer, Ellen, 217
Burke, Thomas, 160
Burket, Edward, 21
Burley, Thomas, 190
Burris, Samuel D., 149–50
Burton, Charles P., 214
Burton, Daniel, 35
Burton, Frances C., 217
Burton, Sarah M., 217
Butler, Absalom, 58
Butler, George, 34
Butler, John, 128
Butler, Sally, 191
Butler, William, 195

Cabrera, Juan Márquez, 34
Caesar (boy), 57
Caesar (doctor), 17
Cailloux, Felicie, 204
Cain, Richard H., 253
Caldwell, Andrew, 30
Calpha, Simon, 53
Cambow, Emanuel, 31
Cameron, Mrs., 126
Cammel, Nicholas, 51
Campbell, Charles, 43
Canada, 149, 178
Cannon, Jesse, 101
Cannon, Martha "Patty," 101
Capers, William, 120
Cardwell, R. P., 215
Carey, Isaac N., 213
Carey, Lott, 85
Carmen, Maria del, 121
Carondelet, Baron de, 65
Carr, John, 242
Carriere, Manuel Noel, 53
Carroll, Jenny, 108
Carter, Isam, 52
Carter, James, 163
Carter, James P., 188
Carter, John, 97
Carter, Lewis, 54
Carter, Lidia, 188
Carter, Robert, 224
Carter, Robert (Nomini Hall), 46
Carter, Sally, 217-18
Carter, Sucky, 218
Carter, Thomas, 30
Cary, London, 132
Casanave, Pierre, 179, 219
Casanova, Joseph, 59
Casar, John, 32
Catalina, 50
Catharine, 58
Cattle, William, 124
Cavelier, Joseph, 193
Chain, Joseph, 131
Chalk, Emeline, 240-41
Chalk, John, 240-41
Charles, 59
Charles, Josephine, 200
Chastang, Foster, 229
Chastang, John, 112
Chaumette, Joseph, 204

Chavers, Edmund, 243
Chavers, Samuel, 233
Chavers, William, 243
Chavis, John, 118, 126
Chavis, Meredith, 134
Chavis, William, 32-33
Chesson, John B., 191
Chew, William H., 237
Christoph, Mrs., 245
Cinderella, 148
Cité, 51
Clamorgan, Cyprian, 189
Clark, Bella, 109
Clark, George, 116
Clark, Henry T., 223, 232
Clark, Martha, 116
Clark, Mary, 116
Clark, Nancy, 116
Clark, William, 124
Clarke, Molly, 112
Clarke, Nancy, 111-12
Clay, Henry, 84
Clay, Mary Ann, 212
Clayton, Francis, 43
Cleeves, James, 31
Cleoeke, 42
Clifton, 245
Coffi, Antonio, 65
Cohen, Lavinia, 243-44
Cohen, Sheldon, 243-44
Coker, Daniel, 124-125
Cole, Bartlett, 102
Cole, Thomas, 65-66
Cole, William (patient), 188
Cole, William (kidnapped), 102
Colet, Naneta, 59
Colin, Augustin, 59
Collins, George, 124
Collins, Stephen D., 232
Colson, William, 85
Conrad, Rufus, 222
Cooch, Thomas, 43
Cook, Ann, 116
Cook, Eliza Anne, 202
Cook, Hannah, 116
Cook, John F., 177, 196
Cook, Mary Victoria, 203
Cooper, William, 124
Corn, Dixon, 232
Corn, Egbert, 232

Corn, Ned, 232
Corn, Richardson, 229
Cornie, Louis, 130
Cornish, Nathaniel, 236
Costin, John, 209
Costin, William, 126
Cotton, John, 21
Courtney, Thomas, 29
Cousins, Granderson, 102
Couvent, Marie, 204
Cox, James L., 192
Cox, William, 37
Cranch, William, 213
Creek, Jesse, 58
Cresap, Thomas, 30
Cromwell, Isaac, 30
Croom, Hilary, 192
Cropper, Elkaney, 213
Cruzat, Francisco, 50
Cuff, Thomas, 190
Cuffee, Mathias, 238
Culms, Elizabeth, 113
Cunningham, Matthew, 154
Cupid, Rachel, 130

Dabney, Richard, 226
Daniel, Joseph J., 156
Darby, 28
Darby, Caleb, 124
Davis, Agnes W., 165
Davis, Jefferson, 250
Davis, Lucretia, 130–31
Davis, Sarah, 190
Dawson, Levi, 47
Day, Cato, 133
Day, Thomas, 134
Decoux, Maria Ana, 50
DeLarge, Robert C., 253
Delille, Henriette, 200
Delphina, Maria Estephania, 121
Dempsey, Nathan, 239
Dempsey, Thoroughgood, 128
Dereef, J. M. F., 231
Dereef, Joseph, 190
Dereef, J. U., 231
Dereef, Richard E., 190, 228–29
Derham, James, 55
DeRosario, John Wallace, 134–35
Dessalines, Jean-Jacques, 103
Destres, Marie Jeanne, 51

Deveaux, Catharine, 132
Dianah, 57
Dick, John, 18
Donato, Auguste, 193
Doram, Dennis, 240
Doram, Joshua B., 240
Dorville, Francisco, 53
Douglas, Agnes, 146
Douglas, Charles, 146
Douglas, Maria, 146
Douglas, Patty, 146
Douglas, Thomas, 146
Douglas, Vincent, 146
Douglass, Frederick, 174–75, 246
Douglass, Margaret, 165
Douglass, Rosa, 165
Dove, Robert, 55
Dreux, Francis, 114
Driggers, Robert S., 218
Driggers, Sarah, 13
Dubroca, Arsene, 112
Dubroca, Arthur, 112
Dubroca, Bazille, 112
Dubroca, Cephire, 112
Dubroca, Hilaire, 112
Dubroca, Louise, 112
Dubroca, Maximillian, 229
Dubuclet, Antoine, 193
Dubuclet, François, 200
Dudley, Edward B., 215
Duncan, Jethro, 134
Dungee, John, 74
Dungee, Lucy Ann Littlepage, 74
Dunlop, M. A., 246
Dunn, James, 16
Dunn, Maria, 161
Dunn, Oscar, 253
Dupart, Carlos, 121
Dupart, Luisa, 121
Durant, Tyra, 227
Durnford, Andrew, 128, 193, 204
Dutchesse, Margery, 16
Dwight, Caroline C., 132
Dwight, Rebecca, 132
Dye, Maria, 213

Eaton, William, Jr., 216
Edge, Jordan, 111
Edge, Rebecca, 111
Edmond, Doctor F., 232

Edwards, Hannah, 116
Edwards, Weldon N., 156–57
Eliza, 98
Ellinghaus, Charles, 114
Ellis, Elizabeth, 17
Ellis, Gideon, 17
Ellis, James, 206
Elzey, Kitturah, 234–35
Emanuel, Nancy, 110
Emanuel, Sylvia, 110
Emory, Nancy, 186
Ephraim, 42
Epps, Allen, 186
Epps, William, 186
Evans, Henry, 120–21
Evans, James, 226

Faison, Thomas, 116
Fauntleroy, Isabella, 43
Fauntleroy, Thomas, 43
Fayerweather, Angelina A., 246
Femmie, Jacob, 50
Ferris, David, 39
Fillmore, Millard, 182
Finney, Levi, 124
Finny, James, 124
Fisher, Mary, 101
Fleet, John H., 202
Fletcher, 225
Flurry, Kinner, 143–44
Folk, Minton, 191
Ford, Edmund, 58
Forrest, Nathan Bedford, 240
Fortiere, Francisco, 53
Fortune, Benjamin F., 168
Fox, Alfred, 226
Francis, Buck, 128
Francis, Dolphin, 128
Franklin, David, 242
Franklin, Edward, 133
Franklin, Nicholas, 120
Freeman, Adeline, 198
Freeman, John, 44
Freeman, Mrs. Coleman, 145–46
Freeman, Willis, 166
Fulcher, Frederick, 222

Gaillare, Mathilde, 113
Gaines, Gustavus, 223–24
Gálvez, Bernardo de, 54

Garetta, Emilita, 159
Garetta, John, 159
Garland, John, 47
Garnes, Anthony, 117
Garnes, Nancy, 81
Garris, James, 116
Garrison, William Lloyd, 149
Gaston, William, 15, 157, 207
Gates, James, 34
Gaudin, Juilette, 200
Gavin, David, 175–76
George, 142
George, Eleanor, 161
George, Sally, 206
Gibbs, Fleetwood, 29
Gibbs, Flora, 30
Gibbs, Grace, 30
Gibbs, Joseph, 30
Gibbs, Mary (elder), 29–30
Gibbs, Mary (Tenn.), 148
Gibbs, Mary (younger), 30
Gibson, Mary (elder), 15
Gibson, Mary (younger), 15
Gibson, Thomas W., 235
Gilbert, Archibald, 54
Gilbert, Thomas, 30
Gillison, Fannie, 171
Goin, Nicholas, 215
Goins, Andrew, 233
Goins, Duncan, 233
Goins, Edward, 233
Goins, Henry, 233
Goins, John W., 233
Goins, Richard, 233
Goldsborough, William, 99
Gooch, William, 15, 23
Gordon, Margaret E., 217
Goyens, William, 166
Grandy, William, 28
Grason, Richard, 214
Graves, Mary, 26
Green, Ann, 230
Green, Anne, 30
Green, James Y., 206
Green, John P., 202
Green, John R., 207
Green, Lucy, 161
Green, Samuel, 149
Griffin, 166
Griffin, Israel, 191

INDEX OF NAMES { 355

Grimes, James, 140, 143
Grimes, Leonard, 146–48
Gross, Nicholas, 240
Grove, Archibald, 222
Guille, Mr., 96
Guimarin, John, 110–11

Haden, William, 133
Hagan, John, 226
Hagleton, Thomas, 16
Haithcock, Thomas, 137, 140–42
Hall, Charles H., 236
Hall, Eli, 140, 143
Hamilton, David, 116
Hamilton, Leah, 185
Hamilton, Paul, Jr., 57
Hammond, Moses, 238–39
Hannah, 29
Hanshaw, John, 216–17
Hanson, James H., 126
Hare, Morris, 188
Harmon, Mitchell, 237
Harmon, William, 229
Harper, Sally, 74
Harris, Benjamin, 206
Harris, Drury A., 186
Harris, Henry C., 122
Harris, James, 126
Harris, Milly, 198
Harris, Pleasant, 191
Harrison, William Henry, 173
Harry, 41
Harry, Evan, 135
Harwood, Richard A., 216–17
Harwood, Silvia, 113
Hassel, Josephine, 231
Hawkins, Catherine, 25
Hawkins, John, 25
Hawley, Anna, 212
Hay, Frederick J., 217–18
Hayward, George, 109–10
Hazle, Richard G., 206
Hebb, William, 77
Hemsely, William, 186
Hervieux, Mariana, 50
Hewitt, Lurana "Raney," 111
Hicks, George, 126
Hill, John H., 168
Hill, Marietta T., 220–21, 248
Hill, Phillis, 132

Hill, Rachel, 116
Hill, Susan, 185
Hill, Thomas Jefferson, 227
Hill, William, 33–34
Hilton, Andrew, 54
Hippolyte, François, 235–36
Hitchens, Edward, 21
Hobbs, Mary, 27
Hobbs, Nathaniel, 55
Hobles, Susan, 108
Hodges, Willis Augustus, 139–41, 143
Holland, Augustus H., 188
Holland, William, 188
Holloway, Richard, 124
Holmes, Johny, 28
Holt, Ann, 35
Holt, George, 35
Holt, Mary, 35
Honore, Zacharie, 193
Hope, Caesar, 108
Horniblow, Molly, 139
Howard, Christina, 120
Howard, Jacob, 128
Howard, Robert, 231
Howard, William (elder), 120
Howard, William (younger), 120
Howell, Jacob, 122
Howell, Latisha, 188
Hubard, John, 28
Huberdeau, Pierre, 27
Huger, Carlos, 124
Hugin, Rose, 30
Hugon, Juan Bautista, 53
Humphrey, Lotte W., 169–70
Humphries, Joseph, 124
Hunt, Gilbert, 198, 200
Hutchinson, Mary Anne, 211
Hutchinson, Silas, 211
Hutt, James, 27
Hyde, Thomas, 129

Ichabud, 43
Inglis, Thomas, 133
Isabele, 42
Isabelle, 112
Isidore, Adelaide, 107
Isidore, Baptiste, 107

Jack (free), 45
Jack (runaway), 148

Jackson, Aaron, 31
Jackson, Abraham, 57
Jackson, Andrew, 84, 118
Jackson, Daphne, 57
Jackson, Hannah, 57
Jackson, Hezekiah, 237
Jackson, James, 64
Jackson, John H., 146
Jackson, Peter, 124
Jackson, Robert, 124
Jackson, Samuel, 43
Jacobo, 50
Jacobs, Asa, 160
Jacobs, Curtis W., 169
Jacobs, Harriet, 139, 145
Jacobs, William, 243
Jacobs, Wilson, 190
James, Cyrus, 101
James, Henrietta, 44
James, Robert, 54
James, Thomas, 53
James, William, 245
Jarrett, Richard, 122
Jeffers, John, 114
Jeffers, Sylvia, 114
Jefferson, Manuel, 227–28
Jefferson, Thomas, 57, 67, 69, 84, 94
Jemima, 43
Jennings, Paul, 195
Jenny, 85
Jimmy (enslaved), 174
Jimmy (free), 28
John, 58
Johnson, Anthony, 32
Johnson, Archibald, 126
Johnson, Catharine Geraldine, 245
Johnson, Ebenezer F., 101
Johnson, Elisha, 144
Johnson, Isaac, 126
Johnson, John Thomas, 202
Johnson, Joseph (kidnapped), 101
Johnson, Joseph (kidnapper), 100–101
Johnson, Polly, 198
Johnson, Thomas, 53
Johnson, William (Miss.), 189, 218
Johnson, William (S.C.), 33
Jonathan, Aaron, 191
Jones, Allen, 177–78, 190
Jones, Britton, 109
Jones, Daniel, 126

Jones, Dick, 191
Jones, James, 101
Jones, Leonard, 57
Jones, Robert A., 128
Jordan, James C., 142
Jordan, Robert, 222
Jorge, 17
Joshua, 44
Juan, 35
Juana, 35
Julia, 98
Julia, Mary Ann, 120

Kain, Hannah, 108
Kate, 45
Keckley, Elizabeth, 246–47
Keene, Thomas, 44
Kelker, Cecile, 159
Kelker, Frederick, 159
Kelker, John, 159
Kellam, John, 47
Kersey, William, 81
Key, Edmund, 117
Key, Francis Scott, 84
Key, William, 188
Keys, Daniel, 236
Keys, William, 236
King, Caesar, 45
King, David, 45
Kingsley, Elizabeth, 148
Kingson, 18
Kitt, Lucy, 161

Labadie, Antoine, 190
Laborissiere, Pierre, 117
Lacewell, James, 190
Lacey, Fanny, 54
Lacey, George, 54
Lacey, Kate, 54
Lacour, Jean Baptiste, 59
Lacroix, François, 221
Lafae, John J., 110
Lamamiere, Francoise, 186
Lange, Alexander, 134
Lange, Elizabeth Clarisse, 200
Leah, 27
Leary, Matthew N., Jr., 228
Lee, Jarena, 118–20
Lee, Nancy, 74
Lee, Robert E., 228

INDEX OF NAMES { 357

Left, 31
Leggitt, James, 42
Lewis, 18
Lewis, Evan, 47
Lewis, Frederick, 126
Lewis, Mary, 26
Lewis, Stephen, 212
Lewter, John T., 188
Lightfoord, William, 206
Ligon, Thomas Watkins, 214–15
Lillington (alias McAuslan), John, 109
Lincoln, Abraham, 170, 221, 235, 246, 248
Lincoln, Mary Todd, 246
Linthicum, George L., 237
Lioteau, Ferdinand, 135
Littleton, Nathaniel, 17
Liverpool, Moses, 126, 133
Locklear, Joseph, 211
Logan, George, 124
Logan, Greenberry, 166
Lomax, Thomas, 230
Lominil, Louise, 135
London, 47–48
Longo, Anthony, 17
Lopez, Frank, 238
Lorimer, Hannah T., 43
Lorimer, James H. T., 43
Louison, 112
Louverture, Toussaint, 38, 103
Lowe, Mr., 126
Lowry, James, 32–33
Lowry, Sinclair, 225
Luke (son of Phebe), 16
Luke (of Leggitt), 42
Lyon, Mary, 203

Macarty, Augustin de, 91
MacDowell, John, 35
Mackey, Julius, 240
Macon, Nathaniel, 94, 157
Madden, Slaughter, 224
Madelon, 59
Madere, Jean Baptiste, 237
Madison, Dolley, 195
Madison, James, 195
Magdelena, 50
Malvin, John, 224
Mangloan, Juan Santiago, 49

Manlove, Alexander, 101
Manly, Arthur, 128
Manly, James, 47
Manly, Joseph, 124
Mann, Sterling, 122
Mansantos, Sophia, 121
Maria, 35
Mariana, 50
Marie, 17
Marie Francoise, 51
Marie Jeanne (alias Rosalie), 120
Marly, Jean Baptiste, 33
Marr, G. W. L., 156
Marsham, Richard, 28
Martha Ann, 142
Martin, Sam, 232
Mary Josephine, 59
Mason, Thomas, 202
Mathews, P. B., 66
Matteaur, Beverly, 226
Matthews, George, 214
Matthews, William, 135
Matthews, William E., 237
Maxwell, Elizabeth, 43
Maxwell, Solomon, 43
Mayo, Joseph, 45
McAuslan, John, 109
McCall, George, 54
McCartee, Margaret, 21
McCracken, J. C., 211
McCulluck, Samuel, 166
McElroy, William T., 187
McEnery, John, 113
McIntosh, James M., 227
McKim, Alexander, 99
Meachum, John Berry, 184, 197
Mead, Betty, 130
Mead, Joseph, 146
Meaux, Elizabeth, 187
Meaux, Spy, 187
Meaux, Susan Mary, 187
Meaux, Vance W., 187
Meeds, Hester, 185
Meeds, Sarah, 185
Meeds, William, 185
Mehardy, Jane, 228
Mejat, Geanty, 112
Mejat, Leon, 112
Melton, Feraby, 191

Melton, Willis, 188
Menendez, Francisco, 18
Meshires, William, 187
Metcalfe, Thomas, 214
Metoyer (alias Lewis), John, 245
Metoyer, John B., 245
Metoyer, Louis, 245
Metoyer, Mrs. John Baptiste Augustin, 245
Meyers, Henry, 230
Middleton, Charles, 131
Middleton, Charles H., 202
Middleton, Mary, 43
Middleton, Robert, 43
Miers, Ann, 26
Miers, Martha, 26
Mifflin, Daniel, 42
Mifflin, Warner, 40, 42
Miles, Harris, 191
Miller, Armistead, 161
Miller, Arthur, 26
Miller, Michael, 28
Miller, Phillip, 53
Millon, Victoria, 121
Milteer, Patrick, 191
Miner, Lewis, 237
Miner, Myrtilla, 203, 220
Mitchell, Ellis, 96
Mitchell, Hannah, 114
Mitchell, James, 124
Mitchum, Arthur, 132
Monroe, James, 84
Montiano, Manuel de, 18
Moore, Ben, 190
Moore, Celia, 97–98
Moore, David, 85
Moore, Grailen, 97–98
Moore, William H., 239
Moreau, Jean Louis, 135
Morell, Junius C., 207
Morgan, Bennett, 31
Morgan, George, 114
Morgan, Jarret, 237
Morgan, Pamelia, 161
Morgan, Thomas, 224
Morin, Charles B., 242
Morris, Samuel, 98
Morsu, Pedro, 50
Mortie, Louise de, 247

Moultrie, William, 63–64
Muraille, James Hector Nicholas Joubert de la, 200

Nahar, Annie M., 246
Najo, Azou, 51
Nancy (baker), 131
Nancy (daughter of Kate), 45
Nancy (servant), 28
Nanny, 17
Napier, William C., 244
Nash, Charles E., 253
Nash, Frederick, 216
Neale, Anthony, 34
Neale, Francis, 128
Nelson, Eliza, 139, 286n4
Newsom, Berry, 137, 140–42
Newsom, Moses, 116
Newsom, Nathaniel, 116
Nicholson, Thomas, 39
Nicken, Edward, 31–32
Nicken, Mary, 32
Nickens, John Cornelius, 236
Noel, Andrew, 104, 135
Nuit, Luis la, 53
Nutinez, Agustina, 35
Nutter, Risdon, 185

O'Brien, Kennedy, 28
O'Neale, William, 187
O'Reilly, Alejandro, 50
Offley, G. W., 127
Offutt, Milly, 187
Oldham, Samuel, 133
Olivares, Marcos, 49
Oliver, 28
Opothleyahola, 227
Overton, Daniel, 31
Overton, Parthenia, 31
Overton, Rachel, 31
Overton, Samuel, 31
Owen, John (elder), 32
Owen, John (younger), 32
Owen, Mary, 32
Owen, Thomas, 32
Oxendine, Wylie, 225

Pablo, 35
Paca, James, 186

Paget, Maria, 50
Palfrey, Henry William, 211
Pamilla, Rebecca, 130
Parker, Joanah, 25
Parker, William, 25
Parsons, Elizabeth A., 198
Pascal, Benjamin, 207
Patience, 98
Patterson, Henry I., 190
Payne, Daniel A., 198–201, 206
Peace, James B., 212
Peake, Mary Smith, 247
Pearson, Richmond M., 216
Peck, Elizabeth, 115
Peck, Harriet, 203
Peck, James, 148
Peggy (of Bond), 17
Peggy (of Leggitt), 42
Pepino, Jane, 241
Peter, 15
Peters, Charles, 53
Peters, Elisha, 168
Peters, Nancy, 168
Pettiford, Moses, 117
Pettit, Dennis, 229
Phebe, 16
Philip, John, 245
Phillip, 59
Phillips, Wendell, 246
Phillis (free), 47
Phillis (of Ridgely), 44
Pile, Henry, 46
Pinchback, P. B. S., 252–53
Pinn, David, 229–30
Pinnion, Harry, 108
Plique, Marguerite Elizabeth, 186
Pollard, Mary Ann, 224
Pollard, Reuben, 224
Pomet, Francisca, 50
Pompey, 42
Pope, Amelia, 144
Pope, Harrison, 144
Popewell, Elijah, 243
Porche, Algae, 241
Poryo, Sophia, 51
Posey, Caty, 108
Pouche, Nanette, 112
Power, John, 26
Prentis, William, 72
Pretlow, Thomas, 42

Privott, Susan, 163
Pugh, William, 244
Pully, Susan, 216–17
Purcell, Sophia, 146

Queen, Richard, 108

Rachel, 42
Rainey, Joseph H., 253
Ramirez, Miguel, 159
Ramirez, Rosa, 159
Ranger, Joseph, 52
Ransier, Alonzo J., 253
Rapier, James T., 253
Read, Amariah, 1–2
Read, Hardy, 191
Reed, Peter, 239
Reid, Benjamin, 211
Reid, David S., 134, 215–16
Reid, Jasper, 211
Reid, Mourning, 211
Revels, Hiram, 250–51
Rey, Henry Louis, 200
Reynolds, Barsha, 191
Reynolds, Benjamin, 188
Reynolds, Hampton, 239
Reynolds, Jesse, 191
Reynolds, Lemuel, 239
Reynolds, Mary, 188
Rial, Jonathan, 132
Richard, 42
Richards, Emanuel, 186
Richardson, James, 110
Richardson, John, 110
Richardson, Samuel, 187
Richer, Fannie, 227
Ridgely, Absalom, 44
Ridgeway, Alfred, 236
Ridgeway, Cornelius, 236
Ridgway, George, 174
Ridout, Horatio, 110
Rigbie, James, 37
Rillieux, Norbert, 204
Rivas, Francisco, 50
Roberts, Filomena, 159
Roberts, James, 85, 87
Roberts, Jane Waring, 86
Roberts, John S. F., 159
Roberts, Joseph Jenkins, 85–86
Roberts, Willis, 87

Robin, 28
Robin, Caliche, 114–15
Robinson, Lafayette, 225
Robinson, Valentine, 30
Rodgers, Solomon, 110
Roger, 30
Romezo, Nicolas, 35
Rooks, Joseph, 115
Ross, James, 43
Ross, William H., 214
Roudanez, Jean Baptiste, 247–48
Roudanez, Louis Charles, 204, 248, 253
Roudanez, Louise, 247
Rudulph, Tobias, 214
Rueben, Felipe, 53
Ruff, Dilsey Maria, 223
Ruff, Sarah, 223
Ruffin, Thomas, 216
Rush, Benjamin, 55

Sabatier, Dorsin, 186
Sabo, Cato, 130
Saltus, Samuel, 124
Sam (of Leggitt), 42
Sam (of Lorimer), 43
Sampson, Benjamin Kellogg, 204
Sampson, James D., 204
Sampson, John Patterson, 204–5
Samuel, 44
Sanette, 114
Santos, Manuel, 113
Sappington, Catherine, 146
Sarah (East Indian), 47
Sarah (of Snow, elder), 17
Sarah (Indian), 29
Sarah (of Jackson), 57
Sarah (daughter of Peggy), 17
Sarah (of Snow, younger), 17
Satchell, Carrie, 246
Savage, Thomas, 31
Savoy, Philip, 52
Sawyer, Dick, 191
Sawyer, Frank, 191
Scarburgh, Edmund, 28
Scomp, Samuel, 101
Scot, Mary, 26–27
Scott, Dred, 5, 210, 263n7
Scott, James (Tenn.), 187
Scott, James (Va.), 98
Scott, John, 129

Scott, Nancy, 98
Seagrove, Adam, 34
Sedella, Antonio de, 121
Selby, George, 74
Selby, William F., 110
Shad, Abraham D., 207
Shad, Amelia, 131–32
Sharp (alias Atkins), Solomon, 98
Shaw, H. W., 223
Shelby (or Shelvy), 98
Sheppard, Bird, 186
Sheredine, Cassandra, 44
Shiphard, Joseph, 122
Shipley, Ann, 215
Shirkey, Philip, 98
Shoecraft, Abram, 111
Shoecraft, Silas, 111
Shorter, Alexander, 237
Shorter, Milly, 108
Shrewsbury, George, 232
Sikes, William, 235
Simpson, Leah, 132
Sinclair, Cornelius, 101
Sip, Ann, 27
Sip, Jo, 27
Sipple, Waitman, 30
Skeeter, Betsey, 1–2
Skeeter, Joseph, 191
Skipwith, Abraham, 44
Smith, Charles, 53
Smith, Henry, 129
Smith, John, 34
Smith, Morgan, 98
Smith, Sophia, 121
Smith (alias Hitchens), Tamar, 21
Smith, William Loughton, 63
Snow, Beverly, 177–78
Snow, William, 17
Sophie (alias Sanette), 51
Sparrow, Ellick, 87
Speight, Jesse, 107
Spellman, Mary, 241
Spellman, Richard, 241
Spencer, John, 29
Spencer, Peter, 154, 207
Spenser, Thomas, 101
Spradling, Washington, 184
Stanly, John C., 133
Stanly, John S., 202
Staten, James, 160

Stephen, 44
Stewart, Barnet, 53
Stewart, Thomas, 55
Stokes, Darius, 123, 206, 209
Stowe, Harriet Beecher, 149
Stringer, William, 98
Sue, 57
Swan, John, 239
Sykes, Isaac, 245
Sykes, Richard, 245
Sykes, World, 122
Sylvester, Abba, 45
Sylvester, Jerry, 45
Sylvester, Joan, 45
Sylvester, Nancy, 45
Sylvester, Thomas, 45
Sylvia, 109
Symons, Jeremiah, 45

Taborne, Luke, 122
Taney, Roger B., 210
Tapia, Chrispin de, 33
Tappan, Arthur, 173
Tasco, Anna, 108
Tasco, Frank, 108
Tasco, Nancy, 108
Tasco, Santy, 108
Tasco, William Henry, 108
Tasker, William, 208
Tate, George, 222
Tate, Jane, 111
Tate, Joseph, 166
Tatum, Howell, 117
Taylor, Billy, 128
Teague, Colin, 85
Teaster, Mary, 111
Thezan, Sidney, 247
Thomas (son of Catharine), 58
Thomas (of Ridgely), 44
Thomas, Davy, 140, 142–43
Thomas, Elizabeth, 47
Thomas, James, 170, 178
Thomas, Philip, 132–33
Thomas, Philip F., 149
Thomas, Robert, 46–47
Thomas, Tommey, 43
Thompson, John, 117
Thompson, John P., 207
Thompson, William, 53
Thoroughgood, Celestine, 198

Tilghman, Enos, 101
Tilmon, Levin, 108–9
Tilmon, Violette, 109
Timy, 98
Titus, 17
Todd, Ann, 142
Todd, Upton, 188
Tom, 55
Toney, 31
Tony, King, 13, 36
Tony, Sarah, 13
Toogood, Benjamin, 190
Toomer, John D., 156
Toulson, Sally, 50
Townsend, Charles, 211
Toyer, Anne, 15
Trapier, Paul, 197
Travis, William, 32
Trévigne, Paul, 248, 253
Triton, Maria, 59
Trusty, Joseph, 131
Turner (alias Johnson), Rachel, 216–17
Turner, Becky, 216
Turner, Isham, 137, 140–42
Turner, Joseph, 164
Turner, Nat, 137, 140–41, 145, 150
Tutten, Mrs., 126
Tynes, Dick, 191
Tyre, Isaac, 102
Tyson, Elisha, 99

Valentine, Charles, 53
Valentine, William D., 172
Vallery, 174
Valmour, J. B., 200
Van Buren, Martin, 173
Vaughan, Ambrose, 159, 289n65
Vaughan, Henry B., 142
Vaughan, Tabitha, 159, 289n65
Veney, David, 225
Vesey, Denmark, 79, 88
Vilars, Julia, 59
Violet, 58
Voshell, James, 27

Wade, Howell, 116
Wade, Richard C., 263n9, 274n108
Wadsworth, Thomas, 42–43
Walden, Drury, 53
Walden, James, 192

Walker, David, 149
Waller, Edward, 53
Warbourg, Daniel, 190
Warbourg, Eugène, 190
Ward, Cyrus, 214–15
Ward, Sarah, 47
Wareham, George, 192
Waring, Colston M., 122
Warington, James, 44
Warmoth, Henry C., 253
Warrior, Clory, 227
Washington, Annie E., 202
Washington, Bushrod, 84
Washington, George, 45–46, 208
Waters, John P., 113
Waters, Thomas, 16
Watie, Stand, 227
Watson, William, 53
Watts, Benjamin, 224
Watts, Daniel, 140, 143
Watts, Jesse, 140, 143
Weaver, Benjamin, 191
Webb, Jane, 31
Webb, Mathew, 66
Webster, Araminta, 132
Weedon, George, 43
Wells, George, 187
Wells, Lewis G., 130
Wells, Samuel, 188
West, George, 55
Weston, Anthony, 231
Weston, Jacob, 231
Weston, Samuel, 231
Wheeler, Charles, 115
Wheeler, Ignatius, 115
White, Betty, 186
White, Charles, 188
White, Edwin, 225
White, Patrick, 29
White, Sampson, 195
Whitfield, Sylvia, 132
Wickham, John, 108
Wiggins, Benjamin, 128
Wiggins, Lucy, 130

Will, 29
Williams, Betsey, 161
Williams, Jane, 226–27
Williams, Lydia, 130
Williams, Mary B., 247
Williams, Peter Alexander, 245
Williams, Till, 32
Williamson, David, 51
Williamson, Sarah, 25–26
Willis, Henry, 55
Willis, Joseph, 120
Willson, John, 75
Wilson, Andrew ("a Christian"), 28
Wilson, Andrew ("a Scotchman"), 53
Wilson, David, 134
Wilson, Emmett, 165
Wilson, Jesse, 157
Wilson, Joseph, 165
Wilson, Josiah, 143
Wilson, Keziah, 212
Wilson, Oscar, 243
Wilson, Richard H., 212
Wilson, Sherry, 149
Wingfield, Elizabeth, 241
Winn, Baylor, 218
Wise, H. A., 223
Witten, Juan Bautista, 117
Woodhouse, Mary, 165
Woodhouse, Mary Jane, 165
Woodland, John, 134
Wormley, William, 149
Wright, James, 30

York, Benjamin, 57
York, Dinah, 57
Young, Allen, 42
Young, Hardy, 190
Young, Nathaniel, 144
Youngblood, Anderson, 166
Youngblood, Dick, 111

Zaire, 59
Zekell, James, 16
Zekell, Jenny, 16

www.ingramcontent.com/pod-product-compliance
Lightning Source LLC
Chambersburg PA
CBHW032012300426
44117CB00008B/999